PIMLICO

460

WITNESSES OF THE RUSSIAN REVOLUTION

Harvey Pitcher studied at Oxford and Leningrad, and in 1963 started the Russian Department at St Andrews University. Since 1971 he has been a full-time writer. His first book to achieve widespread popularity, *When Miss Emmie was in Russia* (1977), was described by Paul Scott as 'a study of the whole adventure' of being an English governess before and during the Russian Revolution. This was followed by other books on the British and American communities in pre-Soviet Russia: *The Smiths of Moscow* (1984) and *Muir & Mirrielees*, about Russia's first department store (1994). Harvey Pitcher is also a leading Chekhov scholar. He is the author of a standard work, *The Chekhov Play: A New Interpretation* (1973) and of *Chekhov's Leading Lady* (1979), a portrait of Chekhov's actress wife, Olga Knipper. With fellow translator Patrick Miles he introduced English readers to the delights of Chekhov's early comic stories. Harvey Pitcher lives in Cromer on the north Norfolk coast.

WITNESSES OF THE RUSSIAN REVOLUTION

HARVEY PITCHER

PIMLICO

Published by Pimlico 2001

2 4 6 8 10 9 7 5 3 1

Copyright © Harvey Pitcher 1994, 2001

Harvey Pitcher has asserted his right under the Copyright, Designs
and Patents Act 1988 to be identified as the author of this work

First published in Great Britain by
John Murray (Publishers) Ltd 1994
Pimlico edition 2001

Pimlico
Random House, 20 Vauxhall Bridge Road,
London SW1V 2SA

Random House Australia (Pty) Limited
20 Alfred Street, Milsons Point, Sydney,
New South Wales 2061, Australia

Random House New Zealand Limited
18 Poland Road, Glenfield,
Auckland 10, New Zealand

Random House (Pty) Limited
Endulini, 5a Jubilee Road, Parktown 2193, South Africa

The Random House Group Limited Reg. No. 954009
www.randomhouse.co.uk

A CIP catalogue record for this book
is available from the British Library

ISBN 0–7126–6775–X

Papers used by Random House are natural,
recyclable products made from wood grown in sustainable forests;
the manufacturing processes conform to the environmental
regulations of the country of origin

Printed and bound in Great Britain by
Mackays of Chatham PLC

Contents

Illustrations   vii
Acknowledgements   ix
Foreword to the Pimlico Edition   xi
Map   xvi

INTRODUCING THE WITNESSES   1

1. RED MONDAY   9
   Events up to and including Monday, March 12

2. THE BIRTH OF FREEDOM   34
   Tuesday, March 13 to Saturday, March 17: agreement reached between Duma Committee and Soviet on formation of Provisional Government

3. ASSUMING OFFICE   53
   Week to Saturday, March 24: profiles of Lvov, Milyukov and Kerensky; recognition of new Government by US and Allies

4. 'WALK AND TALK'   68
   March 25 to April 16: the new spirit of freedom and equality; dual authority of Government and Soviet

5. KERENSKY IN THE ASCENDANT   86
   April 16 to May 17: Lenin's return (April 16); the Milyukov crisis; formation of Coalition Government (May 17)

6. ONE ISLAND, TWO ORATORS   99
   May 18 to June 17: conditions on the island of Kronstadt; Kerensky and Lenin at First All-Russian Congress of Soviets (opens June 16)

7. JULY DAYS   116
   Events up to and including unsuccessful attempt by Bolsheviks to overthrow the Government (July 16–18)

8. THE PLAIN PEOPLE   140
 Impressions of village life, September

9. KORNILOV   160
 *Early August to end of September: the Moscow Conference
 (opens August 25); the Kornilov Affair; the Democratic
 Assembly (opens September 27)*

10. 'SOME MAD SCHEME'   179
 *October 20 (Pre-Parliament opens) to early hours of
 November 7*

11. THE BOLSHEVIKS TAKE OVER   193
 November 7 (9 a.m.) to November 8 (6 a.m.)

12. DOWNFALL OF KERENSKY   213
 Morning of November 8 to November 13 (3 a.m.)

13. MOSCOW   238
 *The Battle of Moscow (November 10–15) and the Red Burial
 (November 23)*

14. THE CONSTITUENT ASSEMBLY   252
 *Attempts to convene the Constituent Assembly
 (December 11–13 and January 18, 1918)*

Afterword   280
Sources and Bibliography   290
Notes and References   293
Index   305

Illustrations

1. Sir George Buchanan
2. Meriel Buchanan
3. The British Embassy, Petrograd
4. Arthur Ransome
5. Morgan Philips Price
6. General Alfred Knox
7. Harold Williams
8. John Reed
9–11. The March Revolution
12. 'Proletarians of all Countries, Unite!'
13. Demonstration of women
14. May Day Parade
15. Trotsky at the Finland Station
16. Kerensky addressing troops at the front
17. Crowds being fired on during the July Days
18. Disarming the 1st Machine-Gun Regiment
19. Kerensky in Petrograd
20. Lenin's secret police photograph
21. Lenin in disguise
22. Kerensky at his desk
23. Kornilov arriving for the Moscow State Conference
24. Smolny Convent and Institute
25. Red Guards outside Smolny
26. Red Guards on street patrol
27. View through the Red Arch towards the Winter Palace
28. The ransacked Alexander II room inside the Winter Palace

The author and publishers wish to thank Mrs Tania Rose for her helpful co-operation in lending the photograph of her father, Morgan Philips Price, and Michael Welch for lending the postcard of the British Embassy. For permission to reproduce the photographs by her father Stinton Jones they are grateful to Mrs Marguerita Conway; for the photograph of Arthur Ransome in the Brotherton Collection to Ransome's literary executors, Sir Rupert Hart-Davis and John Bell; and for the photograph of General Knox (presented to William Gerhardie, dated 'Vladivostok 23 December 1919') in the Gerhardie Archive to William Gerhardie's literary executor, Anne Amyes, and the Syndics of Cambridge University Library. Photographs no. 8, 15, 16, 21, 23, 25 and 28 are reproduced by kind permission of David King. The author wishes to offer special thanks to Dr Catherine Cooke for giving so generously of her time and energy in helping him prepare the illustrations.

Acknowledgements

For permission to quote from *Russia in Revolution* by Stinton Jones I am most grateful to his daughter, Mrs Marguerita Conway; from *Russia's Ruin* by E.H. Wilcox to his daughter, Mrs Barbara Quartermaine; and from *My Reminiscences of the Russian Revolution* and *My Three Revolutions* by M. Philips Price to Pluto Press and to Price's daughter, Mrs Tania Rose, who also generously allowed me to quote from unpublished material in the Price Papers. Permission to quote from *Ten Days That Shook the World* by John Reed was kindly given by Lawrence & Wishart Ltd.

For allowing me to quote from Arthur Ransome's original copies of his telegrams to the *Daily News* and from unpublished letters to his mother, deposited with the Brotherton Collection in the Brotherton Library, University of Leeds, my sincere thanks are offered to his literary executors, Sir Rupert Hart-Davis and John Bell; from the unpublished Memorandum by Sir George Bury in the Lord Davies of Llandinam Papers, to the National Library of Wales; and from an unpublished letter by William Gerhardie in the Gerhardie Archive, to his literary executor, Anne Amyes, and the Syndics of Cambridge University Library. For permission to quote from unpublished material deposited with the Leeds Russian Archive, Brotherton Library, University of Leeds, I am grateful to Francis Bennett (grandson of Reginald Bennett), Mrs Margaret Garlick (niece of Marguerite Bennet), Leslie Metcalf (brother of H.K. Metcalf) and Tim Crook (grandson of Mrs Nellie Thornton). Every effort has been made to trace all copyright holders, but in a few instances this proved impossible.

I take this opportunity of thanking Christopher Sheppard, Sub-Librarian (Brotherton Collection), and Mrs Ann C. Farr, Assistant Librarian, for allowing me to consult the Ransome Archive and kindly sending me a large number of photocopies; Mrs Eirionedd A. Baskerville, Assistant Archivist, Department of Manuscripts and Records, The National Library of Wales, Aberystwyth, for answering queries about Sir George Bury and sending photocopies; Dr P.N.R. Zutshi, Keeper of Manuscripts and University Archives, Cambridge University Library, for allowing me access to the Gerhardie Archive; Mrs Linda Shaw, Assistant Keeper of the Manuscripts, Department of Manuscripts & Special Collections, Hallward Library, University of Nottingham, for answering queries about Sir George Buchanan and his daughter, Meriel Buchanan, and for allowing me access to the Buchanan Papers; and Ellen Scaruffi, Curator, Bakhmeteff Archive, Columbia University Libraries, New York, for sending me details of the Ariadna Vladimirovna Tyrkova-Williams Papers. Lynda Ballinger of HarperCollins Permissions answered my queries with exemplary good humour.

My special thanks go to Richard Davies, Archivist of the Leeds Russian Archive, not only for helping me to find suitable material among the Archive's unique holdings, but also for coping cheerfully with a variety of requests for information throughout the writing of the book.

Professor Edward Acton of the University of East Anglia showed me great kindness in reading through my first draft and giving me the benefit of his comments. Hugh Brogan, Arthur Ransome's biographer, generously found time to answer my long letter about Ransome, and Dido Davies, William Gerhardie's biographer, was likewise informative about Gerhardie and General Knox. Professor W. Harrison, formerly of the University of Durham, answered my letter about Robert Wilton, and David Saunders of the University of Newcastle made extensive enquiries on my behalf with regard to E.H. Wilcox. This led to a helpful correspondence with Wilcox's daughter, Mrs Barbara Quartermaine, and her nephew, Peter Kendall.

My final thanks are offered to John R. Murray, at whose invitation the book was undertaken, and to Grant McIntyre for his editorial supervision.

For the present edition Will Sulkin of Pimlico kindly allowed me to add an Afterword, in writing which I benefited from the advice and comments given me by Martin Dewhirst, Honorary Research Fellow, University of Glasgow, and Professor Paul Dukes of the University of Aberdeen.

Foreword to the Pimlico Edition

To anyone who first began to study Russia in the late 1950s the Revolution seemed an impenetrable event. Within the Soviet Union the historical record on 1917 was repeatedly being written. This happened not because fresh evidence had come to light or an enterprising historian had come up with a new theory. On the contrary, original documents were kept in 'special collections' accessible only to a few trusted scholars, and historians even more than most Soviet academics had to toe the party line. One historian has recalled how in 1972, when he and his colleagues at the Institute of History of the USSR wished to look more closely at the role of the peasantry in the Revolution, their discussion 'was terminated by some instructor in the Communist Party. He simply forbade it, saying, this is the right way of looking at the question and that's the wrong way ...'[1] The party line on 1917 changed in response to political changes at the top. Trotsky was the first to be written out of the story; Stalin, it seemed, had been at Lenin's right hand all along; but later Stalin was discredited and the photographs were shown to be fakes. At each stage of reassessment the Revolution had to be re-set in concrete and presented as the inevitable product of the forces of historical necessity. The events themselves receded further and further into the distance, acquiring an almost mythical, legendary quality.

Looking back at those Cold War years, there seem to have been two kinds of book that one could read in English about the Russian Revolution. There were histories, full of essential facts and dates and footnotes, but devoid of atmosphere and difficult to follow; and there were individual stories, short on precise information and almost certainly biased, but colourful and difficult to put down. The first was read with a sense of duty but little enthusiasm, the second with a mixture of pleasure and guilt. There was nothing at that time to compare with Orlando Figes' *A People's Tragedy* (1996), which in its author's words 'weaves between the private and the public spheres' and tries 'to emphasize the human aspects of its great events by listening to the voices of individual people';[2] but a book with that kind of emphasis could not be written until the Russian archives were opened up in the late 1980s.

First published in 1994, *Witnesses of the Russian Revolution* was intended to fill the gap between the formal history and the individual memoir by giving a consecutive account of the events of 1917, not in the way that a historian might, but using the words of eye-witnesses who saw history in the making. Its scope is more modest than that of *A People's Tragedy*, since the witnesses are not Russian, but British and American. They include diplomats, newspaper correspondents, the military, businessmen, even the occasional English governess. Some have acquired a romantic aura, like the young American radical, John Reed, author of *Ten Days That Shook the World*, who died of typhoid fever in Moscow in 1920 and is buried under the Kremlin wall, and who 'co-stars' with his wife Louise Bryant in the film *Reds*. Some are unexpected, like Arthur Ransome, better known in England today as the author of *Swallows and Amazons* than as the Petrograd correspondent in 1917 of the *Daily News*. Others well known in their time are now almost forgotten, like the Labour MP, Morgan Philips Price, and Harold Williams, a New Zealander married to a leading Russian politician and once described as 'the most brilliant foreign correspondent that our generation has known'.[3] Others were quite obscure, but still have a distinctive contribution to make.

As observers rather than participants, these Anglo-American witnesses had little influence on the course of events, but they are historically significant in that they helped to shape opinion about the Russian Revolution in their own countries. John Reed even inspired a generation of young Americans to join the Communist Party and go to live in the Soviet Union. The legacy of these witnesses lives on. As recently as 1995 Arthur Ransome's views on the Russian Revolution could spark a heated debate, for here is someone, seemingly with no political axe to grind, who gives a very positive account of Lenin's Russia and lends credibility to the still widely-held view that Lenin's Russia can be sharply differentiated from Stalin's Russia.[4]

Deciding when 'the Russian Revolution' starts and finishes is largely a matter of choice. Orlando Figes begins the story in 1891 and Richard Pipes (in the other monumental work in English on the Revolution) in 1899, but the origins of political dissent in Russia go back at least as far as the Decembrists in 1825. *Witnesses of the Russian Revolution* highlights the most critical, dramatic period: not the ten days of John Reed, but ten months from March 1917 to January 1918.

(Since the book is based on Western sources, I use the Western calendar throughout: hence March Revolution and November Revolution.) The decision to break off in January 1918 can be justified on the grounds that the dissolution then by the Bolsheviks of the Constituent Assembly, although it cannot be regarded as an endpoint (in a sense that comes only in 1991), undoubtedly marked a critical turning-point in Russian history. A more practical reason for stopping then is that by the start of 1918 the Anglo-American witnesses had become so few in number that they no longer reflected a cross-section of opinion.

The first thing I wanted to know from these witnesses was what it felt like to be there, to hear about events as they were happening. Clearly, no one witness, however well-informed and energetic, however privileged his or her vantage-point, could see more than a small part of what was going on; but by drawing on a pool of witnesses with different vantage-points, a much fuller picture could be obtained. They witnessed not one revolution but two – the overthrow of Tsarism in March and the Bolshevik seizure of power in November – and described them with an immediacy that later accounts never achieve. To discover so much vivid firsthand reporting, in great part unread since 1917, was very exciting.

Not that there can ever be one agreed way of looking at an event, for what you see matters less than how you see it. One witness sees a rabble of unkempt individuals making a nuisance of themselves in the streets; another sees a heroic popular demonstration; while a third is impressed most of all by the colour and spectacle, by the sight of blood-red flags palpitating in the wind. Different witnesses approach a scene with different expectations and preoccupations. The young American witnesses brought with them the expectation that an entirely new kind of human society was about to come into being, whereas most British witnesses were preoccupied not so much with the Revolution itself, as with its implications for the First World War. It seems odd now that in *The Times* of 19 March 1917 the headlines, 'The Tsar's Final Ordeal. Signing The Writ of Abdication. "I Cannot Part With My Boy"', should appear in a column headed 'Late War News'; it cannot have seemed odd at the time. 'Absorbed as we were in the war,' one British witness later wrote, 'we entirely failed to realize the importance of the Revolution for Russians.'[5]

Our witnesses are not then to be regarded as 'dispassionate observers'. They had their sympathies and prejudices. Already in 1917 they displayed a wide range of pro- and anti-Revolutionary sentiments, and here, too, I have attempted to build up a composite picture by drawing on a pool of witnesses with different views. Although they saw less than individual Russians of what was going on behind the scenes, they do have one important advantage over Russian witnesses: they are not partisan. For a Russian in 1917 not to be partisan would have been impossible. Even though you might not be politically active yourself, you belonged to a particular social class that stood to lose (in some cases, to lose everything) or gain (a bright new future?) as a result of the Revolution. This was bound to colour, and almost certainly to distort, your view of events. Because they are standing further back, our witnesses are able to look at events more as a whole; at the end of the day it was not their problem. For this reason I find it easier to relate to them, to allow for their individual biases, and to make up my mind on that other question: not only what it felt like to be there, but how might one have reacted – how does one react now – to those momentous and challenging events?

That kind of question used to be very loaded. There was, after all, as much of a Cold War mentality in the West as in the Soviet Union. Ask someone what they thought of the Russian Revolution and you might as well be asking, what do you think of the Soviet Union, or more simply: are you a Communist sympathizer? Even to take an interest in the subject was regarded with some suspicion. A gulf divided those who were so anxious for the Soviet Union to succeed that they put a positive interpretation on everything to do with the Revolution, and those who regarded 1917 and its consequences as an unmitigated disaster. The arguments of the former were buttressed by the apparent permanence of the Soviet Union, by the fact that like it or not, the Revolution had been successful and endured. When in 1991 that permanence was shown to be illusory, it became possible to take a fresh and more dispassionate look at the Revolution.

Going back to the original Anglo-American witnesses changed my view of the Revolution completely. I realized that it had become so heavily overlaid with historical interpretation and political controversy that it was impossible to see what was actually there. I hope that by stripping away those extra layers, the colours of the original may show up again more clearly.

The text of the present edition is the same as that of 1994, but this Foreword has been revised and I have written a new Afterword in which I draw some conclusions about the two Russian revolutions, and try to relate 1917 to what is happening in Russia today.

Cromer, August 2000   Harvey Pitcher

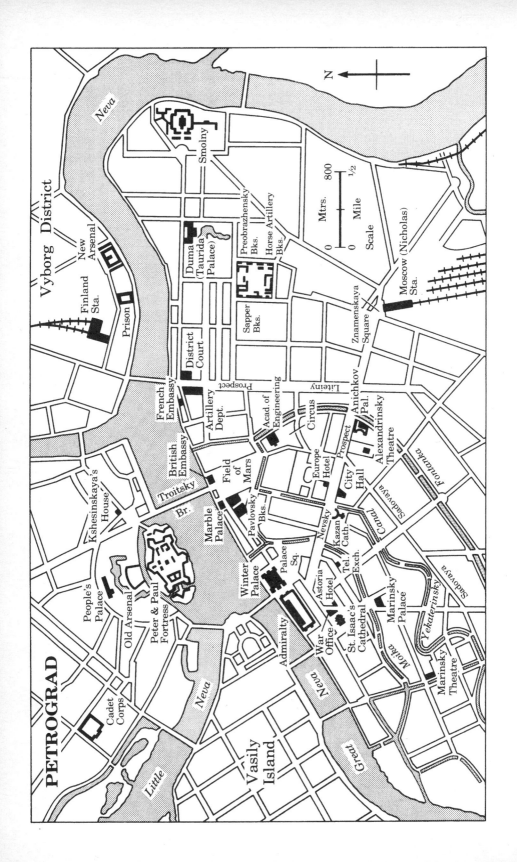

Introducing the Witnesses

Sifting material for this book has brought home to me the sad fact that the human memory cannot be trusted. It is not so much that we forget, but that we select, rewrite the record to make our own actions and judgements appear in a more favourable light, and find it almost impossible to resist the temptation to be wise after the event (how many witnesses of the Russian Revolution claimed later to have been aware all along of Kerensky's limitations – but said nothing at the time!). Hence, the evidence of foreign correspondents always deserves attention, because they are usually writing within twenty-four hours of the event. On the other hand, their views may be coloured by the politics of the newspaper employing them, or their editor may say that he wants 'hard' news only. In books they can spread themselves more, but at the expense of immediacy and verac-ity. Diaries and letters written at the time likewise provide excellent evidence, but they may be too personal, or the writers too far from the centre of events to understand much of what is going on. Being close to the centre is the one advantage that an Ambassador enjoys, but in other respects his position restricts him. His advisers, if well-informed and prepared to go out into the streets, are likely to be better witnesses.

Of the forty witnesses whom I have drawn upon, eight may be regarded as major, and I shall describe here who they were and how they came to be in Russia, and comment briefly on the written records they left behind.

HAROLD WILLIAMS (1876–1928) was the son of a Nonconformist minister who emigrated to New Zealand in 1870. A precocious lin-guist, he stored languages in his brain 'as a musician stores notes', completed a doctoral thesis on the Ilocano language at Munich in 1903, and eventually knew more than fifty languages, over half of which he spoke fluently. But Russia attracted him no less than philol-ogy – as a young man he had been passionately interested in Tolstoy – and in September 1903 he wrote: 'I feel that the liberation of Russia is the great cause I have to work for.' It was at the home in Stuttgart of a leading Russian political exile, Peter Struve, that he met his future wife, Ariadna Tyrkova, another Russian dissident.

Williams worked in Russia as a journalist from December 1904 to March 1918, first for the *Manchester Guardian*, then the *Morning Post*, and finally the *Daily Chronicle*. In 1914 he published *Russia of the Russians*, a compendium of all aspects of Russian life. He was particularly well informed about internal Russian politics through his wife, a member of the Central Committee of the Kadet (Constitutional Democrat) party, founded in 1905. After his return to England in 1918, he began a book about the Russian Revolution which he never completed, while in her biography of him, *Cheerful Giver* (1935), his widow expressed the hope that his dispatches from that period might one day be published in book form; they never were.[1] Tall and scholarly in appearance, Williams inspired much affection among friends both Russian and British. He writes in a very relaxed personal style, so that his articles often read more like private musings on the state of Russia than newspaper reports.

If the name of Harold Williams is now almost forgotten, that of ARTHUR RANSOME (1884–1967) is still widely known as the author of such children's classics as *Swallows and Amazons* (1930), in which very middle-class English children go sailing and fishing: a far cry from the world he moved in earlier, when he fell in love with Trotsky's secretary and was labelled a 'dangerous Red'. The son of a Leeds history professor, Ransome had published a variety of books when he decided in the summer of 1913 to visit Russia: partly to escape from a stormy first marriage and partly to pursue an interest in Russian folklore, which led to his celebrated *Old Peter's Russian Tales* (1916). In October 1915, helped by his friend Harold Williams – 'a very quiet man, unselfish, extraordinarily kind'[2] – he became Petrograd correspondent for the Liberal *Daily News*.

Ransome had taught himself Russian and knew the city well, having compiled a guidebook that was never published because of the war. An American friend described him in 1917 as 'an Englishman of the six-footer, lounging sort, red-moustached and pipe-smoking'[3]; he was also very short-sighted. In spite of health problems, Ransome was a brave and tireless correspondent, who thought nothing of going for twenty-mile walks to gauge the political temperature of the city. Though previously uninterested in politics, he worked hard to understand the complex political situation in Russia. Reuter's correspondent advised him early on to contract, e.g. write 'unwent' for 'did not go'. This saved his employers money but may not have been good for his prose, which even when 'disentangled', still seems unrelaxed. He is at his best describing some striking incident or sequence of events, with plenty of movement and vivid – often humorous – detail, in other words, telling stories, which he so much loved doing.

Ransome's friendship with Harold Williams did not survive the Revolution, whereas that with MORGAN PHILIPS PRICE (1885–1973) lasted many years. Unlike Ransome, Philips Price had politics in his blood, and from 1929 to 1959 he was to be a Labour MP. At Cambridge he studied science and took a Diploma in Agriculture, having inherited a 2000-acre estate when he was twenty-one. He first visited Russia in 1908, and in 1910 joined a scientific expedition which took him to remote parts of the Russian Empire. In 1914 he published *The Diplomatic History of the War*, 'aimed to show that each of the belligerent countries was partly responsible for the disaster', and helped to found the Union of Democratic Control, 'a society for those who had not lost their heads'. Knowing Russia well and speaking the language, but deploring the trend to whitewash the tyrannical regime of Britain's wartime ally, he offered his services in 1914 as Russian correspondent to C.P. Scott, editor of the *Manchester Guardian*.[4]

For most of 1917 Price was not reporting regularly, as Scott had another correspondent, David Soskice, of Russian emigrant stock, who became Kerensky's private secretary. Price concentrated on the activities of the Soviet, and on life outside Petrograd, which other correspondents had little time to cover. *My Reminiscences of the Russian Revolution* appeared in 1921. It is a long book, in which rather dry and tendentious passages of political analysis – Price had by that time been temporarily converted to Marxism – are interspersed with extremely vigorous firsthand reporting. Much use is made below of *Reminiscences*, in conjunction wherever possible with what Price wrote in 1917 itself.

About Robert Wilton, correspondent of *The Times*, there is little to say. He had been in Russia for fourteen years, but his contacts and sympathies were so much with the upper classes that the Revolution left him high and dry. E.H. Wilcox, correspondent of the *Daily Telegraph* (which throughout 1917 also printed Harold Williams' telegrams and provided excellent coverage of Russia), analyses events far more dispassionately, but in neither his articles nor his book does he write about his personal experiences.

The British Ambassador in Russia from 1910 to the beginning of

January 1918 was SIR GEORGE BUCHANAN (1854–1924). 'I may in a certain sense be said to have been born into diplomacy,' he writes, 'for I was born at the Legation at Copenhagen, where my father was then Minister.'[5] He also looked like a diplomat, with his tall patrician appearance, monocle and silvery-grey hair. On his arrival in St Petersburg (renamed Petrograd in 1914), he must have felt that he was about to add another worthy, if unspectacular, paragraph to a modestly successful career. In the event, this cautious and reserved career diplomat became a historically important and surprisingly controversial figure.

Buchanan listened to other people, and as the political situation in Russia worsened during the war, he realized that in Harold Williams he had a unique asset. With considerable misgivings he was persuaded by Williams in the autumn of 1916 to make the acquaintance of some of the more moderate liberal politicians: a move that paid off when these same men assumed power in March 1917.[6] With Kerensky, too, he later cultivated good relations. This did not mean that the conservative Buchanan had been converted into a socialist or even a mild liberal, but simply that pro-war forces must be sought wherever they could be found. 'If we can only keep them in line until the autumn,' he said soon after the March Revolution, 'perhaps some day they will be grateful to us at home.'[7]

My Mission to Russia and Other Diplomatic Memories was published in two handsome volumes in 1923. Buchanan spoke no Russian and conveys little of the hurly-burly of the streets (though he continued to take his daily walk along the English Quay even when in personal danger), but the passages from his diary are interesting, and more useful still are the extracts from his confidential reports, where he outlines the rapid changes in Russian politics in simple language that even the Foreign Office in London might be expected to understand. His humour is so quiet that it can pass unnoticed. By all those who worked under him he was greatly admired; by the Russian *émigrés*, however, he was later much reviled and more or less accused of starting the whole Russian Revolution.

MERIEL BUCHANAN (1886–1959) was Sir George and Lady Georgina's only child. Described in the *Lady's Pictorial* of 24 October 1914 as 'a fair type of a real English girl, pretty, quiet, moderately tall, with a splendid figure and possessing delightful manners', she appeared nursing another future witness of the Revolution, her Siamese cat. The interviewer found it impossible to believe that Miss Buchanan was the author 'of one of the most popular of last year's books, *The White Witch*, she speaks so modestly of her great gift...'[8] Not surprisingly, the aspiring young writer saw in her Russian experiences a heaven-sent opportunity. *Petrograd the City of Trouble 1914–1918* came out in December 1918 and was quickly reprinted. It might have been sub-titled: *What I Saw of the Russian Revolution from the Windows of the British Embassy*, but the author makes a little go a long way, and the Embassy was not a bad vantage-point, especially during the 'July Days'. On the evidence of *Petrograd*, her literary gift was modest – too many stars shine dimly in tender skies – but from time to time she conveys atmosphere in a way that no other witness achieves. Unenthusiastic about the events of March, after November she parades her fastidious distaste for the 'unkempt, unwashed, unshaved, totally ignorant' new rulers of Russia.[9] *The Dissolution of an Empire* (1932), which incorporates large parts of *Petrograd*, is even more anti-Bolshevik.

Looking after the Ambassador's daughter was a duty that fell on various members of the Embassy staff, including MAJOR-GENERAL SIR ALFRED KNOX (1870–1964). An Ulsterman and Tory of private means, Knox had served in India and at the War Office before being appointed Military Attaché at Petrograd in 1911. As a liaison officer during the war, he exasperated the Russian officers assigned to protect him by making for the most dangerous parts of the front line and coolly munching his sandwiches in the midst of hails of bullets; but he earned the gratitude of the Russian Munitions Delegation whom he accompanied to London in December 1915: 'They said that I had fought their battle as if I had been a Russian myself'.[10] During 1917 his assistant in Petrograd was a twenty-one-year-old lieutenant from an Anglo-Russian family, William Gerhardie, the future novelist. Gerhardie hero-worshipped Knox, whom he describes as 'having the air and voice of a man engaged in winning the war while everybody else about him was obstructing him in his patriotic task'.[11] Knox worked very hard, had great personality and a 'fine presence'. He spoke Russian fluently and 'retained a freshness of mind, an eagerness to get in touch with every phase of Russian life, so that he was the real link with the country, the most authentic channel of information for the Ambassador'. Gerhardie liked the way in which Knox treated his Russian batman with the kind of respect that no Russian officer ever showed to a subordinate. He was also 'full of fun'.[12]

With the Russian Army 1914–1917 appeared in two volumes in 1921. Of its 760 pages some 200 cover the period of the Revolution. The long extracts from Knox's diary are more valuable than his later

comments. In March 1917 he saw at once that Russia's future contribution to the war was going to depend on her political future, and
became as much a political as a military adviser to the Ambassador;
and like Buchanan, he saw that he must not let his own political
preferences affect his judgement. Knox has his prejudices (he is
noticeably anti-Semitic), and his vision is restricted by his preoccupation with the war, but within those limits he is an excellent witness: well-informed, accurate, astute, and often very entertaining.

Two other well-known British witnesses, of whom only sparing
use has been made, may be mentioned here. As British consul in
Moscow, R.H. Bruce Lockhart spent little time in Petrograd in 1917,
and *Memoirs of a British Agent* did not appear until 1932. Bernard
Pares, already a Professor of Russian, knew more about the country
than any other witness except Harold Williams, but *My Russian
Memoirs* was likewise not published until 1931, and its author's most
vivid experiences – going on tour with a group of Russians calling
themselves 'The League of Personal Example' and making pro-war
speeches – are somewhat remote from the Revolution itself.

Compared with the British witnesses, the main American witnesses
laboured under several very obvious disadvantages. They did not
arrive on the scene until the Revolution was well under way, they
had comparatively little knowledge or experience of the country, and
none of them had more than a smattering of the language. What they
did have was immense energy and burning enthusiasm. To witness
was not enough; they wanted to be part of the action. As reporters,
they showed colossal nerve. It is hard to imagine any of the British
correspondents barging into the Winter Palace where members of the
Provisional Government were holed up on November 7, or stationing
themselves prominently in the lobby to watch the departure of the
discomfited ministers after their arrest by the Bolsheviks.

JOHN REED (1887–1920) came from a wealthy family in Portland
and studied at Harvard, but had to earn his own living as a journalist when the money ran out. Jack was the rebel of the family.
'Defiance was not a principle with him,' writes his biographer,
Granville Hicks, 'it was an instinct.' In New York he became aware
of 'the cruel inequality between rich people who had too many
motor-cars and poor people who didn't have enough to eat'. For
supporting a workers' strike, he landed himself briefly in jail. As a
writer, Reed made his name with *Insurgent Mexico* (1914), based on
his experiences as a war correspondent during the revolution; in
Mexico, as in America, he identified 'big business' as the real enemy.

In April 1917 his outspoken opposition to America's entry into the European war – 'a clash of traders', he had earlier called it – made him many enemies. Exempted from military service on August 14 because he had had a kidney removed, he set sail three days later with his wife, Louise Bryant, for Russia, where reports of the activities of the Soviet made them think that a new kind of human society was about to emerge.[13]

Ten Days That Shook the World, published in March 1919, deserves its reputation as the best firsthand account in English of the Bolshevik Revolution.[14] The book is well researched and documented: in addition to his own notebooks, Reed had amassed a large collection of newspapers, decrees and proclamations. Skilfully he evokes the time of day, what the weather is like, how the streets look. Most of all, though, Reed found a structure and style to match his unique subject. *Ten Days* is not long, and the concentration on a short time span gives the book great dramatic intensity. Once under way, the narrative fairly plunges ahead, helped by breathless dots and short sentences, often without verbs. Reed clearly sympathizes with the Bolsheviks, but *Ten Days* is not one-sided: dashing recklessly from one camp to the other, the author always gives a clear account of what the Bolsheviks' opponents are doing and saying, even though he disagrees with them.

How much *Ten Days* owes to the manner of its writing becomes obvious when one compares it with Louise Bryant's *Six Red Months in Russia* (1918) or *Through the Russian Revolution* (1923) by Albert Rhys Williams, a Congregational minister from Boston of Welsh extraction. Bryant does not have her husband's journalistic skills or sharp reporter's eyes, while Williams' book reads like a sermon pitched on too high a note. His most exciting experience – interceding on behalf of the besieged *yunkers* in the Petrograd Telephone Exchange on November 11 – is described much better by a fellow-participant, BESSIE BEATTY (1886–1947) in *The Red Heart of Russia* (1918). Beatty was a correspondent for the *San Francisco Bulletin*. Though very pro-Revolution, she was less committed to the Bolsheviks than Reed, and it is instructive to read her accounts alongside his.

Minor witnesses, who appear only occasionally or whose contribution is limited to a particular period, are introduced briefly on their first appearance in the text.

1

Red Monday

Events up to and including Monday, March 12

'The March Revolution,' writes Philips Price, 'came like a thief in the night'. It was not that a revolution was unexpected. Far from it. 'How often,' he goes on, 'had its possibility been discussed in Russia during the two and a half years that followed the outbreak of the Great War! Over samovars and tea-glasses officers and students had speculated whether it would come during the war or after peace. Working men had whispered of it in *traktirs* (tea-rooms) with bated breath. Soldiers had timidly broached the subject to each other in the trenches.'[1]

Western observers, too, had long been weighing up the possibility. 'If there has ever been a Government that richly deserved a revolution,' Colonel Knox wrote in a report on September 19, 1915, 'it is the present one in Russia. If it escapes, it will only be because the members of the Duma [the lower chamber of the legislature] are too patriotic to agitate in this time of crisis.' Corruption and mismanagement, he believed, had reached a point at which the mistrust of authority was penetrating all classes of society. He went to see Rodzianko, President of the Duma, to discuss the internal situation. 'I spoke of the preventable sufferings of the people and of my astonishment at their patience under conditions that would have very soon driven me to break windows. He only laughed and said that I had a hot head.'[2]

In private audiences, Sir George Buchanan repeatedly warned the Emperor how dangerous the situation had become. The last of these meetings took place on January 12, 1917 at the Imperial Palace at

Tsarskoe Selo, south of Petrograd. 'On all previous occasions,' Buchanan writes, 'His Majesty had received me informally in his study, and, after asking me to sit down, had produced his cigarette case and asked me to smoke. I was, therefore, disagreeably surprised at being ushered this time into the audience chamber and at finding His Majesty awaiting me there, standing in the middle of the room.' Buchanan's heart sank, but when the conversation turned to the competence of those entrusted by the Emperor with the conduct of the war, he asked permission to speak with his 'usual frankness'.

On the Emperor signifying his assent, I went on to say that there was now a barrier between him and his people, and that if Russia was still united as a nation it was in opposing his present policy. The people, who had rallied so splendidly round their Sovereign on the outbreak of war, had seen how hundreds of thousands of lives had been sacrificed on account of the lack of rifles and munitions; how, owing to the incompetence of the administration, there had been a severe food crisis, and – much to my surprise, the Emperor himself added, 'a breakdown of the railways'. All that they wanted, I continued, was a Government that would carry on the war to a victorious finish. The Duma, I had reason to know, would be satisfied if His Majesty would but appoint as President of the Council [Prime Minister] a man in whom both he and the nation could have confidence, and would allow him to choose his own colleagues. The Emperor, while passing over this suggestion, referred by way of justification to certain changes which he had recently made in the Ministry. I therefore ventured to observe that His Majesty had of late changed his Ministers so often that Ambassadors never knew whether the Ministers of today with whom they were treating would still be Ministers on the morrow.

'Your Majesty, if I may be permitted to say so, has but one safe course open to you – namely, to break down the barrier that separates you from your people and to regain their confidence.' Drawing himself up and looking hard at me, the Emperor [who was considerably shorter than Buchanan] asked: 'Do you mean that I am to regain the confidence of my people or that they are to regain *my* confidence?' 'Both, sir,' I replied, 'for without such mutual confidence Russia will never win this war. Your Majesty was admirably inspired when you went to the Duma last February. Will you not go there again? Will you not speak to your people? Will you not tell them that your Majesty, who is the father of your people, wishes to work with them to win the war? You have, sir, but to lift your little finger, and they will once more kneel at your feet as I saw them kneel, after the outbreak of war, at Moscow.'...

I next called His Majesty's attention to the attempts being made by the Germans, not only to create dissension between the Allies, but to estrange him from his people. Their agents, I said, were everywhere at work. They were pulling the strings, and were using as their unconscious tools those who were in the habit of advising His Majesty as to the choice of his Ministers. They indirectly influenced the Empress through those in her entourage, with the result that, instead of being loved, as she ought to be, Her Majesty was discredited and accused of working in German interests. The Emperor once more drew himself up and said: 'I choose my Ministers myself, and do not allow anyone to influence my choice.' 'How, then,' I ventured to ask, 'does Your Majesty select them?' 'By making inquiries,' His Majesty replied, 'as to the qualifications of those whom I consider most suited to conduct the affairs of the different Ministries.' 'Your Majesty's inquiries,' I rejoined, 'are not, I fear, always attended with success. There is, for example, M. Protopopov, who, if your Majesty will forgive my saying so, is bringing Russia to the verge of ruin. So long as he remains Minister of the Interior there cannot be that collaboration between the Government and the Duma which is an essential condition of victory.'

The Emperor denied that Protopopov was pro-German, and went on to say that the prevailing talk of revolution need not be taken seriously. Buchanan, however, persisted.

'Your Majesty', I concluded, 'must remember that the people and the army are but one, and that in the event of revolution only a small portion of the army can be counted on to defend the dynasty. An Ambassador, I am well aware, has no right to hold the language which I have held to Your Majesty, and I had to take my courage in both hands before speaking as I have done. I can but plead as my excuse the fact that I have throughout been inspired by my feelings of devotion for Your Majesty and the Empress. If I were to see a friend walking through a wood on a dark night along a path which I knew ended in a precipice, would it not be my duty, sir, to warn him of his danger? And is it not equally my duty to warn Your Majesty of the abyss that lies ahead of you? You have, sir, come to the parting of the ways, and you have now to choose between two paths. The one will lead you to victory and a glorious peace – the other to revolution and disaster. Let me implore Your Majesty to choose the former. By following it you will, sir, secure for your country the realization of its secular ambitions and for yourself the position of the most powerful Sovereign in Europe. But above all else, Your Majesty will assure the safety of those who are so dear to you and be free from all anxiety on their account.'

The Emperor was visibly moved by the warmth which I had put into this appeal, and, pressing my hand as he bade me good-bye, said, 'I thank you, Sir George.'

The Minister of Finance, who had an audience with the Emperor immediately afterwards, later reported that he had never seen him so nervous and agitated.[3]

Bertie Stopford (a diplomatic courier, described by his friend Serge Obolensky as 'a great and muscular Englishman with a droll, elephantine sense of humour'[4]) was coming down the Embassy staircase when he met the Ambassador newly returned from Tsarskoe. 'His Excellency told me... he was half an hour with the Emperor, and was able to tell him everything that he had hoped and intended to tell him. Though he was looking very tired, I could see how pleased he was to have got it off his mind – like some one who had confessed and communicated.' Writing some years later, Meriel Buchanan adds one more significant detail to her father's published account. 'He had noticed that a door leading into the private apartments of the Emperor had been standing ajar, and he had been conscious all during the audience that a third person was present, listening to every word that passed. There seems now no doubt that that third person was the Empress.'[5]

No, a revolution was not unexpected, but its timing and speed seem to have taken everyone completely by surprise. On February 27 the Duma reassembled. Attempts by this 'lower house' to promote reforms had been perpetually thwarted by the 'upper house', known as the State Council, or by the Tsar's personally-appointed ministers, so that it had become a platform for dissent. Demonstrations were anticipated; none occurred. Sir George decided that he and his wife could safely take a short holiday in Finland; Meriel had already gone to stay with a friend in the Baltic Provinces. On Wednesday March 7 the Emperor himself left for General Headquarters at Mogilev. 'Had luncheon alone at Donon's,' Stopford recorded that day. 'Tereshchenko [soon to become an important figure] sat down at my table. Had not seen him for nearly a year. Dined at the French Embassy; heard there had been disturbances in the streets today and some tram-car windows smashed.'[6]

It was only Thursday and Friday that the trouble began to look at all serious. Marguerite Bennet was a Scotswoman of remarkable *sang froid*, who had gone out to Russia in 1911 at the age of twenty-eight to be a governess in the von Meck family, and was now working in Petrograd as office manager for Vickers. March 15 she wrote home to her family:

As you can imagine this has been a very strange time, but I haven't been a bit frightened. This is Thursday and it all began last Thursday, by some of the works striking. In the office in the afternoon we began to hear of this but there was nothing to be seen about the Nevsky, except a few extra policemen & soldiers guarding bridges & so on. Mrs Watson & I got home without seeing anything in the very least exciting. Friday I had to go to the dentist at 11 near here so didn't start to go to the office till nearly 12. I went across the bridge – the trams weren't running, or rather they were, but in a very irregular way – so I walked on. The bridge was guarded, but there was nothing very extraordinary to be seen but heaps of people till I got up near the street where our office is and then there I met the Cossacks trying to keep back a great crowd of people which was coming along. It presented a very strange sight to see the Cossacks coming riding along with their great long lances glancing in the sun. It was a glorious sunny frosty day & all the people were in an excellent mood. They were singing the Marseillaise & when they weren't doing that they were asking for 'khlyeb, khlyeb (bread, bread)'. Suddenly the Cossacks began to charge & to scatter the people in all directions. They rode on the pavement *et partout*. You can imagine how people ran, shouting the Cossacks are coming. Needless to say I ran too – a vegetable shop man invited me to come in & locked the door. That felt rather queer. However it really wasn't anything at all, so I went on to the office & reported to Mr Anderson so they all went out. Mr Anderson found the Nevsky looked like an enormous circus. In the evening when we went home we tried to avoid the Nevsky as much as possible and only crossed it. Cossacks were still tearing up and down, but at that moment where we crossed the crowd was less.[7]

Here the Cossacks appear in a familiar light, displaying all the qualities traditionally associated with them. Awe-inspiring, disciplined and fearless, they dominate the crowd in the streets with almost casual ease, so that when the cry goes up, the Cossacks are coming, no one thinks twice about what action to take. But on that same day, Stopford met another demonstration singing the Marseillaise, and the picture he gives of the Cossacks is quite different. Telling his sledge-driver to wait, he walked a short distance with the demonstrators. 'They were accompanied by Cossacks. They were not harassed at all, and the Cossacks chafed them and talked to the children: all were on the best of terms. I wanted to see how they behaved and how they were treated. *Tout était a l'amiable.*'[8]

In his cable to the *Daily Chronicle* on Saturday morning, Harold Williams sounds more puzzled than perturbed by the situation:

> All attention here is concentrated on the food question, which for the moment has become unintelligible. There is no real want in Russia, and there are towns in the south and east where it is still possible to buy any quantity of bread at peace prices. But difficulties of transport and defects in organization cause constant jerks and jolts in the mechanism which supplies the larger towns, and on the present occasion the jolt is more acutely felt in Petrograd than usual. Long queues before the bakers' shops have long been a normal feature of life in the city. Grey bread is now sold instead of white, and cakes are not baked. I am bound to say, however, that after diligent inquiry I have not been able to discover any cases of actual starvation or even serious underfeeding. The trouble hitherto has amounted in practice to very little more than rather harassing inconvenience...
>
> But this week there was a certain decline in supplies in Petrograd. People still get bread, but with rather more difficulty than usual. This caused disquiet, and the apprehension was intensified by the general lack of confidence in the working of the machinery of supplies.
>
> Unrest expresses itself in the form of street demonstrations of an unusually mild character, wholly unlike any demonstrations I have ever seen in Russia.
>
> Crowds wander about the streets, mostly women and boys, with a sprinkling of workmen. Here and there windows are broken and a few bakers' shops looted. But, on the whole, the crowds

are remarkably good-tempered. . . and presently cheer the troops, who are patrolling the streets. Near the Moscow Station the crowd treated the Cossacks to white bread and cigarettes, and women pleasantly bantered the soldiers.

Occasionally when the mobs on Nevsky grow too dense the troops gently disperse them. There is a curious placidity about the whole thing, a curious absence of excitement and alarm.

At present the main current of movement is not revolutionary. There is nothing like a popular uprising. It is simply an unusually insistent demand for a vigorous solution of the food problem.[9]

Cabling to the *Daily News* on the same day, Arthur Ransome described the general feeling on Friday as one of 'rather precarious excitement like a Bank Holiday with thunder in the air'. He, too, had noted the 'extremely good relations between the crowd and the Cossacks'. While looking the other way, he narrowly escaped being taken off his feet between two Cossack horses being ridden along the broad Nevsky pavement; others were less lucky, but no one was seriously hurt. When a woman shouted, 'Go for the police, not us,' a Cossack replied: 'We shall settle accounts with the police later.' Opposite the Kazan Cathedral he came across a solitary demonstrator, clearly not a workman, but in Ransome's opinion a *provocateur* being employed by the police to stir up trouble.[10]

Saturday afternoon found Stopford walking back to his hotel, the Europe, after another solitary luncheon at Donon's. The day was beautiful, the streets normal and the Nevsky full of 'the usual people'. Going up to his room, he completed a letter and began changing for a concert.

I had put on my boots and my trousers when I heard a sound which I knew, but couldn't recall. I opened my window wide and realised it was the chatter of a machine-gun; then I saw an indescribable sight – all the well-dressed Nevsky crowd running for their lives down the Mikhail Street, and a stampede of motor-cars and sledges – to escape from the machine-guns which never stopped firing. I saw a well-dressed lady run over by an automobile, a sledge turn over and the driver thrown into the air and killed. The poorer-looking people crouched against the walls; many others, principally men, lay flat in the snow. Lots of children were trampled on, and people knocked down by the sledges or by the rush of the crowd.

It all seemed so unjust. I saw red. I put on a jacket without tie or collar or greatcoat, rushed to my third-floor lift, where I was kept waiting some time. I thought, if I could rally the people, we could capture the guns. When I got downstairs I found the hall and doorway crammed. Only with difficulty could I get out. By now those who had crouched near the wall had got up and were running away. The guns had stopped firing. The street was almost empty; there was nothing for me to do, so I returned to the hotel, finished dressing, and walked to the concert... All the sledges had gone home. There were only a dozen people there, who immediately left when I told them what I had seen.[11]

Sunday March 11 was the day when, in the opinion of British engineer Stinton Jones, a government-instigated revolt turned into a genuine revolution. His view is shared by Arthur Ransome, quoting in his telegram from notes that he kept of each day's events:

Sunday about two hundred persons killed wounded stop Local police chief lying dead this house stop Commander military district issues new notice forbidding gatherings promising use of weapons by soldiers who quote will stop at nothing to restore order unquote Still only organized demonstrations are on part of police stop Afternoon revolution definitely begun stop Police disguised overcoats of Litovsky regiment fired on crowd stop Litovsky regiment gone over to people stop Those who provoked disorders now getting more than wanted stop Streets near Duma being held by people and soldiers who have joined them stop Tried get up to Duma but could not my part of town being still hands authorities Duma district hands revolutionaries stop People taking events with astonishing calm stop I scuttled round corner of street to get out of way machinegun fire and found four men peacefully scraping ice from pavements with hoes stop[12]

Also very active was Robert Wilton, who described what happened on Sunday in a telegram to *The Times*, datelined Monday 11.45 a.m.

Scores of people were killed and wounded in various parts of the Nevsky Prospect during the afternoon.

The fine weather brought everybody out of doors, and as the bridges and approaches to the great thoroughfare were for some unaccountable reason left open, crowds of all ages and conditions made their way to the Nevsky, till the miles separating the Admiralty from the Moscow Station were black with people. Warnings not to assemble were disregarded. No Cossacks were visible. Platoons of Guardsmen were drawn up here and there in courtyards and side streets. The crowd was fairly good-humoured, cheering the soldiers, and showing themselves ugly only towards the few visible police. Traffic was impossible, but as the trams were not running and the cabmen had vanished, the obstruction was not serious, except for the unfortunate people who happened to arrive or intended to start at the Moscow Station.

Shortly after 3 p.m. orders were given to the infantry to clear the street. A company of Guards took up their station near the Sadovaya and fired several volleys in the direction of the Anichkov Palace. Something like 100 people were killed or wounded. On the scene of the shooting hundreds of empty cartridge cases were littered in the snow, which was plentifully sprinkled with blood.

After the volleys the thoroughfare was cleared, but the crowd remained on the sidewalks. No animosity was shown towards the soldiers. The people shouted 'We are sorry for you, Pavlovtsy [the Pavlovsky Guards Regiment]! You had to do your duty.'

The same company later returned to its barracks situated in the Field of Mars [a large oblong area covered with sand used as a parade-ground], near the British Embassy. I had just called on Sir George Buchanan, who arrived at 4 p.m. from Finland, where he went for a few days' rest, and I was walking through the Summer Garden when the bullets began to whiz over my head. The Pavlovsky Guards on approaching their barracks on the other side of the Field of Mars found the way blocked by another crowd, who cheered them, but refused to disperse. The Colonel in command ordered the men to lie down, so as to avoid killing people. After several volleys the crowd gave way, and sending his men forward he himself superintended the removal of the wounded.

Following his men, he then crossed the canal bridge. Two individuals, apparently disguised – one as a student, the other as an officer – barred the way. The student wrested the colonel's sword and slashed him savagely over the arm and head, causing serious but not dangerous wounds.[13]

In his book Wilton continues the narrative as follows:

The assailants jumped into a sleigh and vanished, and at the same time shots rang out from the roofs and garrets of surrounding houses and from the adjoining Church of St Saviour. . .

And then followed the unexpected. As soon as the Pavlovtsy entered their barrack-yard, recriminations began among them. One of the men had recognized his own mother amid the slain. Another wanted to know who had fired from the housetops and killed one of their comrades. 'It is the police,' was the unanimous verdict. 'They are provoking bloodshed. They have betrayed us.' Revolutionary sympathizers fed the flame. The whole company decided not to obey orders, but to side with the people. General Khabalov [Commander-in-Chief of the District] was immediately informed of what was transpiring, and loyal troops were sent to surround the mutineers. But the latter had their rifles and ammunition, and it was decided not to resort to extreme measures. The company remained within its quarters. Some of the men ventured out and were arrested.

What Wilton describes as 'the most sanguinary episode in the Revolution' took place some hours after this, when the police, armed with machine-guns and hidden on the tops of houses, fired at enormous crowds in Znamenskaya Square, a traditional gathering-point for demonstrators, in front of the Moscow Station. Later, Wilton tried twice to reach the Station at the far end of the Nevsky, but although the street was quiet and deserted, burly guardsmen held it from end to end with orders to let no one pass.[14]

In spite of the shootings, in spite of the wild rumours spreading through the city, the Léon Radziwills' dance went ahead that evening as planned. Grand Duke Boris graced it with his presence. So, too, did Bertie Stopford, but introduced a discordant note into the brilliant occasion.

I had words with Boris Golitzin about the police shooting the people who, quite quietly, were asking for bread. He sneered, 'You were very much upset yesterday at seeing a few people killed in the street. Tomorrow you will see thousands!' I replied, 'It's damned hard lines asking for bread and only getting a bullet!'

Léon Radziwill very kindly sent me home in his automobile at 4 a.m. The Nevsky, as well as the other streets that radiate from the Admiralty, was being swept by searchlights from the Admiralty Tower; occasional bullets whistled up and down.[15]

At this point the authorities still appear to have the situation well under control.

Sir George and Lady Georgina Buchanan, having reached the Embassy safely on Sunday afternoon, were alarmed to find that Meriel had not yet returned from the Baltic Provinces. In the country, Meriel writes, they knew nothing of the events of the past few days, but having settled to return to Petrograd on Sunday night, they packed themselves into the waiting sledge and drove through the blue darkness of the woods to the little station. The train, coming from Reval, was full to overflowing, but the head of the district police had reserved them a compartment.

We arrived at Petrograd the next morning at a quarter to eight, the train being for a wonder only ten minutes late. The big, dark station wore somehow a disturbed and somewhat perturbed air, and the sight of one of the English officers in full uniform caused us a little alarm. 'I have come to meet you,' he told us, 'because there have been riots here the last two days, and the police won't let motors go about without a pass.'

With all our luggage dumped on the platform, we stood shivering in the cold of that bitter winter morning. 'The maid had better bring on the things in a cab,' I said, 'and we can all go together in the motor.'

'There are no cabs,' I was told gently. 'They have all gone out on strike.'

'Can't the two maids go in a tram?' my friend suggested, 'and then we can take the luggage with us.'

'There are no trams,' came the same answer decisively. 'We shall have to get everything into the motor somehow or other.'

The other passengers were now all crowded on the station steps, some of them sitting disconsolately on their boxes, others talking in excited voices, arguing with the porters, who only shrugged their shoulders and repeated stolidly that there were no cabs. . .

At last the three of us, with our various bags and wraps, the English officer, the two maids, and the rest of the luggage, managed to crowd into the motor, leaving the other passengers gazing after us enviously.

Hardly four yards away we passed a tram with all its windows broken, standing desolate on the lines. A few minutes farther on a soldier with a rifle and bayonet stopped us, and then after a prolonged conversation allowed us to continue on our way.

In the bleak, grey light of that early morning the town looked inexpressibly desolate and deserted, the bare, ugly street leading up from the station, with the dirty stucco houses on either side, seemed, after the snow-white peace of the country, somehow the very acme of dreariness. The few soldiers we passed eyed us suspiciously, here and there a woman with a shawl over her head hurried along, looking furtively round as if she feared at every corner some hidden danger. But beyond that the streets seemed completely empty, nearly all the shops were boarded up, not a face showed at the windows of any of the houses.

Avoiding the big thoroughfares of the Nevsky and the Morskaya, we made a detour by St Isaac's and drove back along the Quay. One solitary policeman with a white, set face watched us pass but made no movement to stop us. A strange spell of silence and dread lay over the frozen river, the palaces all along the Quay seemed to be holding their breath in a terrible suspense, on the opposite shore the Fortress, with the Imperial flag fluttering against the iron grey sky, looked grim and desolate, the huge bridge spanning the river was absolutely empty.

My father and mother had returned from Finland the day before, and met me at the Embassy with obvious relief, and a very little later the breathless silence, that had been so intense and almost uncanny when we drove through the town, was broken, and the first real fighting began.[16]

The English officer – it was Colonel Knox – must also have breathed a sigh of relief when they finally reached the Embassy at 9.30 and he was able to relinquish responsibility for Miss Buchanan and all her various items of luggage. About an hour later he drove to the Artillery Department, a large building on the Liteiny Prospect.

I was talking to friends there in the corridor on the first floor, outside the office of General Manikovsky, the Chief of the Department, when General Hypatiev, the chemical expert, and M. Tereshchenko arrived with the news that the depot troops of the garrison had mutinied and were coming down the street. I heard for the first time that a company of the Pavlovsky Regiment had fired on the police on the previous evening and had been disarmed and confined in the Preobrazhensky barracks. The Preobrazhensky and Volynsky Regiments had now mutinied.

We went to the window and waited. Outside there was evident

excitement, but no sound came to us through the thick double windows. Groups were standing at the corners gesticulating and pointing down the street. Officers were hurrying away, and motor-cars, my own amongst the number, were taking refuge in the courtyards of neighbouring houses.

It seemed that we waited at least ten minutes before the mutineers arrived. Craning our necks, we first saw two soldiers – a sort of advanced guard – who strode along the middle of the street, pointing their rifles at loiterers to clear the road. One of them fired two shots at an unfortunate chauffeur. Then came a great disorderly mass of soldiery, stretching right across the wide street and both pavements. They were led by a diminutive but immensely dignified student. There were no officers. All were armed, and many had red flags fastened to their bayonets. They came slowly and finally gathered in a compact mass in front of the Department. They looked up at the windows, which were now crowded with officers and clerks, but showed no sign of hostility. What struck me most was the uncanny silence of it all. We were like spectators in a gigantic cinema. Tereshchenko, who stood beside me, told me later that as he looked down on the disorderly crowd, he foresaw all the quarrels and licence and indiscipline that were to follow.

General Manikovsky came out and invited Tereshchenko and me in to his room. We were soon joined there by General Hypatiev, and by General Lekhovich, who a few hours before had been appointed Assistant Minister of War.

Hypatiev asked me if I reported such things to England, and I said that I certainly did. He seemed overcome by the shame of the mutiny.

Soon we heard the windows and door on the ground floor being broken in, and the sound of shots reached us.

The telephone rang and Manikovsky took up the receiver. 'They are shooting at the Sestroretsk Works, are they?' he roared in his great voice. 'Well, God be with them! They are shooting at the Chief Artillery Department too!'

An excited orderly rushed in: 'Your High Excellency! They are forcing their way into the building. Shall we barricade your door?' But Manikovsky had kept his nerve, and said: 'No. Open all the doors. Why should we hinder them?' As the orderly turned away, astonished at this new complaisance, Manikovsky sighed, and said to me with the characteristic Russian click of worried anger: 'Look what our Ministry has brought us to!'

Tereshchenko went out, and most of the officers were leaving the Department by a back door. Hypatiev and I went to the staircase and looked over the banisters. Down on the ground floor, soldiers were taking the officers' swords, and a few hooligans were going through the pockets of coats left in the vestibule. I went down and found a N.C.O. of the Preobrazhenskys, who was ordering his men to take only the swords and to steal nothing. I told him who I was, and he helped me on with my coat. I returned upstairs and found Manikovsky had gone.

A party of soldiers was almost timidly breaking the glass of one of the arm-stands to take out the rifles – specimens of the armament of other nations, that were without ammunition and would be of no use to them. As they went off, proud of their capture, an officer caught the arm of one of them – a young soldier with a straight, honest face – and remonstrated with him, and I heard the boy reply: 'I could not help it. They forced me.'

I descended the stairs and my N.C.O. gave me a couple of men to escort me through the crowd. Out in the street a ragged individual expressed his delight with much gesticulation. He yelled: 'They used to beat our friends in the prison over there, to beat them with rods!'

A hundred yards further we met the French Military Attaché, Colonel Lavergne, who was on his way to the Artillery Department in search of some prosaic details regarding the output of shells. My escort recommended him to turn back and we walked together to the French Embassy. There, as the men left us, we stood a moment on the Quay, and looked back at the stream of troops now crossing the bridge to liberate the prisoners in the Krestovsky Prison, and Lavergne suddenly asked me if those men were mutineers and if my escort had been mutineers. They had been so orderly and friendly that he had never dreamed that they were anything but loyal troops!

I walked on to the British Embassy. The Ambassador had gone, as usual, with the French Ambassador to the Foreign Office. I telephoned to him that a large part of the garrison had mutinied and was in undisputed control of the Liteiny Prospect. I heard him repeat my message in French to the Foreign Minister M. Pokrovsky, and to the French Ambassador.

I expected Colonel Engelhardt to lunch, so walked back to my flat. Engelhardt, of course, did not come, for he, with other prominent members of the Duma, was busy trying to bring the torrent of anarchy under control. He had been appointed Commandant of Petrograd...

After lunch I went to see General Khabalov... and passed on the way the still loyal part of the Preobrazhensky and the Keksgolmsky Regiments, which were marching in good order under their officers into the Winter Palace.

I found General Khabalov at the Prefecture... On the street outside a party of Cossacks stood dismounted beside their horses. I climbed the stairs to the first floor. In the centre room of the long group of apartments a few Guards officers were seated, silent and depressed. Young officers of Cossacks were coming and going with reports.

From the centre room, where I waited, through the folding doors officers and officials could be seen in the further rooms walking to and fro in earnest conversation. The Grand Duke Cyril was said to be there amongst others, but I did not see him.

General Belyaev [Minister of War] passed and shook hands with his usual courtly smile. I never saw him again.

General Zankevich, the General Quartermaster, talked bravely. He said: 'These are only depot troops that have mutinied, and not regulars. Regular troops will very soon put the movement down.'

At last General Khabalov came, and I told him that the Ambassador had sent me to ascertain the situation. He said that the position was 'very serious', as a part of the Depot Battalion of the Preobrazhenskys, the whole of the Volynsky, Pavlovsky and Litovsky Battalions and the Sappers of the Guards had mutinied, and the movement might spread. He thought he could trust the Cossacks, and he said he had telegraphed to the front for troops.

I left the Prefecture with the conviction that the old regime was doomed.

From the Embassy, later, I walked with another British officer to the Liteiny Prospect. On the way we passed a very drunken soldier with rifle and fixed bayonet. The great District Court, nearly opposite the Artillery Department, was blazing. It had been set on fire early in the day, partly perhaps in imitation of the storming of the Bastille, but more, no doubt, with the practical idea of destroying all criminal records. We found a barricade across the street with three guns and some soldiers. I asked if I could go to No.9 to see some friends, and the sentry said that I might go anywhere if I only gave up my sword. Another man immediately interrupted him with the remark: 'These are Englishmen! You must not insult them!' However, the guard decided that it was better not to pass the barricade. One of the soldiers grasped my hand and said: 'We have only one wish – to beat the Germans to the end, and we will begin with the Germans here and with a family that you know of called Romanov.' The crowds on the Nevsky on the previous day had been shouting: 'Down with Alexandra!' (*Doloi Sashe!*)

Three men were coming to dine, but Ramsden (one of the secretaries at the Embassy) and Prince B— sent apologies, the first because all hired cabs had disappeared from the streets, and the latter because, as a prominent member of the Court, he had been advised to remain at home. Only Markozov came, having walked the whole three miles from his house. He brought the news that all the regiments except the Moskovsky had joined the movement. After dinner we telephoned to various people, both he (the ex-Guards officer) and I hoping for the success of the Revolution. He left me at 10 p.m. to walk back, but quickly returned to say that there was firing next door, where the headquarters of the Secret Police with its incriminating documents was being burned.[17]

*

As military attaché, Knox had been mainly concerned all day with assessing the state of the troops and the likely outcome of the revolution. For the most detailed account of what was happening on the streets of Petrograd during the course of Red Monday we turn to Stinton Jones, a British engineer with Westinghouse, who had lived in Russia for twelve years and had a Russian wife.[18]

On leaving home early to cross into the city, he found large crowds collected at the bridgeheads, where their way was blocked by cordons of police, all fully armed and ready to open fire at a moment's notice. He was only able to get through by saying that he was an Englishman and mendaciously adding that he was a war-agent on his way to the British Embassy.

In the city, however, large processions of residents and those remaining from the previous night were already making their way by various routes to the Small-Arms Factory & Arsenal. This was guarded by a strong force of police and soldiers. When the huge crowd became threatening, the police opened fire, killing and wounding many. The infuriated mob then immediately rushed the police cordon and broke through. Ordered to fire by the police, the soldiers refused, shot down their own officers and joined the crowd against the police. Then they all broke into the Arsenal and removed its enormous stores of rifles, revolvers, swords and machine-guns, and almost unlimited supplies of ammunition. The soldiers stocked up with ammunition and a number formed themselves into machine-gun detachments, while the crowd seized whatever weapons came to hand. The police meanwhile continued firing, but the people could now join the soldiers in firing back. Everywhere the police were shot down without mercy.

By this time the crowd and soldiers had become a disorderly rabble. Worked up to a frenzy of excitement, they turned their attention to the nearby Krestovsky Prison, which they burst open, killing the guards and releasing the inmates. This added to the already furious mob a large number of the worst possible criminal characters, who were immediately supplied with arms. Many were still awaiting trial, and their first thought was how to destroy all the incriminating evidence held against them in the adjoining District Court. The simplest method was to set light to the whole building, which soon became a blazing furnace. Not only criminal records were destroyed, however, but the archives of centuries: an act of vandalism described by Stinton Jones as 'one of the worst of the whole Revolution'. Both the Court and the Prison burnt for the greater part of the day and night, and were completely gutted.

Various detachments of revolutionaries then went off to attack other prisons in and around Petrograd. Here, too, they killed the guards and released the inmates, whom they armed. The people, Jones writes, 'had many bitter memories to avenge'. At nine every Wednesday morning, from the gates of the prison near the Moscow Station, a procession of 100 to 150 political prisoners would emerge, mostly chained together by the wrist in groups and escorted by police and gendarmes, on their way to entrain for the point on the Siberian Railway nearest to their place of exile. This prison was burnt. When released, however, the majority of political prisoners declined to take up arms, preferring to make the most of their new-found freedom.

Other mobs turned their attention to the police-stations, breaking in and killing the men in charge. Where resistance was offered, brisk fights took place, but the outcome was always the same. Having captured the stations, they immediately set fire to them, making sure that every piece of furniture and scrap of paper in the place should be burnt. In cases where the stations were in a large block of buildings, the mob, not wishing to injure the property of their fellow-citizens, cleared the contents out into the middle of the street and made a huge bonfire of them. In a very short time every police-station was either in flames or its contents were being burnt. The mob took control of the large stores of arms accumulated at each station. Later in the day the headquarters of the Secret Police received similar treatment. This formed part of a large block on the Fontanka Canal, which also contained the flat of the much-hated Minister of the Interior, Protopopov. Here, too, every article of furniture, and every document, book and scrap of paper, was carried out of the Secret Police offices and the Minister's flat, and made into huge bonfires. It was 'entirely just', Jones comments, that incriminating evidence relating to political and religious prisoners and suspects should be burnt, but not documents containing particulars of criminals, to say nothing of the vast volumes of information relating to enemy spies. The homes of judges and police-officers all suffered the same fate.

Police resistance did not cease, however, with the destruction of police-stations. Many policemen had stationed themselves on the roofs of high buildings, where they were armed with machine-guns, placed there, it emerged later, by Protopopov's agents in expectation of demonstrations at the opening of the Duma a fortnight earlier. From these hidden vantage-points they fired into the thickest of the mobs. There would be a momentary hush, followed by the cries of the wounded and a general scurry for cover. As the streets cleared, little heaps, some very still, others writhing in agony, told of the machine-guns' toll. The casualties would have been even heavier had the guns been on ground level and commanded a whole street.

From the doubtful protection of doorways and arches the crowds returned the fire with interest, but did very little damage save to buildings, as few of those possessing arms knew how to use them. The situation of people living in these buildings became very dangerous, Jones writes,

> and in many cases the occupants were shot through their windows quite by accident. On the other hand, the police on the roofs took care to shoot, with deliberate intention to kill, at those who showed themselves at the windows of the houses opposite. As the ammunition used by the police was charged with smokeless powder and these events happened in the daytime, none could tell where the police were, and thus no part of the city was safe.

Knowing that the religious views of the Russians would to a

great extent prevent them firing at churches, the Government had
with diabolical intent caused the majority of the machine-guns to
be placed in the belfries. It was some time before the people
realised where the fire was coming from, and even when they did
they were very loath to return it, as they thought to hit so sacred a
building would be an act of sacrilege. Nevertheless the machine-
guns had to be silenced. In most cases this was done by a patrol of
soldiers and people entering the churches, which they did with a
respect that was almost awe. They then made their way to the belfries... This was not so dangerous a proceeding as it might
appear, as owing to their cramped positions the police could not
put up a very serious hand-to-hand fight. In many cases the police
were simply thrown over the parapets into the roadway below. In
cases where policemen were wounded, no medical assistance was
allowed them, but they were dispatched out of hand.

The people of Petrograd had much to avenge.[19]

All these widespread events were following each other with
'almost bewildering rapidity', and it is hard to imagine that Jones
can have witnessed more than a sample of them. To the following
vivid paragraph, however, he adds in a footnote: 'I detail only what I
saw about me.'

In a short time the whole of the city was aglow with the glare from
the burning buildings which, in addition to the heavy firing, made
the situation appear far worse than it actually was, and had the
effect of clearing the streets of the more serious-minded and
nervous citizens. The mobs presented a strange, almost grotesque
appearance. Soldiers, workmen, students, hooligans and freed
criminals wandered aimlessly about in detached companies, all
armed, but with a strange variety of weapons. Here would be a
hooligan with an officer's sword fastened over his overcoat, a rifle
in one hand and a revolver in the other; there a small boy with a
large butcher's knife on his shoulder. Close by a workman would
be seen awkwardly holding an officer's sword in one hand and a
bayonet in the other. One man had two revolvers, another a rifle in
one hand and a tram-line cleaner in the other. A student with two
rifles and a belt of machine-gun bullets round his waist was walking beside another with a bayonet tied to the end of a stick. A
drunken soldier had only the barrel of a rifle remaining, the stock
having been broken off in forcing an entry into some shop. A

steady, quiet-looking business man grasped a large rifle and a formidable belt of cartridges.[20]

Singing, shouting, roaring, firing off their weapons into the air
regardless of whom the bullets might hit, these mobs wandered
along without leaders, apparently without purpose. Although it was
not yet noon, the whole city and surrounding districts were already
in their hands.

Meanwhile, at the Embassy, shut up in the house and forbidden to
go out, Meriel Buchanan spent most of the morning sitting on the big
staircase, gleaning what information she could from the various
people who came and went.

In the afternoon a few English ladies, braving the very real dangers of the street, came to the weekly sewing party, and sat talking
in hushed tones of what might be the result of all this... A little
later the first motor-lorries passed across the bridge in front of us,
filled with soldiers... Occasionally one could hear bursts of firing in the distance, and news was brought us that the Fortress,
after very little resistance, had surrendered to the people...
More and more motor-lorries began to pass, and the sound of firing seeming to become more persistent, mother sent the English
ladies home while it was still light.[21]

It was not only motor-lorries, however, that began to fill the
streets, for, as Stinton Jones writes,

the crowds commenced to commandeer every automobile in the
city, no matter to whom it might belong. These automobiles they
filled with armed men, with at least two soldiers lying on the
mudguards with loaded rifles and fixed bayonets. These formidable units then rushed all over the city shooting wildly, but with the
chief object of hunting down the police, especially those in the out-
lying districts who had not yet become aware of the true state of
affairs in the city... It was a terrifying sight to see a private lim-
ousine tearing down the road filled with armed men and a
machine-gun mounted on its roof. The gun was of very little use,
as it was with the greatest difficulty that the men themselves could
keep in position, let alone the gun, which wobbled about perilous-
ly. Upon the motor-lorries machine-guns were mounted in such a
way as to command the front edge of the house roofs from the

roadway. When those in charge were certain of a particular building from which the police were firing, the lorry would draw up
and return the fire... Later in the day a large mob broke into the
big Military Garage and commandeered all the cars, including a
number of armoured cars. These were largely responsible for the
speedy way in which the police with their machine-guns were
rounded up, as from the cars they were able to concentrate their
fire on any particular point without suffering injury themselves.[22]

As Knox had learned, the military authorities' only hope of sup-
pressing the movement was to bring in troops that had not been
infected by the mood of revolutionary excitement in the city centre.
Arthur Ransome, whose flat was in the rapidly diminishing area still
under the authorities' control, witnessed an instance of the way in
which this plan repeatedly misfired. 'Went up towards Duma with
troops being led against revolutionaries stop battle proceeding in
Liteiny district where new troops ordered fire hesitated moment
then in extreme brotherly love handed over their rifles to crowd
stop.'[23]

Throughout the day red flags and pieces of red rag were everywhere evident, and hardly a soul was to be seen in the streets without some such decoration. It was, indeed, highly dangerous, Stinton
Jones writes,

> to be among the crowds without such evidence of one's
> sympathies. Personally I took the precaution of wearing a small
> Union Jack in my button-hole. In spite of this, I was repeatedly
> challenged by someone in the mob, whereupon I uttered
> the magic word 'Englishman', showed my flag, and all was well.

Ransome's experiences were similar. At dusk, wearing his big
overcoat and fur hat, he was stopped by a man on horseback, who
took him to be a Russian officer. During the day all officers had been
stopped by the mobs, and as in Knox's case, asked to give up their
arms. If they agreed and handed them over, they were allowed their
freedom, but in cases where they refused, they were shot down and
their arms taken; any particularly unpopular officers who were recognized by units of their regiments were shot without question.
Ransome's position was therefore perilous.

Quote for the people or against people unquote was asked with

revolver in my face stop Replied was English stop Long live
England shouted man and galloped on stop Everywhere great
courtesy towards Allies stop This domestic affair we not drag you
into it represents Russian attitude[24]

Towards evening, according to Stinton Jones, a large number of
people who had stayed indoors all day joined the crowd in the
streets, and this led to an enormous number of casualties.

Machine-guns spitting lead in all directions and thousands of persons were firing indiscriminately. It was all a matter of luck
whether one escaped or no. I myself had many narrow escapes, as I
invariably found myself in the thick of the mob. It was safer,
however, than being in my office with bullets coming through the
windows. In addition to the actual fighting between the people and
the police, numbers of young and irresponsible boys and hooligans
found huge delight in firing off their weapons into the air or at
windows, in fact anywhere that suited their fancy [pigeons being a
favourite target, according to Ransome]. Again, there was great
danger from the happily few drunken soldiers and hooligans.
These took a keen delight in showing small groups of people, especially women and girls, how to load and fire a rifle. This they
would do by placing a cartridge in the breech and then pulling the
trigger, quite regardless as to where the bullet might go.
    In a few hours the value of human life had dropped with start-
ling suddenness. By carelessness in handling weapons quite a
number of people were killed and injured. Little boys also delighted in picking up dropped cartridges and throwing them into the
fires which were burning outside the police-stations and also the
usual fires in the streets to give the people, more especially the
poorer classes and cabmen, an opportunity of warming themselves. During the Revolution these fires were numerous, the
dvorniks [house-porters] seeing the necessity of such fires to warm
their comrades in the streets. It was in these fires that the younger
element delighted to throw loose cartridges they had picked up. In
many cases these children became possessed of fire-arms and, in
imitation of their elders, they delighted to fire them off.
    One little boy of about twelve years of age had secured an auto-
matic pistol and, together with a large number of soldiers, was
warming himself at one of these fires. Suddenly he pulled the trigger and one of the soldiers fell dead. This so alarmed the boy, who

had no idea of the mechanism of the deadly weapon he held, that he kept the trigger pulled back and the automatic pistol proceeded to empty itself. It contained seven bullets, and it was not until they were all discharged that the boy released his hold of the trigger. The result was that three soldiers were killed and four seriously injured. This wholesale destruction was probably an isolated case, but hundreds of people were injured by the careless use of weapons in unaccustomed hands. Quite a number of children shot themselves whilst playing with firearms.

In the evening and throughout the night it was a weird and wonderful sight to see the rabble in the streets waving red flags and singing revolutionary songs, while the sky was aglow from the burning buildings. One particular fire was extremely picturesque, that of the large police and fire station situated near the Moscow Station. All fire-stations throughout Russia are built with a very tall look-out tower usually surmounted by a very high mast. This particular station consisted of four floors above which was built this high tower, the whole reaching to a height of about 150 feet, and when the flames secured a good hold on the building, the tower acted as a chimney and produced a most weird and terrifying picture silhouetted as it was against the night sky.[25]

*

To find out about the political developments that were taking place on Red Monday, we turn to Harold Williams and his wife, Ariadna Tyrkova-Williams.

Early in the morning a friend telephoned to say that the soldiers of the Volynsky Regiment were running wildly about the streets firing aimlessly. They hurried out and made for the Taurida Palace. The Imperial ukase ordering the dissolution of the Duma, Williams reported in the *Chronicle*,

passed unnoticed. M. Rodzianko repeated his warning telegram [of the previous evening] to the Emperor in language of greater insistency: 'The last hour has come to decide the fate of the dynasty; further delay is fatal.' The Emperor made no reply.

The Duma waited loyally. At 1 troops began coming to the Duma to ask for guidance. In the afternoon the Duma formed a Temporary Committee, one member from each party, to keep control of events. The Ministers disappeared.[26]

More and more parties of troops, with numbers of armed citizens, began arriving. They were loudly cheered, and were addressed by the Socialist and Labour leaders. 'I looked at the faces of these mutineers,' Williams wrote later,

> and I shall not easily forget the strained eyes fixed on the speakers, the rough hard features of these young peasants in khaki, the look of bewilderment mingled with fear of these simple ignorant men, transformed by some strange turn in the wheel of fortune into makers of history. They cheered hoarsely, and asked one another who were Kerensky and Chkheidze.
>
> Soon the immense hall of the Duma was crowded with soldiers who listened eagerly to speeches from well-known deputies and from fiery socialist orators, men and women, who had suddenly sprung from obscurity.[27]

At 5.30 a strong revolutionary escort brought in Shcheglovitov, one of the most prominent reactionaries. At the same time, it was intimated that a number of other arrests were imminent: the so-called German Gang was to be removed once for all. Boy and girl students ran about on various errands, and veteran soldiers obeyed them. Food committees and supply committees were set up. Because she was a member of the Municipal Supplies Committee, and had organized a municipal restaurant for a thousand people, Ariadna Tyrkova-Williams now found herself entrusted with the task of feeding tens of thousands of mutineers.

> I tried in the first instance to persuade the soldiers to return to their barracks for supper. I failed; they did not feel in the least like victors, and feared that machine-guns would meet them at the barracks. I telephoned fantastic orders to various tea-rooms and restaurants. To my surprise they were instantly carried out. The words 'Taurida Palace' and 'the Duma Committee' had magic power.[28]

Regiment after regiment came up, led by sergeants, to offer its help. By evening, Harold Williams writes,

> when all the speakers were hoarse and weary, it was certain that the whole Petrograd garrison of 140,000 men had gone over to the Revolution. But their officers were not with them. Uncertain of

their duty, unwilling to break their oath of allegiance, they held back – all but a very few – and passed the day in deep depression while Petrograd was rejoicing.[29]

At about nine o'clock, Ariadna writes, after spending ten hours in a revolutionary crowd, she and Harold decided to have a break. At home everything was as usual: the cook had prepared dinner, the maid was ready to wait. Only the telephone kept ringing. They were bombarded with questions. No one knew what was really happening, but the Taurida Palace was recognized as the centre of Russia. Then came a telephone call from a journalist friend at Taurida itself. An important meeting, he said, was about to take place and Tyrkova-Williams was needed. Harold went with her.

Among the political prisoners released earlier in the day from the Krestovsky Prison were members of the Workmen's Group of the Central Military Industrial Committee, who had been arrested a month earlier. On their release they took possession of a room at the Duma and reconvened the Council (Soviet) of Workmen's Deputies, which had been banned since December 1905. A manifesto was issued inviting the troops siding with the people, and the factories, to choose representatives to attend a meeting of the Council in the Duma premises that evening: one representative per battalion, one per thousand workmen, and one from each factory employing less than a thousand hands.

It was to this meeting, at which the decision was taken to fuse the worker and soldier elements in the revolution by setting up the Council of Workers' and Soldiers' Deputies, thereby creating a political organization of great appeal to the working masses, that Ariadna Tyrkova-Williams had been summoned. 'Lists of deputies from various liberal professions were being hastily drawn up. They wanted to include me, but I refused. My political sympathies were at the other end of the Taurida Palace, where in Rodzianko's study the more moderate wing of the Opposition was organizing a Provisional Government.'[30] Shortly before midnight these moderates decided to take power.

'Thus ended,' in the words of Stinton Jones, 'one of the most historical and probably the most memorable day for the Russian people. To quote a remark heard, "The slowest people on earth had done the quickest thing in history." '[31]

The Birth of Freedom

Tuesday, March 13 to Saturday, March 17: agreement reached between Duma
Committee and Soviet on formation of Provisional Government

On Tuesday morning Meriel Buchanan woke with the feeling that
what had happened on the day before must have been a dream, and
it was not until the sharp crack of a rifle outside made her go to the
window that she was sure she wasn't still asleep. The great square
had a desolate air, the tram lines were blocked with snow, not a cart
or cab was to be seen, to the right across the frozen river the Fortress
stood bleak and grey with no flag fluttering against the sky to give a
sign of life. Bands of workmen and soldiers, carrying a strange
assortment of weapons, were crossing the Troitsky Bridge in small
companies of three or four, and there seemed to be a slackness about
the way the soldiers walked that had not been there before. Now and
then motor-lorries, bristling with soldiers and rifles, like enormous
hedgehogs, decked with huge red flags, lumbered past; and later
private cars began going by, evidently commandeered, their back
windows broken and the wicked-looking nose of a machine-gun
sticking through the opening.[1]

'Today is the critical day,' Colonel Knox noted that morning in his
diary. 'It is a grand sunny day with about twelve degrees of frost
(Réaumur). A biting north-east wind would have been better, as it
would have kept people indoors.' It was not that he feared the old
regime might attempt to reassert itself; what he wanted for Russia now
was a swift, trouble-free transition to constitutional government that
would lead to a wholehearted renewal of her commitment to the war.

Ivan, my orderly, arrives with the news that heavy firing is going on in the Vyborg District, and in the Nevsky direction. The sailors have come in from Kronstadt to join the movement. Bands of excited men are motoring about in cars with rifles, cheering and being cheered by the populace. Ivan thinks that there is 'perfect organization'!...

The telephone does not work. One can only hope for the best. If the officers would only join the movement! I must go out to try to find out things.[2]

Late on the previous evening, Arthur Ransome had made his way to the Astoria, Petrograd's largest and most modern hotel. It had been taken over at the beginning of the war by the military authorities, and was packed out with officers on leave from the front or convalescent, the families of high-ranking officers on active service, and a large contingent of Allied officers. In the vestibule Ransome found the officers debating what to do, while an old general urged them to go quietly to their rooms.

I stayed some time, hoping to witness a meeting between the revolutionaries and the officers, but about midnight started home along the Moika Canal. Meanwhile, the revolutionary left wing had swept forward towards the river passing my house, which now lies in revolutionary territory. But isolated bodies of police on the roofs of houses were keeping up desultory fire. I had a narrow shave from a hand-grenade which was dropped from a roof and exploded in front of me. Twice I was stopped by revolutionary patrols. I found heavy firing going on up and down my street. The naval barracks at the foot of the street were being persuaded by bombardment to join the revolutionaries. I dodged across the street in a quiet moment. There was a horrid row all night mixed with intermittent heavier firing from the siege of the Admiralty.[3]

The officers in the Astoria had given an undertaking that there would be no shooting from the building, in return for which the revolutionaries would leave the hotel unmolested. Accounts vary as to what sparked off the trouble early on Tuesday morning, but the most likely version, given by an eye-witness, George Bury, a Canadian who was in Russia to help in the organization of shipping, is that one of Protopopov's agents, hidden on the top floor of the hotel, turned a machine-gun on the soldiers and people assembled in the square below. The gun, Bury writes, was just over the windows of a suite of rooms occupied by the wife and daughter with their maids of General Prince Tumanov, who is in command of a Cavalry Division at the front. In reply to this provocative gun the revolutionary forces brought up a couple of armoured motors with three machine-guns apiece and opened a furious cannonade upon the Astoria. Whether from careless shooting or inability to locate the provocative gun, this fusillade wrecked the rooms of the Tumanov princesses and did considerable damage to the adjoining suite. The young Princess Tumanov, roused from her bed by the infernal din of this fusillade, rushed to the window apparently in a panic and received a bullet through the neck [she was treated later at the Anglo-Russian Hospital[4]]. The maids fled screaming into the corridors and the Tumanov ladies sought refuge in the bathroom of their suite which was happily protected by a substantial wall. The whole place was in an uproar, for the mob of soldiers, sailors and people had smashed all the great plate glass double windows reaching within a foot of the pavement on the ground-floor and were busy wrecking the interior. The kitchen and stores were wrecked and looted. Happily they found less drink in the cellars than was normally kept there, but enough remained to intoxicate the first comers. [According to Stinton Jones, also an eye-witness, 'some of the soldiers, after they had drunk as much as they possibly could, poured the wine into their top-boots and then wandered away to consume more elsewhere.'[5]] A good deal of blood was spilt on the ground floor and the excited soldiers with a number of sailors proceeded to search the upstairs premises. Every Russian officer was disarmed but the allied officers were treated with much more courtesy, although in the passion of the moment not a few had very narrow escapes of being butchered. Naturally the rage of the invaders was directed specially towards the point whence they supposed the treacherous shooting to have come. How many other lives were lost in this hotel I cannot say, but the shooting and bayoneting went on for some time in the building and the revolving door was running in a pool of blood.[6]

The English officers in residence at the time, Jones writes, naturally did not attempt to join in the fighting.

Their chief concern was for the women and children. These they collected together and formed a guard in front of them. They then informed the mob in the hotel that they themselves would not in any way interfere with their programme provided that the women and children were not molested, but in such an event they would protect them to the last man. This called forth great cheers from the crowd, who promised that they would not interfere with the English or other foreign officers or any of the women and children. This promise they religiously kept, but insisted that all Russian officers must give themselves up without further delay. This they were persuaded to do, with the result that they were all immediately placed under arrest and taken from the building. In the square outside a number of these officers were shot, while others were taken to places of detention under a strong escort of soldiers.

Stinton Jones was standing close to the spot where the officers were executed. They included one general who had performed the mad act of firing into the crowd from a window at the same time as the machine-gun began pouring its stream of lead down from the roof. His body was thrown into the adjoining canal.[7]

Finally, Bury writes,

order and some discipline were restored and sentries posted on all floors to put a stop to looting by the mob, who rapidly assembled in vast numbers filling the greater part of the square. At the moment after midday, when the crowd was thickest on the square, rapid machine-gun firing began again, presumably from the Admiralty 600–700 yards away, or from the Marinsky Palace, about half that distance away in the opposite direction. The crowd of civilians, including numbers of women and girls, soldiers and sailors, dispersed with celerity to cover. Ten men were killed and a number wounded. Firing continued for ten minutes and several shots were loosed off again inside the hotel. Several attempts were made to burn the premises down, the Astoria being known to the mob as originally a German undertaking. It happily remains standing, the lower floors wrecked and looted, and the whole vast structure littered with broken glass and debris.[8]

Once the excitement was over, Bury and his assistant hurried off to the British Embassy to pass on the latest news. Here they found Knox preparing to set off on the two miles' tramp through the snow to find out for the Ambassador what was happening at the Duma, and the three of them decided to join forces. Knox takes up the story:

Half way, a country sledge passed us crowded with peasants in holiday dress. They waved their arms and cheered, and when we cheered in reply, they stopped the sledge and offered us a lift, an old soldier, who smelt strongly of vodka, turning other passengers off the sledge to make room for us. As we drove along, holding on to one another to avoid falling, my soldier friend breathed into my ear that the Emperor was a good man, and fond of the people, but was surrounded by traitors. Now these traitors would be removed and all would be well.

We arrived at the Duma at the moment when the Preobrazhensky Regiment was being interviewed by Rodzianko. The whole wide street before the building was thronged with lorries filled with joy-riding soldiers. Our self-appointed guide walked in front of us, waving his hat and shouting: 'Way for the British representative!' I felt a fool, and no doubt looked it. The Preobrazhensky giants yelled: 'Hurrah!'

Our man conducted us to the great Catherine Hall [which Bury likens to a cathedral nave a hundred yards in length], in a cleared space in the middle of which I saw for a moment Rodzianko and Guchkov. Then I fell back into the crowd, while Rodzianko addressed the men, calling upon them to return to barracks and to maintain order, as otherwise they would degenerate into a useless mob. I overheard one soldier near me say to his companions: 'No. We won't return to barracks, for that will mean guards and fatigues and work as before.' Then I noticed an expression of sad bewilderment and disappointment come over the face of my guide, who had been listening intently to another man of the Preobrazhenskys. Poor fellow! No doubt his simple, honest beliefs had been shattered and he had begun to understand that a revolution was something coarser than the gentle thing he had imagined.

Rodzianko was succeeded by the pale-faced lawyer, Kerensky, who spoke hoarsely from the shoulders of guardsmen. I could not catch much of what he said, but I am told that he is working loyally with the Duma Committee.

The other Labour members have been less patriotic, and are working on purely party lines for the Soviet. The first news-sheet (*Izvestiya*) of this organization, which was published today, contains nothing objectionable, but a leaflet, signed 'Petrograd Committee of the Russian Social Democratic Labour Party and the Party of Social Revolutionaries' is less pleasant reading for an ally, for it incites to class-war. It commences: 'Proletariat of all countries, unite! The movement we long ago inaugurated has grown to fruition, and has cleared our way for the realization of the eternal longing of the proletariat. The people has overthrown the capitalists and in co-operation with the army has annihilated that hireling of the Bourgeoisie, the Imperial Government. The place of the latter has been taken by the Temporary Revolutionary Government, which should be composed only of representatives of the proletariat and of the army.'

Harold Williams, the *Daily Chronicle* man, whom I met at the Duma, told me that things last night were very bad – worse even than they are at present – but that the Duma Committee is now gradually getting the upper hand.

The scene in the Duma today, however, did not show much sign of the re-establishment of order. Few people were working. Soldiers lounged everywhere. There were only about thirty officers, and they seemed ashamed of themselves. One room was being used as an extemporary cartridge factory. In another, bags of flour were piled up for the issue of rations to the troops as they arrived. In another I found poor Engelhardt trying to function as Military Commandant. He sat at a table, on which was a huge loaf of half-gnawed black bread, and tried vainly to make himself heard above the noise of a rabble of soldiers, all spitting and smoking and asking questions...

In my walk back from the Duma, I met Tereshchenko, who told me that efforts were being made to induce the officers to come over in order to restore order. Meanwhile, many officers are being arrested. I am probably the only one in Petrograd that now wears a sword![9]

All the most unpopular reactionaries were being systematically rounded up. While Knox was in the Duma, Stürmer, a former Prime Minister, 'was brought along the corridor with an *opéra bouffe* escort, led by a solemn student with his sword at the carry. The old man, wrapped in a huge fur coat, was unceremoniously hustled along.' Harold Williams saw the Metropolitan, Pitirim, brought in: 'a pale and tottering figure in white cap and black robe, pushed on from behind by not very respectful soldiers. Very different he was when I saw him last, in his palatial apartment at the Alexander Nevsky Monastery, with generals, high officials, and society ladies waiting on his pleasure.' Three search parties were out looking for Protopopov. At 11.15 p.m., Knox writes, a student standing in the open space before the Taurida Palace was accosted by an individual in an old fur coat with muffled-up face: 'Tell me, you are a student?' 'Yes.' 'I ask you to take me to the Executive Committee of the Imperial Duma. I am the former Minister of the Interior, Protopopov'; then in a lower voice with lowered head: 'I also wish well to my country, and that is the reason I have come of my own free will. Take me to the people who want me.'

George Bury is scathing about Protopopov's 'crocodile tears', but claims that in proof of good faith he handed Kerensky, who took him into custody at the Duma, a plan of Petrograd on which were marked all the places and particulars of the machine-guns installed earlier on his instructions.[10]

'All these gentlemen', Robert Wilton wrote in *The Times*,

are comfortably housed in the Ministerial pavilion which had been fitted up for their comfort and convenience in the days of their glory. I paid a cursory visit to this interesting house of detention. The inmates had just been handed a few sandwiches and tea – a luxurious meal at the Taurida Palace in these times. M. Stürmer was busily perusing papers at his writing desk. His colleagues were wandering listlessly to and fro, or sitting in small groups discussing the wondrous events through which they were passing. M. Protopopov reclined on a sofa, a physical wreck.[11]

What retaliation the Emperor might be planning was unclear, but in Petrograd support for the old regime was crumbling by the hour. Knox reckoned that in the present state of disorder a couple of thousand regulars with guns would make short work of the Revolution, but every trainload of troops that arrived 'to quell the rising' was met by a persuasively large reception committee and went over at once to the side of the revolutionaries.[12]

Stubborn pockets of resistance, however, remained. The naval barracks at the foot of Arthur Ransome's street eventually decided to hang out the red flag and opened its gates to the revolutionaries, but it was not until 4 in the afternoon that the Admiralty surrendered. In the meantime Ransome had witnessed another fierce encounter. 'The battle has come to me,' he informed his readers,

and my windows have the best possible view of preparations for the storm of the prison which is next door on my right. Desultory fighting has been going on from the roofs. The revolutionaries announced that they would take the prison at two o'clock. At ten minutes to the hour a motor car stopped in the open space between my windows and the Marinsky Theatre. The Opera on the other side of the square has been turned into a field hospital. The car seemed to have gone wrong and two sailors got out and began to tinker with the engine. Other people got out on the other side. Suddenly machine-gun fire came from the prison, and the onlookers scuttled for shelter. The people round the car ran to the Theatre, each man guarding his face with his arm as if against rain. A consultation took place under the Theatre. A yellow postal delivery car with a red flag and a machine-gun propped up in it ran out from my street, stopped a moment under the Theatre, ran round behind it, and opened fire on the prison from the other side. The defenders replied, and while their attention was thus occupied people ran back to the deserted motor below my windows and put a machine-gun together on the side furthest from the prison. Then the car drove off and four men, with two students holding up a long ribbon of cartridges like a bridal train, carried the gun towards the prison. Fire began from both sides and within a few minutes the prison was opened and the prisoners released. It was quiet for a short time and then policemen, who are hidden in the roofs of the Theatre commissariat (to the great annoyance of inhabitants in the roof of this house where I have quarters in the top storey), opened fire on the crowd now filling the open square below. The space was cleared in a moment and the wounded shifted into the Opera House. Soldiers and sailors sheltering where they could fired at openings in the roofs. During this business a bullet spoilt my telephone connection, which hampered me subsequently, so that I did not learn as soon as I might of the reopening of the telegraph.[13]

Not in the most thrilling drama ever produced on the stage of the Marinsky Theatre, Reuter's correspondent comments, had such scenes been witnessed as those which took place that afternoon outside its walls.[14]

In those first days of the Revolution, according to George Bury, the streets leading to the Duma were filled for miles around with crowds of people, of all classes but mostly in uniform, streaming towards or from the new palladium of the people's liberties.

For half a mile before the actual building was reached the street
was a solid mass of soldiery, in column with flags flying, in groups
and masses mingled with the mob, steadily lurching forward a
few steps at a time with tediously long waits at every ten yards.
With the trained politeness of the drilled man it was much easier
than might have been imagined to make one's way through the
press. However tightly the soldiers seemed wedged together, a
polite 'May I pass, allies?' or 'Let me through, little brothers!'
never failed to get one forward the depth of two or three men's
bodies. It was an interesting, but decidedly trying progress. Lamp-
posts, railings, roofs and windows afforded points of vantage for
adventurous sightseers all along the route. And over all lay the
mysterious silence of a stern decision, broken very occasionally by
a purely local cheer as some familiar regimental colour, some well-
known face was recognized by those immediately near. At the
gates of the semi-circular garden and courtyard space before the
Duma were posted sentries, assisted in the matter of deciphering
the curious scraps of various paper which served as passes by volunteer students and schoolboys, those of the Jewish faith predomi-
nating and apparently deciding all doubts – which were many...
As I made my way to the gate there presented himself the burly
figure of M. Rodzianko, who naturally never thought about passes. A soldier, in the momentary absence of the student settling a
wordy dispute with a doubtful entrant, stopped the President of
the Duma with a rude: 'Where are you shoving to? got a pass?' M.
Rodzianko patiently replied: 'I don't think I need a pass, I am the
President of the Duma,' after which a little cheer from those near
ended an amusing and characteristic little incident...   Inside the
courtyard the masses of soldiery and people were more tightly
wedged than ever: it took twenty minutes to cross some thirty
yards of court and mount the few entrance steps to the Duma portico. The cadets of naval and military schools, drawn up in proper
military array, were swamped beneath a mob of soldiery, but perfectly happy and showing the smiling faces that will no doubt be,
what it certainly has not been in the past, the natural hallmark of the
easy-tempered Russian of the future.[15]

The burly figure of Rodzianko towers over the opening stages
of the Revolution in more senses than one. According to US
Ambassador Francis, he was over six feet in height, weighed almost
three hundred pounds, and had a voice that could be heard easily by

thousands in the open air. A member of the right-wing liberal party known as the Octobrists (who derived their name from the Imperial Manifesto of October 1905 granting the Constitution), he is described by Harold Williams in *Russia of the Russians* (1914) as 'a persistent defender of the ceremonial rights and privileges of the Duma on public occasions'.[16]

On Tuesday evening Ransome decided to walk the length of the Moika Canal and cross the river to visit his friend, the economist Will Peters, in the Vyborg District, a centre of working-class political activism. Palace Square was so quiet and empty that it was difficult to believe in the Revolution, but for the firing in the Nevsky close at hand. To his astonishment he found the Vyborg District absolutely peaceful. Everything was already in the hands of the people and order had been restored.

Re-crossing the river on Wednesday morning, Ransome had to thread his way along the Quay through immense crowds of people and soldiers. In the street outside the Duma the Marseillaise was being played, the whole crowd was cheering like mad, and many people were weeping with excitement. He had to try three ways before he finally managed to enter the building. The main hall was piled with ammunition, sacks of flour and machine-guns. News came in that the Emperor's train had been halted by revolutionary troops at Bologoye, 200 miles from Petrograd. The feeling inside the Duma was one of indescribable enthusiasm coupled with a full knowledge of the difficulties still to be overcome. There was an absolute determination that the war should not suffer. As someone put it: 'We have beaten the Germans here, we will now beat them in the field.' On his way home, he was amazed to see soldiers and officers drinking coffee together in a café on the Nevsky. An Embassy car flying a large Union Jack passed him and was loudly cheered by the crowd.[17]

At 10.50 a.m. Bertie Stopford left his hotel, where there was nothing to eat, and made his way to the Embassy. After luncheon 'the *Daily Chronicle* correspondent' came to tell the Ambassador that new Ministers had already been chosen, with Prince Lvov as President of the Council; that the food supply would now be all right, as the town had been organized into districts; and that 500 officers, including many Generals, had been to the Duma to swear allegiance.[18]

Wilton in *The Times* was no less enthusiastic than Ransome in the *Daily News* about the course that the Revolution was taking:

The astounding, and to the stranger unacquainted with the Russian character almost uncanny, orderliness and good nature of the crowds of soldiers and civilians throughout the city are perhaps the most striking features of the great Russian Revolution...

At the Taurida Palace yesterday [Wednesday 14th] it was wonderful to see the way in which the huge gathering of soldiers and civilians managed to avoid collision. Inside the building the work of the various Parliamentary Committees went on day and night with unflagging intensity. The great hall where the Duma meets was occupied by men of the Preobrazhensky Guard Regiment. These giants were taking a much-needed rest in the seats of the Deputies, with their rifles beside them. The adjoining hemicycle had been fitted up with long tables as a temporary messroom for the Guardsmen.

I was present at the Taurida Palace yesterday afternoon when the Grand Duke Cyril [a cousin of the Emperor], commanding the Sailors of the Guard, came in person with his officers and stated that this historic corps would place itself under the orders of M. Rodzianko. Accompanied by a deputation of sailors, the Grand Duke and his Staff were drawn up in the Catherine Hall. Addressing M. Rodzianko, the Grand Duke said with emotion:

'I have the honour to appear before your Excellency and to place myself at your disposal. In common with our nation, I desire the welfare of Russia. This morning I assembled my men, and explained to them the significance of present events, and I can now say that the whole Naval Guard Corps is at the entire disposal of the Imperial Duma.'[19]

The last word on Wednesday, March 14 goes to our youngest witness, seventeen-year-old Kenneth Metcalf, whose father was in charge of Babcock & Wilcox's Petrograd office at 21 Nevsky Prospect. Writing to his younger brother, Leslie, in England he describes it as 'the greatest day' of the Revolution.

Every soldier in Petrograd came over on the side of the people, and Dad and I watched for half an hour soldiers of the red flag passing along (in perfect order, without officers, about 15 abreast) to salute the 'Dooma' and its new ministers, it was a *grand* sight, we went to the 'Dooma' and there heard Rodzianko the president speak.[20]

By Thursday morning, according to Stinton Jones, 'although spasmodic street fighting continued, serious disturbances were practically at an end. The streets throughout the city were thronged with large crowds, but of a much better class than those of the previous days, and a distinct air of goodwill and security prevailed.'[21]

Robert Wilton instanced an example of this goodwill for readers of *The Times*:

One teashop which I visited displayed the following notice, which, although drafted ungrammatically and badly spelt, showed the right spirit:

'FELLOW-CITIZENS! In honour of the great days of freedom, I bid you all welcome. Come inside, and eat and drink to your hearts' content.'

Boniface, attired in a red shirt, himself welcomed his guests, and distributed rusks, bread, and an unlimited quantity of tea. The place was filled, but perfect order and tranquillity were observed by the guests.[22]

Ransome was relieved to find that the post was working again and that 'the yellow post cars which yesterday carried machine-guns today carry mailbags',[23] while Harold Williams cheerfully reported that the enthusiasm for England was delightful to see.

Our Ambassador, walking home yesterday, was recognized, and a cry was raised by the cheering crowd, who immediately surrounded him and followed him to the Embassy.

British officers were cheered at every turn. A party of British sailors ['tars' in the *Times* version] were amazed at the sight of the accomplished revolution. A great throng followed them on their way, cheering wildly. 'You'd 'a thought it was King George V himself coming in,' said one of the sailors, 'instead of a lot of old muckers. I tell you I was proud at being British.'[24]

This was also the day, however, on which Allied hopes that Russia's commitment to the war would be redoubled were given a sharp jolt. Acting on its own initiative, the Petrograd Soviet issued 'Order No.1', dated March 14 but not circulated until the following morning. Although it was addressed to the Petrograd garrison only, the millions of copies printed soon found their way to the Russian forces in every theatre of the war.

Some of its provisions, Knox comments, were sensible and might have been welcomed had they been issued by the Army Command. Articles 6 and 7 laid down that when off duty, soldiers were to enjoy equal rights with other citizens, and off-duty saluting was to be abolished. This included 'forming front', in which privates had to stand at the salute facing a general till the latter had passed; 'in the crowded Nevsky Prospect', as Knox points out, 'this custom was a nuisance to everyone, and must have been a special worry to a modest general'. High-ranking officers were no longer to be addressed by such titles as 'Your High Excellency', but as 'Mister General' or 'Mister Colonel'. The old grandiloquent forms of address, Knox adds, 'were taught to raw recruits on joining, together with such stock forms of reply as, for instance, "I am unable to know". It was always much easier for the Russian soldier to use this form of reply than to trouble to think, and its continual repetition became very irritating when, for instance, one lost one's way near the front.' All rudeness to soldiers, especially the use of the condescending second person singular, was forbidden.

Articles 1 to 4, however, were essentially political in character. Military units of every kind were to form administrative committees consisting of elected representatives of the rank and file; each company was to send a delegate to the Soviet; in all their political actions, the troops must obey the Soviet and its committees; and the orders of the Military Committee of the Duma were to be obeyed only when they did not contradict those of the Soviet. Article 5 stated that arms of all kinds should be under the control of the committees and on no account handed over to the officers, 'even if the officers so order'. This last phrase, with its implicit incitement to disobey orders, together with the instruction to form committees, seemed to Knox deliberately calculated to undermine all sense of military discipline.

> In my daily visit to the Duma on the 15th, I found the officers terribly depressed...
>
> I saw Rodzianko for a moment and told him that I was frightened that things were taking a turn that might endanger the continuance of the war. He said: 'My dear Knox, you must be easy. Everything is going on all right. Russia is a big country, and can wage a war and manage a revolution at the same time.' It was, however, precisely because Russia was a big – and unwieldy – country that the situation was dangerous. In Petrograd there were

some 219,000 factory hands and some 150,000 mutinous troops, and these constituted inflammable material that internationalists were working day and night to ignite. . .

Leaflets were distributed advocating the murder of officers. The outlook was black on the evening of the 15th.[25]

Ransome, however, took a less pessimistic view in his Thursday evening telegram. 'The town is comparatively quiet, the only disquieting signs being the continued distribution of proclamations by the extreme party seeking to undermine the authority of the Duma. These are read everywhere, but from the comments I have heard from soldiers and sailors they meet with small sympathy, while the middle classes as a whole fully realise that the division of authority at this moment would be disastrous.' But he concludes by saying that 'the next twenty-four hours will decide the question between the Duma and the extreme party who demand general confiscation of the land and the handing of all power to the soldiers and workpeople. Most of the best Labour representatives are using all their influence on the side of the Duma.'[26]

Stopford, too, had heard that 'the situation was getting serious – not in the streets, which were quieting down – but amongst the Social Democrats, who were throwing printed inflammatory manifestos out of automobiles.' The Emperor's train was said to have left Bologoye and reached Pskov. On his arrival at the Embassy that afternoon, Stopford met the Ambassador coming down the staircase and helped him on with his coat. 'Just then he was called to the telephone, and when he came out said the Emperor had abdicated – the Heir Apparent was to reign under the Regency of Mikhail Alexandrovich.'[27] While the Duma Committee's two delegates were on their way to Pskov, however, Nicholas decided to abdicate both for himself and the twelve-year-old Tsarevich. The throne was to pass direct to Grand Duke Michael, the Emperor's younger brother, but when the latter met the Duma Committee on the following day, he decided not to accept it unless that proved to be the wish of a duly elected Constituent Assembly. Bulletins posted up in the office windows of the evening newspapers announcing these two decisions produced an impression of frenzied joy, and the people immediately set about removing the portraits of the Emperor and destroying the Imperial eagles on all public and private buildings. Such was the popular enthusiasm for this task that several American eagles suffered the same fate.[28]

In the meantime the political tension had eased considerably with the reaching of agreement between the Duma Committee and the Soviet. A Provisional Government had been formed, and an eight-point programme of reform proclaimed. 'This agreement has cost a great effort and considered concessions by both sides,' Harold Williams reported on Friday.

The composition of the new Government is extraordinarily moderate in the circumstances... There has been, and still is, danger from extremists, who want at once to turn Russia into a Socialist republic and have been agitating amongst soldiers, but reason has been reinforced by a sense of danger from the Germans and the lingering forces of reaction gaining the upper hand, and it is noteworthy that the soldier delegates from insurgent regiments have preferred the more moderate view.

In numberless talks I have had with soldiers I have been struck by their fundamental reasonableness, their sense of order and discipline. They wish to be free men, but very strongly realize their duty as soldiers. The more moderate Socialists, the so-called Plekhanov party, who stand for war, are very useful as mediators, and as soon as the new Government secures its ground the influence of the extremists will be diminished.

Very important, too, will be the influence of the front, where in the presence of the enemy practical sense is strong.[29]

Knox shared the general view that the new Government contained the most prominent men of non-official Russia, and that its loyalty to the Alliance was beyond question, but his misgivings about the future of the army had not been dispelled.

It seemed necessary to ascertain the real attitude of the Labour Group towards the war, so I asked Harold Williams, who knew everyone, to introduce me to some of its leaders. As we entered the Duma on the 16th we ran into M. Sokolov, a barrister and socialist labour leader. I told him that with all our sympathy for the struggle for freedom, we were naturally anxious regarding the continuation of the war. I assured him that, from the knowledge gained by constant intercourse with the officer class during the war, I was convinced that practically all of them had been in favour of political change, but pointed out how difficult the position of the Russian officer had been made by the issue of

Paragraph 7 of the Provisional Government's programme [stating that the troops who had taken part in the revolutionary movement were not to be disarmed, and were to remain in Petrograd], and by Order No.1 of the Soviet. I handed him a copy of this latter Order, and told him I considered it a deathblow to the Russian army.

Sokolov replied that it was essential to retain in Petrograd troops that the new Government could trust. Knox, however, remained of the opinion that the Petrograd garrison had degenerated into an armed mob: dreading the idea of fighting at the front, they preferred to remain in the capital to demonstrate, and had succeeded in forcing their will on the Government with the connivance of the Soviet.

As for Order No.1, Sokolov 'donned his pince-nez to read it, as if he had never seen it before.' ('This was interesting,' Knox adds in a footnote, 'in view of the general belief that Sokolov wrote the Order himself.') He then said that it was 'not very well written,' but he justified the order regarding the retention of arms on the grounds that it was not yet known which officers could be trusted. He assured Knox that there would now be an unbounded enthusiasm for the war and that work in the munition factories would be resumed on Monday 19. Appearances, however, Knox thought, were against such optimism.

> The 'heroes of the Revolution' seemed only to want to bask in the limelight, and could not understand an ally's anxiety to 'get on with the war'. One soldier said to me in the Duma on the 16th: 'We have suffered 300 years of slavery, you cannot grudge us a single week of holiday!'[30]

The Canadian, George Bury, shared Knox's opinion. He could not forget that a war unparalleled in the history of the world was still awaiting settlement. Seen in that light, the impressions received by the appearance of the Petrograd streets were the reverse of pleasant.

> From Wednesday onwards they were crowded uncomfortably with a tangled mob of civilians, soldiers armed and unarmed, sailors, who for the most part maintained some sort of formation and always had their arms, women and girls. Quite a number of the latter had adopted a sort of over-adorned military costume, with boots and breeches, and fancy variations of ornamental

military headgear. They passed almost unnoticed: the Russian people for the moment seemed unsusceptible of any save political impressions... Over all public buildings [including the Winter Palace] and many private ones red flags flew conspicuously, not a national flag was anywhere shown... Petrograd, having won an easy victory by the defection of the troops, was seemingly engaged in endless joy-rides in confiscated motor-cars... The worst feature was the troops, who far outnumbered the civilian public, and looked as slovenly and useless as a drilled man in uniform ever can look, slouching along with the mob.[31]

Ransome and Williams, however, strike a very different note from Knox and Bury. On Saturday, March 17 Ransome sent off no fewer than eight telegrams, including one in which he suggested that the *Daily News* should immediately open a 'Red Flag' subscription for the families of soldiers who had gone over to the people and been killed in the Battle of Petrograd. Friday was a day of brilliant sunshine, so he took a twenty-mile walk round the city. The streets were still crowded but already less picturesque, with fewer citizens striding about using swords as walking-sticks. The newly constituted citizen police was keeping admirable order; many of the released convicts had been recaptured. Agitators were numerous, urging the people not to trust the government and the soldiers not to obey their officers, but he did not think they were being taken very seriously. (In *The Times* Wilton observes: 'I regret to have to say that some students of both sexes are blindly cooperating in this anarchistic propaganda.'[32]) As for the political situation, 'today the outlook is distinctly more hopeful and it is possible that a breach between the extremists and the moderates may be avoided, both agreeing to support the present Temporary Government until a Constituent Assembly decides the fate of Russia by the votes of all her 170 million people. The organization of this gigantic general election will naturally take time.' Kerensky, the Labour member and newly appointed Minister of Justice, was distinguishing himself by his utmost devotion to the good of his country.

It is impossible for people who have not lived here to know with what joy we now write of the new Russian Government... Only those who knew how things were only a week ago can understand the enthusiasm of us who have seen a miracle take place before our eyes. We knew how Russia worked for the war in spite of her

Government. We could not tell the truth. It is as if honesty had returned... Russia has broken her chains and stands as the greatest free nation in Europe with republican France and liberal England. Nowhere outside Germany had Prussianism gone so far as here. Nowhere has it been so absolutely defeated.[33]

Throughout the week Harold Williams had been keeping a close eye on the often confused developments in the Duma, hurrying round to brief the Ambassador, and also finding time to compose and send off his telegrams to the *Daily Chronicle*. It was not until Friday that he was able to savour the talk of the streets, finding it endlessly interesting and full of delightful humour.

It is as though the Russian people dared for the first time display its talent frankly and boldly.

'Heigho,' said the soldiers, 'now we shall have a short service in church, because the priest always took such a long time praying for the Tsar and the Government, and the poor orthodox Russian people only by a little bit at the tail-end.'[34]

But it is in his telegram of Saturday, March 17 that he gives fullest expression to his feelings about the Revolution:

It is a wonderful thing to see the birth of freedom. With freedom comes brotherhood, and in Petrograd today there is a flow of brotherly feeling.

Everywhere you see it in the streets. The trams are not yet running, and people are tired of endless walking. But the habit now is to share your cab with perfect strangers.

The police have gone, but the discipline is marvellous. Everyone shares the task of maintaining discipline and order. A volunteer militia has been formed and 7,000 men enrolled as special constables, mostly students, professors, and men of the professional classes generally. These, with the help of occasional small patrols of soldiers, control the traffic, guard the banks, factories, and Government buildings, and ensure security.

Everyone is happy in this sense of free order. The strong sense of common responsibility for order has united all classes in one great army of freedom. Cabmen delight in liberty from the police, who blackmailed them, and for the first time talk freely, and speculate with all the curious humour and originality of the Russian peasant.

Soldiers, with all their freedom, are displaying a sense of order and discipline that would be hardly conceivable in any other nation.

Throughout the revolution, when the city was actually under the control of thousands of soldiers, they behaved with few exceptions like thorough gentlemen. We heard of no cases of cold-blooded murder. Only those officers or police were killed who opened fire on the soldiers. Private property nearly everywhere was scrupulously respected, and in most cases robbery was due to criminals disguised as soldiers.

Good news comes this evening that the moderate group in the Soviet is gaining the upper hand, and the prospects are brighter than ever.

Prince Kropotkin (now living in Brighton) and Plekhanov, veteran Socialist exiles, who champion the war as a war of defence and liberation, have been urgently invited to return to help in the work of reconstruction.

Possibilities of work are boundless, and the sense of rich opportunity and personal responsibility is thrilling the hearts of even the humblest. The barrier that separated the Intelligentsia from the people is broken down, suspicion removed, and all are joining hands in the common work.

Life is flowing in a healing, purifying torrent. Never was any country in the world so interesting as Russia is now. Old men are saying 'Nunc dimittis', young men singing in the dawn, and I have met many men and women who seemed walking in a hushed sense of benediction.[35]

Assuming Office

Week to Saturday, March 24: profiles of Lvov, Milyukov and Kerensky; recognition of new Government by US and Allies

At 1 a.m. on the morning of March 16 the Imperial train carrying the ex-Emperor left Pskov and returned to General Headquarters at Mogilev. Sir John Hanbury-Williams, who had been chief of the British Military Mission in Russia since 1914 and become well known to the Emperor and his family, received an invitation to visit him there at 6 p.m. on the 19th.

> At the entrance I was stopped by a sentry with the red band of revolution round his arm. He at first would not hear of my admission, but I explained who I was, and at the same moment the faithful old body servant of the Emperor appeared and told the sentry to let me pass unhindered.
>
> Each step I took seemed to bring back some memory to me, the stairs along which the little Tsarevich used to run to bid us good-bye, the ante-room, which used to be full of officers and ministers on official visits, and where I had stood talking to the Empress on the last occasion upon which I saw her. Such scenes seem to rush pell-mell through one's brain on such occasions.
>
> I had no time for a set or stilted speech, and all I could say when I saw that familiar face again was: 'I am so sorry'.
>
> I think, indeed I know, he understood.
>
> I walked into the room, being left alone with him.
>
> Apparently everything had been packed up, as the room, which used to be bright with flowers and the photographs and so on on his big table, looked now quite bare.

But he was sitting at the table in his khaki uniform, just as he used to sit when I went in to see him.

He looked tired and white, with big black lines under his eyes, but smiled as he shook hands with me, and then asked me to come and sit on the sofa where we could talk.

I asked him if he had been able to sleep, and how the children who were ill at Tsarskoe Selo were getting on.

He told me that he had been able to get a certain amount of sleep, and that the news of the invalids was better. An officer had brought him a letter from the Empress hidden in his tunic. This he said had been a great comfort to him in his anxiety for her and the children.

We then talked over plans for his future, as he evidently saw that plans were no longer in his own hands. . .

The proposal that the Tsarevich should take his place with a Regent he could not accept, as he could not bear the separation from his only son, and he knew that the Empress would feel the same.

He was much touched with the offer we had made to accompany him to Tsarskoe Selo, and hoped that he would not have to leave Russia. He did not see that there could be any objection to his going to the Crimea, which he hoped would be allowed, and if not, he would sooner go to England than anywhere.

He never referred to any anxiety in regard to his own safety, which was typical of him.

The question of his eventual place of asylum is for many and various reasons a difficult one.

He expressed a wish to write to me personally and not through some other channel, and then added that the right thing to do was to support the present Government, as that was the best way to keep Russia in the alliance to conclude the war. On this he laid great stress. He feared the revolution would ruin the armies.

As I prepared to leave he asked me for my photograph, which I sent him tonight, and said he would send me one of his.

As I said 'good-bye' in anticipation of the more formal farewell tomorrow, he turned to me and added: 'Remember, nothing matters but beating Germany'.

I went away sad and depressed, fearing that he has still hopes, though I have none.

It was a black night in more senses than one as I walked home.[1]

Three days later, 'Nikolai Alexandrovich Romanov' was at Tsarskoe Selo, where he found his children in various stages of recovering from or going down with measles. The newspapers, Ransome cabled on the 23rd, had printed detailed accounts of his journey to Tsarskoe,

> where he is now under the guard of soldiers of the new govern-
> ment. But against the scene of the biggest revolution in the history
> of the world, the drama of individuals, however important a part
> they may once have played, sinks into insignificance. The stage is
> held by the nation itself, and the tragicomedy of persons who have
> lost crowns and courtiers whose gilt chairs have been knocked
> from under them becomes mere byplay in the corner.[2]

On that same day Harold Williams wrote of the Emperor:

> Since the Revolution rent the veil he has said nothing, done noth-
> ing, to show that he ever held the spirit of a Monarch. He has
> expressed no will of his own, no outcry, no protest, has submitted
> tamely, has expressed no opinion, has said: 'Yes, very well. I agree.
> I abdicate for myself and my son. Thank you. Good-bye,' as
> though he were discussing the weather at an afternoon call.[3]

New figures now found themselves at the centre of the nation's drama. Rodzianko, having played his part, disappeared into the wings. So did the Duma of which he was still President, its central role passing to the Temporary or Provisional Government, so called because it proposed to hold office only until such time as a Constituent Assembly had been elected by the democratic vote of the whole Russian people.

The new Prime Minister and Minister of the Interior was Prince Georgii Lvov (1861–1925). He had been hastily summoned to Petrograd from Moscow, where his wartime work as President of the Union of Zemstvos – an organization formed by the *zemstvos* or local government bodies to provide additional medical services for the army – had enhanced his high reputation among Russian liberals. This 'quiet, grey-haired man' (Ransome), who spoke 'in rather jerky little monotones' (Bruce Lockhart), had none of Rodzianko's impos-ing presence. When the American journalist, Isaac Marcosson, went to see him at the Taurida Palace, he found 'a slight, bent, bearded lit-tle man, whose manner was kindly almost to benevolence, and who met me with a grave but charming courtesy'. He was sitting at an

elaborate desk littered with papers: the same desk from which
Protopopov had issued the orders that gagged and bound Russia.

> I remarked on the tide of time that had landed him in the seat of
> Stürmer and Protopopov.
> 'Ah,' he replied, and his eyes lighted up, 'they were the slave
> drivers.'
> 'And you?' I asked.
> 'We are the servants of the people,' he answered. 'Autocracy in
> Russia is dead for ever.'[4]

In his book published in 1930, Samuel Hoare, who had met Lvov in
1916, described him as 'a man better qualified to be Chairman of the
London County Council than to be the chief of an unstable
Government in the midst of a great revolution' (a description that
Bruce Lockhart found so apt that he used it in his own book two
years later)[5].

An altogether more formidable figure was the Foreign Minister,
Pavel Milyukov (1859–1943). It was he, not Lvov, who chose the new
ministerial team. A professional historian and member of the Duma
from 1907, Milyukov was the leader of the Constitutional Democrats
or Kadets, who had been part of the 'Progressive Bloc' during the
war (uniting all parties in the Duma except reactionaries and socialists), and who now dominated the new administration. 'His manner
and speech, although decided, was courteous. He had a smooth face
with the exception of a slight moustache and was about five feet
eleven in height, muscular and active with no surplus flesh' (US
Ambassador Francis). Through his wife, Harold Williams had
known Milyukov for many years; at one time they used to travel
home after work on the same tram. He 'has a capacity for work',
Williams writes of him in *Russia of the Russians,*

> and a tenacity of purpose exceptional among Russian public men,
> and therein lies his strength as a leader. He is an *intelligent* with no
> experience in affairs except what he has gained in recent years,
> and this explains to a considerable extent both his defects and his
> qualities. He has a wide knowledge of European politics, and is an
> able and resourceful speaker. The mistakes he makes – serious
> ones, sometimes at critical moments – are those that academic men
> do make when they overreach themselves in trying to be
> practical.[6]

It was a novel experience for Williams to go to see him on March 17, not in his simply-furnished flat, but in the big red Foreign Ministry building opposite the Winter Palace. Upstairs a uniformed messenger told him that the Minister was lunching.

Down a long corridor he led me into a great room splendid with tapestry and gilding. I sent in my card and waited, scanning the big white bees woven into the pink silk upholstery of the chairs and sofa. It was just as of old, no sign of change. 'This way,' said the attendant when he appeared, but it was a new way, not into the Minister's reception room, but into a smaller room far down the corridor, where I found M. Milyukov and his wife finishing a simple hasty lunch suited to these busy democratic times. I congratulated them both warmly, and we talked of all the great events. 'How are things?' I asked. '*Nichevo*' (the nearest English equivalent of the favourite Russian expression is 'All right'), said M. Milyukov with an inflection that denoted that things were going well.

This is probably the occasion to which Bernard Pares is referring when he writes that as soon as Milyukov was in office, Harold Williams visited him and urged him not to talk for the time being about Russian claims to Constantinople. 'Milyukov quite agreed that this was unsuitable, but made a vigorous speech on the subject almost the next day.'[7]

To the political right of the Kadets in the new Cabinet were three members of the Octobrist party, including the Minister of War, Guchkov. The Minister of Finance, Tereshchenko, at thirty-three the youngest member of Cabinet – 'his English is flawless... he is the one man who gives you the immediate impression of swift and dynamic American business methods' (Marcosson)[8] – had no political affiliation. Two portfolios were offered to politicians from the left. Chkheidze (1864–1926), the Georgian leader of the Mensheviks in the Duma, was invited to fill a specially created post as Minister of Labour, but declined, since the Executive Committee of the Petrograd Soviet, of which he was chairman, had voted against joining the new Government. Kerensky, however, though a deputy chairman of the Executive Committee, accepted the post of Minister of Justice. In so doing, he had to appeal over the heads of the Executive Committee to the rank and file members of the Soviet. Appearing in the stormy assembly, Harold Williams reports,

Kerensky mounted a table, and with flashing eyes and passionate utterance, announced that he had accepted the new post.

> 'Comrades, in entering the Provisional Government I remain a Republican. In my work I must lean for help on the will of the people. I must have in the people my powerful support. May I trust you as I trust myself? (Tremendous cheers and cries of "We believe you, comrade".) I cannot live without the people, and if ever you begin to doubt me, kill me. I declare to the Provisional Government that I am a representative of the democracy, and that the Government must especially take into account the views I shall uphold as representing the people, by whose efforts the old Government was overthrown.[9]

Kerensky resigned as deputy chairman of the Soviet, but remained on the Executive Committee.

Alexander Fyodorovich Kerensky was thirty-six. A lawyer, he was the leader in the Fourth Duma of a small group known as the Trudoviks, but soon became the spokesman for the left wing as a whole. According to E.H. Wilcox, such was his popularity with the Petrograd working classes that in the industrial quarters of the Vyborg District, and in the shipyards and ironworks, the questions, 'What has Alexander Fyodorovich said?' and 'What will Alexander Fyodorovich say?', became the final standards of judgement on every political issue.[10] Unlike the self-effacing Lvov, Kerensky was a 'high-profile' politician: he liked to be seen in public, never seems to have refused an invitation to dine at one of the Allied Embassies, and gave numerous interviews.

Harold Williams and Alfred Knox went to see him on Monday, March 19. Both left fairly long accounts of the meeting, Williams in his dispatch and Knox in his diary. Their appointment was for the unprecedented hour of 9 a.m., 'a welcome change', Knox writes, 'from the old regime, when it was impossible to see anyone before 11'. Williams arrived first. There was a general air of desolation about the huge Ministry building, deserted by all the old officials, but the hall porter said:

> The Minister is here: he slept here last night. But he hardly sleeps at all. Yesterday he went to bed at half-past five in the morning, and was up at eight. It is not like the old days, when hundreds of people had to wait hours to see the Minister. There was

Shcheglovitov – he would go on playing with a racket and ball in the quadrangle while the crowd waited and waited in the reception-room, and if his secretaries waited for him he would say, 'I must have my exercise'.

Altogether the porter was delighted with the new regime.

Knox arrived, and they walked up the great stairs. At the end of the corridor they saw Kerensky coming to meet them, accompanied by friends. 'Never was there a more democratic Minister,' Williams comments, while Knox was struck by the hollow sound of the Minister's footsteps as he walked towards them through perhaps a hundred yards of reception apartments.

Kerensky, Williams writes,

is a young man in the early thirties, of medium height, with a slight stoop, and a quick, alert movement, with brownish hair brushed straight up, a broad forehead already lined, a sharp nose, and bright, keen eyes, with a certain puffiness in the lids due to want of sleep, and a pale, nervous face tapering sharply to the chin. His whole bearing was that of a man who could control masses. He was dressed in a grey, rather worn suit, with a pencil sticking out of his breast pocket. He greeted us with a very pleasant smile, and his manner was simplicity itself. He led us into his study, and there we talked for an hour. I cannot give all the details of the conversation. We discussed the situation thoroughly, and I got the impression that M. Kerensky was not only a convinced and enthusiastic democrat, ready to sacrifice his life if need be for democracy – that I already knew from previous acquaintance – but that he had a clear, broad perception of the difficulties and dangers of the situation, and was preparing to meet them.

Knox, too, was impressed: 'Kerensky seems shrewd, energetic and a man. He has a certain charm of manner.'

On the urgent question of the resumption of their normal occupations by the workmen and soldiers, Kerensky informed them that the workmen in most factories were returning to work that day: an eight-hour day was to be declared, but machinery would be kept working for the full twenty-four hours.

'Their mood has changed,' said the Minister. 'They are tired of demonstrating, and want to work.' The Government has decided to pay wages to the workmen for the week of the strike, which is to be regarded, not as a strike, but as an act of national heroism. This should greatly stimulate the energy of the workers and inspire them to make up for lost time.

As for the soldiers, Williams continues, Kerensky informed them that here, too, order was being quickly restored.

Last week's ridiculous manifesto [Order No.1], issued in the name of the Council of Workmen's Deputies [the Soviet], calling on the soldiers not to obey their officers, M. Kerensky sharply character-ized as an act of provocation. There had been a few instances of grave disturbance of discipline, but the Minister was confident that this phase would soon pass, together with the other eccentric-ities. He declared:
'The general effect of the liberation will, I am convinced, be to give an immense uplift to the spirit of the troops, and so to shorten the war. We are for iron discipline in working hours, but out of working hours we want the soldiers to feel they are also free men.'
British discipline is, in fact, the ideal.

Kerensky's comments on the 'immense uplift to the spirit of the troops' seem to have impressed Williams more than Knox, who noted only that Kerensky thought 'I would see the men back at their drill in less than a week'. Knox raised the question of the dis-turbances reported to have taken place on the Northern and Western fronts following receipt of the news from Petrograd. 'Kerensky hoped the Germans would try to advance, for that would bring the officers and soldiers together.' He fully under-stood that the Allies would like Grand Duke Nicholas to be retained as Commander-in-Chief (in August 1915 he had been dis-missed by his nephew, the Emperor, who took over the military command himself), but the soldiers were against it, and there was a general feeling amongst the Left that with Guchkov as Minister of War, his retention would lead to the re-establishment of the Dynasty. As to other representatives of the old regime, they would be secured against violence: 'I earnestly hope that the revolution shall be as far as possible bloodless.'
Kerensky spoke repeatedly of his sympathy for England, saying that he was one of the few Russians to stand up for her at the time of the Boer War. However,

'I must tell you frankly... that we Russian democrats have been latterly rather worried about England, because of the close relations between your Government and the corrupt Government we had. But now, thank God, that is over, and our deep, strong feeling for England, as the champion of liberty, will come into its own again.'

In the light of Williams' remark that he could not give all the details of the conversation, it is interesting to note where Knox's account differs from his. In Williams we read: 'The Government is sending emissaries all over the country to explain their new policy. Many of the ablest men in the Duma are charged with this responsibility. "Our aim," said M. Kerensky, "is to use talent wherever we can lay hands on it." ' Contrast this with Knox: 'He said that there was a certain amount of friction with the Duma, who wanted to control the Provisional Government, but this would be avoided by giving important missions to prominent members of the Duma to visit distant parts of the Empire!'

Knox also records that Kerensky was instituting a search for proofs of the correspondence of the Romanov family with Germany, and adds in a footnote that no proofs were ever found, 'for the simple reason that... the Emperor, the Empress and their family lived and died in complete loyalty to the Alliance'. Knox asked what was to be done with the Emperor. He would go to England, Kerensky replied. On that most vexed issue of all, dual power, Kerensky 'allowed that the present position with two Governments was impossible, and assured us that the Soviet was losing ground'.

'We both went away hopeful,' Williams concludes, 'and, personally, I thought as I walked down the Nevsky through a snowstorm, that if all went well Russia might actually prove to be an even freer country than England.'

Both, however, had stated their most important conclusions at the start of their accounts. Kerensky, Williams writes, 'is of great importance at the present moment, because he represents in the Provisional Government that great heaving sea of democracy on whose right guidance the stability of the new regime so essentially depends'. Knox expressed the same thought more forcefully, and rather less optimistically:

There is only one man who can save the country, and that is Kerensky, for this litle half-Jew lawyer has still the confidence of the over-articulate Petrograd mob, who, being armed, are masters of the situation. The remaining members of the Government may represent the people of Russia outside the Petrograd mob, but the people of Russia, being unarmed and inarticulate, do not count. The Provisional Government could not exist in Petrograd if it were not for Kerensky.[11]

Before leaving, Knox pressed on Kerensky 'the necessity of making each regiment swear allegiance to the Provisional Government, pending the decision of the Constituent Assembly, as to a permanent constitution. He made a note of this, and asked me to speak to Guchkov.' Wasting no time, Knox went straight round to the Ministry of War. Guchkov received him at 11 a.m., together with General Kornilov (1870–1918), who had just arrived to take command of the Petrograd Military District. Kornilov said that units would have to be brought to some sort of order before the oath was administered. (It never was.) They welcomed the suggestion that British officers who spoke Russian might be of use in barracks to reason with the men. Kornilov himself was about to visit the Volynsky Battalion, 'the most turbulent of the lot', and Knox and Major Thornhill were to be busy on work of this kind for the next four weeks.[12]

While Knox worried over army discipline and Williams followed the course of mainstream Russian politics, Arthur Ransome's attention was beginning to turn in another direction. Answering a knock at his door one day, he was handed an envelope addressed to 'the correspondent of the *Daily News*'. It contained a ticket of admission to the Soviet 'with the right to speak but not to vote'. He interpreted this as a reciprocal favour by the Soviet for his having passed on to the Embassy in February a statement from the arrested War Industry Committee. Though he never exercised the right to speak, he made full use of the right to listen, and so, as he writes in his *Autobiography*, 'from the very first days of the revolution, had a better chance of knowing what was happening than most of the foreign correspondents who for a long time took no interest in any Russian politicians Left of the Kadets'. He also paid a visit, as reported to the *Daily News* on March 19, to the offices of the Social Democratic party's newspaper, *Pravda*, which had been suppressed at the beginning of the war, but was now appearing again. There was 'a general air of extremism' about the soldiers, students, and girls wearing their red ribbons, but the party programme, which he thought 'not unfairly represented the views of Labour', did not strike him as so very extreme; in any case, they recognized that nothing could be done until the meeting of the Constituent Assembly.[13]

On Thursday, March 22 the US Ambassador was the first to give the Provisional Government official recognition: 'an achievement', Buchanan comments drily, 'of which he was always very proud'.[14] Determined that Republican America should be the first to recognize Republican Russia, Francis had been moving heaven and earth to obtain his government's approval as quickly as possible, so as to steal a march on his fellow-diplomats. Buchanan was conveniently laid up in bed for a few days with a bad chill. Francis was also determined to let Petrograd see how much importance America attached to the event, and drove up the Nevsky Prospect to meet the new Government's representatives 'with my coachman in full livery on the box and the chasseur also in full livery standing behind me. I was accompanied by the Counselor, the four Secretaries, the Military and Naval Attachés in full uniform, the Commercial Attaché and two Attachés on special mission.'[15]

Two days later, it was the turn of the British, Italian and French Ambassadors. Buchanan in his memoirs salvages some glory from the event by quoting a large chunk of the speech in French with which he opened the proceedings. His impression of the new Ministers did not, however, inspire him with great confidence for the future: most of them already showed signs of strain and struck him as having undertaken a task beyond their strength.[16] Knox in his diary gives a more unbuttoned account:

The Ambassador is not well yet, but got up at 6 p.m. to announce the recognition of the Provisional Government by the Allies.

Each Ambassador brought his Councillor and his Naval and Military Attachés, and we assembled at the State Council – a weird-looking crew!

Grenfell [British Naval Attaché] was resplendent with epaulettes. I was common-looking in putties. There was a general atmosphere of depression, and Galaud, the French Naval Attaché, a jovial fellow as a rule, by way of cheering us whispered that there would soon be a general massacre of foreigners and that we would lose the war.

We filed upstairs and were met and welcomed by M. Milyukov. We wandered into a long room. M. Milyukov fetched the remainder of the Ministry, who stood in an informal group, while Sir George Buchanan, as doyen, made an inspiriting appeal for the

re-establishment of discipline in the army and the energetic pro-
secution of the war. He then delivered a message from Mr Lloyd
George, which M. Milyukov translated into Russian.

The Italian Ambassador, M. Carlotti, associated himself with the
'nobles paroles de Sir George' and somewhat bored us by reading a
report of an interminable debate in the Italian Chamber on the
subject of Russia. Then M. Paléologue had his say. He said that he
believed in the patriotism of the Ministry and in its loyalty to the
Alliance; he was also told that all the Russians were patriotic,
'though appearances were against it'.

While the diplomats spoke, the ministry stood looking at the
ground, bowing at the conclusion of each speech. I could not think
of it as a ministry of victory. I did not like to look at their faces,
when they were all looking at the ground; it seemed too aggressive and unfair, so I looked at the ground too, and then I saw their
boots. What an extraordinary collection of boots they were! I have
never seen such boots!

M. Milyukov replied with a declaration that Russia would fight
till her last drop of blood. I have no doubt that Milyukov would,
but can he answer for Russia?

When this was over and the groups broke up and mingled, I
attacked General Manikovsky, who was acting for M. Guchkov as
Minister of War. I said that these were merely diplomatic words,
but what of the situation at Dvinsk, where Neilson had told me
that the men were streaming back from the trenches with the officers powerless to control. I said the same thing to M. Kerensky. He
said that the great preoccupation of the Government was to restore
discipline in the army, and more especially in the navy. He spoke
of the proclamations issued on the 22nd. But what is the good of
proclamations? It seems to me that we are moving straight to anarchy and a separate peace.[17]

*

This recognition of the new Government by America and the Allies,
which took place less than a fortnight after Red Monday, is a convenient point at which to pause and take stock of how our witnesses
are responding to the Revolution.

With the exception of Sir John Hanbury-Williams, all would share
the sentiments expressed by an Englishman, John Pollock, who was
working for the Red Cross in Russia, when he writes on March 24:

With the announcement of the Constituent Assembly and the arrest of the Emperor, the Russian revolution has come to the end of its first phase. The air that Russians breathe is free. All that an Englishman and a lover of their country can do is wish them God-speed in a task that cannot but be troubled, and to show by his sympathy that in the main, in spite of excesses and crimes wrought by the ignorant and the exasperated,. . . nevertheless he feels that. . . right has triumphed and the curtain been drawn upon the long drama of brutal despotism, unsweetened by any grace of chivalry or touch of ideal.[18]

All would agree, too, that the Revolution had been unplanned and leaderless (though Wilton, having written at the time that there was 'no evidence of any concerted organization on the part of the Revolutionaries, military or civilian,'[19] changed his mind before writing his book). As Ransome puts it: 'Let there be no mistake in England. This was not an organized revolution. It will be impossible to make a statue in memory of its organizer, unless that statue represents a simple Russian peasant soldier.'[20]

For Alfred Knox, however, asking himself night and day whether the Revolution is going to make it easier or harder for the Allies to win the war, this simple Russian peasant soldier is not so much a revolutionary hero as a highly unpredictable quantity. More than anyone else, Knox fears the damage that Order No.1 and anti-war agitation may do to the troops. But is Knox, the military man obsessed with military discipline, in danger of losing his sense of proportion? Other witnesses take a more sanguine view. 'Returning from the Duma today,' Ransome writes on the 17th, 'I met a steadily marching crowd singing an old peasant song. I thought that it was a demonstration but found that the men were new recruits called to the colours and about to be trained for the Russian army.' And Wilton, writing a day later and worried like Knox about the effect of extremist propaganda upon largely ignorant young peasant soldiers, has 'reason to believe that a great improvement has been noticeable in the barracks since yesterday'.[21]

The most exuberantly enthusiastic witness is Arthur Ransome, for whom 'the biggest swiftest-realized revolution in the history of the last three hundred years' (March 15) has become by March 23 'the biggest revolution in the history of the world'.[22] At thirty-three, he was young and adventurous enough to respond with romantic intensity to the spectacle of a people rising up dramatically *en masse* to overthrow its age-old oppressors.

By his own account he was still at this stage of his life a completely non-political person. In England he had been too busy writing to bother about politics; no Russian political party had interested him at all. About the war, however, he did have decided views. Unlike Philips Price, he believed completely in the justice of his country's cause and in the paramount importance of defeating 'Prussianism'. The failure of Protopopov's plans, he reports on March 19, meant that from a British point of view the situation had improved vastly, 'because Russian retirement from the war, instead of being inevitable, has become highly improbable'; and he describes with obvious relish how an agitator had been shouted down by the crowd for referring to the Germans as 'brothers'. This is the same telegram, however, in which he describes his visit to *Pravda* and outlines the 'not so very extreme' programme of the Social Democratic party. He cannot have been unaware that this party was also the source of the anti-war literature that he so much deplores earlier in his telegram, but the inconsistency does not appear to strike him.[23]

Harold Williams uses a different kind of language from Ransome ('The wonderful and incredible thing has happened...'; 'A great people has displayed its finest qualities...'), but it has the depth of feeling of one who had suffered under the old regime far longer and experienced the abortive revolution of 1905. Williams, of course, *was* a political person, at least so far as Russian politics was concerned, with an allegiance to one particular party, the Kadets. More than any other witness, he feels a sense of responsibility towards the Revolution. He desperately wants it to succeed, and he wants public opinion in Britain, and the British Government, to help make it succeed. What he tells the Ambassador is not the same as what he tells the readers of the *Daily Chronicle*. To them he is comfortably reassuring: difficulties lie ahead, granted, but they will be overcome; there have been a few excesses, true, but in the circumstances it is quite remarkable how well everyone has been behaving. He tries to make British readers feel involved in these distant events: 'the enthusiasm for England is delightful to see'; 'British discipline is, in fact, the ideal'. Whereas Wilton refers unequivocally to 'the treasonable incendiary Order No.1',[24] Williams, not wishing to cause alarm and despondency at home, does not mention it (neither does Ransome), until in the course of the Kerensky interview he refers retrospectively to 'last week's ridiculous manifesto... which Kerensky sharply characterized as an act of provocation.'

Williams gives his most considered assessment of the situation at this stage of the Revolution in his telegram of March 18:

> Army and country have accepted the new Government practically unanimously. Democracy has come to power. The Government is composed of the best men in the country.
>
> Every man and woman in Russia is now able to speak and work freely. Russia has found her multitudinous voice. It is now possible in Russia to speak the truth about Russia. The old fear has vanished. There is room and space at last for honesty and for honest, straightforward work. The possibilities are magnificent. The only cloud on the horizon is the chaotic fanaticism of extremists.
>
> The Council of Workmen's and Soldiers' Deputies is now an unwieldy body of over a thousand members elected by the workmen of all the factories and the soldiers of each company of the insurgent regiments. This body is swayed by Socialists, some of whom are moderate and reasonable, and realise all the complexity of the present situation, while others are extremists who are eager to give immediate effect to their doctrines. The result is that the council is forced into precipitate and contradictory decisions, which complicate the action of the new Government.
>
> But the forces of order and reason are very strong, and are growing in energy every day. The one passionate desire of the majority is that the new freedom should not be endangered by any recklessness, and that the war shall be fought by New Russia to a brilliant finish.[25]

'Walk and Talk'

March 25 to April 16: the new spirit of freedom and equality; dual authority of
Government and Soviet

Today is the second Sunday after the revolution [March 25]. The
Nevsky Prospect is crowded with processions carrying red banners with various inscriptions. Through the processions the trams
move at a snail's pace and the *izvozchiks* abandon the effort to force
a passage.

It is a sort of national holiday, but not very exciting after all that
we have passed through. A red flag is exciting when Cossacks are
lurking round the corner ready to shoot, but when the revolution
is victorious and the people free to demonstrate as they please,
they walk in procession more for the mere fun of it, and have the
air of cheerful flaneurs.[1]

This comment is characteristic of Harold Williams, who always
attempts to convey the mood of an occasion, and is less responsive
than other witnesses to the purely visual stimulus of the Russian
Revolution. For many Russians, though, the Revolution clearly needed to be *seen* to have triumphed, to be celebrated in visual terms with
the same sense of drama and mass spectacle that characterized the
ceremonies of the Orthodox Church. It had its own distinctive colour,
which was to acquire enormous associations in the years to come. At
the same time it had ceased to be a chaotic sequence of often violent
events and become something simpler and grander: 'The Revolution',
or even, in Kerensky's phrase, 'Her Royal Highness the Revolution'.[2]
Those cheerful Sunday afternoon strollers with their red banners
were able to feel part of something much larger than themselves.

The triumph of the Revolution was celebrated with a fine sense of the dramatic on Saturday, March 31, when a concert on behalf of the victims was held at the Marinsky Theatre, scene in the past of so many glittering Imperial occasions. The politely worded invitations received by the British, French and Italian Ambassadors did not come from some court functionary, but from the concert's organizers, the 'turbulent' Volynsky Regiment, who had been given the credit for being the first regiment to come out in favour of the people. Inside the theatre all the Imperial eagles and coats of arms had been removed, and the box attendants had exchanged their sumptuous uniforms for plain grey jackets. The Ambassadors sat in one of the Imperial boxes on the grand tier, with members of the Government, wearing ordinary frock-coats, in a box just opposite. But as the French Ambassador, Maurice Paléologue, points out, the attention of the audience – bourgeois, students and soldiers – was directed not at the Ambassadors or even the Government, but at the great Imperial box in the centre, the gala box, for there, turning wondering eyes back on the assembly, sat some thirty persons, old gentlemen and several old ladies with grave, worn, curiously expressive and unforgettable faces: those veteran terrorists and revolutionaries who only three weeks before had still been in prison or exile.

The concert began with the Marseillaise (in its endlessly repeated, more soulful, Russian version, which had taken the place of the national anthem), played on stage by a military band with the men of the Volynsky Regiment standing in groups behind them. It was greeted with tumultuous shouts and cheers; so was the long speech by Kerensky that followed. In the interval Buchanan, entering into the spirit of the occasion, suggested that the three of them should pay their respects to the Government box. Thence they were conducted to the central box and introduced to its occupants. 'No one,' Buchanan wrote, 'would have conceived such a thing possible a couple of months ago.'[3] When the Ambassadors returned to their own box, it seemed to Paléologue as if a murmur of sympathy passed through the audience, a kind of silent ovation.

Five days later, with the streets ankle-deep in slush and the skies grey and lowering, the Revolution buried its dead. This, too, was a largely symbolic occasion, since many of the victims had already been buried privately. There were said to be 200 coffins, but when Stopford visited the mass grave on the following morning before the coffins were covered, he counted only 'over 150'. He had noticed in the procession that sometimes a simple plank of wood was carried alongside the coffins to represent another victim who had already been buried.[4]

Fearful of some kind of right-wing agitation, the authorities had urged people to keep off the streets, but their warnings went unheeded and Petrograd proved 'as safe as a Sunday School Convention' (Marcosson).[5] The event was seen by a number of witnesses, of whom Harold Williams gives the best account.

'No Tsar was ever given a burial like this.' My neighbour in the crowd spoke the truth. Today's public funeral of the revolution's victims was indeed very unlike any other funeral in Russian history.

From six gathering places in various parts of the city processions, each bearing a quota of red coffins, slowly made their way to the Field of Mars. [Here the sense of spaciousness, Williams writes elsewhere, 'is increased by the fact that only on one side is there an uninterrupted row of buildings'.[6]] Petrograd, purged of its police, seemed to feel its responsibility. The bearing of the people was perfect. There was no crushing, no ill-temper, no impatience. The crowds watching the procession were less numerous than might have been expected, and for a very simple reason. The great bulk of the population was actually taking part in the procession itself.

The gigantic numbers involved [estimated at nearly a million] will be realized when I say that from 9 in the morning till late in the evening a constant stream filed past the grave. All classes and nationalities were represented. Factories, trade unions, technical schools, societies, and hundreds of other units were represented.

There was a big red banner with the words in Polish: 'The rights of nations to determine their own destinies'. There was a group of Finnish workmen and a little later a group of Letts. So the procession passed in orderly linked ranks [the distances between groups, according to Stopford, were regulated by men or women carrying small white flags on poles, who signalled down the line for advancing or halting[7]].

There were dozens of military detachments, with military bands, playing at times the Marseillaise or one of the new revolutionary songs. Even more impressive was it when a whole section of the procession sang the 'Eternal Memory' [the chants for the dead] as only Russian crowds can sing.

The prevailing note was not one of mourning. The dead in those red coffins had not died in vain. In bygone years the Field of Mars has witnessed many a State review. Today the new Russia also reviewed her forces.

As each coffin was lowered the guns of the Peter & Paul Fortress thundered a salute. The Fortress is the last resting place of many Romanovs, and the temporary enforced abode of many of the blackest adherents of the old regime. The stronghold of Old Russia has become the saluting battery of the New.[8]

According to the French diplomat, Louis de Robien, the scene was especially impressive at night, under the illumination of six big naval searchlights.[9] Williams does not draw attention to a feature of the event that troubled several witnesses: that apart from the spontaneous singing of the 'Eternal Memory', it was devoid of any religious character. Stopford understood that the clergy had not been invited to attend, since they had given the Tsarist police permission to place machine-guns on the roofs of churches. Robien noted also that none of the banners in the procession made any reference to the war.

For several days afterwards soldiers continued to parade at the Field of Mars and to sing the Marseillaise, prompting Sir John Hanbury-Williams, who was shortly to leave Russia, to write in his diary: 'I really believe the latter [the victims of the Revolution] will rise from their graves and ask them to stop singing if they keep at it all the time. Pleasant for our Embassy, which adjoins.'[10]

On April 6 the British Ambassador was himself at the receiving end of a deputation. It consisted of some four thousand Cossacks, described by Meriel Buchanan as 'fierce-looking men, sitting their horses like no other men on earth, with fearless, honest eyes and bronzed, bearded faces.'[11] Their general, her father writes,

had originally asked me to come and review them on the Field of Mars, and had kindly offered to place a 'quiet' horse at my disposal. I had to tell him that this was an honour which I, as Ambassador, could not accept, so it was arranged that the regiments should march past the Embassy instead, while I watched them from the balcony. After the march past the commander, with a delegation of some fifty Cossacks, came up to my study and made a patriotic speech in favour of continuing the war.[12]

Throughout April the popular demand for demonstrations, processions, meetings and speeches – what one unidentified English journalist neatly summarized as 'walk and talk'[13] – continued unabated.
Colonel Knox, impatient to get on with the war, did not approve.

> There was everywhere a passion for speech, the right to which had
> been so long denied, and a moment of silence seemed to everyone
> a moment lost. There were continual 'meetings' in the streets, and
> these gradually multiplied in number and decreased in volume – a
> development popular in that it enabled more men and women
> simultaneously to hear the sound of their own voices. A new verb
> was coined, *'mitingovat'*, to attend meetings. A man would ask his
> friend what he was going to do that evening, and the reply would
> be: 'I will attend meetings a little' (*ya nemnogo mitinguyu*).[14]

Bernard Pares, returning to Petrograd from the front, found the
streets 'full of an atmosphere of exaltation and vague optimism'.
Marvellous street placards advertised every imaginable fad or idea.
Numerous little cliques with high-sounding titles proclaimed ambi-
tious schemes for saving Russia and even the world. 'One strange
poster bore the heading, "Self Organization". Apparently Russia was
to be saved by a general dispatch of postcards to a common anonymous address.'[15]

But leaving aside the self-indulgent talk and the cranky excesses,
there can be no doubt of the transformation of Russian life taking
place as a result of the new spirit of freedom and equality generated
by the Revolution. Arthur Ransome found it all tremendously exciting. 'Every man walks with new pride and self-respect.' And not
only every man: a fat old woman on the pavement, when politely
asked to let other people pass, replied: 'Freedom has come. Where I
wish, there I will walk', and continued down the middle of the pavement. On meeting a huge procession of women on their way to the
Duma to ask for their rights, Ransome had no doubt that a
Government which in three short weeks had freed the Finns, the
Poles and the Jews, would grant their demands also. 'Universal suf-
frage, which guarantees the vote to the mountaineers of the
Caucasus, the wandering tribes of Central Asia, and the half-savage
fishermen of the Siberian rivers, will not be denied to the women of
Russia who have taken so great a part in the hundred-year story of
the revolutionary movement.' He gleefully passes on the story of a
small district of half a dozen villages in Central Russia, which had

declared itself an independent republic and informed Petrograd that it was ready to enter into *pourparlers* with the Russian Republic on the subject of mutual tariffs (letting it be known that it had a considerable quantity of onions and other vegetables which it was ready to offer on reasonable terms). He admits that the new spirit may have its negative side. 'Old bottles artificially weakened by the late government have been badly strained by the new wine of revolution. The delight of holding meetings in a country where till the revolution meetings were forbidden has not yet worn off, and continual discussion, together with the dismissal of directors and their replacement by elected representatives of the work-people, have temporarily lowered industrial productivity.' But these are no more than passing difficulties.

> Freedom is like a new toy and everyone wishes to play with it. The Duma has upset the Government which was the force immediately above it. Therefore, the socialists wish to upset the Duma which more or less controlled them. And the populace upset the police which was immediately above them. The soldiers discover the possibility of controlling the officers and the peasants consider what they shall do with the landowners. Each man translates freedom as escape from under his immediate superior. [According to Knox, children had been seen parading in Petrograd with banners inscribed: 'Down with the parental yoke!'[16]] In any other country but Russia the result would be a hopeless vista of disorder. But here, apart from the sound sense which characterizes the people, there is the enormous momentum of habit and custom which presently will reassert itself. For the moment Russia is stretching herself and realizing that the fetters have at last left her limbs free.[17]

Few other witnesses, however, shared Ransome's optimistic reading of the situation. They would have been more likely to agree with Buchanan's opinion that Russia's new-won liberty was already degenerating into licence.

> The Russian idea of liberty is to take things easily, to claim double wages, to demonstrate in the streets, and to waste time in talking and in passing resolutions at public meetings. Ministers are working themselves to death, and have the best intentions; but, though I am always being told that their position is becoming stronger, I

see no signs of their asserting their authority. The Soviet continues to act as if it were the Government. . .

The military outlook is most discouraging. . .   Nor do I take an optimistic view of the immediate future of this country. Russia is not ripe for a purely democratic form of government, and for the next few years we shall probably see a series of revolutions and counter-revolutions. . .   A vast Empire like this, with all its different races, will not long hold together under a Republic. Disintegration will, in my opinion, sooner or later set in, even under a federal system.[18]

A humbler member of the British community in Petrograd, twenty-year-old governess Rosamond Dowse, puts her finger on the problem of 'freedom' in the following reminiscence (in fairness, it should be added that free travel on public transport was one of the privileges granted by the Provisional Government to the Petrograd soldiers):

When the trams started running again, people got on them and clung on outside like a bunch of grapes or swarm of bees. In Russia one had to get on at the back, pass through the car, and get off in front, paying the conductor when you saw him. Once when looking up at a tram to see how I could get in, two burly Russian soldiers who were standing on the step invited me to join them and each put an arm round me to hold me on, so I felt reasonably safe and glad of the ride as I had some way to go. When I descended and thanked them I gave them my fare and asked them to give it to the conductor when they saw him. 'Oh, don't bother,' said one, 'you needn't pay now we have freedom.' 'Oh, indeed not,' said I, 'I am English and we are free but we still pay our fares on buses and trams.'[19]

For well-to-do members of the British community, that 'hopeless vista of disorder', to use Ransome's phrase, was beginning to look unpleasantly close. At Thornton's Mill 3000 Russian workers were employed. After the Revolution they immediately elected their own factory committee, which insisted on having a say in running the mill and presented demands for an eight-hour day and a huge increase in wages. No sooner had the management come to an agreement with the committee than some extremist would demand further concessions.[20] In their own homes, too, the British residents found their comfortable lifestyles being undermined by the new spirit of freedom and equality. One of the attractions of living in Russia had always been that domestic servants were plentiful, and could be expected to work very long hours for very little pay. Now they, too, took to the streets, demanding an eight-hour day (though some thought this meant beginning work at 8 and ending at 8), and demonstrating for days on end. Even the *dvorniks* were not what they were. The police, once the paymasters and bullies of this army of spies on the dwellers they were supposed to serve, had ceased to exist, so there was no one to keep them up to the mark. The traditional saying that 'the *dvorniks* make the spring' – by clearing the melting snow from the pavement and street in front of their houses – did not apply in 1917, and the streets of Petrograd remained filthy.[21] Moreover, as Ransome reports, 'yesterday, lest things be too solemn, a deputation of *dvorniks* (yardmen or porters) presented a petition that in these times of freedom and equality their humiliating title of yardmen should be changed officially to that of house directors.'[22] As for travel in the new Russia, that, too, took on an entirely different character. A member of the British Embassy staff travelling to Moscow found that his reserved coupé was already occupied by eight Russian soldiers, taking advantage of their free travel. 'I am very sorry to disturb you,' he said, 'but this is my coupé; I am going to Moscow on official business.' He showed his ticket, whereupon one of the soldiers at once replied good-naturedly: 'It is all right. We have not the slightest objection to your riding down with us.'[23]

Colonel Knox, of course, felt most concerned about what the new spirit of freedom and equality might do to Russia's armed forces, especially as regards their attitude to the war.

Between March 20 and April 16 he and Major Thornhill visited most of the Guard depot units in Petrograd and its vicinity. Knox was not encouraged by what he saw. All the best officers had been expelled. No drilling took place, and the main idea seemed everywhere to do as little work as possible. As for the war itself, that had receded into the background.

Their visits tended to follow a similar pattern:

I used to attempt a short address, telling the men that I had heard in the Duma that the Russian soldier would like to hear something of the discipline and of the life in the British army. I told them of the fights in which I had seen their unit at the front, and of how they had suffered from the lack of heavy guns and shell; that

England was now sending them heavy artillery, her sailors braving the German submarines to deliver the guns in Russia... After some minutes of this sort of thing Major Thornhill used to say some words about discipline in the British army, about our system of training and the relations between officers and men. Then we invited questions, and did our best to reply.

Generally several members of the battalion committee made speeches in reply. They all spoke fluently and well, for the Russian is a natural orator, and with one or two exceptions they were loud in their enthusiasm for the continuance of the war.

In one battalion they had to listen to an interminable speech from a follower of Tolstoy, who extolled the Brotherhood of Nations that he hoped would follow the conclusion of the war, while in another a private soldier, who had been an actor in civil life, proved very talkative.

I had asked the men to forbear from 'experiments' at such a time, and pointed out that the experiment of electing officers had only been made once, as far as I knew – in the great French Revolution – and the result had been Napoleon. The ex-actor said: 'With the "broad Russian nature" experiments are possible that could not be tried in Western countries.'...

The 'broad Russian nature' was always the excuse for every extravagance. What was wanted was a little narrow common sense.

At the Izmailovsky Battalion the old colonel, who was 'strict', had been expelled. His replacement was as hoarse as any Duma orator from public speaking.

He told us that he had established a 'Regimental University', in which he delivered lectures himself on the 'Psychology of the Masses', while his second-in-command discoursed on the 'Military Law of Various Nations'. I ventured to remark that the subject he had chosen seemed rather recondite, but he said that, on the contrary, it was of extraordinary interest... This poor fellow somewhat later commenced writing the regimental orders in verse, and was removed from his command by the district staff.

The officers of the Finlyandsky Battalion made a poor impression.

The men chaired us into the dining-room at 4 p.m., when we had finished our talk, and as we sat down to tea no less than twelve of the officers went straight to resume the game of bridge that they had only interrupted for an hour.

What was wanted was games of another type – some such grand class leveller as football – to bring all ranks together.

On the face of it, however, their visits were a success. 'We were always received politely and we were always cheered; we were often tossed by the men in the traditional Russian way, and chaired to our car in the street.' But, Knox concludes, 'any impression we may have made was wiped out in a few minutes by the next agitator'.[24]

That the general feeling at this time was still strongly pro-war, however, is made clear by Sukhanov. A member of the Executive Committee of the Soviet (and author of the best Russian eye-witness account of the Revolution), Sukhanov was an internationalist committed to liquidating the war. He found it very disturbing that the soldiery of Petrograd refused to allow any talk about peace, and that the proletariat at the core of the Revolution was being 'more and more submerged amongst these impenetrable little peasants in their grey greatcoats'.[25]

It was, in any case, the soldiers at the front who would determine what further part Russia played in the war (to be strongly pro-war was easy when you knew you were safe in Petrograd). Knox left on a short visit to the Northern Front on April 16, but before doing so, took every opportunity of urging his views on members of the Provisional Government. When Buchanan read Prince Lvov a formal note from Knox pointing out that the Petrograd garrison was idle, that there was no excuse for allowing agitators to visit troops at the front, and that if the present agitation were allowed to continue, there would be no discipline left, the Prime Minister blandly replied that the Russian Army was a better fighting machine than ever before, and quite well able to deal with agitators.[26] On his arrival at the Embassy on April 8, Knox found the Ambassador in conversation with Kerensky. The latter, Buchanan reported to the Foreign Office,

does not favour the idea of taking strong measures at present, either against the Soviet or the Socialist propaganda in the army. On my telling him that the Government would never be masters of the situation so long as they allowed themselves to be dictated to by a rival organization, he said that the Soviet would die a natural death, that the present agitation in the army would pass, and that the army would then be in a better position to help the Allies to win the war than it would have been under the old regime.[27]

Writing up the same conversation in his diary, Knox adds that in answer to the remark, no doubt contributed by himself,

> that no other country at war allowed its Press to attack its Allies, he replied that the paper in question – the *Pravda* – had no influence and might be disregarded...
>
> The Provisional Government could depend on the regiments at Petrograd to quell disturbances, but things would not be allowed to go so far.
>
> He said that we must allow that the Provisional Government was composed not of children, but of grown-up men with brains, who knew Russia, and that its members felt that they were pursuing the only course possible to enable them to gain their ends.
>
> Kerensky seems honest, but he altogether over-estimates any possible effect of overtures from the Russian Socialists to the German Social Democrats, and he altogether underestimates the effect of the rot in the Russian army.[28]

Arthur Ransome did not ignore the army question, but here, too, he took the optimistic view that the dangers of slack discipline and anti-war propaganda would soon pass. He was more concerned, however, with political developments. His telegram of April 8 ends with a romantic flourish.

> The Revolution is only three weeks old. The golden towers of Utopia gleam almost within men's reach. The freed men of Russia, their eyes bright with that vision, turn with impatience from the drab sober visions offered them by the class with which they have least in common.

That class was the bourgeoisie. Russia, Ransome pointed out, had proportionately the smallest bourgeoisie of any country in Europe, yet the greater part of its government was bourgeois. The 'drab sober visions' were those of Foreign Minister Milyukov, whose views concerning war aims, especially his desire for Constantinople, were regarded by almost the whole of the Russian people as 'dangerous imperialistic moonshine'. Kerensky, however, had officially declared that Milyukov's view was not that of the Government. Ransome had come to the conclusion, reached somewhat earlier by Williams and Knox, that Kerensky was the key figure in the situation. On March 30 he describes him as 'one of the heroic figures of the Revolution', who had been working night and day for unity between the Soviet and the Government. 'Every day without conflict is a day gained, and that so many days have been gained is largely due to this one young man, whose health is such [Kerensky had had a tubercular kidney removed] that he may be deliberately sacrificing his life for his country.'[29]

On April 10 Ransome reported on the All-Russian Conference of the Kadet Party. Harold Williams refers to the Kadets at this time as the ablest and best organized party in Russia, bringing 'strong clear brains' to bear on the new problems,[30] but Ransome could not see them in such a positive light.

That party now finds itself in the wholly unexpected position unconsciously illustrated by Milyukov when, in addressing it, he described how on the Monday morning of the Revolution he looked from the window on the barrack yard next door, and saw the soldiers waving their caps and going out to join the people. This is the Russian Revolution, I thought, but it will be suppressed in a quarter of an hour. But in a few hours I learnt that it was indeed the Russian Revolution, and that it would not be suppressed so easily. Precisely because that party was looking from the windows while the workmen and soldiers were taking the stupendous risk of armed rebellion, it is no longer unquestionably representative of Russia...

Throughout the conference the tone of the discussion was more significant than individual speeches. The feeling throughout was one of disquiet at the existence in the country of two powers, in the Government and the Soviet, and of fear, rather than belief, that real power was in the hands of the latter... The clear-sighted, intelligent bourgeoisie that once had to behave tactfully with regard to the powers above it, now has to use similar tact in dealing with the powers below.[31]

No sooner had the Kadets dispersed than those 'powers below' were holding a Conference of their own. Arthur Ransome appears to have been the only British correspondent to attend:

It is one month after the Revolution, and something very like a proletariat Parliament is sitting in the White Hall once occupied by the Duma. It is the Conference of Councils of Workers' and Soldiers' Deputies [Soviets] from all parts of Russia and from the armies at the front. Colonels and captains are to be seen here and there, but for the most part it consists of private soldiers and workmen, the latter noticeable in the sea of uniforms by their black coats, coloured shirts and jerseys. These were the people referred to by the Kadet Party when they spoke of double authority; the people who presently at any rate determine government policy, since they are necessary as the government's support; and the people whose representative, Kerensky, is the strongest man in the Council of Ministers.

The opening of the Conference on April 11 was turned into another highly-charged emotional occasion. Breshko-Breshkovskaya (1844–1934), a revolutionary of noble Polish origin, was known as 'the Grandmother of the Russian Revolution'. Most of her life had been spent in prison or exile. Now she had come straight to the Conference on her return from Siberia and was still carrying the bouquet of flowers presented to her at the railway-station. The whole gathering stood and cheered as a 'little, kindly old lady with nearly white hair and pink cheeks' came in on the arm of Kerensky, who was looking very ill and trembling with excitement. Recalling the occasion a few months later, Ransome wrote that Kerensky greeted her 'with an impassioned speech, she all the while stroking his head like a mother calming the enthusiasm of an already overstrained child.'[32] At last she, too, made a speech. It was very quiet after Kerensky's. In it she urged that Hohenzollern should not be allowed to conquer what had been taken from the Romanovs.

> I have never seen such enthusiasm. Soldiers and sailors leapt from their places, rushed to the tribune, and in some cases kneeling before her cried: 'We have brought you from Siberia to Petrograd. Shall we not guard you? We have won freedom. We will keep it.' She gave away some roses from the bouquet with which she had been met at the station, and I saw a soldier who had secured two petals wrap them up in paper while tears of excitement ran down his face. Finally Grandmother was lifted shoulder-high in her chair and carried out of the building.[33]

Two issues dominated the Conference: the war, and relations with the Provisional Government. 'The spirit of the army,' Ransome reported, 'became very clear during the debate. I did not hear a single "militaristic" speech. Soldier after soldier said: 'We want to end the war, we want peace, but we do not want peace with defeat, we do not want to smudge our new freedom with dishonour.' Peace should be based on the principles of 'no annexations or contributions' (i.e. no country should stand to gain in any way from the war) and of the right of each subject race to determine its own future. An extremist who argued, 'If there are to be no annexations and no contributions, why do we continue the war? Surely we do not go on simply because we have to serve the bourgeois classes of England and France?', was received with howls of indignation. After Breshko-Breshkovskaya's address it came as no surprise to Ransome when a resolution in favour of making every effort to strengthen the front and rear against the enemy was passed by 325 votes to 57.[34]

The debate on relations with the Provisional Government, however, 'was marked by great divergence of views'. The difficulty, according to Ransome,

> lies in the fact that the Government and the Conference represent different classes of the population... The Socialists know that through the existence of the Soviet thay have so far been able to keep the Government fulfilling the will of the revolutionaries... The outcry against divided power has been raised exclusively by the bourgeoisie and the landed class who are fundamentally opposed to that will. The bourgeoisie would naturally prefer that the revolution should be administrative and not social, and the revolutionaries not without justification believe that they are willing to use the war and public patriotism to further this purely class desire. Frequent mention is made of possible counter-revolution... not the return of Tsarism... but any turn of affairs which should set the minority in control of the majority.

A military doctor argued that all the power was falling into the hands of the landowners and rich bourgeoisie, while another speaker said it was not a Government of Public Confidence but of Public Panic. Outright hostility to the Government was shown, however, only by the extremists, 'who are in an almost ridiculous minority'. The Conference passed a resolution recognizing that the Government was so far fulfilling perfectly the will of the people, and guaranteeing to support it so long as it continued along that road, 'and to resist it only if it should attempt to put itself beyond democratic control'.[35]

On Friday, April 13, a British Labour delegation, consisting of Messrs Thorne, O'Grady and Sanders, arrived in Petrograd in company with three French Socialist delegates and the veteran Russian Socialist leader, Plekhanov. At three o'clock on Sunday they all went to the main hall of the Duma where the Conference was still in session. The amphitheatre, Harold Williams writes,

> which one had been accustomed to see occupied by the sober figures of Deputies, was filled with picturesque soldiers and workmen, all intent on the new and serious business.
>
> The entry of the delegates and Plekhanov was the signal for cheering. Business was interrupted as Messrs Plekhanov, Thorne, O'Grady, Moutet and Cachin were led up to the Speaker's chair, and M. Chkheidze, president of the Soviet, said a few words of welcome. It was an amazing sight to see Mr Thorne, with a big fur coat over his arm, standing amid the throng of Russian Socialists on the official tribune of the Duma.
>
> M. Cachin, the French delegate, made an impassioned speech to the audience, which did not understand a word, but responded to the thrilling inflections and dramatic gestures of the French orator. The cheering was still more lusty when his speech was translated by a member of the Russian Executive Committee.
>
> Then Mr O'Grady spoke. He began in a low voice, and I was afraid his speech would be less effective than the Frenchman's. But in two minutes he had raised his voice to Trafalgar Square dimensions, and the decorous Duma has never heard such a volume of thunderous sound as Mr O'Grady poured forth on the uncomprehending soldiers and workmen. They were greatly impressed, and when the translator announced that Mr O'Grady was chairman of the National Federation of Trade Unions there was a tumult of applause, which was renewed again and again during the translation of the speech.
>
> Neither M. Cachin nor Mr O'Grady mentioned the war. They conveyed greetings from the Western workers, and spoke glowingly of the liberative effect of the Russian revolution on the world. M. Plekhanov did speak of the war, and most definitely and emphatically, and his words were cheered to the echo.

Then, on the spot where only a few months ago I had heard Stürmer mumbling his lying assurances about loyalty to the Allies and war to victory, M. Plekhanov seized Mr O'Grady by one hand and M. Moutet by the other, and raising them on high, presented to the wildly-cheering throng a real and thrilling symbol of allied democracy. 'It was admirable, it was moving,' said M. Cachin, as we walked out. 'It was the most historical thing I've ever been at in my life,' said Mr Will Thorne. It was certainly a most hopeful beginning.[36]

Ransome devotes only half a dozen lines to this event: compared to the tremendous receptions given to Breshko-Breshkovskaya and Plekhanov, the arrival of the Allied delegates 'naturally uncaused very great excitement'. Philips Price was present when the delegates visited Moscow and met a deputation from the local Soviet to discuss the revolutionaries' peace programme. The British position was uncompromising.

No peace, they said, could be obtained by such means. Only the complete military defeat and crushing of Germany for many years to come would bring peace in the world. 'But even if that were the best tactics to adopt for destroying Prussian militarism, which is as much our enemy as it is yours,' said one of the Russians, 'is that any reason why we should not renounce the old annexationist plans of the Tsar's late regime and publish the secret treaties? The Tsar made us fight for Constantinople, which is not Russian, and never was.' One of the British delegates thereupon jovially burst out: 'If you don't want Constantinople, then, damn it, we'll take it!' I remember a long silence after this remark, then handshaking and the withdrawal of the deputation.[37]

*

Five weeks have passed since the Revolution. Our witnesses do not appear to have great confidence in the members of the Provisional Government, although Harold Williams, if he shares their doubts, refrains from rocking the boat by saying so openly. Bernard Pares feels that government has disappeared. Colonel Knox – still not recovered from the shock of seeing that collection of boots? – has little faith in the new authorities' ability to control the situation in the army. Nor does the Government appear to be showing much confidence in itself: Prince Lvov told an Englishman at this time that they were 'merely a straw rushed along by a turbulent current'.[38]

An exception is made in the case of Kerensky, still regarded as the one bright star in the political firmament, although Knox is beginning to have reservations about him, too.

With regard to the Soviet, opinions are more divided. This is because our witnesses' *own* class and political sympathies – quite apart from the Russian context – are being brought into play. Philips Price, arriving in Moscow from the south on April 2, found the crowds 'consisted broadly of two elements. On the one hand there was a well-dressed section of middle-class people, students, officers, advocates, doctors; on the other hand there were common soldiers, workmen, small handcraftsmen, who could be detected at once by their weather-worn, collarless shirts... Two social groups were engaged in spiritual conflict.' His sympathies lie with the second group.[39] So, too, do those of Arthur Ransome, the more so, since the Soviet's whole-hearted commitment to a 'defensive' war does not conflict with his desire to see Germany defeated. In his *Autobiography* he describes how he inadvertently gate-crashed a Russian Cabinet Meeting.

> I had overheard someone say that it would be a pity not to know what was being decided in the Marinsky Palace [where the Provisional Government had installed itself, leaving Taurida to the Soviets], so I went there and found much of it in darkness. I wandered through the dark corridors without being stopped by anybody. Light was coming through chinks and I was feeling my way along the chinks to find the handle of a door, when the door flew suddenly open before me and I fell head first into the room where the Council of Ministers, sitting in red plush chairs with gilt legs, was being addressed by Milyukov.[40]

Those red plush chairs have little to do with the Revolution as Ransome understands it; they are too reminiscent of 'the tragi-comedy of... courtiers whose gilt chairs have been knocked from under them'. Harold Williams tries to strike a balance, distinguishing the moderate and reasonable element in the Soviet from the chaotic fanaticism of extremists, but when he describes the Duma amphitheatre being 'filled with picturesque soldiers and workmen, all intent on the new and serious business', he betrays a slight condescension: these men may have a useful supporting role to play, but that is all. By contrast, Ransome and especially Philips Price take the view that the Soviet already is the effective ruler of Russia. In an article datelined 'Moscow, April 11' Philips Price writes: 'It gives its orders to the middle-class intelligentsia parties which nominally run the country in the shape of the Provisional Government, but watches over it and sees that it does what it is told.'

Feelings among the witnesses themselves were beginning to run high. Robert Wilton had been openly critical of the Soviet's 'mischievous' activities almost from the first day of the Revolution. Great indignation is being expressed in Moscow, Philips Price writes,

> at the abominable behaviour of the Northcliffe Press in England, especially of its correspondent, Wilton, in Petrograd, whom, by the way, I know quite well, for spreading the provocative reports about the Union of Soldiers and Workers [the Soviet], and trying to discredit them in Western Europe... I only hope that they [the Russian people] will turn the *Times* correspondent out of Petrograd.[41]

As it happened, Wilton fell ill around this time as a result of stress and overwork (so, too, did Harold Williams later in the month) and the *Times* coverage of Russia became very thin.

In his report to the Foreign Office of April 16, Sir George Buchanan refers to 'the arrival of fresh Anarchists from abroad'.[42] This arrival is more significant than all the other arrivals described in this chapter, for among the latest group is an exiled revolutionary known as Lenin.

Kerensky in the Ascendant

April 16 to May 17: Lenin's return (April 16); the Milyukov crisis; formation of
Coalition Government (May 17)

Buchanan's reference to 'Anarchists' was unfortunate. There *were*
Anarchists in Petrograd, and it was not long, Ransome reports,
before they took to the streets and 'solemnly protested' against Lenin
being regarded as one of them.[1] But Buchanan was not the only witness to blur the distinctions between the various Russian left-wing
parties. This vague terminology does not necessarily imply ignorance so much as a reluctance to inflict baffling Russian names upon
English readers. Both Ransome and Williams for a long time
shunned the term 'Soviet', referring instead to the 'Council of
Workmen's and Soldiers' Deputies', and preferred to call the
Bolsheviks 'extremists', 'Leninites' or 'Maximalists'.

Whatever deficiencies there may have been in Buchanan's political
education were, however, made good, and in his memoirs he depicts
the views and aims of the different Socialist groups as follows:

The Social Revolutionaries [SRs] were agrarian, in contradistinc-
tion to the Social Democrats, who represented the interests of the
proletariats of the towns. The watchword of the former had
always been, 'Land and Liberty'. During the latter part of the last
and the commencement of the present century they had adopted
terrorism as a weapon for attaining their ends...

The Social Democrats, on the other hand, had, after the conference held in London in 1903 – at which the Leninites outvoted
their opponents on the question of the party organization – been
split up into Mensheviks and Bolsheviks, or Minority and Majority

Socialists [later, to confuse the issue, the Bolsheviks became the smaller party], though moderates and extremists would have been more appropriate terms. The former, like most of the SRs, had advocated collaboration with the advanced Liberals for the overthrow of the Empire, and, now that this had been done, they aimed at the establishment of a Republic on democratic lines. The Bolsheviks, on the contrary, would have nothing to do with any bourgeois group, no matter how advanced it might be. With them it was the masses which alone counted, and it was to the workmen and to the peasants that they turned for the support necessary to enable them to carry out their programme – the establishment of the dictatorship of the proletariat and the transformation of the whole social system. . .

As regarded the war, both Mensheviks and SRs advocated the speedy conclusion of peace without annexations or contributions. There was, however, a small Menshevik group, led by Plekhanov, that called on the working classes to co-operate for the purpose of securing the victory over Germany, which would alone guarantee Russia's new-found freedom. The Bolsheviks, on the other hand, were out and out 'Defeatists'. The war had to be brought to an end by any means and at any cost. The soldiers had to be induced by an organized propaganda to turn their arms, not against their brothers in the enemy ranks, but against the reactionary bourgeois Governments of their own and other countries. For a Bolshevik there was no such thing as country or patriotism.[2]

The Bolsheviks were the smallest of the three Socialist parties, but had well-organized support among the working classes in the big cities. Both they and the Mensheviks were Marxists. The Mensheviks interpreted Marx more strictly, believing that socio-economic change was inevitable, whereas the Bolsheviks, especially Lenin, adopted a more flexible, even opportunist approach. The SRs enjoyed the greatest support among the people as a whole, especially in the rural areas. Although they were not Marxists, there was more co-operation during 1917 between them and the Mensheviks than between the Mensheviks and the Bolsheviks. Kerensky joined the SRs after the Revolution and became known as a 'March SR'. All three Socialist groups, however, felt that they had more in common with each other than with the liberal Kadets.

The leader of the SRs, Chernov (1876–1952), also returned from exile in April. He was, in Buchanan's opinion, a man of strong character and considerable ability. He belonged to the advanced wing of the SR party, and advocated the immediate nationalization of the land and its division among the peasants without awaiting the decision of the Constituent Assembly. He was generally regarded as dangerous and untrustworthy, and I found him the reverse of sympathetic.

The leader of the Mensheviks, Tsereteli (1882–1959), a Georgian of princely family who had spent several years in Siberia under a sentence of hard labour, impressed Buchanan more favourably.

> With a refined and sympathetic personality, he attracted me by his transparent honesty of purpose and his straightforward manner. He was, like so many other Russian Socialists, an Idealist; but, though I do not reproach him with this, he made the mistake of approaching grave problems of practical politics from a purely theoretical [i.e. Marxist] standpoint.[3]

With Lenin, the leader of the Bolsheviks, Buchanan appears not to have had any personal contact.

Born in 1870, Vladimir Ilyich Ulyanov (Lenin) was eleven years older than Kerensky. Both grew up in Simbirsk, where Lenin's father was an inspector of schools, and Kerensky's a headmaster. Lenin's youthful interest in revolutionary socialism intensified in 1887, when his elder brother was executed for his part in the attempted assassination of Alexander III. In 1897 he was banished to Siberia, and on his release in 1900 emigrated to Western Europe, returning to Russia only once, in October 1905, when he led the Bolshevik faction during the last stages of the abortive 1905 Revolution. To all but his fellow Bolsheviks – and not even to many of them – Lenin was personally unknown in 1917. He was the legendary revolutionary figure, the 'veiled oracle' of the Bolshevik movement, as E.H. Wilcox calls him.[4]

The return to Russia of Lenin and his fellow exiles was to provide Edmund Wilson with the memorable title of his study of socialist thought, *To the Finland Station*, published in 1940. By then the terminal for trains arriving from Finland had become a shabby little stucco station more appropriate to a provincial town, but in 1917 it still had a rest-room reserved for the Emperor, and it was there, on the evening of April 16, that the Georgian, Chkheidze, dutifully waited to greet Lenin on behalf of the Petrograd Soviet. The train was very late, and did not arrive until ten minutes past eleven. Inside and outside the station the Marseillaise resounded, a large bouquet was thrust into Lenin's hands, and a guard of honour presented arms. The whole event had been brilliantly stage-managed by the Petrograd Bolsheviks. Chkheidze, a Menshevik, made a cautious speech of welcome, stressing that now was the time for the revolutionary democracy in Russia to close ranks. There was nothing cautious, however, about Lenin's speech of reply, addressed not so much to Chkheidze as to his own supporters crowding into the room behind him. What had happened in Russia, he told them, was simply the first step in a world-wide socialist revolution. From the Finland Station Lenin was driven in a motorcade to Bolshevik headquarters. At every crossroad fresh crowds gathered, and from the turret of the armoured car in which he was travelling Lenin addressed them in the same uncompromising terms.[5]

If, as his diary suggests, Arthur Ransome saw Lenin arrive at the Finland Station and make a speech, it is surprising that his telegrams give no indication of this. Meriel Buchanan had never heard the name of Lenin before. She did not remain in ignorance long. One of the first houses to be pillaged by the mob after the Revolution was that of the ballerina, Ksheshinskaya, the Emperor's former mistress, facing the Embassy on the other side of the river. 'It had stood empty and desolate ever since, but on April 17 I noticed suddenly an enormous scarlet flag flaming vividly above the walls.'[6] On making enquiries, Meriel learned that it had been taken over by a political group called the Bolsheviks as their Party headquarters. 'From a kiosk in the garden,' E.H.Wilcox writes (Francis calls it 'a circular pagoda, or bandstand') 'inflammatory harangues were delivered daily to open-mouthed crowds of workmen and soldiers in the street on the other side of the palings. Money Lenin had in abundance, and the smartest motor-cars in Petrograd carried his army of orators into the remote working-class districts on the rim of the city.'[7] Ransome casually dismisses Lenin's proceedings at this time as 'so exaggerated that they have the air of comic opera', but Harold Williams, though equally dismissive, gives Lenin more careful attention.

> Lenin, leader of the extreme faction of the Social Democrats, arrived here on Monday night by way of Germany. His action in accepting from the German Government a passage from Switzerland through Germany arouses intense indignation here [the ensign in charge of the guard of honour at the Finland Station publicly dissociated himself from Lenin on learning the details of

the journey]. He has come back breathing fire, and demanding the immediate and unconditional conclusion of peace, civil war against the army and Government, and vengeance on Kerensky and Chkheidze, whom he describes as traitors to the cause of International Socialism.

At the meeting of Social Democrats yesterday his wild rant was received in dead silence, and he was vigorously attacked, not only by the more moderate Social Democrats, but by members of his own faction.

Chkheidze said that probably the Russian Revolution would absorb Lenin, but if he remained outside it would be no great loss.

Lenin was left absolutely without supporters. The sharp repulse given to this firebrand was a healthy sign of the growth of practical sense in the Socialist wing, and the generally moderate and sensible tone of the conference of provincial workers' and soldiers' deputies was another hopeful indication of the passing of the revolutionary fever.[8]

Lenin had arrived on April 16, or April 3 (Easter Monday) in the Russian calendar. As a first step towards introducing the Western calendar, it was decided to celebrate May 1/April 18 as International Labour Day. The whole town, according to Ransome, had worked on Sunday so as to be able to celebrate with a good conscience. Watching from his window, he found it difficult to believe that only six weeks earlier he had been witnessing the battle for the prison next door, now a picturesque ruin decorated with flags.

Immediately below in the great square two processions are meeting. One of them includes a detachment from one of the regiments which first threw out the red flag in the days of revolution. The other procession, noticing this, breaks into wild cheering which spreads over the whole sea of people far away into the distance. . . The soldiers wave their caps and shout in reply. In all directions as far as the eye can see red flags are waving above the dense crowd, which leaves just enough room for the perpetually passing processions. On either side of them a long string of men and women walk along holding hands like an endless farandole.

In contrast to the grey skies under which the victims of the Revolution had been buried, the sunshine on this day of celebration was superb. Visually, May Day 1917 must be regarded as the high point of the entire Russian Revolution. The ice on the river was beginning to melt, and Louis de Robien describes how the deep violet blue of the water showed up the immaculate whiteness of the ice-floes, while the pale blue of the sky stood out in sharp contrast to the warmly lit red of the flags and banners, which palpitated and floated, swelled out and bowed low in the violent gusts of wind.[9]

Philips Price felt that the halcyon days of the March Revolution reached their climax on May 1:

> I do not think I ever saw a more impressive spectacle than on this occasion. It was not merely a labour demonstration, although every socialist party and workmen's union in Russia was represented there, from anarcho-syndicalists to the most moderate of the middle-class democrats. It was not merely an international demonstration, although every nationality of what had been the Russian Empire was represented there with its flag and inscription in some rare, strange tongue, from the Baltic Finns to the Tunguses of Siberia. The First of May celebration, 1917, in Petrograd and throughout the length and breadth of Russia was really a great religious festival, in which the whole human race was invited to commemorate the brotherhood of man. Revolutionary Russia had a message to the world, and was telling it across the roar of the cannons and the din of battle.

'It was like a dream,' Bernard Pares comments, 'and the people themselves seemed dreamy; but it was a good dream.'[10]

Yet even while these celebrations were going on, the Provisional Government was passing through a political crisis: one that a British journalist may have inadvertently helped to hasten. On the day after his arrival in Moscow from the south, Philips Price learned that the Foreign Minister, Milyukov, was returning to Petrograd on the night train after a short visit. He went to the station in search of an interview, sent in his card and was summoned to Milyukov's compartment about ten minutes before the train was due to leave.

> I found him surprisingly frank. In a few sentences he said that nothing would satisfy the Provisional Government but the end of the Austrian and Turkish Empire and the annexation to Russia of Constantinople and the Straits. I was so astonished at the bluntness of the Foreign Minister's statement to me that I sat dumb for a while in the carriage and had to be reminded that I had better

get off the train, as it was just going to start. I hurriedly thanked
M. Milyukov and rushed off to the telegraph office which, though
it was nearly midnight, was still open for press telegrams.

The interview was published in the *Manchester Guardian* on April 26.
On the next day it was telegraphed back to Russia, and when Philips
Price arrived in Petrograd soon after, he found that it 'had created a
big stir'.[11] Then on May 1 Milyukov cabled a Note about war aims to
Russian Embassies abroad for transmission to Allied governments.
Its ambiguous tone caused extreme dissatisfaction in Russian left-
wing circles, as Ransome reports in his morning telegram of May 3.

> The position is curious. Milyukov, the Foreign Minister of demo-
> cratic Russia, is probably the strongest imperialist in the country,
> and retains his position solely on account of his great personal
> influence, although twice already before this Note words of his,
> once about the preservation of the old dynasty and then about
> Constantinople, have nearly caused a definite split in the country.
> The extremist [Bolshevik] *Pravda* points to Milyukov's Note as
> proof of the failure of the moderate methods of the Soviet. Other
> papers point out that Milyukov's Note is written in the dead lan-
> guage of old diplomacy from which the Revolution was to have
> freed Europe.[12]

Philips Price was present at the sitting of the Petrograd Soviet on
May 3, when the Bolshevik group demanded 'All power to the
Soviets', arguing that the Soviet had allowed power to slip from its
grasp into the hands of the Provisional Government. The Bolsheviks,
however, 'were at this time only a small minority of the Petrograd
delegates, and they were confined to the skilled workers of the big
metal works and arsenals, the sailors of the Baltic Fleet and the yards
at Kronstadt and a small part of the Petrograd garrison.' The Soviet
as a whole preferred to keep to its policy of controlling events without assuming the full responsibility of government.[13]

On the afternoon of May 3 Ransome found the whole of Marinsky
Square filled with a dense mass of troops. In the centre were men of
the Litovsky Regiment carrying huge red banners inscribed: 'Down
with Milyukov!' Speakers among the soldiers were saying: 'Since he
no longer fulfils the will of the people, why should he be a member
of the people's government?' There were strong rumours that he
would resign. In the evening more regiments turned out carrying

anti-Milyukov placards. Meanwhile, inside the Marinsky Palace, urgent talks were being held between the Government and the Executive Committee of the Soviet. The latter telephoned all the barracks asking the troops not to come out, and did their utmost to prevent demonstrations and preserve order. It was the Leninites, Ransome felt, who were profiting most from the situation: Milyukov's Note had given them a new impetus and they were addressing meetings everywhere, though their reception was almost invariably hostile. Milyukov's supporters then tried to turn the current of feeling in a new direction: crowds of students rushed about the streets shouting 'Down with Lenin!', and when Milyukov came out after midnight and made a speech from the palace balcony, the crowd was 'more or less friendly'.[14]

On May 4 Bernard Pares was lunching at a restaurant on the Nevsky when he heard firing. A small party of armed Bolshevik soldiers had just passed the Kazan Cathedral. A much larger pro-Government procession had also gathered, unarmed and consisting of people from all classes of society. He went out and joined them as they made their way to Marinsky Square, which they nearly filled. That afternoon on the Nevsky Arthur Ransome met three processions of Leninites demonstrating against the Government, all obviously poor folk and including many women. Each procession was headed by a small body of civilians carrying rifles (factory workers known later as 'Red Guards'). Near the City Hall they met opposition: shots were fired, one man was killed and two wounded. Further conflicts took place that evening. In the meantime, however, the Executive Committee of the Soviet had decided to accept the Government's explanation of the Note and to regard the incident as closed. At a full meeting of the Soviet this was agreed to by everyone except the Bolsheviks, and all demonstrations were banned for the next two days. But while the Soviet was thus engaged in securing peace, the extremists, among whom Ransome includes 'both imperialists and Leninites', were still manifesting. 'Between 9 and 10.30', Buchanan writes, 'I had to go out three times on the balcony of the Embassy to receive ovations and to address crowds who were demonstrating for the Government and the Allies. [Pares acted as interpreter, shouting down his words in Russian.] During one of them a free fight took place between the supporters of the Government and the Leninites.'[15]

What the outcome of this conflict had been, Buchanan did not feel quite certain: Milyukov was much elated, whereas the Soviet continued to act as if it were master of the situation. But on May 21 he reported to the Foreign Office:

> The last two weeks have been very anxious ones, as the victory which the Government had won over the Soviet in the matter of the Note to the Powers was not nearly so complete as Milyukov had imagined. So long as the Soviet maintained its exclusive right to dispose of the troops, the Government, as Prince Lvov remarked, was 'an authority without power', while the Workmen's Council was 'a power without authority'. Under such conditions it was impossible for Guchkov, as Minister of War, and for Kornilov, as military governor of Petrograd, to accept responsibility for the maintenance of discipline in the army. They both, consequently, resigned, while the former declared that if things were to continue as they were the army would cease to exist as a fighting force in three weeks' time. Guchkov's resignation precipitated matters, and Lvov, Kerensky and Tereshchenko came to the conclusion that, as the Soviet was too powerful a factor to be either suppressed or disregarded, the only way of putting an end to the anomaly of a dual Government was to form a Coalition. Though this idea did not at first find favour with the Soviet, it was eventually agreed that the latter should be represented in the Government by three delegates – Tsereteli, Chernov and Skobelev. Milyukov was at Headquarters when the crisis broke out, and he had on his return to choose between accepting the post of Minister of Education or leaving the Cabinet. After a vain struggle to retain charge of the Foreign Office he tendered his resignation.

Buchanan's feelings about Milyukov's departure were mixed: it weakened the more moderate section of the Government, but as Foreign Minister, Milyukov had been so obsessed by Constantinople that he had never voiced the views of the Government as a whole. Ransome was more outspoken. Though a wonderful leader in opposition, Milyukov had not acted responsibly as a Minister, and with his resignation there would be 'a considerable clearing of the air'. The youthful Tereshchenko became Foreign Minister, while Kerensky took over the War Office and the Admiralty.[16]

And so on May 17, two months after the Provisional Government had been formed, the first Coalition Government came into existence, with Prince Lvov still nominally in charge but Kerensky as the dominant figure. The problems that it faced were formidable,

Ransome reports: a rising tide of anarchy at home, especially in the country, where forests were being cut down, land seized and country houses sacked indiscriminately, and disorganization in the armed forces, which were having to continue a war beyond their strength. The main plank in the Coalition platform was the quickest possible attainment of a general peace, based on the principle of no annexations and no indemnities, and obtained in close unbreakable unity with the Allied democracies.

This is the aim put forward by Kerensky in his great effort to restore discipline in the army... His task will be lightened the moment the Allies take the wind out of the sails of anti-Ally propaganda in the army by clearly expressing agreement with Russia. I do not think it an exaggeration to say that the Coalition Government will stand or fall by the Allies' reply to its declaration. If the Coalition is broken by failure in the main task it has set itself, it will have small chance of resisting attacks from the extremists, who regard its very formation as a concession... The extremists are in a minority among articulate Russians, but have a disproportionate influence among what Russians themselves call 'the dark masses', meaning by this the inarticulate uneducated people, on whose ignorance agitators play in the most shameless manner, insisting always on the supposed distinction between the aims of the Allies and those of the Russians. The more serious newspapers eagerly await the Allies' declaration, believing that if the Allies and Russians can agree on an absolutely definite statement of war aims, the onus of prolonging the war will fall on the Germans, so that it may be possible to reunite the army and persuade it to advance. As I foresaw, the extremists are already attacking the Coalition as a 'war cabinet'. This does not lighten their task. If, however, the Allies' declaration cuts the ground from under the agitators' feet, Kerensky's influence is such that the situation may yet be saved.[17]

These comments make clear in passing how the position of the Bolsheviks has been strengthened, because they now represent the only alternative to official Government policy. As for the Allies, although Buchanan was to do his best to smooth the British Government's relations with the Coalition, they were far too preoccupied with their own wartime problems to pay more than superficial attention to what was happening in Russia, and to make the kind of positive declarations that Ransome felt were needed. Revolutionary Russia's message to the world went unheeded. As a delegate to the Peasants' Conference in Petrograd, a young peasant soldier from the front, put it to Philips Price: 'The Russian people is like a nightingale sitting upon a tree and singing day and night, but it does not know to whom it sings or who is listening.'[18]

All hopes thus rested on Kerensky's shoulders. If anyone could galvanize the army into new life, Buchanan realized, it was he. The British Ambassador had been pleased to be able to report to the Foreign Office on April 23 that he had overcome Kerensky's initial suspicions about his real opinion of the Revolution, and was gradually making friends with him.

> Unfortunately, he can talk but little French, but when he dined at the Embassy, Lockhart (our consul-general at Moscow), who talks Russian fluently, acted as our interpreter, and we had a long and straight talk... I was rather amused at his coming to dinner accompanied by his *officier d'ordonnance*, whom I had not invited. It was a curious proceeding on the part of a Socialist Minister who never wears anything but an ordinary workman's black jacket.[19]

Meriel Buchanan, who in general is extremely hostile to Kerensky, writes that in the spring of 1917 he was at the very height and zenith of his power,

> enjoying a popularity that was almost unequalled. I remember, during some big charity entertainment [the annual benefit performance held on April 30 for the military heroes, the Knights of St George], his appearance in one of the boxes causing the whole audience, oblivious of the performance then going on, to rise in a sudden burst of enthusiasm, many people even leaving their seats and flocking to the middle of the theatre the better to be able to see him. In the entr'acte some half-dozen soldiers carried him through the theatre on a chair which they finally placed on the stage. Dressed in the little black workman's coat which he always wore – prompted by his love of a somewhat theatrical appearance – his arm, owing to a slight accident, in a sling, his face paler and more cadaverous than ever, his deep, fierce eyes sweeping the crowd that thronged cheering and clapping to the very edge of the stage, he stood there a moment in silence, and then in the midst of a sudden hush began to speak in that harsh, unmusical voice that was

yet so strangely compelling and enthralling [Bernard Pares refers to the 'almost military thrill of that sharp vibrant voice']. His speech was short and full of fire and enthusiasm, but it was, above all, the man's personality that was so arresting, in spite of the fact of its not being sympathetic. His thin, cruel-looking face stood out from all others as a painted face of extraordinary vividness on a dark canvas, his small, deep-set eyes held one with the quick power of their shifting glance, his voice rapped out his words with a sharp incisiveness that wasted nothing but went straight to the point with a brutal swiftness. A storm of cheering that seemed to rock and shake the theatre greeted his speech, and he was carried back to his box in triumph.[20]

Kerensky the public orator was not the same person, however, as the Kerensky of private conversation. Bernard Pares, to whom Kerensky gave an interview on May 1, found him 'very simple and direct', and states that his personality made a very pleasant impression on him, as it did on many others.[21]

Both Harold Williams' deputy and Arthur Ransome in his telegram of May 13 have left careful accounts of the speech that Kerensky made to a conference of delegates from the front. It was not a cheerful speech, Ransome writes, but one of ringing honesty, while his fellow journalist describes it as a speech of grave warning.

Comrades, soldiers and officers! I don't know what you feel there in the trenches, but I know what is going on here... Russia will only be able to play a decisive role in the history of the world if she can prove her ideals just and her democracy too strong to be struggled against. But two things are necessary to realize this objective – namely, organization and patience... Comrades, you have been able for ten years to suffer and keep silence. Why can't you be patient now? Surely the free state of Russia is not a nation of rebellious slaves? (*These words produced great consternation.*) My strength is failing; I no longer feel my former courage; I am no longer sure that the Russian people are not rebellious slaves, but responsible citizens worthy of the Russian nation. (*He paused and then continued at the top of his voice.*) They say there is no more need for a front, since there is already fraternity. Are the troops fraternizing in France? Fraternity is all very well when both sides fraternize. But, comrades, are not the enemy's forces already flung across to the Anglo-French front and is not the Anglo-French advance already brought to a standstill? There is no Russian front. There is only one united Allied front. (*Tremendous applause.*) We are not a group of weary folk. We are a nation. (*He paused again.*) Would that I had died two months ago, when I should have died with a great dream that once for all in Russia new life had flamed into being. If we do not all recognize instantly the tragedy of the moment, if we do not understand that responsibility lies on all of us, if our state organism does not run like well-adjusted clockwork, then all of which we have dreamed and towards which we have struggled will be thrown back for years and perhaps drowned in blood. The fate of the country is in your hands, and it is in most extreme danger. Beware! We have tasted freedom, and are becoming intoxicated. But we need now the greatest possible sobriety and discipline. History must be able to say of us, 'They died, but were never slaves.'[22]

6

One Island, Two Orators

May 18 to June 17: conditions on the island of Kronstadt; Kerensky and Lenin at
First All-Russian Congress of Soviets (opens June 16)

General Knox – he had been appointed to the temporary rank of
Brigadier-General on April 27 – would certainly have applauded
Kerensky's fine words, especially his reference to a united Allied
front; but how could one man stop the rot in the Russian army? Knox
had recently seen for himself the deplorable state of things on the
Northern front, where 'units have been turned into political debating
societies', and parleying 'takes place daily with the enemy, who
laughs at the credulity of the Russian peasant soldier'. It was all part
of 'an extraordinary wave of extravagant humanitarianism': prisoners
of war liberated by the peasants were working on the landlords'
estates, while in Moscow German and Austrian officers walked about
freely. 'Surely,' Knox exclaims in exasperation, 'there has never been
another country at war in which the prisoners of war declared a
strike for better pay and conditions of life!' As for Petrograd,

> things are growing worse daily. The tens of thousands of able-
> bodied men in uniform who saunter about the streets without a
> thought of going to the front or of working to prepare themselves
> for war, when every able-bodied man and most of the women in
> England and France are straining every nerve to beat the common
> enemy, will be a disgrace for all time to the Russian people and its
> Government.
>
> Even Lenin disclaims the idea of a separate peace, but his agita-
> tion tends to the same end by the utter ruin it is bringing on the
> Russian army.

Knox was quick off the mark to congratulate Kerensky, arriving at the new Minister of War's official residence on the morning of May 18 before the Minister himself. Kerensky was planning to leave for the South-West Front in five or six days,

'when he has restored order here'. Hope that springs eternal! I told him I was glad of his appointment, for I considered him to be the only man who could save Russia... When I was going away he asked me not to frighten the Ambassador by collecting 'pessimistic information'!

Tereshchenko was in cheerful mood when he told Buchanan that Kerensky had ordered all deserters to return by May 28 or face severe punishment, but even this news failed to raise Knox's spirits. 'We will wait and see!' he writes bleakly in his diary. 'After all, both Kerensky and Tereshchenko are only boys, and naturally full of boyish enthusiasm!'[1]

That Kerensky's order was not entirely ignored, however, we know from a young member of an Anglo-Russian family, Edith Kerby, who was travelling across Russia at that time from the Far East on the Trans-Siberian Express. At every station hundreds and hundreds of returning soldiers tried to board the train, bayonet fights broke out frequently on the platforms, and many soldiers travelled all the way back on the train roof. About half-way through the journey they suddenly heard a terrible commotion and the train came to a halt in a densely wooded area. The restaurant car had caught fire and was burning fiercely. Without further ado, it was uncoupled, toppled over and left to burn itself out by the side of the track. This meant that for the remaining week they were dependent on the simple food that peasants sold at the wayside stations. It became almost a battle for survival, but often a kindly disposed soldier from her compartment would bring Edith back something. Yet in spite of these privations, the experience was one she would not have missed for the world. She sat talking politics with the soldiers by the hour, listening avidly to every word they had to say about the Revolution, which had happened while she was out of Russia. The days seemed to flash past. They were due to arrive in Petrograd on May 26. The 'Express' was two days late, but the soldiers were still in time to meet Kerensky's deadline.[2]

Kerensky himself had already left for the front, to prepare the troops for a new offensive. He is 'to start going round units,' Knox records, 'the same old game as poor Kornilov played. His speeches will be more frothy and the effect will last an hour or two longer.' Even the usually buoyant Ransome does not sound very optimistic. 'Kerensky always carries his audience with him and has probably done enormous good on the front, but Russian audiences so much enjoy good oratory that it would be unwise to count too much on the practical effects. Other speakers are doing their best to undo Kerensky's work.' In Petrograd, too, his enemies were busy, accusing him of being the new Bonaparte. 'There is a group of wreckers here,' Harold Williams' deputy writes on May 31, 'and when they begin a campaign against Kerensky a number of the more unstable Socialists begin to wobble. If there were no noise, the unstable Socialists would probably support Kerensky, but once the hue and cry is raised they grow fearful for their own popularity.'[3]

Williams himself returned to Petrograd in early June after a long period of convalescence in the Caucasus. 'The atmosphere is distinctly thundery in Russia,' he writes on June 6, 'but whether a storm is coming no one can say. We hear mutterings on the horizon; we see flashes that may or may not be summer lightning; we watch the barometer from hour to hour, and count up the signs and wonder.' Two days later he describes how Petrograd has changed in his absence:

Once stiff, taciturn, and rather morose, it has suddenly become loquacious and noisy. The hum of argument never ceases day or night. Hundred-tongued rumour is the field of a battle royal.

Politics pursue one everywhere. You cannot buy a hat or a packet of cigarettes or ride in a cab without being enticed into a political discussion. The servants and house porters demand advice as to which party they should vote for in the ward elections. Every wall in the town is placarded with notices of meetings, lectures, congresses, and electoral appeals, and announcements, not only in Russian, but in Polish, Lithuanian, Yiddish, and Hebrew.

Meetings are crowded, and who does not speak at meetings now? There are ministers, workmen, returned exiles, soldiers, officers, students, escaped prisoners of war, cripples, sailors, Englishmen, Frenchmen, Serbs, Belgians, Italians, Americans. There is fierce argument between the parties, violent applause, violent hissing. The battle of the meetings flows over into the unceasing buzz and murmur and perpetual cut and thrust of the streets and the trams and the workshops and the barracks. Two men argue at a street corner and are at once surrounded by an excited crowd. Even at concerts now the music is diluted with political speeches by well-known orators.

The Nevsky Prospect has become a kind of *Quartier Latin*. Book hawkers line the pavement and cry sensational pamphlets about Rasputin and Nicholas, and who is Lenin, and how much land will the peasants get. Returned exiles flit through the crowd, recognisable by the Rue Bertholet cut of their clothes and their hair.

Even that ancient institution, the 5 o'clock procession of *chinovniks* going home from Government offices, has lost its typical colouring. One misses at first the staid, familiar figures, till one suddenly realises that those rather long-haired young men, swinging or slithering along with portfolios under their arms, must, of course, be the new *chinovniks*.

Newsboys used to carry papers in a bag. Now there are so many papers and such a demand for them that the hawkers have had to improvise stalls at the street-corners, and one may pause there and watch the play of political sympathies and antipathies as the hard-faced young workman buys the Maximalist [Bolshevik] *Pravda* or the dreamy student buys the Radical [Menshevik] *Den*, or some stout, elderly gentleman buys the [right-wing] *Novoe Vremya* with a melancholy air of resignation.

Then on certain days the streets fill with processions, and the pulse of disputation beats more strongly. Last Sunday crossing from the other side of the Neva I saw near Kshesinskaya's house a meeting of Leninites. Next door the Salvation Army were holding a service. Crossing the bridge was a long church procession with icons and crosses and glittering banners and a sweet, slow chanting of ancient prayers. But in front of the procession the red flag was waving.

On the Nevsky the scene changed again. Here was a procession of armed but tame-looking Anarchists with black flag and black coffin, while a troop of laughing Cossacks followed at a distance. Further up near the City Hall a Salvation Army band was crashing out some sickly Western air, and a plain clothes militiaman leaned on his gun and listened.

I have been absent from Petrograd for a time, and listening to the talk in the streets I notice a change. The frank joy of the early state of the Revolution has given place to bitter party strife, and growing resentment against the extremists and disturbers of order.

The desire for order is becoming a passion with the crowd, and the national instinct, at first baffled and stunned by the vehement outcry of preachers of immediate social revolution, is beginning to reassert itself. I sometimes begin to fear the reaction may be too violent.[4]

At the end of May reports began to appear in the Petrograd press that the local Soviet at Kronstadt, the famous island fortress guarding the approaches to the capital, had declared itself independent of central Government. The regime on the island had always been exceptionally harsh, and in the first days of the Revolution the sailors had revenged themselves on their officers with a corresponding degree of violence and brutality: the lucky ones were those thrown into prison. Extremist agitation, Williams writes, found the soil excellently suited, and the Soviet took entire charge. 'A curious local patriotism developed, accompanied by contempt for bourgeois Russia.' The man thought to have most influenced the decision of the Kronstadt Soviet to declare independence was another leading political exile who had only just arrived in Russia: Trotsky (1879–1940).[5]

Philips Price suspected that the right-wing press was spreading rumours about Kronstadt 'for sinister purposes', and (alone among our witnesses) decided to go down to investigate for himself. What he saw during his short visit provides us with a series of striking images of how lives had been turned upside down and roles reversed as a result of the Revolution.

On a fine morning at the beginning of June he boarded a little steamer, which sailed down the Neva, past the great dockyards, and out into the blue waters of the Gulf of Finland. After an hour and a half they pulled up alongside the quay of a long, flat island.

I got out and walked along the little streets of an old town. Life was going on just as usual, and I saw no outward signs of disorder. In a large house in the main street I found the headquarters of the Kronstadt Soviet. With some little misgiving I passed by the sentries and asked to see the President. I was taken into a room, where I saw a young man with a red badge on his coat looking through some papers, who appeared to be a student. He had long hair and dreamy eyes, with the far-off look of an idealist. This was the elected President of the Kronstadt Workers', Soldiers' and Sailors' Soviet.

'Be seated,' he said. 'I suppose you have come down from

Petrograd to see if all the stories about our terror are true. You will probably have observed that there is nothing extraordinary going on here; we are simply putting this place into order after the tyranny and chaos of the late Tsarist regime. The workmen, soldiers and sailors here find that they can do this job better by themselves than by leaving it to people who call themselves democrats, but are really the friends of the old regime. That is why we have declared the Kronstadt Soviet the supreme authority in the island.'

I asked him if the Soviet recognized the Coalition Government, and he replied: 'Of course we do, if the rest of Russia does, but that does not prevent us from having our own opinions as to what the Government ought to be. We would like to see the whole of the government in the hands of the All-Russian Congress of Soviets.'

After further conversation he suggested that I might like to see the fortress and the naval and military prisons, and offered to take me round himself. This student-president and I thereupon went out and walked down the main street. He began to be very friendly and confidential in true Russian style, and, although I had known him for barely half an hour, took my arm and began to tell me about himself and Kronstadt. 'I was a student of technology at the Petrograd Institute,' he said. 'During my studies I had frequent occasion to come down here and see what was going on. You can have no idea of it. The soldiers and sailors were treated on this island like dogs. They were worked from early morning till late at night. They were not allowed any recreations for fear that they would associate for political purposes. Nowhere could you study the slavery system of capitalist Imperialism better than here. For the smallest misdemeanour a man was put in chains, and if he was found with a Socialist pamphlet in his possession, he was shot. There was terror indeed. The ruling classes of Russia had to keep this regime going in Kronstadt in order to cow the men into submission, for, herded together on this island in a half-communal state, they could so easily combine to overthrow the power of their officers. The latter only kept the system going by a corps of picked gendarmes and a system of spy-provocateurs. A very large percentage of the soldiers and sailors of Kronstadt were drawn from the artisan class and from the better educated type of peasant, who had knowledge of some craft. Most of them could read and write. This fact made Kronstadt one of the most advanced revolutionary centres in Russia.'

While talking over these things, we arrived at the big square in front of the cathedral. A large crowd of workmen, soldiers and sailors had gathered there. Presently there came from the cathedral a procession with red banners, and, borne aloft by sailors, some five or six urns. 'These are the bones,' said my companion, 'of some comrades who were executed here after the 1905 Revolution by the Tsarist reaction, because of their revolutionary activities. One of them had attempted to bring food to his comrades who were beleaguered and starved out by the Tsarist gendarmes on a small island off the Finnish coast. Another had attempted to rescue his friend from prison the night before he was to have been executed. We never knew where these comrades were buried, but we found out later that their bodies were thrown into a pit. We found the pit, dug up the bones recently, and are giving honour to those who died for the freedom which we now enjoy.' A grave had been dug near the monument of Admiral Makarov. Soldiers and sailors spoke a few words in memory of their comrades, and the urns descended into the earth. And yet those men had died eleven years ago. They were personally unknown to all but a very few of the garrison of Kronstadt that day. But they had died for the same cause, the same mystic power had driven them to rebel and to strike a despairing blow for freedom...

I was taken to a prison on the south side of the island, where were kept the former military police, gendarmes, police spies and provocateurs of fallen Tsarism. The quarters were very bad, and many of the cells had no windows at all. Great hulking men with coarse animal features were lounging about dark and narrow corridors. Some of them still had on the uniform of their former profession. Here was a gendarme in that long grey cloak that once was the terror of striking and petitioning masses. In reply to a question he said, 'If only they would take us out and put us to do some work! We are strong and can serve our country, whether it is Monarchy or Republic.' Beside him was a military policeman. His coarse, heavy features were untouched by any signs either of anger or of repentance. He seemed to be thinking only of food, drink and sleep. A happy existence indeed for a man situated as he was!

At that moment I saw in front of me the lean figure of a man in civilian clothes. His bloodshot eyes, looking out from under dishevelled hair, were like those of a hunted animal that hears the hounds approaching. 'So you have come at last,' they seemed to say; 'am I to be hanged or shot? or what form of death has been prepared for me?' I was just going to ask him what he used to do and how he came to be there, but at the moment he suddenly vanished into darkness and left me wondering if this might be some Kronstadt Azev [the notorious Tsarist *agent provocateur*], on whose heels stalked revolutionary justice.

As I passed out of the prison, a bent old woman came up to my companion, and with tears in her eyes begged him to give her some news of her only son. He was a gendarme, and on the first day of the Revolution had, with some half-dozen others, occupied the watchtower with machine guns and had swept the main street with a deadly fire, which had laid low three of the revolutionary leaders besides many dockyard labourers. She was a widow, and had no one to earn for her now. She knew nothing of politics, she said, and wanted only peace. The President of the Soviet was touched, and thought for a moment. Human sympathy told him to unbend. Revolutionary discipline told him to be firm. 'The whole case of these men is being dealt with,' he said. 'We are even allowing the Government to send down a commissioner to examine with us the indictments. Your son will probably be free before long.'

We passed on to the prison on the north-east of the island. The sentries gave a friendly nod to the President and said 'Good morning, comrade,' as we passed them. Inside the iron doors we entered a low room in which, sitting and lying on iron bedsteads, were a number of half-dressed, unshaved, unkempt men. They were the erstwhile satraps of Tsarist might in Kronstadt. There was a naval staff officer – a man over fifty, whose imprisonment had begun to tell on him. 'Look at this,' he said, as he took my hand and placed it on his projecting hip-bone; 'what have I done to deserve this?' I passed on to a Major-General, formerly in command of the fortress artillery of Kronstadt. He stood in his shirt-sleeves – no medalled tunic decorated his breast any more, although he had fought at Port Arthur and in the Polish campaign. His red-striped trousers of Prussian blue bore signs of three months' wear in confinement. Sheepishly he looked at me, as if uncertain whether it was dignified for him to tell his troubles to a stray foreigner. 'I wish they would bring some indictment against us,' he said at length, 'for to sit here for three months and not to know what our fate is to be is rather hard.' 'And I sat here, not three months, but three years,' broke in the sailor guard who was taking us round, 'and I didn't know what was going to happen to me, although my only offence was that I had been distributing a pamphlet on the life of Karl Marx.' I pointed out to the sailor that the prison accommodation was unfit for a human being. He answered, 'Well, I sat here all that time because of these gentlemen, and I think that if they had known they were going to sit here they would have made better prisons!'

Next I came upon a young artillery officer who seemed to take his troubles in a very sportsmanlike way. 'I never ill-treated my men,' he said, 'but they arrested me with a lot of officers whom they had a grudge against, and rightly so, for they treated their men like dogs. I used to have trouble with my brother officers, and indeed they turned me out of the Naval Club, because I protested against some of the things that went on here. And for this I sit alongside with them.' Further on I came upon a Vice-Admiral. His spirit seemed very nearly broken, for his face was thin and pale, his voice weak and his hands shaky. 'I did my duty to my Tsar,' he murmured. 'I always served my country and was ready to die for it. I fought in the Japanese war and was wounded twice in this war. If I was strict with my men, it was because I loved the Tsar and my country, and knew that only thus could Russia be great and her people happy' – and so saying he wept.

That evening I was taken to the house of Admiral Veren, who had been murdered on the first day of the Revolution. I found the Anarchists in possession. In the sumptuous halls where once councils of war were held by medalled officers I now saw unkempt, long-haired revolutionary students and sailors. I was introduced to their leader, a veteran fighter, who had taken a prominent part in the mutiny of the Potemkin on the Black Sea in 1906. I expected to find the most desperate characters among this lot, but I confess that they turned out very harmless. Their revolutionary ideas did not go beyond the speedy application of Marxism and the class war, while the Anarchists I found to be peaceful Tolstoyans who would refuse to shed blood on principle. As it was already late they invited me to supper and to sleep the night.

Next day I was taken to visit the battleships and training ships in the harbour. I first went to the Naval Staff. The commander of the fleet I found was now a young lieutenant. He received me very cordially, called me 'Comrade', and took me to his cabin for lunch, which consisted of the same food as that eaten by the sailors. He wore no epaulettes on his uniform, he was not saluted by the sailors, and when they spoke to him they called him 'Comrade'.

All the officers of the fleet in Kronstadt are now elected by the crews of the ships on which they serve, and the Council of Sailors' Delegates elects the officer commanding the fleet. My first question was how did this new principle of electing officers affect the work and efficiency of the fleet. The Chief of Staff, although himself an old sailor, and not accustomed to this new way of doing things, said that on the whole he thought it worked well. At first there was some difficulty. The sailors elected officers just because they liked them and not because they knew their job. But after a while, he added, the men got to know who were efficient as well as those who were nice to their men.

On the following day I visited the dockyards and foundries of Kronstadt. I found all the men working busily, and the rumours of disorganization prevalent in Petrograd quite unfounded. The first results of the March Revolution had been to call into being the so-called *'fabrichny komitet'*, or factory committee, which is the Russian form of 'shop stewards'. They had extended to the dock-workers in the form of 'district unions'. These committees and unions were the elementary industrial unit upon which the Soviet idea was based, and in Kronstadt I found them already well developed. They were formed by the men of all grades, skilled and unskilled, who met for half an hour after the day's work. While I was going over the yards and foundries I found the central offices of one of these committees. In the corner of a workshop there was a table and chair and a notebook, in which the secretary set down resolutions and minutes. That was the office. And yet in those unimposing quarters important public work was already being performed. Delegates went forth from this place to the Kronstadt Soviet, which was the *de facto*, if not the *de jure*, political authority on the island, controlling militia, prisons, public services, food supplies, and so on. From here also went forth delegates, who were assuming direct control in industrial affairs. They claimed and exercised the right to inspect the accounts and books of the management, saw to it that no materials left the premises without good reason, and in general ways looked after the welfare of the industry and of its members. These rudimentary proletarian organizations, therefore, had divided their activities into two branches, one political and the other industrial. Both these branches, however, sprang from the same roots.

The factory committees and dock unions which I saw in such active development at Kronstadt were really the fighting organs of the revolutionary workmen. In Petrograd they had, in the first days of the Revolution, been formed out of a few energetic spirits among the skilled artizans... In Kronstadt, where there was an unusually large number of skilled workers and sailors, the factory committees had reached a high state of efficiency, as early as June 1917. The greatest employer in the island was the State. But, nevertheless, the work of the State officials was subjected to rigid scrutiny, for the men were fully alive to the fact that in a capitalist state the bureaucracy is only the agent of 'big business'.

But there were also private capitalist concerns in Kronstadt, and chief of these was the cable factory. This, I found, was already under the control of the factory committee. The owner, who had tried to close down the works and to sell some of the machinery to a foreign bank, was arrested, the whole business requisitioned in the name of the Kronstadt Political Soviet, and administered by the factory committee... And now I discovered the real cause of the outcry against Kronstadt in Petrograd bourgeois circles: Kronstadt had gone one stage beyond the rest of the country and was openly threatening the capitalist system.

Before leaving Kronstadt I attended a sitting of the Workers', Soldiers' and Sailors' Soviet, the political body. The sitting took place in the former Naval Officers' Club. In the great salon, where formerly balls and banquets were given, and whose walls were still hung with pictures of the Russian Navy welcoming Tsars and foreign Sovereigns, the Kronstadt Soviet deliberated. The admirals and generals and officers, picked from the flower of the aristocracy who formerly haunted its precincts, were now in the prisons that I had visited. Their places were taken by brawny common sailors, lusty great peasant soldiers and horny-handed mechanics, just come from their day's work. A keen and energetic bunch they were, these Kronstadt sons of toil, who hailed from every part of Russia. The pick of the land, the flower of Russia's revolutionary greatness. No feats of intellect in university or college had these men performed. They had a native instinct, which enabled them to see direct and call a spade a spade, to read the signs of the times and to act, when action was needed.

The question on the order of the day was, whether the Coalition Government's Commissioner should be accepted on the island. The tone of the debate was throughout moderate, and a compromise was ultimately reached, by which the Commissioner was to be received on the island as the 'guest' of the Soviet.

I found on examination that the Bolsheviks were a minority in the Soviet. The greater number of delegates belonged to no party at all. [Contrastingly, in *My Three Revolutions* Philips Price states that they were 'all Bolsheviks'.] But in actual fact they were doing everything that the Bolsheviks were officially preaching.[6]

In the event, two 'guests' were received by the Kronstadt Soviet: the Socialist Ministers, Tsereteli and Skobelev. From his own considerable experience Tsereteli described prison conditions on the island as the worst he had ever seen, and it was agreed that steps should be taken to bring the prisoners speedily to trial. As for the issue of Kronstadt's independence, Ransome found the situation almost impossible to fathom: the Kronstadt Soviet, having at first climbed down, appeared to change its mind as soon as the Ministers had departed.[7]

While Kerensky was making countless speeches at the front and at home, Lenin's public appearances were comparatively rare. Philips Price heard him for the first time on May 20 at the Conference of Peasant Deputies. At the opening session Kerensky made a brilliant speech, after which, amid indescribable enthusiasm, he was surrounded by delegates and carried round the building on their shoulders, while hundreds of peasant soldiers cried: 'You are our leader, and we swear to go wherever you order us.'[8] Only a handful of the thousand or so delegates were Bolsheviks. 'Lenin held his audience well,' Philips Price writes, 'drawing frequent applause from them, but as soon as he had finished, from one end of the hall to the other speakers got up and began to pull his argument to pieces.' They rejected the idea that what applied to the town also applied to the country.[9] Later, Philips Price wrote that Lenin 'did not then make an outstanding impression on the conference or on me... He seemed to be a man with a one-way mind full of fixed ideas, incapable of compromise.'[10] Of Lenin as an orator E.H. Wilcox writes:

Neither his physical nor his mental equipment is of a sort to appeal to the crowd. He is a little man of commonplace figure, with no other outward mark of distinction than the high bald dome of his forehead. His slovenliness is merely that of indifference, and has none of the calculated picturesqueness which excites curiosity and rivets attention. His gesture as he speaks is casual and spasmodic. His speech is swift and fluent, simple in its form and free from ornament, but crowded with facts. He frequently introduces political and economic conceptions which can hardly be intelligible to untrained minds.[11]

On June 16 the First All-Russian Congress of Soviets opened. This was a larger and more representative assembly than the one held in April, and the delegates, as Philips Price describes, came from all parts of Russia:

> Here was a picturesque group of Ukrainians round a samovar and an accordion. There was a group of sunburnt soldiers from the garrisons in Central Asia. There were some dark-eyed natives from the Caucasus. There were lusty soldiers from the trenches, and serious-looking officers; there were artisans from the Moscow factories and mining representatives from the Don.[12]

They were to meet, eat and sleep in the enormous red and white buildings, only seven years younger than Petrograd itself, of the Cadet Corps, where Ransome visited them on the eve of the Congress:

> Hundreds and hundreds of beds with red blankets were arranged in rows, and I saw crowds of deputies sitting on their beds and talking like boys in a gigantic dormitory. Here and there a deputy weary from his journey snored under his red blanket. In one dormitory are the Cossacks all together. Downstairs there is a great refectory in the basement under a low ceiling, where group after group of dusty soldiers sat drinking tea and emphasizing their political views by thumping the heavy tables.[13]

The Congress proceedings are described most fully by Philips Price in an article for *Common Sense*, datelined June 26, and in *My Reminiscences of the Russian Revolution*, written after he left Russia at the end of 1918; the following account is based on the former, except where indicated.

It was soon clear that there were to be three main parties in the assembly. On the left of the platform were the Bolsheviks, led by bullet-headed Lenin, and numbering in all 105. 'This was the "Cave of Adullam", to which all irreconcilable Marxists, Syndicalists, and even Communist-Anarchists came for shelter and comfort... We knew that they were bitterly opposed to the Socialist participation in the "bourgeois" government.' In the centre was the great amorphous mass of the Mensheviks, led by Tsereteli and Dan: 247 of them, according to *Reminiscences*. 'It was they who had solved the Milyukov crisis by coming into the Provisional Government. Seeing the danger of a full proletariat revolution in an economically undeveloped and unorganized country, they stood for a policy of temporary conciliation between the masses and the capitalists.' The whole of the right side of the hall was filled by the SRs, numbering 321 (how Philips Price arrived at this total is not clear; 285 is the accepted figure): 'an essentially Russian political party... they are the product of the Russian mind, ever seeking something abstract, something which will relieve the spirit of man in the evil surroundings of the world.'

On June 17 a resolution of confidence in the Coalition Government was moved. The Menshevik, Lieber, opened the debate on behalf of the Executive Committee of the Soviet, and was followed by his fellow Menshevik, Tsereteli, 'a spare, thin man with the dark complexion and the deep kindly eyes of a Caucasian... Statesman and diplomat in him are combined in one... Not a sound was heard in the great hall as in soft Georgian accents he addressed the audience.' His argument was like the threads of a carefully woven carpet, and at the end of his great speech the delegates rose to their feet and gave him an ovation lasting several minutes.

There then rose upon the tribune a man whose name has been on all lips for many weeks past... Lenin. He is a short man with a round head, small pig-like eyes, and close-cropped hair. [In *Reminiscences* this reads: 'a thick-set little man with a round bald head and small Tartar eyes', and the next three sentences have been omitted.] The words poured from his mouth, overwhelming all in a flood of oratory. One sat spellbound at his command of language and the passion of his denunciation. But when it was all over one felt inclined to scratch one's head and ask what it was all about.

'Where are we?' he began, stretching out his short arms and looking questioningly at his audience. 'What is this Council of Workers' and Soldiers' Delegates? Is there anything like it in the world? No, of course not, because nothing so absurd as this exists in any country today except in Russia. Then let us have one of two things: either a bourgeois Government with its plans for so-called social reform on paper, such as exists in every country now, or let us have that Government which you (*pointing to Tsereteli*) long for, but which you appear to be frightened of bringing into existence –

a Government of the proletariat, which had its historic parallel in 1792 in France.'

'Look at this anarchy, which we now have in Russia,' he went on. 'What does it mean? Do you really think you can create an intermediate stage between Capitalism and Socialism? Can Tsereteli's fine plan for persuading the bourgeois Governments of Western Europe to come to our point of view on the peace settlement ever succeed? No, it will fail ignominiously, as long as power is out of the hands of the Russian proletariat. [The next two sentences are not in *Reminiscences*.] That power I and my party are prepared to take at any moment. (*Shouts of derisive laughter resounded all over the hall*.) Look at what you are doing,' he cried, nothing daunted, and pointing a scornful finger at the Socialist Ministers. 'Capitalists with 800 per cent. war profits are walking about the country just as before. Why don't you publish the figures of their profits, arrest some fifty of them and keep them locked up for a bit, even though you may keep them under the same luxurious conditions as you keep Nicolas Romanov. (*A yell of delight came from the corner of the hall where the Bolshevik delegates sat*.) You talk about peace without annexations and contributions. Put that principle into practice in your own country, in Finland and the Ukraine. You talk to us about an advance on the front. We are not against war on principle. We are only against a capitalist war for capitalist ends, and until you take the government entirely into your hands and oust the bourgeoisie you are only the tools of those who have brought this disaster upon the world.'

And with these words this demagogue finished his fiery speech [this sentence not in *Reminiscences*].

There was a hush in the hall as there rose up a short, thickset man with a square face and close-cropped hair. He wore a brown jacket and gaiters, his face was pale with nervous tension, and his eyes blazed like fiery beads. It was Kerensky, the popular hero of militant revolutionary Russia [in *Reminiscences* this reads: 'the popular hero of the moment, who was believed to be about to lead the Russian Revolution to the successful realization of its ideals, who was expected to bring land to the hungry peasants, land and peace to the weary soldiers, without annexations or indemnities']. Standing bolt upright, with his right arm clasping the button of his breast pocket, he began his speech in quiet, measured tones.

'We have just been given some historical parallels,' he said. 'We have been referred to 1792 as an example of how we should carry out the revolution of 1917. But how did the French Republic of 1792 end? It turned into a base Imperialism, which set back the progress of democracy for many a long year. Our duty is to prevent that very thing from happening, to strengthen our new-won freedom, so that our comrades who have come back from exile in Siberia shall not go back there, and so that that comrade (*pointing a scornful finger at Lenin*), who has been living comfortably all this time in Switzerland, shall not have to fly back again. He proposes to us a new and wonderful recipe for our revolution: we are to arrest a handful of Russian capitalists. Comrades, I am not a Marxist, but I think I understand Socialism better than brother Lenin, and I know that Karl Marx never proposed such methods of Oriental despotism. (*A hurricane of applause rose from the body of the hall and shouts from the corner of the discomfited Bolsheviks.*) I am accused of opposing the national aspirations of Finland and the Ukraine and of reducing the principle of peace without annexations to ridicule by my action in the Coalition Government. But in the First Duma it was *he*,' he added, turning savagely on Lenin, 'who attacked *me* when I stood up for a federal republic and national autonomy; it was *he* who called my Socialist Revolutionary comrades Utopianists and dreamers. [The next two sentences are not in *Reminiscences*.] Today I say only one thing. I recognize the rights of the Ukraine and Finland, but cannot agree to their separation until the Constituent Assembly of the Russian people has sanctioned it.'

Turning to the question of fraternizing on the front, Kerensky evoked a storm of laughter as he referred in sarcastic terms to those naïve people who imagine that friendly meetings between a few parties of Russian and German soldiers [in Ransome's account, 'when a Russian soldier gives a German soldier a crust of bread in exchange for a thimbleful of vodka'[14]] can usher in the dawn of Socialism throughout the world. Our Bolshevik comrades,' he added, 'had better be careful, 'or they may wake up one day and find they are fraternizing with the mailed fist of Wilhelm!' His face flushed, and his voice became harsher with excitement, as he braced himself up for his supreme effort. 'You tell us that you fear reaction,' he almost screamed; 'you say that you want to strengthen our new-won freedom, and yet you propose to lead us the way of France in 1792. Instead of appealing for reconstruction, you clamour for further destruction. Out of the fiery chaos that you wish to make will arise, like a Phoenix, a dictator.' He paused and walked slowly across the platform towards the corner where the group surrounding Lenin sat. Not a sound was heard in the hall, as we waited spellbound for the next sentence. '*I* will not be the dictator that you are trying to create,' and so saying he turned his back scornfully upon Lenin, while the assembled delegates thundered their applause... It was a memorable speech of a fascinating personality, and in its way did much to consolidate the Russian revolutionary democracy assembled in that hall and to disperse the forces of chaos and disorder.

In *Reminiscences* those words of approbation are omitted, and instead, after Kerensky has turned his back on Lenin, Philips Price writes: 'The latter was calmly stroking his chin, apparently wondering whether the words of Kerensky would come true, and on whose shoulders the cloak of dictatorship, if it came, would rest.'

The resolution of confidence in the Coalition Government was eventually passed by a huge majority, only the Bolsheviks and a handful of their sympathizers voting against.[15]

July Days

Events up to and including unsuccessful attempt by Bolsheviks to overthrow the
Government (July 16–18)

'It is now most lovely weather here,' Arthur Ransome writes to his
mother on June 1,

> bright sunshine all day, very hot, and light all through the night.
> At midnight you can see the time by your watch. The trees are
> showing green. Some of them have leaves, and within a week it
> will be absolute summer. . .
> I have a funny truant feeling, even when, walking along the
> Quay to the Embassy, I find myself really enormously enjoying the
> wonderful beauty of the river there, which is very broad, with a
> fine bridge, and the fortress with a spire like a thorn from the
> cathedral in the middle of it, and close by a pale blue mosaic
> dome, and cupolas on tall stem-like towers belonging to the
> Mohammedan mosque. It's a gorgeous scene, and the sky is
> always different giving it new character every time. It's most
> queer how naughty I feel in being able to enjoy it as much as I do.

To indulge in such feelings seemed inexcusably frivolous when life
in Petrograd was so grim. 'People in England,' he writes to her later,

> even intelligent birds like yourself, have not the faintest notion of
> the condition of things here. I think of England as of a sort of
> dream country in the world and in the war but not of it.
> Everybody, I know, is either working or fighting, but for some rea-
> son or other the war does not hurt every man woman and child in

England permanently continuously as it does those of the continental nations, and Russia most of all. Partly it is the laziness of
our imagination, partly because the actual sufferings of England
are so much less. You do not see the bones sticking through the
skin of the horses in the street. You do not have your porter's wife
beg for a share in your bread allowance because she cannot get
enough to feed her children. [They ate well, though, when he
caught enough roach one evening in the suburbs 'to feed a family
of eight for lunch'.] You do not go to a tearoom to have tea without
cakes, without bread, without butter, without milk, without sugar,
because there are none of these things. . . That is why those
English newspapers who rail at the Russians are criminally wrong.
It is because things are like that here that German agents and
extremists who promise an immediate millennium do succeed in
carrying away the absolutely simple minded Russian soldier. . .

He envied Harold Williams, who had broken down after the rush
of the Revolution and been given a long holiday by the *Chronicle*.
'Unfortunately for me though I nearly collapsed at one time I didn't
quite, and got all right again without a holiday.' At the beginning of
June he was feeling physically better than for a long time, but then
he 'crocked' and by mid-July had been suffering alternately from
dysentery and headache for about a month. Meanwhile, he had
been worked off his head and his feet into a state of near hysterical
delirium, and was tired out beyond any previous conception he
ever had of the meaning of the words. 'I fall asleep at once if I put
my elbows on the table, so I work on a chair as far from the table as
possible.'

His tiredness was understandable. He was sending off telegrams,
often of considerable length, almost daily to the *News*, and in crisis
periods, as many as six a day. Though some of his material was second-hand, much had to be obtained personally by witnessing events,
attending meetings or interviewing people. He was also contributing
articles to the *Observer*. J.L. Garvin, its right-wing editor, sent him 'a
long and most excited telegram about allied policy because I had
had to telegraph that the Russian socialists were by no means satisfied with the same', whereas Gardiner, the editor of the *News*, sent
him a £50 bonus. 'My first inclination was to send it back and say I
wasn't in the habit of taking tips. Then I remembered the amount of
fishing tackle I could buy with it after the war. . . and that I belong
to the casual labouring proletariat.' He would have liked to get

down to the front, but dared not leave Petrograd 'for more than twenty-four hours because of the chance of some new political crisis or rather a new manifestation of the almost permanent crisis'.

As for politics, he continued to protest his undying hatred for them.

> O not for me the Treasury Bench,
> The Woolsack or the Speaker's Chair!
> I'll never make a Tory blench
> Nor raise my party leader's hair!
> There's no portfolio I'd bear
> Could compensate me for the stench
> Of that opinionated air.

Politics made him feel as if his mouth were full of sawdust. 'If I do ever get home... I shall drink too much beer, and shun the acquaintance of all people who know the difference between a liberal and a conservative... I shan't read a newspaper EVER.' Unfortunately, though, there was no getting away from politics in his job. When his mother 'sailed right in' and told him that he wasn't the right person to muddle in politics, he replied:

> Well, all right. But at the present moment and in the present place I shouldn't be playing fair to anyone if I didn't sweat my eyes out trying to get an exact knowledge of what is happening and what may happen. However I hate it. And I won't do it any longer than juty compels. Juty is a beastly thing. It's like a hot compress on the vitals.

As for Petrograd politics, they were enough to turn the sanest man crazy. Images of Petrograd as a madhouse recur in Ransome's letters. 'Russians returning, *Russians*, mind you, simply throw up their hands and describe it as Bedlam. One lives the whole time in an atmosphere of mental conflict of the most violent kind.' 'Books aren't written by the warders of lunatic asylums. And I feel like a horribly observant warder who cannot help imitating the grimaces of the patients.'

As that image suggests, he *was* becoming emotionally involved, however reluctantly, in Russian politics. The letters to his mother during June and July bring this out more clearly than the telegrams. In another striking image he writes:

You see here, politics are sort of spread out naked, and you work among them as a vivisector works among the nerves of a live organism open and visible on his operating table. Whereas in England politicians are sort of bound by tradition and the nature of things to be no more than a kind of consulting physicians, rather shy even of using their stethoscopes.

What worried him most was England's failure to understand the Russian situation. 'It is a wretched business due to our national unwillingness to look facts in the face. And, of course, partly to our blank ignorance of what the facts are.' Every British action, such as the refusal of the seamen's union to allow the anti-war Ramsay Macdonald to travel to Russia (Buchanan himself had changed his mind about this and informed the Foreign Office that the visit 'might do good'[1]), seemed calculated to reinforce the impression of Britain as an entirely hostile country.

I see the Anglo-Russian friendship, everything I've sweated at all these years crumbling day by day, while Russia is being turned into a large helpless market ready for German goods and German influences and full of a dull resentment against England... As far as I can judge from the newspapers that come out here nobody at home realizes at all how very serious the position is. I suppose they've got enough to think of, poor things, but, as far as world politics goes England is like a baby playing in a back garden. She is losing support here every day. Posters against her are distributed in the main streets, printed in Russian on one side and in German on the other.

On June 30 he had a 'tremendous talk' (reported to his mother, but not to the *News*) with members of the Executive Committee of the Soviet. The most hopeful view taken by the very pro-English members of the most moderate party was that if they 'can keep things going until the meeting of the Constituent Assembly (October), and if, when the Assembly meets peace negotiations have not begun, a separate peace will be inevitable. No power on earth will keep the Russian army in the trenches this winter.'

Ransome's own mood now oscillates between a vague general optimism – 'Underneath it all, I have got real faith in the bedrock sense of Russia. Russia always does come through all right in the end, and she will...' (June 16) – and a more clearly formulated

pessimism: 'Meanwhile she herself is going steadily towards bank-
ruptcy... and starvation and a class warfare in which everyone
who wears a collar will be counted an enemy of mankind' (June 17).[2]

By this time, what an Englishman writing home from Petrograd
describes as the 'baiting of the bourgeoisie' or collar-wearing class
was already in full swing.

> Much time is spent in discussing who is a 'bourgeois' (the
> Russians use the French word) and who not. To be a 'bourgeois' is
> the greatest imaginable disgrace. When boys quarrel in the street
> and one of them wishes to hurl a deadly insult at his opponent he
> shouts 'Bourgeois!' That is a slur which really can only be washed
> out with blood.[3]

Even more extreme than the Bolsheviks in their antagonism to the
bourgeoisie were the Anarchists. Though few in number, they were
very vocal, never missed a chance to demonstrate, and had considerable influence on the workers and soldiers. As with all such movements in Russia, Anarchists came in different shades. Those whom
Philips Price met on Kronstadt turned out to be peaceful Tolstoyans,
whereas the ones observed by Harold Williams were armed but
tame-looking. 'Tame' is not an adjective, however, that can be
applied to the Anarchists whom W.G. Shepherd, correspondent of
the United Press of America, goes to see on June 21.

> On Thursday night I was granted the distinction of being admitted
> into General Durnovo's villa, which has been seized, and is being
> held, by Anarchists. The Government had given until three o'clock
> in the afternoon to surrender, but the fortified Anarchists tele-
> phoned to seven factories in the vicinity, and 3,000 workmen
> armed with rifles arrived. The men were prepared to defy the
> authority of the Government. The garden surrounding the palace
> was dotted with huge, well-made black banners, bearing the
> motto, 'Death to all capitalists'. As I approached the gate a youth
> with a rifle said, 'Come on in, old boy: you are American.' When I
> explained I was an American reporter the welcome became aston-
> ishingly hearty. Broken English-American twang assailed me on
> all sides, and, to the surprise of the crowd assembled on the side
> walk, who looked on the Anarchists as super devils, I was led
> through the portals into the building. 'How many of you are from
> the United States ?' I asked. 'Fifteen,' came the answer. 'What are

you acting like this for?' 'We are Anarchists, and always were in the United States, but never had a chance of action. Now we have our chance we are making the best of it.' 'Don't you believe in war? Doesn't your present action prevent Russia helping the United States?' I asked. The answer was, 'To hell with war! We have got a bigger war against the capitalists.' 'Do you favour a separate peace?' was my next question. For answer I was told, 'We favour any old kind of peace. We are all likely to be killed here to-morrow, or as soon as the Government calls out the troops, and we are not cowards.'

The palace had been turned into a filthy hole. The men were unwashed, unshaved. 'Did you send the story about us taking the *Russkaya Volya* office?' asked one. 'Yes.' 'Were you fellows in that?' The reply was, 'Sure, we did not know whether the Petrograd public would stand behind us, and finding they would not, we surrendered.' 'What do you think of this?' said a youth from an automobile factory at Detroit, showing me a big revolver. 'That's the argument we are going to use,' he said, 'and we have got a lot of big potatoes (Russian jargon for bombs) upstairs.' I was escorted to the doorway. 'Be around at eight o'clock on Friday morning,' said an expert machinist from Cleveland. 'The Government are going to send troops, and we are ready to die before we surrender the palace. If you are a war correspondent you will see war in these gardens.'

Officials have stated that the American Anarchists were the most violent. Today's experience proves that they include the most extreme New York 'gun-men'. Most of these came on the ship United States, via Norway. I saw several young and pretty girls about the rooms. I was offered vodka, of which they said they had plenty. They are having the most lurid time of their lives. Petrograd agrees with them, in the expectation of seeing a pitched battle at the palace.[4]

Just as the Bolsheviks had occupied the Kshesinskaya mansion, so the Anarchists had seized General Durnovo's palace, an elegant building overlooking the river, as a symbolic act of defiance, since the General had been a much-hated Minister of the Interior under the Tsar. It was in the Vyborg District, the working-class Bolshevik stronghold. What more natural, when threatened by the Government with eviction, than that the Anarchists should seek help from their closest neighbours, physically and politically? According to Harold

Williams, it was as a result of Bolshevik intrigue at the All-Russian Congress of Soviets that the Anarchists who had raided the offices of the *Russkaya Volya* newspaper were allowed to go free. For a whole week, he writes, the Vyborg District was 'simmering with incipient revolt'. No Government troops appeared; no pitched battle was fought. Instead, the Bolsheviks called for an armed anti-Government demonstration on Saturday, June 23. The All-Russian Congress did not get wind of this until the previous afternoon. 'Prompt action by the moderates,' Ransome reports, 'once again saved the situation.' They immediately issued an appeal against the demonstration, and members of the Congress went from regiment to regiment and from factory to factory warning the soldiers and workers not to take part. It was an anxious night, but at 4.30 a.m. the Bolsheviks announced that they had decided to call upon their supporters to put off the demonstration.[5]

'The feeling of Petrograd,' Ransome reports next day, 'is rather like that of a person half awake and not quite sure whether he has been visited by a burglar or a bad dream. Very few people knew of the threatening trouble until they heard it had been avoided. Even now opinion is very various as to the exact nature of the danger.' He himself attaches more significance to the counter-revolutionary threat from parties on the right, who 'would be glad of an excuse to take things into their own hands' and forestall the moment when they find themselves in a minority in the Constituent Assembly, than to the danger from extremists on the left, 'who are always ready to prod them [the moderate majority] into action against the right, and as shown by the last few days, are ready to risk all and themselves seize power.' On June 26 he reports: 'The extremists profit unscrupulously by the difficulties of the moderate party. I do not consider the danger great at present, but fear that when the material conditions of the country become still worse, the moderates will find people slipping away from their support towards those who promise them earlier relief.' Meanwhile, the Anarchists remained defiant.[6]

All parties now agreed that there should be an *unarmed* general demonstration on Sunday, July 1. It was a fine cool day, and the streets, Harold Williams writes, were a mass of colour.

> The people who carried flags and those who followed them looked as placid and cheerful as children marching to a Sunday school treat. The workers were dressed in their best, and the soldiers looked unusually spruce. They sang revolutionary songs,

rather uncertainly as yet, because of the novelty, and many kept their eyes fixed on little song-books. Bolshevik flags were in a huge majority. The favourite inscription was: 'Down with the ten capitalist Ministers!'

There was no doubt that what Ransome calls the 'referendum of red flags' had been won by the Bolsheviks, even though the demonstration had been called for by the moderates. 'As there are only nine ministers not socialists,' he points out, 'the choice of the number ten is a good example of Bolshevik cunning. The object is to get the appearance of a protest against Kerensky. There are many simple-minded people who are willing to carry a banner disapproving of the capitalist ministers who would indignantly refuse to take any sort of share in an attack on Kerensky.'[7]

But then the mood in Petrograd changed abruptly. At noon on July 2 telegrams were received from the front announcing a brilliant start to the long-awaited Russian offensive. The heroism of this effort, Ransome wrote to his mother, 'can only be appreciated by those who know the situation of affairs behind it.'[8] Patriotism re-asserted itself. Bolsheviks who tried to persuade the crowd that the reports of victory were false had to be rescued from lynching by the Cossacks. On that same day Government troops took possession of the Durnovo Palace and arrested its occupants. The 'big potatoes' upstairs, it seems, either never existed or were not used.

Undeterred, the Bolsheviks soon made another, more serious, attempt to seize power. Mrs Nellie Thornton, wife of one of the three Thornton brothers who owned the Thornton Woollen Mill Company, which had a massive mill on the Finnish side of the river Neva nine miles outside Petrograd, relates how she found herself caught up in an early stage of what later became known as the 'July Days':

It was a warm July evening [Monday, July 16], one of those sultry evenings one occasionally gets in Petrograd, when there seems literally no air anywhere, and the oppression is felt like a heavy weight on all around.

A little English friend, a girl of 11 or 12, came in to ask me to lend her a few books. She told me that some war pictures [newsreels?] were to be seen in the town, taken during the recent push on the Russian front. I invited her to see them with me and we decided to take along two more little friends.

We left home in the Rolls Royce and drove along the Schlüsselburg road. Everything seemed as usual, except that the road was rather crowded with promenaders, who seemed to be on their way to town. We arrived on the Islands, where we saw several cars, and people walking about. After a few minutes we reached the last Island looking out on to the Gulf. Here we got out, and I asked my English driver to buy me some chocolate, while we took a little walk.

We soon went back to our car and decided to go on to see the pictures. As we drove along the Kamenno-Ostrovsky Prospect we met great crowds of people at all the street corners, who shouted all kinds of unpleasant and insulting words at us, such as: 'Oh you cursed capitalist! Down with you, hounds and blood-suckers!', and many offensive remarks of this kind.

I began to fear some trouble was brewing, but took no notice of all this. Just then, at the corner of the Bolshoi Prospect, a voice called out: 'Don't go on, you'll lose your car if you do.' We still drove a few yards further, then a soldier dashed out and came up to me, saying: 'Mrs Thornton, go back at once, or you will get hurt and be arrested and your car taken from you.' My driver, Allen, pulled up, and we made a dash back, the soldier swinging on to the step. He offered to conduct us through the crowded corners, and help us to get home safely, telling me he knew my husband and brother-in-law.

We went along for a couple of streets, when we suddenly met a whole lot more soldiers. These shouted insolence at us, and a moment after, round the corner came six lorries armed with Maxim guns, all pointing different ways.

We were ordered to stop, and in a moment were surrounded by some 20 or 22 men. They declared us under arrest, and four jumped on to the foot step of the car, and ordered Allen to drive on. They had guns and bayonets, and looked most unpleasant and warlike.

I asked one where he was taking us, and he replied to the regiment. On asking where this was, he replied you will know when you get there. He made us drive on and on, and at last when I saw we were getting away out of the town, I again spoke and begged him to tell me where we were bound, but he was most unfriendly and replied it is not your business but mine.

So we were forced to go on, Allen obliged to obey orders, although he was simply furious and ready to say anything. I begged him to be silent, and to try to control himself, which for my sake he did.

At last we reached Lessney, and after a few moments were ordered to drive into a huge and secluded yard. This was a large square with a barrack in the middle, surrounded by a high brick wall.

The moment we got into the square, I saw we were in a trap and could not get away. Strange to say, all my fear went and I became an infuriated creature, ready to fight to the death. In a moment some two thousand armed men rushed at us, and I thought we were to be shot. I stood up in the car, trying to protect the children behind. I must confess it was a terrible moment, and I broke into a perspiration and could not for a few seconds collect myself.

After a moment, I spoke to the men. 'Comrades,' I said, 'what do you want from me? I am a helpless woman lured here by your soldiers. I know nothing, I want nothing from you. I am not a Russian and don't care for any of your politics. It does not matter to me what party you uphold, or wish to throw over. I am a British subject, the wife of an English manufacturer working for your Russian soldiers. He works like any other workman, and is not the idle bloated capitalist you talk about. I also work, and help to nurse and look after wounded and sick men. What grievance can you have now against me? I ask you as men to let me go, as I am afraid of you, and I appeal to your better feeling and your manhood to spare me for my three little girls' sake, who are trembling behind. I will not give you my car, as this is the private property of a British subject, my husband. I live some 25 versts [16 miles] from here, and if you take the car I must walk home with the children, as all trams and driving are stopped. I have a bad heart, and the children cannot go so far, so God knows what will happen to us if you take away our car. If you are base enough to have other motives, then in mercy spare the three girls. Let them go at any cost.'

After a lot of talk of this kind, three of the soldiers who were in favour spoke up for me. It was agreed that we should be allowed to go with an escort of soldiers, who were to see us home and then return with the car. I asked the soldiers why they wished to take away my car. They replied: 'To show you we have the power. We shall now drive your car and make you walk barefoot, then you will know what is what.'

The Rolls-Royce set off again with its extra occupants. At every corner they met soldiers who shouted at them, but they drove on, their escort declaring them to be the arrested capitalists. As they could not get through the town, they decided to drive round by Ochta. This made it necessary to drive past the Durnovo Palace (referred to by Mrs Thornton as 'the home of the great Anarchist Lenin'). The soldiers assured her they could get by if they got up enough speed. So they came along at fifty-five miles an hour, but as soon as they approached, they heard the whistles go, and a black mass of Anarchists (who had evidently returned to the building after the Government action) rushed out and surrounded the car. The same talk went on again, and she had to beg the crowd to let them go.

Eventually they got away, and came home accompanied by the three soldiers with fixed bayonets. 'I cannot describe how very thankful I was, nor how grateful to the soldiers who saved us.' Gratitude did not extend to parting with the car. 'On arriving home we informed the soldiers that if the British Embassy told us to give up our car we should do so, not otherwise. As they saw the cause was lost they eventually left, and I was thankful to get them out of the premises.'[9]

*

Early that morning Sir George Buchanan had learned by telephone that the four Kadet Ministers had resigned, thereby bringing the Coalition Government to an end after only two months. Tereshchenko, whom he saw later in the day, criticized the Ministers for taking this step when the country was facing dangers from within and without, but spoke confidently of the internal situation, and when Buchanan left him at 6 o'clock, had not the slightest suspicion that a storm might be brewing.[10]

After dinner on that sultry evening, Sir George decided to seek some fresh air by driving to the Islands. Meriel describes how the chasseur came up to announce that the carriage was ready and then stood hesitating for a moment at the door.

'It would be better for your Excellency not to go out,' he said at last. 'The streets are not quiet.'

'But what is happening?' my father asked. The man shook his head. 'I don't know, Excellency. It would be better not to go.'

My father, however, insisted, saying that he would not go far, and he and my mother started out.

From her window Meriel watched their carriage trying to cross the bridge, but being forced to turn back because of the dense block of trams and motors. Then she noticed the huge red flag being slowly hoisted from the roof of the Kshesinskaya house across the river. For a short time during the Russian military offensive it had been taken down, the windows were darkened, and the house seemed to be empty. Now it fluttered a patch of brilliant scarlet against the grey shadow of the mosque behind, and in the distance she faintly heard the sound of cheering.

At a quarter past nine her parents returned, saying that farther along the Quay everything was perfectly quiet,

> but meanwhile the crowd in front of the Embassy grew ever denser, all the trams had stopped, the bridge was a seething mass of people, and several private motors that passed were held up by soldiers who turned out the occupants without any ceremony and themselves took possession of the cars, swarming into them like a lot of insects, five or six inside, two on either step, two or three on the box, two more lying along the mudguards. And presently two fully-armed regiments came marching across the bridge, carrying banners inscribed in flaring white letters with 'Down with the Capitalist War! Down with the Upper Classes! Long live Anarchy! Bread, Peace, Freedom!'

Sir George did what he usually did in such situations: asked Meriel to telephone General Knox. Everything in Knox's part of town was quiet, however, and he knew nothing of any disturbances. But as more and more soldiers and armed workmen crossed the bridge, the anxious Buchanan telephoned again and asked Knox to come round to the Embassy. Unable to find out by telephone what was happening, Knox went round on foot to the General Staff at about 11, only to be told that the trouble was not regarded as serious.[11]

Meanwhile, one of the correspondents had telephoned the Embassy to say that there was fighting on the Nevsky. It was probably Harold Williams. 'We have had a night of it,' he reports next morning.

> Again there has been bloodshed on the streets of Petrograd – this time more than at any period since the revolutionary week. All night long armed soldiers and workers marched about the streets demonstrating, for or against what nobody could tell, least of all

the demonstrators themselves... The previous attempt of the Leninites to organize an armed demonstration was frustrated at the last moment by the efforts of the Soviet. This time they worked more secretly, and sprang the demonstration on the harassed population of Petrograd as a complete surprise.

About seven in the evening several factories in the quarter on the north side of the river struck work. Soldiers in motor-lorries from Leninite and Anarchist regiments scoured the town and called on workers and soldiers to come out into the streets. Some consented and some refused, and a strange movement began. Armed battalions marched about commandeering motor-cars, trams were stopped, lorries and cars with machine-guns whizzed and rumbled some-whither and no-whither, crowds of idlers gathered in the central streets, meetings were improvized, there were fierce disputes.

A characteristic incident was the seizure of a small station on the Finland railway by men from a machine-gun regiment, who put machine-guns on the line and refused to allow any trains going to Finland to pass, although they passed the incoming trains. ['The effect,' Ransome writes, 'was much as if passengers catching their evening trains at Victoria learnt that armed mutineers held Clapham Junction.'[12]]

On the Nevsky Prospect, about ten o'clock, the shooting began. Who began it is not clear, but men on motor-lorries with machine-guns began firing indiscriminately into the crowd, which scattered in panic – soldiers and all. This happened several times on the Nevsky and in other parts of the town...

Late in the evening life in the streets became a complete and unintelligible chaos. It was a hot, close evening. The streets were unlighted. In the dusk of the falling night crowds wandered aimlessly and excitedly to and fro. Lorries and cars buzzed about filled with yelling soldiers, and having the nozzles of the machine-guns pointed threateningly at the crowd. Groups gathered at corners to discuss, to exclaim, to wonder, and to inquire. Yard-keepers and their families sat placidly at the house gates. The talk was curiously mingled. One or two soldiers talked against the offensive, and complained of Kerensky; others cursed the Leninites. Shots rang out from the Nevsky, and a group of idle soldiers hastily moved down the street. One soldier boy complained: 'Somebody ought to explain something. What's the sense of all this, fellows rushing about with machine-guns making a row, no one knows why? Why doesn't Kerensky come and tell us what it's all about?' [He had left by train for the front earlier that evening, shortly before disaffected troops arrived at the station to arrest him.]

At the end of the Liteiny a huge procession passed with banners: 'Down with the Capitalist Ministers! [who had in fact already resigned] All Power to the Soviet! Down with the War!' [Ransome mentions in addition banners inscribed 'Down with Kerensky!' and in the case of one Anarchist banner, 'Down with the blood-thirsty Kerensky!'[13]]. It was a strange sight, this grey, silent, moving mass in the dusk, with a blur of guns, the caps and bayonets of men on the lorries, and the bent figures of soldiers on artillery horses, all silhouetted against the pale sky... Hour after hour crowds trudged the streets... soldiers and workers, workers and soldiers, in an endless, armed stream.

The official Leninites denied responsibility for the demonstration. They said it was the work of counter-revolutionaries, whose names they know. But in the Taurida Palace they refused to vote condemnation; they sat on the fence and promised they would try to make the demonstration peaceful. There happened last night to be a meeting of the new Town Council in the City Hall on the Nevsky... I saw the Leninites there; they were pale and haggard, and most obviously frightened...

When I returned home about four o'clock this morning the streets were quiet; here and there stood a wrecked and abandoned motor-car. I passed the *Novoe Vremya* offices; they had been seized by an armed band ['some extreme gentlemen', as Knox calls them], who were printing their own proclamations [signed 'Petrograd Federation of Anarchists', according to Knox, and ridiculing Kerensky as a 'little Napoleon' who had sacrificed 500,000 men in his recent offensive[14]].

Today, so far, everything is quiet...[15]

This quiet did not last long. Hopes of a swift restoration of normal life, Ransome reports, soon vanished. The workmen turned up at the factories at the usual time on Tuesday morning (the 17th), but listened to orators there and decided not to work after all. Kshesinskaya's house became the rallying-point for the mutineers, and all that side of town was picketed by small bodies of soldiers and armed workmen. To all outward appearances, Knox writes, the town was completely in the power of the insurgents all day. Ransome agrees, but notes how a 'more or less passive hostility on the part of the population' was making the demonstrators more nervous than the onlookers. 'At the bridge over the Moika Canal two armed sailors were anxiously scanning the approaches while a small boy on the bridge fished unconcernedly for sticklebacks... Two or three shots fired in accidental alarm sends the fiercest-looking demonstration scuttling.'[16]

Soon after midday several thousand sailors arrived from Kronstadt and made their way to Kshesinskaya's house. According to Ransome, 'Lenin, although ill, scored a tempestuous success, appearing to the sailors and greeting them as "genuine revolutionaries".' (Lenin had arrived in Petrograd only that morning. On July 12, ostensibly for health reasons, he had gone on a visit to Finland, but whether, as he told the sailors, he was really ill or whether there was some hidden motive behind his absence from Petrograd at such a critical time, are questions that have provoked much ingenious speculation among historians.) A monster armed procession led by the sailors then set off for the Taurida Palace to put their demands to the Soviet. Knox met them coming south as he was walking across the Troitsky Bridge to lunch: an evil-looking crew with such inscriptions on their banners as 'A separate peace with William!' and 'Down with the French and English capitalists!' Meriel Buchanan watched them as they marched past the Embassy, armed with every kind of weapon and cheered by the soldiers in the Fortress, who had gone over to the Bolsheviks. 'Looking at them, one wondered what the fate of Petrograd would be if these ruffians with their unshaven faces, their slouching walk, their utter brutality were to have the town at their mercy.' More panics followed on the streets. After a general flight on the Nevsky, Ransome writes, 'things dropped by the bolting public were taken into the Public Library, but not before daring gleaners had found a harvest. I saw one respectable old lady with great presence of mind grab up several galoshes which are now almost unobtainable.'[17]

Tereshchenko had telephoned the Embassy about lunchtime to say that as soon as loyal troops arrived from the front, the disorders would be put down with a firm hand, but otherwise the Government appeared to be taking no action.[18] 'At 3 p.m.,' Knox writes, 'the situation was critical.' When the socialist Minister, Chernov, came out of the Taurida Palace and tried to address the mutineers, he was very roughly handled, 'and was only saved by the intervention of two anti-war socialists a shade more unpatriotic than himself' (one of whom was Trotsky). 'It was about this time, when the fate of the Government seemed in the balance, that a group of officials at the Ministry of Justice took the step that saved the situation': with the Minister's consent they released material proving that the Bolsheviks had received money from the German General Staff. 'The news spread rapidly and had an excellent effect on the wavering troops.'[19]

That evening of July 17, Meriel Buchanan writes,

stands out very clearly in my memory, not perhaps so much for the actual events, but for a rather unexplainable atmosphere of dread that seemed to brood over the town. I suppose the weather really had something to do with this feeling, for heavy thunderclouds lay piled in ominous masses behind the Fortress; the river lay dark and sullen, with an oily reflection on the grey waters, and only now and then little puffs of a hot dry wind blew clouds of yellow dust up from the Field of Mars across the Square.

One or two people were dining with us that night... and we had just reached the pudding when the chasseur – rather white and agitated – appeared in the doorway. 'Excellency, the Cossacks are charging across the Square,' he announced.

Leaving our pudding untasted we made a slightly undignified rush to my father's study, from where a good view of the Square could be obtained...

Here Knox, always well armed with facts and figures, takes up the story; he had moved into the Embassy temporarily earlier in the day. 'Some ninety Cossacks had charged across the Field of Mars on 200 Kronstadt sailors, who fled precipitately into the Marble Palace. We arrived late for the fun, but saw the Cossacks ride past, many of them with three or four rifles slung across their backs. They rode past the front of the Embassy up the Quay.' The party returned to the dining-room (this is Meriel again) to finish their pudding but had hardly done so when a sharp volley of firing brought them to their feet once more. They hurried back to the study. Nothing was to be seen on the Quay itself. Then suddenly above the crack of the rifles came the report of a field-gun.

Hardly a minute later, with a wild scurry of flying hoofs, two riderless Cossack horses dashed past... The firing had died down to an almost startling silence, broken only by a low rumble of distant thunder and the patter of one or two heavy drops of rain... Unable to tear ourselves from the windows we wandered aimlessly from room to room, while rapidly the thunder-clouds darkened behind the Fortress.[20]

There was one more incident still to come, however, which Knox describes as follows:

Two Cossacks returned on foot, escorting a prisoner, who appealed to a crowd of idle Pavlovsky men to rescue him. One Cossack dropped him, but the other, a big fellow, held on to him like a man. He was one against twenty, and the cowards surged round him and overpowered him. The prisoner got free and at once bolted. A hero of the Pavlovsky drew the Cossack's sword, and, while the others held back, gave him a swinging blow with it on the head. It seemed like cold-blooded murder of a man who had remained true to his salt, and we in the window above, being diplomats, could do nothing, not even shout, much less run down to tackle one or two of the brutes.

The Cossack, however, was only stunned for a moment, and then collected himself and ran off after his squadron. The other man ran in the opposite direction, and the insurgents fired several shots at both, but without hitting either.

A few minutes later there was a stampede of riderless horses down the Quay, and some five of them fell on the pavement at the corner in front of the Embassy. We learned later that the squadron had been ambushed and had suffered several casualties from machine-gun fire.

There was heavy rain on Tuesday night and on Wednesday morning, and this helped to cool down excitement.[21]

Wednesday the 18th is described by Sir George Buchanan as a more or less quiet day. All the bridges were raised early to prevent the rebels from communicating with each other. 'I believe that on this side of the river,' Ransome writes, 'the trouble is definitely over, but up to the moment when I came in to telegraph this could not be said of other parts.' In the Vyborg District many armed workers and soldiers were in the streets, 'some evidently unwilling to realize that the apparent success of Monday has turned to nothing'. Government action was expected shortly against Kshesinskaya's house (where Lenin amongst others was being guarded by the more determined of the Kronstadt sailors, though the red flag had been taken down) and its near neighbour, the Fortress.[22]

That night, according to Meriel Buchanan, was unbearably hot.

I remember getting up at about three in the morning to open the window a little wider... As I stood there trying in vain to get a little breath of air the whirr of a motor broke the silence... Two officers, followed by a sailor and a Cossack, got out and walked up to the bridge, standing there in earnest conversation... I was filled with a very violent curiosity to know what it was they were discussing. However, after a minute or two they got back into their motor again and drove off, and since nothing seemed to be going to happen just yet, I got sadly back into bed again and – still wondering – fell asleep.

At six, however, I was woken up again by a violent report just outside, and getting up hastily saw that the whole Square was a mass of soldiers and sailors, who were all drawn up to attention and all seemed in some state of excitement. Quite who it was or what it was who had fired I could not make out, but I saw that the bridge had been swung back into position and one or two officers stood on it, looking anxiously across. Evidently something was going to happen, and probably whatever it was had to do with the mysterious action the Government intended taking against the Bolsheviks. Hearing at the same time a certain amount of movement going on in the house, I put on a dressing-gown, opened my door and ran straight into Colonel Thornhill with an overcoat on over his pyjamas.

'Oh!' I was a little taken aback. 'Were you coming to call me? Is anything the matter?'

'Yes,' he answered briefly. 'Will you please go up and call your people and tell them they must go down to the coach-house at once. The Government are attacking the Fortress and the Bolsheviks will probably use their big guns.'

'May I dress first?' I asked meekly, but was told with some severity: 'No, please go and tell your father at once.'

So obediently I went up and called my father and mother, and also woke up my maid, who was fast asleep, and was more than a little startled when I shook her violently and told her she must get up at once.

Coming downstairs again I ran into General Knox. He met my cheerful smile with a frown. 'You oughtn't to be here at all,' he told me severely, and then said he was looking for my father, as the officer in command of the Government troops who were attacking the Fortress wished to speak to him.

In the bright morning sunshine we must have looked a somewhat dissipated and motley assembly, arrayed as we were in an
odd assortment of garments. There was General Knox in a beautiful dark red dressing-gown, Colonel Thornhill, who had been out
on the Quay, in khaki, my father, his grey hair a little rumpled and
more curly than ever, with a greatcoat on over his pyjamas, my
mother fully dressed, and one of the maids hovering in the background wrapped in a thick coat. But the officer in command of the
operations behaved as if there was nothing unusual in the circumstances, and as if it was the most natural thing in the world to be
received on the Embassy staircase at six o'clock in the morning by
an Ambassador wearing a greatcoat over his pyjamas and with a
pair of bedroom slippers on his bare feet.

He told us he was confident of being able to take the Fortress,
but that the Embassy being in the direct line of fire it would be
wiser for us to go to the back of the house and – in the eventuality
of very severe fighting – be prepared to leave altogether at a
moment's notice.

So accordingly we once more packed our bags, and the Siamese
cat was again – protesting even more violently – put into her travelling basket [they had received a similar warning on the previous
day]. Disregarding the order to go to the back of the house, we
crowded to the windows of the drawing-room, from where one had
the best view of what was going on.

It was broad daylight now, the sun blazing down out of a cloudless sky, the scarlet flag on the Fortress hanging limp and straight
in the hot still air. All down the Quay soldiers were kneeling
behind the low stone parapet with their rifles resting on the wall
and their eyes fixed on the opposite shore. A little farther down
several machine-guns were hidden in a big stack of wood, and the
whole Square was packed with troops, infantry and artillery, and
one or two companies of the Military and Naval Cadet Schools.
Now and then a little volley of shots sounded from the opposite
shore, once some bullets spattered on the parapet, making the soldiers kneeling behind it duck their heads quickly; another time
one struck the walls of the Embassy with a sharp ping and the
sound of falling plaster. At intervals companies of soldiers, preced-
ed by armoured cars, advanced cautiously across the bridge. Once
an armoured car from the opposite shore came menacingly to
meet them, and the soldiers in the Square put their rifles to their
shoulders – then after a second's breathless tension the Bolshevik

motor turned and scuttled off in the opposite direction, and a little ripple of amusement ran down the lines of troops along the Quay.

Presently, beginning to get rather hungry, we went to have our breakfast, though the fact that there was no milk or butter and hardly any bread did not quite add to one's enjoyment of the meal.

More and more troops were advancing across the bridge ['we had a weary time watching the preparations', comments Knox, who had seen such things before[23]], and now and then the crack of rifles or the rattle of machine-guns could be heard from the opposite shore, but still the guns of the Fortress remained silent, and presently we all went to dress.

At about half-past ten M. Tereshchenko telephoned to my father begging him to come at once with my mother and myself to the Foreign Office, as he did not consider the Embassy to be safe. My father absolutely refused to leave, and my mother would not go without him. They wanted, of course, to turn me out, and General Knox told me that I was more trouble than all the Russian army, but while they were still arguing about my fate a message was brought us that Lenin's palace had been taken by the Government troops and that the Fortress was expected to yield very shortly, and I hastily seized on this to assure them that now it really was not worth my leaving the Embassy.

Occasional bodies of troops could still be seen advancing across the bridge, and now and then a certain amount of shooting could be heard, and it was not till nearly one that the Fortress actually surrendered, without having used those much-threatened big guns [the sailors, according to Harold Williams, did not know how to fire them[24]], or put up really any very great resistance.[25]

'Thornhill and I left the Embassy this morning,' Knox begins his diary entry for Friday, July 20:

Events have moved with dramatic quickness. Kerensky returned from the front last night [escorted from the station to the Winter Palace by Cossacks on white horses, according to Bertie Stopford[26]] and, in a stormy meeting of the Ministry, demanded dictatorial powers in order to bring the army back to discipline. The socialists disagreed. Lvov and Tereshchenko did their utmost to reconcile the diverging views. Kerensky left to meet the Mitava Hussars (14th Cavalry Division). While addressing the men he was handed a telegram telling him of the disaster on the South-West Front, where the Germans have broken through. He took back the telegram to the Ministerial Council and the attitude changed. Lvov has resigned and Kerensky will be P.M. and Minister of War. . .

There is little sign of strong measures. Apparently only individuals suspected as German spies are to be arrested and the organizers of the military rising of the 16th and 17th are to go unpunished.[27]

Knox had almost had a fit the previous day on learning that after the '700 blackguards' in the fortress had surrendered,

they were disarmed – and released! When I heard of this release at the Staff today I went for Polovtsev and Balaban [the Petrograd military commanders] and said that either the Russians were the cleverest people in the world or else the biggest fools. I pointed out that they had everything in their hands if they would only take strong measures, but that there would be an end of their co-operation as allies if they allowed the present opportunity to pass. Polovtsev said that he had not got a free hand, and had only orders to arrest Roshal, the Kronstadt leader, and he only sighed at my bloodthirstiness and said that I was 'a hot-headed Irishman'.[28]

After his whirlwind visit Kerensky set off again for the front at noon on Friday. That evening Ransome was reassured by the sight of a cavalry regiment, just arrived from the front to support the Government, riding from the station. They were men who had been away since the start of the war, and it was strange to see them pointing out to each other such things as the bullet marks on the Astoria Hotel which had long ceased to interest anyone in Petrograd.

Dusty and sunburnt. . .   they moved through the streets on little grey horses. One man with the reins loose on his horse's neck played the accordion accompanied by another who beat time on a tambourine. They brought with them into the hot damp July evening in Petrograd something of the old vigour of the front, something of the vivid contrast there has always been between the front and the rear. I never felt so strongly that Petrograd was the sick city of Russia as when I read the little dusty red flags fastened on their long green lances. Here were the original watchwords of the Revolution – 'Long live the Russian Republic!' 'Forward in the name of Freedom!' 'Liberty or Death!' – whereas for weeks here in Petrograd we have seen only the banners of party struggles.[29]

Harold Williams reflects on the events of the previous days in an article datelined Sunday, July 22, in which he begins by describing Friday evening:

Rat-tat-tat, a sudden crackle, and then silence. It was a spectral night. A sullen gleam on the river, lights of trams gliding across the bridges, and beyond the grey shadowy mass of the quarters on the northern shore. Again rat-tat-tat, a crackle, and silence. Where are they shooting? Disarming the rebels, perhaps. There on the Vyborg side are the barracks of a rebel regiment. But why that sudden angry spurt farther down the river near Vasily Island? Who knows. Perhaps the scoundrels are shooting again from housetops, or firing round corners on the loyal troops, or sniping from swiftly-flying motors, just as they did in the days of the real Revolution. These Leninites copy the methods of the old police. Perhaps they are the old police under a new guise. Where can you draw the line?

The night is still again, and gathers up wrath and vengeance. A cabman drives me slowly home... A sentry stops me to draw out a tattered scrap of paper; he glances at it, and waves me on. A dim line of figures is crouched along the pavement; it is a queue waiting through the night for the morrow's bread. The shadows glimmer and waver. There is something eerie in the night. When will this agony end? When will Russia be strong again?

Prince Lvov has resigned; Kerensky is Premier. That must be good, because Kerensky has energy and fire, and will see that the traitors get their due. But the rest? Nekrasov came in for a moment... He has very nearly boxed the political compass. But even he has backed out. He was afraid of Chernov's agrarian programme. Why this sudden declaration of land nationalization, to what end? And who is Chernov? Tsereteli, Minister of the Interior, yes. Tsereteli is good, and he has the Soviet behind him. But what is the Soviet now? It is tottering; it is clutching at power. And why does it not come out firmly and disown the criminals? Twenty-five per cent of the Soviet were Leninites. And until a few days ago the talk in the Soviet was Comrade Lenin, Comrade Trotsky, Comrade Zinoviev. Will the Soviet, can the Soviet purge itself? Will a Socialist Government last two days?

The streets are angry, very angry. Today the crowd caught two Leninites who had been firing from a house-top with a machine-gun, and tore them to pieces. Women swear death to all Leninites and Germans. The Soviet dare not hesitate, or it is lost. There must be a strong national Government. And so the sultry night wears on. Hour by hour Fate weaves its web. At last the morning comes. The town is quiet today. The 1st Machine-Gun Regiment marched in to the Palace Square [having 'coolly put off the surrender while it sounded other units of the garrison', according to Knox[30]], gave up its arms, and asked for mercy. It had no support, no pity. It will be disbanded. The other rebel regiments are being quietly disarmed. There was trouble with the workmen's 'Red Guard' last night, on the north side of the river. They tried to resist, and there was a sharp exchange of shots. In other quarters workmen threw down their rifles before the soldiers came.

Nearly all the factories are working today, and in some the men are collecting for relief of the families of the victims. The Cossacks are the heroes of the hour. At the height of the disturbances they were sent out, and had orders not to take rifles with them. Attacked by the rebels, they lost heavily, defended themselves with swords alone, and in the end only twenty out of a hundred returned. Warrants are out for the arrest of the Leninite leaders, but most of them, including Lenin, are in hiding.[31]

Ransome, characteristically, takes a more optimistic view of the situation, writing on July 19:

The unfortunate disorders of the last few days may be looked upon as the growing pains of political good sense in Revolutionary Russia. The disorders have been regrettable, but were committed by one side only, and that side itself regrets them. That such an end should have been reached is a triumph for the moderate party, who, with cool heads and unstained hands, see the smoke of anarchy dispersing and the political atmosphere clearer than it has been for many weeks.

And his long telegram of July 21 concludes:

It is possible that the alarms and excursions of this week may have a result exactly opposite to German wishes, in unifying Russia, in destroying the Bolshevik organization, and in illustrating to the army and the fleet before it is too late the danger that threatened them from agitation and mutual distrust in the face of the enemy... The final exposure of the coincidence between German aims and those of the Bolsheviks may stiffen the thousand-mile line.[32]

He still holds to his view that danger to the revolution comes from minorities on the right as well as on the left. Whereas Williams makes no criticism of the Kadet ministers, who had been compelled to resign 'after much long-suffering' from a Coalition Government that was not a genuine Coalition at all[33], Ransome at first was very critical – 'impossible unblame Kadets for risking throwing country into melting pot' – though later he admits that 'Bolshevik agitation was certainly blowing up for trouble before the Kadet resignations'. He appreciates that it is an understandable fear of giving encouragement to troublemakers on the right that stops the Soviet backing the idea of a strong national government or disowning the Bolsheviks as criminals in the way that Williams would have liked. Whereas the latter portrays the Bolsheviks as vicious scoundrels scarcely distinguishable from the old Tsarist police, Ransome is able to discern certain redeeming features: some of them, 'as even their opponents recognize, are perfectly honest men'; the 'better elements of Bolshevism' had been brought to their senses by the revelations of German financial support; and the 1st Machine-Gun Regiment had 'passed a resolution showing that its action was not directed against the Soviet, thereby illustrating what has been most noticeable throughout the disorders, that the mutineers were almost all supporters of the very organization whose authority they were being used to undermine.'[34]

One thing, however, seemed clear. 'Events of this week', he writes to his mother on July 23, 'have definitely knocked on the head all chance of my getting home this year.' Like so many other confident predictions made in and about Russia in 1917, this proved quite false.

8

The Plain People

Impressions of village life, September

In the feverish days of July, when the Bolsheviks were trying to seize the government, one morning I saw a riderless horse come tearing around a corner, snorting blood, shot through the neck; and as it galloped along a canal, a big black-bearded peasant on a barge piled high with wood rose slowly up from a pit in the logs and scowled about in a puzzled way, while from not far off there came the rattle of a machine-gun. I wondered what he was thinking of this city revolution, the shouting crowds, the volleys of shots, the armoured cars that were racing by with shrill screams of warning. For so much depended on what he thought, this man who had come floating down from the boundless fields and forests where the great mass of the Russians dwell.

The writer is an American, Ernest Poole (1880–1950), whose novel about New York, *The Harbour*, 'a dramatization of labour under present conditions', was described by one reviewer as 'the first really notable novel produced by the New Democracy'. Since 1914 he had been living in New York, with trips to London and Berlin and out along the western front, and in the summer of 1917 he arrived in Petrograd to cover the Revolution for the *New Republic* and the *Red Cross Magazine*. His Russian experiences are described in two books, *'The Dark People': Russia's Crisis* and *The Village: Russian Impressions.*[1]

Although he had visited Russia some years before, Poole did not speak the language and had to rely on interpreters. He tried three at first, two Bolsheviks and a Kadet, but each looked at Russia through the eyes of his own political party. Then he thought of Tarasov, a Russian friend from his first visit, and finally tracked him down working in a Moscow bank. Tarasov arrived in Petrograd in the middle of the July Days. 'You'll leave the bank?' 'Of course! Why not? What is a bank?' The advantage of Tarasov was that he belonged to no party at all. He had been a farmer, a chemical engineer, a high explosives expert, a maker of violins, a banker's clerk, a business promoter, a dreamer, an anthropologist for two years, a traveller, a great reader and an eager translator of all kinds of foreign books. He was also a mixer. His father had been a peasant's son, his mother was of noble birth, and this combination gave him access to all classes of Russian society.

Poole had had enough of the cities,

with their shrill hates and jealousies, their war scandals and intrigues. Again and again there had come to me a feeling of the presence all around me, far and near, of the millions of villages in the world where the silent mass of the plain people dwell. . .

My eyes ached from the red glare of the Present. I wanted to live for awhile in a place where life ran deep, and was quiet enough so that one could feel the Present not by itself but as a gap, or a bridge, between the Past and Future.

Also, I wanted a little real food. The restaurants of Petrograd had held more noise than nourishment.

So their travels began, and at the end of August they set off on what proved the best journey of all. For Tarasov himself was a small landowner and they were to visit his estate some five hours from Petrograd. They travelled by train and then steamer, down a wide river that ran smoothly between high banks, in a flat country with fields on each side, and woods and rolling meadows. Tarasov had a word with the captain, the latter promptly blew two piercing blasts, they hastened below with their luggage, and from the open gangway there, as a dory came alongside, threw in their bags and jumped after them.

At once the steamer went ahead, and we were left in the dory with a grey old peasant. He rowed us to the high wooded bank. We paid him a rouble, went ashore across a raft of huge brown logs, and climbed a steep and winding path through a grove of white birches, maples and firs. We passed an old well with a bucket and came to a large log cabin above. And here Tarasov drew a quiet breath and said:

'This is the place where I was born.'

In the days that followed, Poole discovered that the social life of the district was centred on a large village across the river about a mile from Tarasov's home. Here was the post office, with a big red poster on the wall inscribed 'Fight till Victory', appealing for the Government's new Liberty Loan, but the glum postmaster told them the peasants were 'sick of paying, paying'. Here was a grocer's shop, where the woman in charge did not seem very concerned about the bare shelves. A stout peasant woman came in with a sack of potatoes and a package of wool, and after much discussion went out with a carefully weighed chunk of sugar, a small packet of tea and a paper of pins and needles. 'No money had passed between them. Just plain old-fashioned barter here.' This was embarrassing for Tarasov and Poole, who were badly in need of provisions but could only offer money. The woman, however, smiled good-naturedly at Tarasov and said: 'Was not your father always doing kind things for my family? Surely I'll take your money now.' And she did – she took a lot of it.

The proprietor of the tea-house, who had long been a friend of Tarasov's, told them about his work as a member of the local food supplies committee controlling thirty-nine villages, including the little hamlets near Tarasov's farm.

In each village we have a peasant, who brings us a report every week of what grain and fodder his neighbours have. But the reports are all the same. The peasants will not give up their grain until they can get real goods in trade; and as yet, we can get so few goods from the towns that we cannot persuade the peasants to take their grain out of their barns.

The only hope that I can see is in our Co-operative here. Our co-operative store has still quite a stock of goods, and the steadier peasants all belong. We have eighteen hundred members now. Each paid five roubles to buy a share. There were six thousand purchasers last year; and because we charge higher prices to out-siders than to members, so many more peasants wish to join that we are almost ready to announce a second issue of stock.

Of course, our progress has been blocked by the war and the revolution. Goods have gone up to ruinous rates. Already we are nearly out of horseshoes, axes, harrows, ploughs. Last spring we had not ploughs enough to do the needed ploughing, and that is why our crop is short. There is not enough rye in the district to take us through the winter, let alone to feed the towns. And so the town people will starve for awhile – and sooner or later, I suppose, they will finish with their wrangling, start their mills and factories, and turn out the ploughs and tools we need.

Our Co-operative is even now preparing for that time ahead. We are not only growing here but we are getting in closer touch with other societies like ours. We have already joined the Union of Co-operatives. In every province in Russia there is such a union; and the Unions get big credits from the People's Bank in Moscow, which is like a mother of them all. The Unions have altogether more than thirteen million members now. So we are no small affair. We are a power in Russia today.

He took them to see the community centre which the Co-operative had organized. The first building contained a general store, where five or six peasant women and girls were gossiping in a leisurely way and looking over some calico prints and ribbons, two small babies' caps, a blanket, several bottles of 'pain killer' and various kinds of groceries; while behind the store were sheds with sacks of seeds, bags of fertilizer, some barrels of cement and a few farming implements. A larger building nearby contained a little farmers' bank; a rear room was being used by the local food supplies committee, and also as headquarters of the new Soviet. 'The Co-operative had seized the chance', Poole comments, 'to gather in unto itself the revolutionist government here and steady its activities.'

The third building was a hospital, built some three years before the war. The ground floor had been taken over by the government for wounded soldiers, but they had all left now, and the Co-operative was looking out for a new doctor and nurse. However, the midwife, a peasant from the area, was still functioning on the floor above, where she had two rooms for herself and two for serious maternity cases. 'Just think!' she exclaimed. 'A real American here!' Her talk was interrupted by the entry of her son, a tow-headed lad of about twenty in student's uniform. Though illegitimate, he was a recognized leader in the community – 'and this was no uncommon case of Russian village tolerance'. He talked eagerly of his work as secretary of the food supplies committee, and of how he was trying to hold the younger men in line and keep them from rioting. The way to do it was to keep things humming. Fun was a good safety valve. The last play in the schoolhouse had netted 700 roubles. 'The next play will be given tonight, and the proceeds are to go to the building fund for the new People's House to be built by the Co-operative. The sooner that building is started, the better it will be for the whole revolution here.'

The play was one of Ostrovsky's classic satires on petty bourgeois life. Poole could barely follow the story, but with deepening surprise he watched these village players and the spell that they were casting.

Like most amateurs, they dragged their lines; but it was just this leisurely art, this lack of all impatience for having anything happen, this deep and delighted absorption in the characters themselves, which was creating this atmosphere, holding this peasant audience, of which the players were a part. . .

For a time I lost the drift of the play and sat there in the darkness, watching the rows of faces and those shining motionless eyes. I remembered the war. It seemed far away. So, too, the revolution. . . Now it was eleven o'clock and they had just finished the second act. . .

One Sunday, Tarasov took Poole to dinner with a peasant family in a hut close to the waterside. The wife was strong and capable, with reddish hair, a freckled face and bright honest friendly eyes.

While she moved about her kitchen she talked of the high prices. In Petrograd the price of stove wood rose each week; and this, she said, was partly because the peasant boys and women here demanded such big wages for loading the wood onto barges.

'They hardly know what to ask,' she laughed. 'It is like a game. Every week they keep asking more, and always they get it, and so we go on. And so long as things are in such a state, why should not our people get all they can? Petrograd got all the profits once, and always it was at our expense. Now our turn has come. Why shouldn't we take it?'

'Yes, we are living pretty well,' she continued quietly, 'in spite of the disorders in towns. We have plenty to eat, for we catch our own fish, raise our own chickens, our wheat and rye and vegetables. As for clothes, in almost every hut we have old looms and spinning wheels that we have not used for years – but now all the old grannies are fixing them up. We grew flax in our fields this summer; there are still enough sheep to give us some wool; and so this winter we'll make our own clothes.'

1. Sir George Buchanan (1854–1924), British Ambassador to Russia: born into diplomacy, 'he also looked like a diplomat, with his tall patrician appearance and silvery grey hair'

2. Meriel Buchanan (1886–1959), 'a fair type of a real English girl, pretty, quiet, moderately tall, with a splendid figure and possessing delightful manners'

3. British Embassy, Petrograd, showing the balcony from which Buchanan addressed the crowds

4. Arthur Ransome (1884–1967), Petrograd correspondent of the *Daily News*, 'an Englishman of the six-footer, lounging sort, red-moustached and pipe-smoking', seen here travelling in Revolutionary Russia

5. Morgan Philips Price (1885–1973), Petrograd correspondent of the *Manchester Guardian*: he risked starvation in order to be 'one of the very few who saw the great Russian Revolution as an eye-witness'

6. General Alfred Knox (1870–1964), who had 'the air and voice of a man engaged in winning the war while everybody else about him was obstructing him in his patriotic task'

7. Harold Williams (1876–1928), Petrograd correspondent of the *Daily Chronicle*, 'a very quiet man, unselfish, extraordinarily kind': after a drawing by Georges Dantal

8. John Reed (1887–1920), author of *Ten Days That Shook the World*: 'defiance was not a principle with him, it was an instinct'

9, 10 & 11. Photographs by Stinton Jones of the March Revolution: guns behind a barricade commanding the Liteiny Prospect and bridgehead; two soldiers with fixed bayonets lying along the mudguards of a requisitioned car; soldiers with red flags leading an immense crowd in the Nevsky Prospect, all singing the Marseillaise

12. Newsreel, April 1917:
     the banner reads
     'Proletarians of all
     Countries, Unite!'

13. Demonstration of women in support of the Petrograd Soviet of Workers' and Soldiers' Deputies, Nevsky Prospect, spring 1917

14. Field of Mars, May Day 1917

15. Trotsky addressing the crowd on his arrival at the Finland Station, May 17, 1917

16. Kerensky (left) as Minister of War in June 1917 exhorting troops at the front, 'in that harsh, unmusical voice that was yet so strangely compelling and enthralling', to prepare for a new offensive

17. Crowds being fired on during the July Days

18. Troops loyal to Kerensky surrounding disarmed men of the 1st Machine-Gun Regiment on Palace Square, July 21, 1917

19. Kerensky striking a Napoleonic pose as he walks among enthusiastic crowds in Petrograd: photograph by E.P. Stebbing

20. Lenin's photograph taken after his arrest in 1895, found in the files of the secret police (*okhrana*) after the Revolution

21. Lenin, in hiding after the July Days, disguises himself by wearing a wig and shaving off his beard and moustache, enabling him to be given a false worker's pass

22. Kerensky at his desk at the Winter Palace, August 21, 1917

23. General Kornilov being carried down the station steps by fellow officers after arriving in his own train from Headquarters on August 26, 1917, for the Moscow State Conference

24. Smolny Convent and Institute before the Revolution

25. Red Guards take up suitably aggressive poses to be photographed on top of a captured British armoured car outside the main entrance to Smolny

26. Red Guards on street patrol

27. Looking through the Red
Arch towards the Winter
Palace: 'Like a black river we
poured through the Red Arch
. . . In the open we began to run
. . . and jammed up suddenly
behind the pedestal of the
Alexander Column' (John Reed)

28. The ransacked Alexander II room inside the Winter Palace

Her log hut was fresh and clean. The small living-room had heavy beams supporting the low ceiling. The wide brown planks of the floor were polished from much scrubbing. The partition walls were painted blue; and so were the doors and the cupboards built into the corners. There were flowered plants in the little windows. I saw a Singer sewing machine. Certainly they had prospered here. They not only farmed and fished; her husband was the foreman of a logging gang on the river and one of the leading men in the village.

They had no children, but on one wall hung a photograph of a young officer with his wife and baby. He was their nephew, Tarasov said. He had been badly wounded and was home on leave. On his grey jacket, which hung by the door, were pinned a medal and three Crosses of St George, for the boy had distinguished himself during the great Brusilov drive down into the Carpathians. It was there he had won his commission. Soon he limped in from the garden, a lean sinewy lad dressed in grey uniform trousers and a soft linen yellow blouse with a sash around the waist. A veteran at twenty-two, he had had three years of war. His face was gaunt, with high cheek-bones and clear, steady blue eyes. Although friendly enough in his greeting, he did not seem to care to talk.

The head of the house then came in, a strong grizzled man in his fifties. Encouraged by Tarasov, he was soon expressing his views on the Revolution. He insisted that the new government must be forced to give the peasants more land; and to prove the justice of his claim he went back many years in his life.

When we pulled down the old hut to build this one, we found in the attic a pile of receipts for the taxes paid to the government for the land we were given in 1861 [the time of the Emancipation of the serfs]. My grandfather, my father and I have paid so many taxes for our five *desyatinas* [thirteen acres] here, that the land could be quite covered with the money that we gave for it. My father and I were made to pay thirty-six roubles every year, and to get that money in the old days cost us plenty of sweat and blood. All through the summer we worked on the farm. From October until May, we fished and logged on the river. And when there was no other work to do, we used to drag up sunken logs from the river bottom. That was a slow, hard job... It took nearly a day to get one log; and for this we received between one and two roubles.

As soon as the ice broke up in the spring, we were always either fishing or working this small farm of ours. So we laboured; so we saved... But this is what I want to say. I say this land is all our own, and that now we ought to have still more, because since 1861 we have paid the government many times its value. The Tsar is our debtor, so now I claim it is quite right and legal for us peasants to take more land for ourselves. Nor will we ask for it as alms. We will take first the lands of the Crown and then the private owners' estates. The trouble will come in dividing it up. How that will be done, I do not know. It must be managed in such a way so as not to stop the farming – for God knows we need all the grain we can raise.

I don't believe that the cities will be able to help us in this, for they know nothing of our real needs... They complain that our wood contractors charge too much for fire wood. But how can they expect us to sell it at a lower price, when here in the stores we have to pay such enormous prices for everything that comes to us from the city? We are afraid to mow fast in the fields; for we know that if we should break our scythes, there are no others to be had. And we have to mow, or we shall starve. Yet now they say in the cities that we should sell at prices fixed by the new government. But we will not sell at *any* price! They won't get any grain from us, so long as things go on like this!

Just take a trip to Petrograd. Go to any railroad siding there and you will see perfect hills of scrap iron. Why can't they melt it up again and put it to use? Soon we shall have no axles left, no tyres for our wagon wheels, no chains for the logs, no ploughs for the fields, no horseshoes for our horses! But still they do nothing! The blind fools! The trouble with those people is that they think all the best things are made in the cities. It is not so. Here we grow the flax and grain; here we raise the meat they eat, and the wool to keep them warm; we cut trees to build their houses and firewood to heat their stoves. They could not even cook without us! Other country districts turn out the coal and the iron ore. All the real things in Russia are done in the villages. What kind of crops do they raise in the towns? Only Grand Dukes, Bolsheviks and drunkards! I tell you it would be possible to have a whole country without any cities – only small towns and villages, all joined together by railroads.

This whole revolution was manufactured in the towns, and it is as flimsy as other town productions. Look how shallow it runs.

They say, 'This is a democracy. We speak for all the people.' But how can they claim to speak for us when we have never heard of them? What right have they to speak in our names and say that the peasants want this and that, when we have not yet opened our mouths?

That is how they are in the towns. They want to change Russia in a day. What idiots! It cannot be done. If I have a piece of virgin soil to turn into arable land, first I shall have to plough it well, then harrow it and seed it down, and by the time I have produced the right rotation of crops on that field, I will have spent perhaps five years – and all for the simple matter of a few *desyatinas* of soil. But here these people in cities are proclaiming such reforms as have never been tried throughout the world – and yet they try to rush them through! Are these town people gods that they will rebuild the whole world in a day, and the minds and habits of all people on it?

They have begun from the wrong end. If they had been wise, at the very start, as soon as they had dethroned the Tsar, they would have brought iron discipline into the Russian army, both at the front and at the rear; and in the towns they would have said to all the loafers, 'You must work!'

What armies of idlers are in the towns. I shouldn't wonder if four-fifths of the people in Petrograd simply loafed, all of them waiting for Russia to starve, while out here every pair of hands could be used at a big profit. I am sure that by next March, Petrograd will have nothing to eat. Then swarms of these loafers will come to us. And what shall we do? For half of them are soldiers, and our peasant pitchforks are no good against their rifles. Perhaps the outcome of it will be that we shall be forced to feed these beasts and starve ourselves – all because they are loafing now!

The peasant broke off with an anxious scowl; and his nephew, the young ensign, said in a quiet, toneless voice:

Why should you let them take your grain? Why not fight for it like men? I can raise a company here that will stand against that city crowd. They are nothing but garrison troops who have never seen a gun pointed their way. . .

It is hard to tell what will happen before all this has come to an end. But some of us will keep waiting until we see a real chance for an army. It may be a year – it may be two. But we are waiting, men like me, all over Russia.

As they were about to leave, another friend arrived, a former peasant who was now part-owner of a saw-mill down the river. They visited him and his family next day. On the baby grand piano in the front room stood a large gramophone with a horn of vivid green. The windows had lace curtains; in each was a geranium plant. The elder daughter had married a Guards officer the year before. Now her younger sister was eagerly telling Tarasov about the previous winter. She had nothing to say of the Revolution; she had apparently missed all that. For her there had been something vastly more engrossing – her first year in boarding-school. Would she, too, Poole wondered, marry a Guards officer? Would there be any Guards? What was coming in Russia? Certainly such people as these would oppose any extreme levelling down. Even the good-natured mother, whose main concern was to keep their glasses constantly replenished with tea, spoke with a sharp bitterness against the river hooligans who had tried to start riots in the area – 'with their lies and their crazy nonsense about robbing honest people like us of what we have spent our lives to get!'

They left these brand-new bourgeois, with their vigour and zest and smiling self-reliance, and walked off down the river-bank. Poole liked the saw-mill owner and his family, but he was growing hungry for a glimpse of the *other* people. 'Let's see a few of these hooligans,' he proposed to Tarasov.

'You have shown me the respectable lot – and they're all very fine – but they're not enough.'

Tarasov walked in silence. His expression had grown grim.

'All right,' he said.

In the dusk, which was fast deepening, we tramped along the river-bank. Presently from down by the water we heard a gay hubbub of voices, sudden laughter now and then; and coming around the corner of an old log stable, we saw a score of men and boys, their faces lighted in the dark by a large bonfire there, with a couple of black iron pots swinging slowly over the flames. Close by the door of the stable was a short stocky man with black hair, who was busy with an axe and knife cutting up the carcass of a cow. He claimed that they had bought it from a peasant up the river. As he tossed the great chunks of meat into a barrel beside him, and sprinkled in coarse salt from a bag, he explained that they were raft men who had put in to camp for the night. Soon the crowd caught sight of us and called to us to come and sit down.

So we had another tea party, but there was nothing bourgeois here! This spot had often been used before by such gangs for a bivouac. A huge log served as a table, and on logs on either side sat two rows of men and boys hungrily devouring enormous chunks of black bread, and drinking from their dirty tin cups strong tea and a meat soup they had made. There were two small pails of blackberries into which each dipped his hand. They were a noisy rollicking crowd.

'Where are you from?' Tarasov asked.

'Most of us from Novgorod,' cried a short tow-headed chap, with a bullet head and wide square jaws. 'Where the devil else could we have come from? See what hooligans we are. Only in Novgorod, brother, does God make such specimens!'

'That's a lie,' said a tough red-headed boy, who looked about fifteen years old. His mouth was quite full at the moment; with an effort he gulped down his food. 'We come from all over,' he declared. 'I come myself from just down the river. God only knows where I shall end. Before I get through I shall make every river in Holy Russia give me a ride. That's the fellow I am!'

Then a thin, stoop-shouldered, gaunt-looking man, with a ghost of a twinkle in his eye, said solemnly to Tarasov:

'It was sad news for us, *barin*, when our beloved little Tsar was kicked off his golden throne. Sorrow weighed down upon our souls to such a degree that we left our raft and climbed far up a wooded hill to a holy monastery there, which had the same name as our Tsar. Saint Nicholas was its patron saint. And so, to the glory of Nick the Saint and of Little Nick the Tsar, we went in and took the holy relics, stuff all made of gold and silver – jewels stuck in everywhere. And we piled them all upon our raft, so that none of those sinful Bolsheviks should get a chance to rob the good God. When we came near to Petrograd, we hid them all in a little wood. And there, when it had been arranged, we sold them one night to three Petrograd Jews. Then we made them kneel on the ground and beg us not to cut their throats. We let them load the holy stuff into an old automobile – and off they went, while we sang them a song.'

'These Bolsheviks,' growled a man with a square head and a short heavy beard already half grey. 'Bolsheviks, Bolsheviks – how they shout about being free men. What do they know about being free? They know nothing but books, they sit indoors and scribble and read and talk like clerks – and they are so busy making us free that they have no time to be free themselves! Let them come and find what freedom is! We'll show 'em!'

There was a chorus of cries.

'Turn their stomachs inside out,' declared the tough red-headed boy. 'Then take those stomachs in a pile down to the river and scrub them well – and give them back to the little men, and say, "Now, brothers, see how good it feels to be free of all your thinking!"'

One of the youngsters started a song, and the rest came in on the refrain – to the glory of their wandering life. Here indeed were Ishmaelites, abhorred by respectable villagers. There were perhaps a million such men on the long winding rivers of Russia, from Archangel to the Volga and far down to Astrakhan. Their ranks were recruited constantly from villages along the way; for the river called, and the peasant boys strolled into the bivouacs at night, and soon they joined the wanderers; working and sleeping on their rafts, stopping now and then to buy or steal the meat and other provisions they needed. They earned good wages, and some of them sent money home to their families, but most had sprees in the larger towns – or at least they did in the old vodka days.

Tarasov, as we walked away, told of other wanderers – of the armies of labour that roamed about from one big job to another, on railroads, bridges, dams, canals; and of the travelling blacksmiths and tailors and shoemakers who made a semi-hobo class... They would be multiplied tenfold, for as the armies disbanded, innumerable recruits would come to join these wandering hooligans. I wondered what part they would play in the tumultuous months ahead. The Great Revolution had so many parts, so many jarring factors. I recalled the radical working men whom I had seen in the cities, the thrifty prosperous peasants that my friend had shown me here, and the many more in Russia who lived in darkest poverty... And I wondered what these elements, clashing one upon the other, would make of it all before they got through.

One element already being crushed out of existence was the aristocracy. Tarasov's nearest neighbour was Prince C. They heard that not long before their arrival his home had been raided by a crowd of young peasants and soldiers, and decided to visit him.

His two-storey yellow frame house, weatherbeaten and forlorn, stood on the bluff overlooking the river, with white birches and firs behind it. As we drew near, we caught sight of him standing motionless under the trees, a grey-headed figure in a white blouse, impassively smoking a cigarette. Although he saw us coming, he gave no sign of welcome. His greeting was wholly indifferent; his voice little more than a murmur. He shook hands in a way that seemed to say, 'What does anything matter nowadays?'

He was nearly alone, he told us. All his servants had left him but one – the young widow of a soldier who had recently been killed at the front. She lived here with her three small children, and cooked for the Prince and looked after his house. He asked us to come in for a while. It was a desolate place inside. The rooms, with their stiff ugly old chairs, tables, sofas, mirrors, all looked empty and comfortless, like mere relics of the past. The Prince had once been very gay, and there had been wild parties here of men and women from Petrograd, with music and dancing all the night. Mere memories now, the ghost of old days. He spent his time reading or walking about or staring down on the river. Under the Old Regime, he said, he had had an official position here. That was why the peasants had raided his home.

'We have come to get your accounts of our money!' they shouted, as they burst into the house. 'If you are a thief, by Christ we will kill you!'

As the Prince told his story, a slight smile of amusement came upon his wrinkled face. He described how they had scowled and panted over his desk, elbowing each other aside. Soon they had gathered his papers all up and had bundled them into a burlap bag, which they had taken off to the village. He had heard nothing from them since.

'And they are our government,' he remarked.

Now we were out again under the trees. He lit another cigarette and relapsed into his indifference. We left him there in the gathering dusk.

They learned more of what had happened to the Prince from the tea-house proprietor, who as well as being a member of the food supplies committee, had been chosen by the peasants at the start of the Revolution to be head of the local militia, assisted by the man who kept the Co-operative store.

From the revolutionary committee of the district we got two swords and two revolvers – not very much for an army – but we managed to keep the peace until about three weeks ago, when a mob of peasants and hooligans tried to break into the store. We stood in front and kept them off – while they buzzed and talked and shouted.

'This is a very bad business,' we told them. 'You'd better go home and keep the peace.' And most of the older peasants went home. But the younger ones decided to raid the house of your neighbour, Prince C. As you will remember, some years ago, by order of the government the Prince had been appointed the honorary chairman and treasurer of the Co-operative. And last winter, when the time came to pay us a dividend, the Prince had insisted that the money be used instead to build a People's House with a moving picture show. The peasants had been enraged at the scheme because it was done without their consent. So now they decided to search his house and go through his account books. There were nearly six hundred there in the street, all shouting and working themselves up. It was an ugly business. I tried to talk sense into them and show them how crazy was their plan.

'What can you do,' I shouted, 'if you all rush into the Prince's house? Suppose you get his papers. How can you understand them? Brothers, you must all wait here and let the storekeeper and me go up and talk this out with the Prince. For we are used to such things as accounts, and we will bring you back the truth.'

But one young peasant shouted at me, 'You fellows know *too much* of accounts! You are merchants! We want none of your tricks! Now it is revolution and we will do these things ourselves!'

So off they rushed like a herd of young bulls. But it took a long time to get them all into boats and across the river; and after that, when they had climbed the long hill and walked a mile in the rain, by the time the first ones reached the place, they were cooled off and they waited around. At last, when the others had come up, they broke into the house and went through his rooms till they found his desk, and from this they took out all the papers. They brought them back to the village, and here all night they shouted and argued and tried to make something of it all. But the columns of figures in those accounts were as mysterious to them as the spells of the village sorcerer. By morning these fine revolutionists had their tongues hanging out of their mouths. They slept all day, and that was the end of the only riot we have had here.

But there is always danger still from these chaps; and the soldiers from the towns are always looking for trouble. The troops who come home from the front on leave are different, they are a steady crowd – but these fellows who have been loafing in towns are nothing but bums and robbers. . .

The trouble is that men like me have no guns behind us, and so it is hard to keep order. The new government in Petrograd does not give us any support. They allow only two militia men here to keep order in thirty-nine villages. We should have at least fifty armed men. We should have telephones, besides, to every little village, and a policeman in each one; and we should have two or three automobiles for bringing them all together at once to any spot where they are needed. As it is, the young river hooligans steal horses and cattle – and what can we do? Besides, if we had a telephone, when a fire broke out in a village they could send a call for help. As it is, if a village starts to burn, there is nothing to do but pray to God.

Three months before, with other heads of militia, he had been summoned to the chief city of the province to 'listen to a fine address by the President of the Zemstvo there, who would tell us poor peasants what to do'. But the President apologized and sent in his place a young assistant, who told them they must talk to all troublemakers in a quiet sensible way, ask them to be patient, and so prevent all riots and mobs.

I got sick of his talk.

'Now then, fellow,' I called out, 'for Christ's sake tell us something real. What are my duties and what are my powers as head of militia? There is no judge in my neighbourhood now. Am I to be judge? Some peasants have come with their quarrels and asked me to judge them. Shall I do it or shall I not? I did not know, so I did it. I judged their cases as best I could.'

Then the other sixty militia heads began to speak up, one by one, and to say that they had done the same. And we asked the young assistant whether it was legal. But he confessed he did not know. He went to get the President, and that great official now deigned to come in. He had a big belly and fat wrists; as he walked, he had to carry four chins. He was a well-fed gentleman. Gold spectacles were in his hand. He looked at us with amusement and said:

'Oh, that's all right, fellows. Just do your best.' He walked out of the hall. And that's all the practical information we ever got out of the town! We came home thanking God and the Saints that we had been born in villages!

Since then we have settled things for ourselves. And we have been supported by all the more sensible peasants here. Quietly we are planning things out. We have made up our minds we must get more land and also better farm machines. But in Petrograd they only talk, and God knows what the results will be. For the peasants are getting so sick of it all. It is hard to hold the young ones in. Soon they may join the hooligans and the barracks soldiers in the towns, and then with the Bolsheviks they may smash the government. And all because this government will not stop its empty talk and give us what the peasants need! This fellow Kerensky, they tell me, is a well-meaning honest man, and a wonderful speaker, too. When he speaks, he lifts you into the clouds. But the clouds are a very foggy place from which to settle the question of land.

*

At about the time when Poole and Tarasov were clambering on board the steamer at the start of their return journey to Petrograd, Philips Price decided to feel the pulse of Russia by setting out from Petrograd for the central provinces and the towns and villages alongside the Volga. By mid-September he had reached Samara, the great wheat centre of south-east Russia, where you could still buy white bread, a luxury long since unobtainable in the north.

His first object was to get in touch with the Samara Soviet of Peasants' Deputies.

I found their bureau installed in the old Tsarist Governor's house, which it shared along with the Soviet of Workmen's and Soldiers' Deputies. The people who were inspiring the Peasants' Soviet were all members of the SR Party, of the Centre or Chernov group. There were two or three very intelligent women and some young peasant soldiers who were taking an active part in the work of the Soviet. I noticed in talking to them on the agrarian problem that they adopted a somewhat apologetic tone, as if something were happening on the land for which they were not responsible. 'They accuse us in Petrograd of being robbers and of destroying the landlords' properties,' said one of the Deputies, 'but the fact is, we have done everything to restrain the peasants and have, at the last conference of the SR Party for the province, drawn up a memorandum of general directions to be followed by the local Land Committees. In this we have laid down that landlords' estates are to be temporarily taken on public account.' They then asked me if I would visit the villages and see for myself what was going on there. A young peasant soldier member of the Soviet was going home for a few days and offered to take me with him.

Late in the evening we arrived at his village after driving across the open country in a *tarantass*. We drove down the broad, unpaved village street, on both sides of which stood rows of wooden gabled houses. The street was almost empty. An old peasant was returning home from ploughing, and a small boy was trying to direct a huge drove of sheep and cattle back from pasture with the aid of a tiny twig. Some women were digging manure in a back yard. A feeling of depression lay everywhere. It is true that a red flag, flying from the roof of the windmill on the outskirts of the village, was a joyful sign of the great deliverance last March. But on entering the house of my host, an old peasant, I soon felt that the gloom which had been temporarily lifted by the fall of Tsarism, was settling down again with the prospect of an indefinite continuation of the war. In the living room the walls were still covered with religious pictures, and the little oil lamp burnt before the icon in the corner. But beside all these I saw nailed up on a background of red cloth the appeal of the Petrograd Soviet of Workmen's and Soldiers' Deputies to the proletariat of all the world to lay down their arms – the symbol of the new religion, whose influence was penetrating even to remote villages of the great plain.

We sat down on the wooden benches and waited. A purring samovar and a pot of cabbage soup with bits of meat were brought by the womenfolk, and the family gathered round the table and silently ate. Two years ago there had sat at this board the old father and mother, their sons, daughters-in-law and grandchildren. Of the four sons of the house only one was still alive, because he was unfit for service. The whole work of managing the homestead and cultivating the portion allotted to the family by the commune had fallen on the old man, the surviving son, and the three widows. A boy of twelve, the eldest son of the first son, spent the days looking after the sheep in the distant meadows. The united families thus lived under the same roof and carried on a common domestic economy, the ties which united them having apparently been strengthened by the calamities and losses inflicted on them by the war. . .

On the following day the old peasant and his son went off to one of their allotments to plough. I accompanied them. We arrived on the spot soon after dawn and found the bread-winners of three other families already there. To my surprise, my host and his son began to plough along by the side of the others – four teams in all going on the same plot. These four families had clubbed together in a little ploughing *artel*, and all had agreed to plough, reap and harvest their respective allotments in common. Here, therefore, was another communal unit, a group of families living under different roofs, and associating to work their land in common. Each family, however, retained the products of its allotment for itself. The ploughing went on with several breaks till nightfall. Then the horses were tethered and turned loose to graze, and we went into a little hut, made out of mud and wattle. A meal was cooked on an open fire, and we lay down to rest on the straw-covered floor and listened to the hooting of the night owls, the chirping of the crickets, and the gentle sigh of the soft autumn wind coming across the steppe.

These little communal units were themselves part of a larger commune. On Sunday the *selsky skhod*, now renamed the 'village Soviet', met outside the common barn in the middle of the village street.

The heads of families and every working hand, including sons, if there were any now, were present. I also saw quite a number of women. These were either widows or women who were doing field work in their husbands' absence. Here, in fact, was the most elementary unit of Russian rural society. It has existed for centuries and is rooted deep in the Middle Ages. It is essentially democratic, for women here have equal rights with men. The Revolution when it came had only to make use of this institution and it penetrated at once into the village. But it was easy to see how primitive were its foundations, and how much remains to be done before the new spirit of organization which a modern State demands can get a hold on Russian rural society.

The proceedings of this commune, if picturesque, were not exactly business-like. Bearded patriarchs with fur caps were divided into groups, chatting loudly; one was holding forth on the vexed question of corn prices, another on the price of soap; some women in picturesque peasant costume were complaining about the absence of sugar in the village; gypsies were selling furs; soldiers back on leave were relating stories of life on the front. Mangy dogs were walking in and out of the crowd; a ragged beggar suddenly interfered in the middle of a discussion on the land regulations and asked for alms in the name of the Mother of God. Then the village priest broke in, and, gathering round him a little crowd, appealed for funds in support of the parish school. 'Eh, little father,' said someone, 'you want to show us the way up there, but we have had a revolution and are contented down here for a while.'

The president of the commune, sitting on a wooden box and chewing nuts, would occasionally bawl out, 'Comrades, to order; let us get to the business of the day,' and would then relapse to his nuts again. It was only my companion from the Soviet of Peasant Deputies who succeeded, after some difficulty, in getting this confused mass together and explaining to them that the provincial Land Committee wanted an inventory of the livestock and seed-corn in the commune. After endless conversation something was drawn up.

When he reported to them, however, that the Peasants' Soviet in Samara had recommended that a final decision on the landlords' estates be deferred until the convening of the Constituent Assembly, there was a general outcry. 'What guarantee have we that the Constituent Assembly will meet?' said one peasant. 'We have worked that land for the *barin* for the last fifteen years, and it is time that we had it for ourselves.'

Finally, it was agreed that the regulations of the Soviet of Peasants' Deputies in Samara should be disregarded, and that the landlords' demesne and latifundium for that district should be annexed to the commune. But what was to happen to the live and dead stock on the demesne farm? asked someone; it would be ruinous to divide it. But that had not entered into anyone's calculations. The chief thing in the mind of the peasants was to get the land into their own hands, and so to face the authorities with a *fait accompli*. Then it would be possible to keep the land-hungry proletarians of Petrograd and Moscow from coming and claiming a share, and counter-revolutionary generals, if any came in the future, would have a difficult task to return the land to the landlords. In this decision everyone seemed to be united. The well-to-do peasant with an ample waist, spotless blue serge tunic and peaked hat agreed, because he hoped that the lion's share of that land would come to him, as none but he had sufficient horses and capital to work it. The members of the family where I was staying thought the same, for, although they were poor and had not enough land, still they had enough strong hands to manage another couple of *desyatinas* next year. And the poor peasant with only one horse, who sat on a soap box against the barn, also agreed, because he hoped that, if he got a share of the landlords' livestock, he would be able to cultivate his allotment next year, instead of having to let it to the well-to-do peasant with the ample waist, who would pay him next to nothing in rent. All classes in the village were agreed, though for different reasons. The village commune was still a happy family on this Sunday afternoon. The process of splitting up into classes had not yet come, for the classes, rich, poor and middle peasant, although they had already appeared, had a common object, namely, the liquidation of the last relics of feudalism.

On the following day Philips Price went to visit one of those relics, the man who had until recently been the local squire. His house, surrounded by groves of poplar trees, was in the middle of a wide expanse of beautiful black earth steppe, very different from the thin earth, with sand just below the surface, of the peasant allotments.

I walked through the shrubbery up to the wooden, two-storied manor house, plastered with stucco. Grass was growing on the roof, and in the dilapidated greenhouse a cow was finishing off what remained of the ferns. An old servant answered the bell and took the 'English reporter' to the squire, who was in his study packing up to go away the next day. He was an ex-soldier of general's rank, who had been educated in that most aristocratic of institutions in Tsarist Petersburg, the Corps of Pages, had served in the Life Guards, and had been through the Russo-Turkish war with the old Grand Duke Nicholas. What a change he had lived to see in Russia! 'I am going to leave and turn my back on this place for good,' he said, after he had asked me to be seated, 'because I hear that the commune has passed a resolution that all spare rooms in this house are to be turned over for the use of a new school. At any rate, in the Crimea I can find rest, unless this anarchy has broken out there. If no parts of Russia remain safe, I shall have to ask the hospitality of your country.' He used not to like Englishmen, he said, because Lord Beaconsfield robbed Russia of the fruits of Plevna and the Shipka Pass, but the enemy was much nearer home today, and he seemed to look on Englishmen as his friends, and supporters of 'law and order'. He sighed as he quoted the lines of Pushkin's poem, the *Brother Robbers*: 'We live without power or law; like flocks of ravens they come and sweep over the land.' He was referring to the Peasants' Soviets and to my companion whom I had left behind in the village. 'These people,' he said, 'are the ruin of Russia; everything used to be so quiet and so contented. I gave the peasants seed-corn and manure when they were in difficulties. No one wanted any change. Then people came from the town and stirred it all up. Those stupid Kadets ought to have stopped this rabble long ago in the first days of the Revolution.'

This relic of the old Russian agrarian aristocracy, of the type that one reads of in Turgenev's novels, was just on the eve of being swept away... yet one had a pang at the thought of the complete disappearance of this type, for on the bookshelf opposite me lay a collection of poems written in his youthful days by the occupant of this old manor. They were fruits of that leisure which has given many gems of art, literature and music to Russia and to the world. Was it not in surroundings like these that the great master of letters, Leo Tolstoy, lived and laboured? But the sands were running out... the cold wind from Sovietdom was blowing now and was sternly sweeping aside these hot-house plants of nineteenth-century aristocratic culture.

Even the monks of the local Holy Trinity Monastery had had their revolution, throwing out their corrupt abbot and setting up a kind of Monks' Soviet under the presidency of a brawny young fellow who would have been more at home, Philips Price thought, at the plough than in a monastery.

'As far as this part of Russia was concerned,' he concludes, 'it was clear that the agrarian revolution had already begun by September 1917.'[2] More primitive and less organized than the peasants in the north described by Ernest Poole, with their food supplies committee and co-operative ventures, their three-storey school-house and amateur theatricals, these peasants in the Samara Province had gone further down the revolutionary road by taking the law and the land into their own hands.

9

Kornilov

Early August to end of September: the Moscow Conference (opens August 25), the
Kornilov Affair and the Democratic Assembly (opens September 27)[1]

After the storms of July there was a brief lull; and although, as
Bernard Pares comments, 'that of itself, in a revolution, promised but
little, the public got a certain sense of sequence and of recovery.'[1]
Kerensky managed at length to form a new Coalition Government,
consisting of six Socialist and eight non-Socialist ministers. There
would be universal praise, Ransome felt sure, for the appointment as
Minister of Education of the Kadet, Oldenburg, who also happened
to be a friend of his and a great authority on Russian folklore.[2] The
Bolsheviks, though far from suppressed (early in August they held a
secret conference in Petrograd), appeared quiet, their leaders either
in hiding or under arrest, while the appointment as Commander-in-
Chief of the redoubtable General Kornilov promised to bring some
order into the chaos at the front.

August that year was exceptionally hot, too hot, even, for demonstrating. Brushing aside the memory of his ill-timed visit in March,
Sir George Buchanan took a week's holiday in Finland. The work of a
newspaper correspondent had to continue, but after sending off his
telegram on August 11, 'and mopping up the consequent nose-bleed-
ing which too often accompanies that job', Arthur Ransome resolved
to strike; he flung some tackle into a bag, grabbed his rod, telephoned
a friend, and set off for Lakhta. 'The train', he wrote to his mother,

> crosses a long bridge over the river where we fish, and the station
> is two miles further along a very dusty road, and I filled myself
> with joy by jumping out of the train at the bridge, and landing

BEEootifully, running like a hare and not even falling on hands and knees. So I saved the two miles walk, and lay on the bank of the river until my astonished friend turned up hot and dusty from the station. I know what you are remembering... that shameful tramway episode of early youth. Well, this was better, and I felt so bucked about it, it put a glow on the whole day. We got a boat, and found a jolly place by reeds, and we caught fifteen fish, perch, half a dozen of them being really respectable ones. Then coming back I got a cab with a really good horse, which in these days is a rarity, and had a spanking run home. Altogether a ripping half holiday...[3]

The next event of importance did not take place in Petrograd, but in Moscow. Moscow had accepted the March Revolution very smoothly. 'Not a shot did we hear,' writes an English schoolmaster, R.O.G. Urch, 'and as far as we know none was fired.'[4] When Pares arrived in the summer, however, Moscow was 'in an extraordinary state... everything was becoming more and more dingy, though the transition had a certain coarse glamour of its own.'[5] To Kerensky, anxious to give his new personal leadership a national and not only political character, the ancient capital seemed nonetheless a more suitable venue than the sick city of Petrograd for the staging of a grand State Conference, at which, in traditional style, he would call upon leading figures from all walks of life to rally to the defence of Russia in her hour of need. Delegates were summoned from a wide variety of public bodies. Each group was to nominate a speaker to present its ideas on a common national programme, but there would be no voting.

Arriving in Moscow on August 24, the eve of the Conference, Philips Price found alarming rumours going about the city. 'The atmosphere was electric. One instinctively felt that unseen powers were at work, one acting from the right and the other from the left.' The Bolsheviks distributed leaflets denouncing the proceedings as a counter-revolutionary fraud, and succeeded in calling out a number of workers on a one-day strike, including those in hotels and restaurants, but the organizers of the Conference had taken the sensible precaution of laying in a large supply of sandwiches and refreshments.

The Conference was being held in the Bolshoi Theatre, with its impressive Imperial décor and huge seating capacity. Philips Price sets the scene there on the 25th:

The spectacle was brilliant. The whole of the right side of the stalls was filled with the representatives of the four Dumas and the middle-class parties – all respectable people with frock-coats and collars. On the left came the Soviet delegates of the unshaven chin and the working-day shirt, with a fair sprinkling of common soldiers. In the middle, as if crushed between two millstones, came the Co-operators and the free professional associations. In the boxes and the balcony sat the groups of the small nationalities and various officers' associations. In the former Imperial box sat the diplomatic representatives of the foreign Powers and the agents of the Allied Military Missions. On the platform were the Ministers of the Provisional Government, and behind them the press delegates and visitors.[6]

One visitor with a good seat was R.O.G. Urch, who describes how the poet Balmont, looking 'quite pretty, with his long hair and short, pointed beard', warmed up the audience before Kerensky's appearance by reading selections from his own poems. Urch, who cannot have seen Kerensky before, was somewhat taken aback:

He came on to the stage in a sort of improvised or home-made semi-military tunic. While cheers were raised again and again and clapping filled the theatre for some minutes, the tired man stood there in an attitude far from heroic, looking like one dazed or despondency personified.

He had come from a gruelling week of speeches at the front and no wonder he looked tired. But why should he be despondent?

A hush came, and he began to speak; but even during his speech I think he never raised his eyes to the level, to say nothing of looking up at the balconies and boxes.

'*Razviye. . .*' (Can it be. . .), he rasped out without warning, as the noise died down.

He paused for what seemed minutes, then went on to tell of what he had seen at the front. He told of heroes in the Army and heroes in the rear, of the determination of new-born Russia to continue fighting in the cause of the Allies, to fight the whole way to a general victory. His hearers were spellbound. They had, it was clear, expected and wanted to be spellbound, for Kerensky had then reached, if not passed, the peak of his fame and popularity in Russia.[7]

The speech, though unscripted, was very long – according to one source, it took two hours to deliver[8] – and at the end Kerensky was given a remarkable ovation; but it did not meet with quite the universal approbation that Urch suggests. Some of his remarks were received in pointed silence by those on the right, rather more remarks in pointed silence by those on the left. After Kerensky had finally left the stage, a man came on with a large photograph of him to be auctioned for the war fund; it fetched a huge sum.[9]

Harold Williams, of course, had heard Kerensky many times before, and he gives this assessment:

Kerensky was not in his best speaking form. He seemed to be hampered by the effort of speaking, not as his natural self, but as the virtual ruler of Russia. His phraseology was at times unnecessarily ornate and stilted, his assertion of his personal authority and of the unlimited power of the Provisional Government was a little forced. Not in its calculated eloquence, but in its strange revelation of the Premier's personality in hard and difficult conditions the speech was tragic. In form it was a stern challenge, an aggressive assertion of authority. In effect it was almost a plaintive appeal for support.[10]

On Sunday, while the various parties and groups were meeting privately, General Kornilov, escorted by a faithful bodyguard of Turcomans, arrived from Headquarters in his own train. According to Wilton of *The Times*, Moscow gave him an enthusiastic welcome. Accompanied by more automobiles than Kerensky, he drove first to the Iberian Chapel, where he entered the tiny sanctuary alone to pray to the wonder-working icon of the Iberian Virgin for the regeneration of Russia, before entering Red Square on foot. This had always been a part of the Tsar's ceremonial entry into Moscow. Kerensky, Wilton writes,

was coming out of the Imperial apartments in the Kremlin to go for a drive in one of the Emperor's motor-cars when he heard the cheers of the multitude. He immediately gave orders to drive in the opposite direction. The great day was to be on the morrow. That evening I was having tea with some of the gorgeously attired Turcoman princes in Kornilov's saloon carriage when Kerensky summoned him to the telephone and 'requested' the Generalissimo not to speak at the Conference. He replied that he did not intend to discuss politics, but only the affairs of the Army. Surely he had the right and the duty to do so. Kerensky could not find a convenient rejoinder. But Kornilov felt that relations were becoming 'strained', and, for the first time, showed some signs of nervousness. His entourage determined to redouble their precautions, fearing lest some attempt should be made to arrest him.[11]

Next day, Philips Price writes, there was a profound hush in the Theatre as Kerensky's voice was heard saying: 'I call upon the Commander-in-Chief in the field, General Kornilov.'

Upon the tribune rose a wiry little man with strong Tartar features. He wore a general's full-dress uniform with a sword and red-striped trousers. His speech was begun in a blunt soldierly manner by a declaration that he had nothing to do with politics. He had come there, he said, to tell the truth about the condition of the Russian army. Discipline had simply ceased to exist. The army was becoming nothing more than a rabble. Soldiers stole the property, not only of the State, but also of private citizens, and scoured the country plundering and terrorizing. The Russian army was becoming a greater danger to the peaceful population of the western provinces than any invading German army could be. Thereupon there were cries from the Soviet benches of, 'You officers are responsible,' followed by uproar. Kerensky rose, and amid dead silence asked the Conference to receive with sorrow rather than with anger the Commander-in-Chief's description of a great national tragedy. Abandoning the combative strain, General Kornilov began more objectively to review the situation and made a series of astonishing revelations. The stocks of food and forage, he said, were so low and the transport in the rear so inferior that not only had an offensive been impossible for a long time past, but it was doubtful whether the army could be demobilized in an orderly manner. Everyone held his breath at this statement. Here, from the mouth of an Entente-phil Commander-in-Chief, one heard that in actual fact Russia could no longer continue the war! He then referred to the Soviets as institutions the value of which 'should be recognized', but whose 'spheres of activity should be strictly defined'. The impression left on my mind was that Kornilov was honestly trying to find a way out of the impasse, but that he was being pushed by unseen powers behind him, and that he was vain enough to allow himself to be flattered by them.

Kornilov was followed by General Kaledin on behalf of the Cossacks. He took a more uncompromising line: all Soviets should be abolished, in the rear as well as at the front. Chkheidze reminded him that it was the Soviet which had carried through the Revolution, and that it alone could guarantee its safe development.

On the final day of the Conference (Tuesday, August 28) there was great enthusiasm when Bublikov, on behalf of the industrialists, congratulated Tsereteli on his noble appeal to all sides to sink their differences in fighting for a general peace, and shook him warmly by the hands. Was this the golden bridge, Philips Price wondered, that was going to span the gap between the classes? Comrade Ryazanov, however, did not share the general enthusiasm. We of the extreme Left – he dared not describe himself openly as a Bolshevik – are simply waiting for the war on the eastern front to liquidate itself, he told the Conference, which greeted his words in stony silence. But a more dramatic illustration of the antagonisms underlying the Conference came when Esaul Nagaev, a young Cossack soldier from the ranks, rose to speak on behalf of the Cossack Workers' Section of the Soviet.

Dressed in the plain tunic of a Cossack of the 'restful Don', he turned towards the box where General Kaledin, surrounded by officers of the League of the Cross of St George, was seated and courageously looked him straight in the face. In his fiery glance I seemed to see the Russian spirit of rebellion against class privilege and oppression – the spirit 'that despises suffering, tyranny and death'. 'I tell you, General Kaledin, from this tribune,' he said quietly and firmly, 'do not dare to speak in the name of the working Cossacks and troopers of the rank and file. We delegates of the Cossack Workers' Soviet, which is daily increasing in numbers and influence, repudiate your authority, usurped behind our backs.' 'Traitor! Arrest him! How many German marks did he get for this speech?' came from the box where the Knights of St George were seated. A scene of indescribable confusion followed. The whole of the left body of the hall rose, yelled and shook their fists at the officers and generals. After several minutes of deafening uproar, Kerensky's voice could be heard, half screaming for silence. 'As chairman of the State Conference,' he said, 'I call upon the person who uttered that remark from the box to come forward and apologize.' There was dead silence, as everyone's eyes were turned upon the spot where General Kaledin and the Knights of St George sat. The General sat calm and stolid. His conscience was evidently clear. But most of the Knights of St George had vanished – no one knew where. After a few minutes Kerensky quietly said, 'Esaul Nagaev, I hope you are satisfied with the silence of a coward.' A deafening cheer sounded throughout the theatre, and Nagaev finished his speech without further interruption.

The Conference had failed, Philips Price concluded, in its task of reconciliation.[12]

Harold Williams, while describing it as a brilliant display – 'the Constituent Assembly will almost certainly be at a lower level' – was likewise conscious that it had shown up 'a sharp and clear dividing line between right and left'. His article written on September 2 shows him more despondent than ever before:

Life in Russia is a troubled dream. One sleeps to see in fresh and bewildering disorder the visions of the day, and one wakes to find the phantoms of the night, tangible and audible, continuing their irrational play in the very light of the sun.

There is a deep logic in events – the logic of history – but there is little in Russia now that lends itself to the calculations of a narrow, practical reason. Men are little, reputations are ephemeral, the comforting shelter of illusions is torn down, the elemental forces of national psychology are laid bare. The whole process is far too big for any of us to grasp, and we wonder and wait. People go on with their daily tasks, make their little plans and projects, but the wind of fate is sighing through the crevices of all their schemes, and they talk the louder so as not to hear it. . .

Municipal elections are being held in Petrograd now. . .   The Bolsheviks, or Extremists, are hard at work once more. . .   Last evening I looked in at an electoral meeting on the outskirts of the town. A schoolroom was full of working men and suburban peasants and tradesmen. A young Jew was speaking, and glibly, dexterously, and suggestively instilled the Bolshevik poison. He taunted the SRs and the Mensheviks with their new policy of compromise with the bourgeoisie.

'Of course, comrades,' he said, 'they tell you that you can't get Socialism at once. We are like men crushed under the heavy stone of capitalism. Some say we can't lift the stone at once, we must do it gradually. But we Bolsheviks say, if all workers unite, we can in one great effort throw off the weight and bring Socialism immediately. They tell you that Russia is economically backward, that you can't have Socialism now because Russia is poor and half ruined. That's untrue, comrades. All the trouble comes of the accursed war, and if all workers of all countries unite to stop the war we shall be free. Who made the war? The capitalists of all countries put their heads together and decided that this was their last chance to keep the wretched working man in chains. The capitalists made the war, and the workers shall stop it. No, comrades, stand by us, vote for us and not with the cowards who compromise with the rich oppressors of the people.'

And so on and so on. There was loud applause from a section of the audience, and the rest were grim and silent. 'Nice promises,' said a woman at the door, 'but why didn't he boast how they shot down defenceless women in the street a month ago?'[13]

In his report to the Foreign Office of September 3, Buchanan found it curious that all the party leaders seemed to think they had scored a success at the Moscow Conference, but nobody was agreed as to what the Conference had actually accomplished.

Kerensky, whose head has been somewhat turned of late and who has been nicknamed 'the little Napoleon'... made a distinctly bad impression by the way in which he presided over the Conference and by the autocratic tone of his speeches. According to all accounts, he was very nervous; but whether this was due to overstrain or to the rivalry which undoubtedly exists between him and Kornilov it is difficult to say...

Kornilov's conduct, moreover, was hardly calculated to lull the suspicions with which he was regarded by Kerensky. He made a dramatic entry into Moscow, surrounded by his Turcoman guard... There is little love, I imagine, lost between the two men, but our chief safeguard lies in the fact that, for the moment at any rate, neither can get on without the other...

Rodzianko and others have been talking far too openly about a counter-revolution and have been saying that a military *coup d'état* is the only thing that can save Russia... In a telegram which General Barter sent me on his return to Headquarters from Moscow, he spoke as if some sort of *coup d'état* might be attempted at any moment [on August 22, during a brief visit to Headquarters, Stopford noted that according to the other Allied representatives, General Barter 'has the complete confidence of Kornilov, whom he sees twice a day and plays cards with'.[14]] I have told him that anything of the kind would be fatal at present, and would inevitably lead to civil war and entail irreparable disaster.[15]

On that same day, September 3, Riga was evacuated by the Russian army. The Germans were now within striking distance of Petrograd. Bessie Beatty, an American journalist who had been living at the restored Astoria Hotel since June, became aware of a new kind of queue: the trunk queue. There were already bread queues, made up of working-women, servants, a few students, and school-children poring over their books; tobacco queues consisting largely of soldiers, in cheerful mood as they were buying to sell again; chocolate queues limited to members of the bourgeoisie; kerosene queues of poor people renting rooms without electricity; and theatre-ticket queues, which became shorter as the bread queues grew longer. But the trunk queues were the strangest of all. Here were respectable people whom fear had obliged to forget their respectableness. 'They were afraid of Germans, of Socialists, of peasants, of soldiers. They feared to lose their peace, their comforts, and their lives. They feared to stay in Petrograd, and they feared equally to leave.'[16]

The rumours of a projected *coup d'état* now began to take a more material shape. Buchanan was even told by journalists and others in touch with its promoters that success was guaranteed, and that the Government and Soviet would capitulate without a struggle.

On Wednesday, September 5, a Russian friend of mine, who was the director of one of the principal Petrograd banks, came to see me and said that he found himself in rather an embarrassing position, as he had been charged by certain persons, whose names he mentioned, with a message which he felt that it was hardly proper for him to deliver. These persons, he then proceeded to say, wished me to know that their organization was backed by several important financiers and industrials, that it could count on the support of Kornilov and an army corps, that it would begin operations on the following Saturday, September 8, and that the Government would then be arrested and the Soviet dissolved. They hoped that I would assist them by placing the British armoured cars at their disposal and by helping them to escape should their enterprise fail.

I replied that it was a very naïve proceeding on the part of those gentlemen to ask an Ambassador to conspire against the

Government to which he was accredited and that if I did my duty I ought to denounce their plot. Though I would not betray their confidence, I would not give them either my countenance or support. I would, on the contrary, urge them to renounce an enterprise that was not only foredoomed to failure, but that would at once be exploited by the Bolsheviks. If General Kornilov were wise he would wait for the Bolsheviks to make the first move and then come and put them down.

Sunday, September 9 was a cloudless summer's day. Though it was not a game at which he excelled, Sir George left the Embassy early for a day's golf at Murino, some miles outside Petrograd, where the British colony had laid out a rough course. On his return at 7.30 he found a telephone message from Tereshchenko asking him and the French Ambassador (now M. Noulens) to come to the Foreign Ministry immediately after dinner. Here they learned of the complete breach which had just taken place between Kerensky and Kornilov. Next morning Tereshchenko told them that troops loyal to Kornilov were advancing on Petrograd, and advised the diplomatic body to leave at once for Moscow or Finland. Sir George said that he could not possibly run away and leave the British colony unprotected; Lady Georgina decided that she could not leave Sir George; and Meriel, as usual, played for time.[17] On Tuesday afternoon, anticipating a shortage of food, she and her mother went to the British Red Cross store to collect provisions.

> While we were there the door was suddenly opened by a tall Cossack officer in a dark-brown soutane, the orange ribbon of St George gleaming on his chest, his incredibly slender waist tightly bound by a silver belt. A little startled, we stared at him, wondering what his appearance meant, where he had come from, and how he dared, in that uniform, walk down the streets guarded on all sides by Kerensky's armed workmen.
>
> Apparently unconscious of the sensation his entrance had made, calm, unperturbed and courteous, he clicked his heels together and explained in perfect French that he had come to ask us if we would give Red Cross stores, bandages, medicines and liniments, to General Kornilov's army when they entered the town.
>
> Technically my mother knew that she had really no right to promise any form of support to a man who, in the eyes of the Government to whom my father was accredited, was a rebel and a

traitor; but in our hearts we were all on the side of Kornilov, and besides, there was no denying the fact that this young Cossack officer, with his trim waist, his very blue eyes and perfect manners, was very alluring; and so, after a moment's hesitation, my mother consented...[18]

The promise, however, was never redeemed. By Wednesday it had become clear that the *coup* was going to fail. Fraternization took place between the troops advancing on Petrograd and those sent out to meet them. 'Kornilov's venture,' Buchanan writes, 'had from the outset been marked by the almost childish incapacity of its organizers, and ended in a complete fiasco.'[19] Kornilov himself was placed under arrest awaiting his trial for high treason.

The rights and wrongs of the Kornilov Affair have been hotly debated ever since. Was Kornilov really a rebel? Did Kerensky lay a trap for him? Was there a genuine misunderstanding between them? Or some element of collusion or complicity? What was the role of Vladimir Lvov, the former Procurator of the Holy Synod, who acted as intermediary? 'He misrepresented Kerensky to Kornilov and Kornilov to Kerensky,' Buchanan writes, 'but whether he was a knave or a fool I cannot say. He was in any case an arch mischief-maker.'[20]

Our witnesses take up predictably varied positions. At the Moscow Conference Philips Price had concluded that while Kornilov himself might be an honest man, he was susceptible to the flattery of 'unseen powers' pushing him from behind. Price was in Nizhny Novgorod at the start of his provincial tour when the news broke that Tartar and Cossack divisions were advancing on Petrograd. He observed how at once 'Bolshevik sailors of the Volga fleet joined hands with Menshevik railwaymen and SR peasants to present a united front to reaction.' In Petrograd likewise, he concludes, the Knights of St George and 'the money-bags from England' (one of Kornilov's adjutants, he claims, had arrived from England in early August with a large sum of money that was used to finance a group of 'patriots' in Moscow) had proved powerless against the combined forces of the revolutionary democracy.[21]

Ransome felt that Kornilov was a good man 'placed in a false position by unscrupulous politicians'. To Harold Williams, too, the General's actions seemed quite out of character. 'Kornilov, a man of strong will and great courage, is a child in politics; and he was under the influence of two doubtful individuals, his secretary, Zavoiko, and a member of the First Duma, Aladin.' Kerensky himself told Buchanan in London in 1918 that he had always regarded Kornilov 'as a patriot and an honest man, but as a very bad politician'. Though Buchanan's own sympathies were with Kornilov, he had always discouraged the idea of a military *coup d'état*, believing that Russia's best hope of salvation lay in close co-operation between the two men. For others the situation was more clear cut. General Knox, who was in London at the time of the *coup* reporting to the War Cabinet, blamed the officer elements round Kornilov for exaggerating 'to a criminal degree' the strength of the forces at their disposal; but he blamed the Prime Minister even more for refusing to liquidate the incident quietly and peacefully. 'Unfortunately, Kerensky was far from the great man that the times required.' Bertie Stopford had the windows of his hotel room open all day Tuesday 'in order to hear the first signs of the Cossacks' arrival. As the afternoon advanced and I heard no firing, my heart sank, with a presentiment that the *coup d'état* had failed.' Robert Wilton, a welcome guest, as we have seen, in Kornilov's entourage, made no secret of his sympathies, and *The Times* came down openly and emphatically on the side of Kornilov.[22]

As Buchanan had anticipated, the Kornilov Affair played into the hands of the Bolsheviks. Ransome pointed out that by intensifying class feeling and polarizing public attitudes, 'these two extremes help each other'; moderate opinion was the loser.[23] The Bolsheviks had in any case by this time recovered much of the ground lost in July. Helped by a low turn-out, they failed only narrowly to beat the SRs in the Petrograd municipal elections held before the *coup*; in the Moscow municipal elections held after the *coup*, voters were even more apathetic and the well-organized Bolsheviks scored a runaway victory. By galvanizing the opposition to Kornilov, they had regained political respectability on the Left, so that nothing, Ransome reported on September 13, had roused more applause at a meeting of the Soviet than 'the announcement of the coming possible release of some of those arrested in connection with the July disorders'.[24] Trotsky was released on September 16 and took command of Bolshevik operations in Petrograd; Lenin was still in hiding in Finland. In both the Petrograd and Moscow Soviets, as opposed to the All-Russian Soviet, the Bolsheviks acquired a majority.

Harold Williams sought desperately to find some underlying sense in what seemed to him a more and more incomprehensible situation:

Russia is very much bigger than all the formulas offered in explanation of her strange caprices, and the process by which she is finding herself is broader and deeper than any of us can quite understand. Kerensky said in Moscow that the Provisional Government can afford itself the luxury of risings and plots. That is not true of the Government as a particular group of men or of any one man, but it is true of Russia. Russia can and will survive convulsions that would wreck States that are more compact and highly organized.

It can hardly be said that the men on top are guiding Russia except in a very limited sense. They are rather guided by an inevitable and inexorable course of events. And for us Allies and friends faith in Russia is not so much faith in particular persons as in that larger process, which with all its elements of suffering and tragedy is tending toward final liberation.[25]

Because the Kadets' attitude towards the *coup* had been ambivalent – Milyukov had offered to mediate between Kerensky and Kornilov – the Soviet now refused to recognize the second Coalition Government, and decided to call a conference of its own with a view to determining the composition of a government that would better reflect the wishes of revolutionary democracy. Kerensky, meanwhile, carried on the Government as head of a Council of Five.

'There are moments when one would prefer to be silent about what is happening in Russia,' Williams wrote on September 26, the day before the opening of this Democratic Assembly.

It is possible, perhaps, to cultivate an attitude of cool detachment, to observe events from a purely historical standpoint, to calculate that the calamities of today are a particularly stern form of discipline, and that Russia will be stronger in the end for what she is suffering today. Without some such outlook in the more vitalizing form of active faith in the future, it would be impossible to endure the stress of the present. At times the atmosphere is suffocating, the stress is almost intolerable. Russian patriots of every shade of opinion are subjected to an almost unrelieved moral torture, and none living here, unless he has a heart of stone, can fail to share their suffering. The bright hopes of the revolution are darkened, the collective energy of the people is paralysed, the whole life of the nation is entangled in a network of almost insoluble contradictions, patience and hope are exhausted by a series of fruitless compromises between warring forces. If these forces were only positive instead of being negative, if they only displayed real energy and real organizing power, then the crisis might be short, sharp, and decisive, but it is protracted by an extraordinary lassitude, born of the long war and the oppression of the old regime.

This lassitude was concealed for a time by the excitement of the revolution, but the freshening impulses of the revolution were frittered away in words and too soon paralysed by bitter party strife. And now the general weariness is expressing itself in a profound moral reaction. I lived through the reaction that followed the last revolution, in 1906, and again I see the familiar signs – the chase after pleasure, the reckless gambling, the steady decline of interest in politics, the sudden demand for 'penny dreadfuls' of the Nat Pinkerton type. The other evening, in a workmen's quarter, I saw a ball going on next to a house where a Bolshevik meeting was being held, and, generally speaking, in the workmen's quarters dances are more popular now than political meetings. At the same time, the difficulties of living in the towns, the steady rise in prices, the shortage of food, the impossibility of getting any satisfactory share of material goods in exchange for money, have increased the general discontent and established a general attitude of profound disillusionment.

The Kornilov Affair has intensified mutual distrust and completed the work of destruction. The Government is shadowy and unreal, and what personality it had has disappeared before the menace of the Democratic Assembly. Whatever power there is is again concentrated in the hands of the Soviets, and, as always happens when the Soviets secure a monopoly of power, the influence of the Bolsheviks has increased enormously. Kerensky has returned from Headquarters, but his prestige has declined, and he is not actively supported either by the right or by the left... The Bolsheviks hope to capture it [the Democratic Assembly], and by its means to establish a purely Socialist Ministry, but, so far as can be judged, the feeling of the great majority of the delegates is in favour of a real coalition of all parties...

So we live from day to day, amidst rumours and phantoms and a general depression that at times has the quality of a nightmare.[26]

The Democratic Assembly, held in the Alexandrinsky Theatre in Petrograd, seemed to Williams outwardly not unlike its Moscow predecessor, but it was less imposing, rather more casual, and bore more signs of hasty improvization. The atmosphere of tense anticipation so noticeable in Moscow was lacking. A large number of the Moscow delegates were there, but the right wing was wholly absent, and their places were taken by representatives of various revolutionary organizations, including many Bolsheviks. Out of over a thousand delegates the proportion of Bolsheviks, judging by the response to the various speakers, was a little over a third.[27]

Both Ransome and Williams were in the audience to hear Kerensky's speech on the opening day. 'Dressed in a creased khaki suit,' Williams writes, 'and looking worn and unhealthily stout,' he stood up in the former Imperial box facing the stage, and received an ovation of cheers so energetic that it was not immediately clear, as Ransome points out',

> that a large section of the Assembly was resolutely silent. Then he came through the Theatre and reached the tribune by a bridge arranged over the orchestra. Standing by the tribune, he greeted the Assembly in the name of the Government. Then dramatically leaving the tribune, he stepped forward on the temporary bridge and said: 'I now speak not for the Government but for myself.' I find it hard to write of the speech that followed. I was within a yard of Kerensky as he spoke, I saw the sweat come out on his forehead, I watched his mouth change as he faced now one, now another group of his opponents, and I am still under the powerful impression of Kerensky's tremendous effort.[28]

'Kerensky's speeches are always a puzzle to me,' Williams writes.

> He is much more agreeable in private than on the platform. Personally, I dislike his public manner, the rasping voice, the almost mechanical projection of sounds by a succession of forward thrusts of the chin, and a constant jerking of the right hand, the monotonous declamatory tone, the calculated pauses, and the painful emotionalism. It all looks like second-rate acting, and yet, if I may speak of my personal impression, though I am irritated by the manner there is something in the personality of the man. I wish I could analyse the impression to the end. It is something disturbing, at times oppressive. It is not exhilarating or uplifting in any Western sense; in fact there were moments today when I felt

as though I were living through some particularly distressing chapter of Dostoievsky. Part of me resents it violently and another part is profoundly moved...

I shall not attempt to summarise Kerensky's speech. It was rambling, discursive, and had very little of that stiff official tone that was so marked in the Moscow speeches. But it was aggressive. It was mainly a personal defence against the charges of complicity in the Kornilov Affair, and it was full of hard blows against the Bolsheviks. The man who spoke was not the rather pompous Premier who appeared in Moscow. He was not the old Kerensky, with his appeals to ideals and affections. He was a new and harder Kerensky, embittered in the perpetual struggle with chaos.[29]

As for the Bolsheviks, it was clear to Ransome from the first few moments that they had come to the Assembly with a definite intention, and that Kerensky was fighting for the Government's life against determined enemies. 'All the time his speech was punctuated by scornful remarks, by jeers, and by shouted insinuations.' Watching some of the interrupters closely during Kerensky's speech and on the following day,

it was evident they had come prepared to interrupt. They alone at a moment of terrible difficulty brought to the Assembly the irresponsible nonchalance of the debating society, sitting there smiling, indifferent to words that to their speakers represented blood and tears... watching their opportunities and making use of them with a unanimity that could only be the result of a concerted plan.

Williams, however, felt that the Bolsheviks' sneering comments had only increased the fervour of the rest of the Assembly.

One young soldier provoked a violent scene. When Kerensky spoke of saving the country he shouted, 'A rotten country it is, too,' and there was a storm of protest, and the youth was within an ace of being ejected by force.

Kerensky's speech ended as it had begun, with a tremendous but one-sided ovation. Ransome had the impression that the Bolsheviks were slightly in the minority and that within the Assembly the weight of feeling favoured Kerensky and the principle of coalition, but that the balance was reversed among the excited groups of disputants outside the Theatre. Williams for once sounds the more sanguine:

> Kerensky has come out of the mists that have enshrouded him since the Kornilov Affair...
>
> I do not know whether there was anything of what is called statesmanship in today's speech; I do not know whether Kerensky is a great or a small man; that is not for us to judge who are too near him and narrowly scan his defects and his qualities. But there is no other man in Russia at this moment who can take his place, and it was a relief to see that he won the sympathies of the conference today and that the great majority enthusiastically supported him...
>
> The Assembly felt that today personal estimates of Kerensky yielded to an oppressive sense of the tragedy of Russia, and the Premier appeared again as a symbol. That was the net result of today's meeting. There will be trouble and attacks and conflicts during the next few days, but for the present I think it may be said that Kerensky has got his way.[30]

Trouble and attacks and conflicts there certainly were. Compared to the well-organized Moscow Conference, the Democratic Assembly was a shambles. Voting was chaotic. The Bolsheviks, Ransome reports, attempted to improve their chances by bringing in a hundred fresh delegates from the factories and regiments, demanding places and votes for them on the grounds that the proletariat was improperly represented. This was turned down, but the incident showed that the Bolsheviks were evidently prepared to challenge the Assembly's authority. They also protested violently against secret voting; 'this fear of the ballot,' Ransome comments, 'is an unfortunate characteristic of the Bolsheviks.' The Assembly agreed by a show of hands to named voting, with the result that when a resolution in favour of coalition was proposed on October 2, voting took nearly five hours, as each delegate went up on stage, had his mandate stamped and his vote registered, and then crossed the plank over the orchestra. The narrow majority of 78 did not satisfy anyone. After an interval two amendments were put to the vote, this time simply by counting the pink tickets held up by delegates: the first, for excluding from the coalition all those who took part in the Kornilov Affair, passed overwhelmingly, the second, for excluding the Kadets, by a majority of 73. Uproar followed, since this contradicted the primary resolution on coalition, which had been taken to imply some kind of Kadet participation in government.

Discussion shifted to a search among the party leaders for a common programme on which the government should be organized. Kerensky stepped in, saying that if the Assembly decided on a non-coalition government, he would accept the decision but resign, as he believed it would be a turning-point towards the liquidation of the Revolution and the ruin of the country. He also proposed the creation of a Pre-Parliament: 'a sort of second edition of the Moscow State Conference' (Philips Price)[31] that would sit permanently until elections for the Constituent Assembly.

The meeting of the full Assembly announced for 6 p.m. on October 3 did not begin until 11 and lasted until 4 a.m. In what Ransome describes as 'a great speech' Tsereteli outlined the results of the discussions earlier in the day. Each point in the common programme was passed by an overwhelming majority.

> However, when it came to voting on the resolution as a whole, Lunacharsky and Kamenev announced that the Bolsheviks would vote against, basing this action on an alleged change in wording, 'take steps in the formation of a government' having been changed to 'take part in the formation of a government'. They said this dodged the real object of the resolution, since it expressed willingness to collaborate with the existing Government. The result was a tremendous row. Tsereteli said that in dealing with the Bolsheviks it was necessary to have two secretaries and a notary as witnesses.

An interval was announced to allow tempers to cool. Afterwards, Tsereteli declared that his remarks were directed at individual Bolsheviks, and not at a Party which included people with whom a notary and secretaries were not necessary. Thereupon the Bolsheviks left the Assembly *en masse*. Without them the resolution was passed by a huge majority, and the upshot was that Kerensky went ahead with the formation of yet another Coalition Government. For Ransome, however, what had emerged most clearly from the Assembly was 'the definite hostility between the Bolsheviks and the rest of the democracy'.[32]

Arthur Ransome had been a conscientious correspondent: he had sat up late, queued for tea and sandwiches in the intervals with the delegates, and listened to their animated talk in the smoke-filled buffets. Not so, Harold Williams. The optimism that he had felt after

Kerensky's opening speech seems to have evaporated quickly. On the third day he spent a short time at the Assembly when the Co-operators were speaking.

> The great co-operative organizations of Russia are absolutely democratic. They existed before the revolution... they hardly ever touch politics. They simply work, and through their work have laid the basis of a new life in the Russian villages... I listened to Birkenheim, the most prominent and capable of the co-operative leaders... the frank, sober, sensible speech of a practical man, and it ended in an appeal for the formation of a strong Coalition Government.
>
> But, listening to the speech and looking at the audience, I felt something like despair. The whole enterprise seemed so utterly hopeless. The appeal was cold, the protests were chilly, with a sort of dreary, empty cynicism. There was no life or spirit in the meeting. There was a creeping sensation of mental and moral slackness.
>
> I looked again at the apathetic faces of the audience, and I felt as though I were looking at the dying embers of the revolution. Those two young soldiers in front of me, with their stupid, heavy faces, what notion had they of statesmanship? And that young officer, with the flabby cheeks and silly, empty eyes, who ostentatiously read Lenin's paper while the Co-operators were speaking, how was he saving Russia? What are the Germans doing while these men are playing with politics?
>
> I went away with a feeling of intense depression. I suppose the Assembly will in the end pass some kind of resolution... But, after all, it matters little what resolutions are passed. The fate of Russia is not to be decided here. Other forces are at work, real, stern, inexorable, which are guiding Russia, to what destinies who in this bitter and tragical time can foresee or foretell?[33]

'Some Mad Scheme'

October 20 (Pre-Parliament opens) to early hours of November 7

Arthur Ransome left Petrograd for Britain on October 9. The *Daily News* had agreed after all that he should have a holiday, and by taking it then, he could be back well before the Constituent Assembly elections on November 25: that will be 'our toughest time', he told his mother. Philips Price did not return from his tour of the provinces until late October, by which time Harold Williams had left to join his wife in the Caucasus at Kislovodsk, where she was completing a cure. But if British press coverage of events in Petrograd was thus reduced – the more so, since Ransome and Philips Price alone had left-wing contacts – the Americans were now present in full force. John Reed and Louise Bryant had entered Russia in mid-September. They soon teamed up with fellow-Americans Bessie Beatty and Albert Rhys Williams, while Alexander Gumberg, a Russian from New York who was well known to the Bolshevik leaders, often made a fifth and acted as interpreter for all of them.

September and October, John Reed writes, are the worst months of the Petrograd year.

Under dull grey skies, in the shortening days, the rain fell drenching, incessant. The mud underfoot was deep, slippery and clinging, tracked everywhere by heavy boots, and worse than usual because of the complete breakdown of the Municipal administration. Bitter damp winds rushed in from the Gulf of Finland, and the chill fog rolled through the streets.[1]

Philips Price soon learned that the city was having to rely on its old accumulated stores, since food trains from the south were being looted by hungry peasants and by the town populations of the northern provinces.[2] Each week the daily allowance of bread fell. 'One of the things that strike coldness to one's heart,' Louise Bryant writes, 'are the long lines of scantily clad people standing in the bitter cold waiting to buy bread, milk, sugar or tobacco. From four o'clock in the morning they begin to stand there...' In shop windows she noticed the strange remnants of what seemed another age: corsets (of the most expensive wasp-waist variety, once worn by women long since vanished from the city), gold-rimmed and diamond-studded dog collars ('whatever class lines there were among dogs fell with the Tsar') and tons of false hair: short hair was now the fashion.[3]

Newspapers and pamphlets were still being published in hundreds of thousands, for Russia, in Reed's words, 'absorbed reading matter like hot sand drinks water', and lectures, debates and speeches still went on 'in theatres, circuses, school-houses, clubs, Soviet meeting-rooms, Union headquarters, barracks... Every street-corner was a public tribune. In railway trains, street-cars, always the spurting up of impromptu debate, everywhere...' Reed and Rhys Williams were happy to accept invitations to speak at public meetings organized by the Bolsheviks, and to bring fraternal greetings from the American workers. Ambassador Francis was not so pleased, and had Reed followed.[4]

By October the Bolshevik 'islands', as Philips Price calls them, which in the middle of the summer had included only Kronstadt, some Petrograd factories, Schlüsselberg and Tsaritsyn, had increased and become 'a veritable archipelago', raising once more the possibility that the Bolsheviks might attempt to seize power. In mid-August E.P. Stebbing (a former Anglo-Indian official who was in Russia on an economic inquiry) had written that even if Kerensky were to fall, which many people seemed to think not unlikely, 'no one considers that the reign of the Bolsheviks will be very lengthy. They are far too ignorant and have not the faintest idea of what governing or national economics mean, to say nothing of the delicate nature of relations with foreign powers.' Harold Williams took a similar line in the wake of the Kornilov Affair: 'A Bolshevik Government might provide a very dramatic and exciting episode. It would probably effect a good deal of material damage and would certainly do great injury to the principle of democracy. But it would be short-lived, and the wounds it might cause would soon be healed.' Ransome commented on October 2 that having refused a coalition with the bourgeoisie, the Bolsheviks were 'beginning to prepare the ground for the refusal even of a democratic coalition, demanding what amounts to a Bolshevik dictatorship'; but since he left Russia a week later, he does not seem to have regarded the threat as imminent, nor does he sound very concerned, perhaps because he assumed that any such development would be superseded by the election of the Constituent Assembly.[5]

Buchanan, reporting to the Foreign Office after the Democratic Assembly, wrote that the Bolsheviks,

> who form a compact minority, have alone a definite political pro-
> gramme. They are more active and better organized than any
> other group, and until they and the ideas which they represent are
> finally squashed, the country will remain a prey to anarchy and
> disorder. Unfortunately the more moderate Socialist leaders, like
> Tsereteli and Skobelev, whose mission it is to combat their extreme
> doctrines in the Soviet, can never quite forget that, however wide
> the gulf that separates the Bolsheviks from themselves, they are
> nevertheless comrades and fellow-fighters in the Socialist cause.
> They will, therefore, never sanction the adoption of strong mea-
> sures against the Bolsheviks as a party, that has brought Russia to
> the verge of ruin, but only against individual members of it, who
> are proved guilty of treasonable conduct. If the Government are
> not strong enough to put down the Bolsheviks by force, at the risk
> of breaking altogether with the Soviet, the only alternative will be
> a Bolshevik Government.[6]

In a Memorandum written on November 2 after his return to Petrograd, Philips Price points out that the Bolsheviks have acquired an immense following among the lower strata of the masses.

> The soldiers in the garrison towns in the rear follow them to a
> man; and small wonder; for what interest have they to leave the
> towns and go to sit in trenches to fight about something that is of
> no interest to them, especially when they know that at the front
> they will get neither food to eat nor proper clothes against the
> winter cold? The workers in the factories are also strongly inclined
> to go with the Bolsheviks, because they know that only the end of
> the war will give them the food, for the lack of which they are
> half-starving now.

He wonders what the consequences would be if the Bolsheviks were to attempt 'some mad scheme' for overthrowing the Provisional Government,

> declaring an immediate peace at any price and establishing a 'Commune' in Petrograd and some of the more revolutionary urban centres. This of course would lead to the most indescribable anarchy. True it would bring peace... but it would be certain to end in the ruin of the revolution and possibly in the re-establishment of Tsarism or of some reactionary dictator, who would destroy the new-won political liberties. It is sufficient to remember the history of the Paris commune. Probably something of the same thing would happen here, for the peasants and soldiers would not endure the dictatorship of the Petrograd workers.[7]

Unknown to Philips Price, such a scheme was already afoot. Lenin, still a wanted man, had slipped back undetected into the Vyborg District of Petrograd and on the evening of October 23, heavily disguised, made his way to a meeting of the Bolshevik Central Committee. Here he argued the case for an immediate armed insurrection; Kamenev and Zinoviev were in favour of a longer-term strategy; but the majority agreed with Trotsky that they should attempt to seize power, but not until nearer the time of the Second All-Russian Congress of Soviets, at which the Bolsheviks expected to have a majority: their action could then be justified as a seizure of power on behalf of the Soviets, intended to save the Revolution from the counter-revolutionary forces poised to destroy it. The Congress was due to open on November 2.

In late October and early November John Reed and his companions divided much of their time between two buildings. At the Marinsky Palace on October 20 members of the Pre-Parliament, now known as the Council of the Republic, listened to an inaugural address by Kerensky, but three days later, at its first working session, the Bolsheviks, led by Trotsky, walked out and did not return. On October 29 Reed sat in the Palace's white marble and crimson hall, listening to 'a tall, impeccably-dressed young man with a smooth face and high cheek-bones, suavely reading his careful non-committal speech'. This was Tereshchenko, re-stating his country's foreign policy – he was due to leave shortly for the Allied Conference in Paris – and in Reed's opinion failing to satisfy either right or left. Kerensky himself came twice to the Council to plead passionately for national unity, once bursting into tears at the end.[8]

The other building was the Smolny Institute. Ransome reported on August 4 that the Soviet had been transferred there while the Taurida Palace was being redecorated after the wear and tear it had been subjected to since the Revolution. 'In its dusty park,' he writes, 'deputies compose their speeches in the hot weather and read Karl Marx under the trees.'[9] John Reed made his way there in the autumn on a street-car,

> moving snail-like with a groaning noise through the cobbled, muddy streets, and jammed with people. At the end of the line rose the graceful smoke-blue cupolas of Smolny Convent outlined in dull gold, beautiful, and beside it the great barracks-like facade of Smolny Institute, two hundred yards long and three lofty stories high, the Imperial arms carved hugely in stone still insolent over the entrance. . .
>
> Under the old regime a famous convent school for the daughters of the Russian nobility, patronized by the Tsarina herself, the Institute had been taken over by revolutionary organizations of workers and soldiers. Within were more than a hundred huge rooms, white and bare, on their doors enamelled plaques still informing the passer-by that within was 'Ladies' Class-room Number 4' or 'Teachers' Bureau'; but over these hung crudely-lettered signs, evidence of the vitality of the new order: 'Central Committee of the Petrograd Soviet' and 'Central Executive Committee' and 'Bureau of Foreign Affairs'; 'Union of Socialist Soldiers', 'Central Committee of the All-Russian Trade Unions', 'Factory-Shop Committees', 'Central Army Committee'; and the central offices and caucus-rooms of the political parties. . .
>
> The long, vaulted corridors, lit by rare electric lights, were thronged with hurrying shapes of soldiers and workmen, some bent under the weight of huge bundles of newspapers, proclamations, printed propaganda of all sorts. The sound of their heavy boots made a deep and incessant thunder on the wooden floor. . . Signs were posted up everywhere: 'Comrades: For the sake of your health, preserve cleanliness!' Long tables stood at the head of the stairs on every floor, and on the landings, heaped with pamphlets and the literature of the different political parties for sale. . .
>
> The spacious, low-ceilinged refectory downstairs was still a dining-room. For two roubles I bought a ticket entitling me to dinner, and stood in line with a thousand others, waiting to get to the long serving-tables, where twenty men and women were ladling

from immense cauldrons cabbage soup, hunks of meat and piles of *kasha*, slabs of black bread. Five kopecks paid for tea in a tin cup. From a basket one grabbed a greasy wooden spoon... The benches along the wooden tables were packed with hungry proletarians, wolfing their food, plotting, shouting rough jokes across the room...

Upstairs was another eating-place, reserved for the Central Committee – though everyone went there. Here could be had bread thickly buttered and endless glasses of tea...

In the south wing on the second floor was the great hall of meetings, the former ballroom of the Institute. A lofty white room lighted by glazed white chandeliers holding hundreds of ornate electric bulbs, and divided by two rows of massive columns; at one end a dais, flanked with two tall many-branched light standards, and a gold frame behind, from which the Imperial portrait had been cut...[...]

Just across the hall outside was the office of the Credentials Committee for the Congress of Soviets. I stood there watching the new delegates come in – burly, bearded soldiers, workmen in black blouses, a few long-haired peasants. The girl in charge – a member of Plekhanov's group – smiled contemptuously. 'These are very different people from the delegates to the First Congress,' she remarked. 'See how rough and ignorant they look! The Dark People...' It was true; the depths of Russia had been stirred, and it was the bottom which came uppermost now. The Credentials Committee, appointed by the old Executive Committee, was challenging delegate after delegate, on the ground that they had been illegally elected. Karakhan, member of the Bolshevik Central Committee, simply grinned. 'Never mind,' he said, 'when the time comes we'll see that you get your seats...'[10]

Reed spent a great deal of time at Smolny, where security precautions became increasingly strict.

One day as I came up to the outer gate I saw Trotsky and his wife just ahead of me. They were halted by a soldier. Trotsky searched through his pockets, but could find no pass.

'Never mind,' he said finally. 'You know me. My name is Trotsky.'

'You haven't got a pass,' answered the soldier stubbornly. 'You cannot go in. Names don't mean anything to me.'

'But I am the President of the Petrograd Soviet.'

'Well,' replied the soldier, 'if you're as important a fellow as that you must at least have one little paper.'

Trotsky was very patient. 'Let me see the Commandant,' he said. The soldier hesitated, grumbling something about not wanting to disturb the Commandant for every devil that came along. He beckoned finally to the soldier in command of the guard. Trotsky explained matters to him. 'My name is Trotsky,' he repeated.

'Trotsky?' The other soldier scratched his head. 'I've heard the name somewhere,' he said at length. 'You can go in, comrade . . .'[11]

On October 30 Reed made his way up to a small room in the attic of Smolny, where Trotsky, sitting on a rough chair at a bare table, talked rapidly and steadily to him for more than an hour. He spoke of the powerlessness of the Provisional Government and the failure of conciliators like the SRs and Mensheviks to face up to the irreconcilable class struggle ('only by the victory of proletarian dictatorship can the Revolution be achieved and the people saved'), of the importance of the Soviets as the most perfect representatives of the people, and of the schemes to destroy them being hatched in the corridors of the Council of the Republic by bourgeois counter-revolution. As for foreign policy, a Bolshevik Government would address itself directly to all peoples over the heads of their Governments and propose an immediate armistice.

'At the end of this war I see Europe re-created, not by the diplomats, but by the proletariat. The Federated Republic of Europe – the United States of Europe – that is what must be. National autonomy no longer suffices. Economic evolution demands the abolition of national frontiers. If Europe is to remain split into national groups, then Imperialism will recommence its work. Only a Federated Republic of Europe can give peace to the world.' He smiled – that fine, faintly ironical smile of his. 'But without the action of the European masses, these ends cannot be realised – now. . .'[12]

On the following morning, with Louise Bryant and the Associated Press correspondent, Reed went to the Winter Palace to interview Kerensky – the last time that the latter received journalists. (Bryant had almost interviewed him once before, but when she was ushered into the beautiful little private library of Nicholas II by one of

Kerensky's many female secretaries, the Minister-President was lying on a couch 'with his face buried in his arms, as if he had been suddenly taken ill, or was completely exhausted. We stood there for a moment and then went out.'[13]) After waiting in the Tsar's billiard-room, they were conducted to the library by a naval adjutant. 'Kerensky walked towards them,' Reed's biographer writes, 'his face an unhealthy colour, his hair bristling, his hands nervous. Reed had watched him in the Democratic Assembly and the Council of the Republic, seen the man's strange magnetism work miracles, seen him mount from eloquence to hysteria and collapse in weeping. Even now he felt something of his charm and surrendered to the impression he gave of passionate sincerity.'[14] The interview was short. The Russian Revolution, Kerensky stressed, was not over, it was only just beginning ('words more prophetic, perhaps, than he knew,' Reed adds.) When the Associated Press man asked why the Russians had stopped fighting, Kerensky was annoyed.

> 'That is a foolish question to ask. Russia of all the Allies entered the war first and for a long time she bore the whole brunt of it. Her losses have been inconceivably greater than those of all the other nations put together. Russia has now the right to demand of the Allies that they bring greater force of arms to bear... Why aren't the Russians fighting? I will tell you. Because the masses of the people are economically exhausted – and because they are disillusioned with the Allies!'[15]

These words caused some consternation when cabled back to the West.

The opening of the Congress of Soviets had to be postponed from the 2nd to the 7th, because not enough delegates had arrived. On November 3 the Bolshevik Central Committee held another closed meeting. Tipped off, Reed was waiting in the corridor outside the door. One of the Committee members, Volodarsky, outlined to him what Lenin had said:

> 'November 6 will be too early. We must have an all-Russian basis for the rising; and on the 6th all the delegates to the Congress will not have arrived... On the other hand, November 8 will be too late. By that time the Congress will be organized, and it is difficult for a large organized body of people to take swift, decisive action. We must act on the 7th, the day the Congress meets, so that we

may say to it, "Here is the power! What are you going to do with it?" [16]

By this time Lenin was not the only person in Petrograd talking of a Bolshevik rising; the element of surprise, as he had forecast, had been completely forfeited by the decision to wait for the Congress. 'The Bolshevik trial of strength is expected for Wednesday, November 7,' Knox wrote on the 1st. In the factories, Reed noted, the committee-rooms were filled with stacks of rifles, couriers came and went, and the Red Guard drilled. According to Buchanan, rumours of a rising had been circulating for some weeks,

> and it was generally expected that it would take place a few days before the meeting of the All-Russian Congress of Soviets. Tereshchenko had even admitted that most of the troops of the garrison had been won over by the Bolsheviks, but Kerensky was more optimistic. He had in my recent conversations with him more than once exclaimed, 'I only wish that they would come out, and I will then put them down.' [17]

On the 3rd Buchanan wrote in his diary: 'The arrival this afternoon of a guard of cadets of the military school for the protection of the Embassy indicates the approach of a storm.' At 12.30 on November 5 one of the cadets sent him a message that the Bolsheviks would oust the Ministers from their departments in the course of the next few days; in Meriel's version, the cadets 'had just had a telephone message from a reliable source saying that the Soviet had taken over the Government, and that all the Ministers were going, though they were to be allowed to remain in office for five more days till the new Government had been formed and elected.' [18] This news was all the more sensational, since three of the Ministers – Tereshchenko, Konovalov and Tretiakov – were expected for luncheon that day at the Embassy. At one o'clock, however, they arrived quite unperturbed, and laughingly said that reports of the fall of the Government were, to say the least, premature. All three assured Buchanan that the Government had sufficient force behind them, though Tretiakov said that Kerensky 'was too much of a Socialist to be relied on to put down anarchy'. Buchanan told them he could not understand how a self-respecting Government could allow Trotsky to go on inciting the masses to murder and pillage without arresting him. The conversation then turned to personal arrangements. Tereshchenko was due to leave on the 8th for the Paris Conference, and the Buchanans were to travel with him, as the British Government wished to consult Sir George about the Russian situation. Turning to Tereshchenko, Buchanan said: 'I shan't believe we are really going till we are in the train.' 'And I,' he replied, 'not till we have crossed the Swedish frontier.'[19]

Reed spent part of that day at the Marinsky Palace.

> As I came in the Left SR Karelin was reading aloud an editorial from the London *Times*, which said, 'The remedy for Bolshevism is bullets!' Turning to the Kadets he cried, 'That's what *you* think, too!'
>
>   Voices from the Right, 'Yes! Yes!'
>
>   'Yes, I know you think so,' answered Karelin, hotly. 'But you haven't the courage to try it!'

Yet in spite of the bitter wrangling, it seemed to Reed that no real voice from the rough world outside could penetrate that high, cold hall.

At Smolny that evening, in room 10 on the top floor, the Military-Revolutionary Committee – sanctioned by the Soviet to organize the defence of Petrograd against the Germans and the counter-revolution, but controlled by the Bolsheviks – was working round the clock. Reed heard how a regiment ordered to Petrograd by the Government had affirmed its loyalty to the Soviets. As he entered the great hall, Trotsky was just finishing a speech.

> 'We are asked,' he said, 'if we intend to have a *vystuplenie* [rising]. I can give a clear answer to that question. The Petrograd Soviet feels that at last the moment has arrived when the power must fall into the hands of the Soviets. This transfer of government will be accomplished by the All-Russian Congress. Whether an armed demonstration is necessary will depend on. . .   those who wish to interfere with the All-Russian Congress. . .'

On leaving Smolny at 3 a.m., Reed noticed that two rapid-firing guns had been mounted, one on each side of the door, and that strong patrols of soldiers guarded the gates and nearby street corners.[20]

Next morning, November 6, Knox watched about a thousand women march past the Embassy on their way to be inspected by Kerensky on Palace Square. 'They made the best show of any soldiers I have seen since the Revolution, but it gave me a lump in the throat to see them, and the utter swine of "men" soldiers jeering at them.'[21]

Kerensky, Reed heard, had gone to the Council of the Republic to offer his resignation. He hurried down to the Marinsky Palace, 'arriving at the end of that passionate and almost incoherent speech, full of self-justification and bitter denunciation of his enemies'. While Kerensky was speaking, a paper was handed to him.

'I have just received the proclamation which they are distributing to the regiments. Here is the contents.' Reading:
The Petrograd Soviet of Workers' and Soldiers' Deputies is menaced. We order immediately the regiments to mobilize on a war footing and to await new orders. All delay or non-execution of this order will be considered as an act of treason to the Revolution. The Military-Revolutionary Committee. For the President, Podvoisky. The Secretary, Antonov.'

Kerensky in his turn denounced the order as an act of treason, but when he stepped down, pale-faced and wet with perspiration, and strode out with his suite of officers, the Council did not rally behind him: however much the SRs and Mensheviks deplored the policy of the Bolsheviks, which they saw inevitably leading to counter-revolution, they blamed the Government even more for its failure to resolve the burning questions of land and peace. They did, however, recommend the formation of a Committee of Public Safety to work in concert with the Government.[22]

Rumours had spread through the town, Meriel Buchanan writes, that all the bridges were to be taken up.

In the grim, bleak light of the winter evening a mass of people poured across the Troitsky Bridge, cab-drivers whipping up their tired horses to a frantic gallop, motors hooting desperately, tram bells clanging... The shops had been closed an hour earlier than usual, and business people, peaceable citizens, women and children were hurrying to get home before the trouble started. Here and there sullen soldiers, armed with rifles and bayonets, stood and watched the passing crowds, or a workman, his gun slung over his shoulder, jeered savagely as he pushed his way among them... By eight o'clock in the evening the streets were absolutely deserted, only now and then small companies of soldiers or two or three armed workmen hurried past.[23]

Meanwhile, Reed writes, at Smolny, as night fell,

the great hall filled with soldiers and workmen, a monstrous dun mass, deep-humming in a blue haze of smoke. The old Executive Committee had finally decided to welcome the delegates to that new Congress which would mean its own ruin – and perhaps the ruin of the revolutionary order it had built. At this meeting, however, only members of the Executive Committee could vote...

It was after midnight when Gots [SR] took the chair and Dan [Menshevik] rose to speak, in a tense silence, which seemed to me almost menacing.

'The hours in which we live appear in the most tragic colours,' he said. 'The enemy is at the gates of Petrograd, the forces of the democracy are trying to organize to resist him, and yet we await bloodshed in the streets of the capital, and famine threatens to destroy, not only our homogeneous Government but the Revolution itself...

'The masses are sick and exhausted. They have no interest in the Revolution. If the Bolsheviks start anything, that will be the end of the Revolution...' (Cries, 'That's a lie!') 'The counter-revolutionists are waiting with the Bolsheviks to begin riots and massacres... If there is any *vystuplenie*, there will be no Constituent Assembly...' (Cries, 'Lie! Shame!')

'It is inadmissible that in the zone of military operations the Petrograd garrison shall not submit to the orders of the Staff... You must obey the orders of the Staff and of the Executive Committee elected by you. All Power to the Soviets – that means death! Robbers and thieves are waiting for the moment to loot and burn... When you have such slogans put before you, "Enter the houses, take away the shoes and the clothes from the bourgeoisie"' (Tumult. Cries, 'No such slogan! A lie! A lie!') 'Well, it may start differently, but it will end that way!

'The Executive Committee has full power to act, and must be obeyed... We are not afraid of bayonets... The Executive Committee will defend the Revolution with its body...' (Cries, 'It was a dead body long ago'!)

Immense continued uproar, in which his voice could be heard screaming, as he pounded the desk, 'Those who are urging this are committing a crime!'

Voice: 'You committed a crime long ago, when you captured the power and turned it over to the bourgeoisie!'

Gots, ringing the chairman's bell: 'Silence, or I'll have you put out!'

Voice: 'Try it!' (Cheers and whistling.)

'Now concerning our policy about peace.' (Laughter.) 'Unfortunately Russia can no longer support the continuation of the war. There is going to be peace, but not permanent peace – not a democratic peace... Today, at the Council of the Republic, in order to avoid bloodshed, we passed an order of the day demanding the surrender of the land to the Land Committees and immediate peace negotiations...' (Laughter, and cries, 'Too late!')

Then for the Bolsheviks, Trotsky mounted the tribune, borne on a wave of roaring applause that burst into cheers and a rising house, thunderous. His thin, pointed face was positively Mephistophelian in its expression of malicious irony.

'Dan's tactics prove that the masses – the great, dull, indifferent masses – are absolutely with him!' (Titanic mirth.) He turned towards the chairman, dramatically. 'When we spoke of giving the land to the peasants you were against it. We told the peasants, "If they don't give it to you, take it yourselves!" and the peasants followed our advice. And now you advocate what we did six months ago...

'I don't think Kerensky's order to suspend the death penalty in the army was dictated by his ideals. I think Kerensky was persuaded by the Petrograd garrison, which refused to obey him...[...]

'No. The history of the last seven months shows that the masses have left the Mensheviks. The Mensheviks and the SRs conquered the Kadets, and then when they got the power they gave it to the Kadets...

'Dan tells you that you have no right to make an insurrection. Insurrection is the right of all revolutionists! When the downtrodden masses revolt it is their right...[...]'

Martov constantly interrupted: 'The [Menshevik] Internationalists are not opposed to the transmission of power to the democracy, but they disapprove of the methods of the Bolsheviks. This is not the moment to seize the power...'

Again Dan took the floor, violently protesting against the action of the Military-Revolutionary Committee, which had sent a Commissar to seize the office of *Izvestiya* and censor the paper...[...]

Amid the wildest confusion Ehrlich offered a resolution, appealing to the workers and soldiers to remain calm and not to respond to provocations to demonstrate, recognizing the necessity of immediately creating a Committee at once to pass decrees transferring the land to the peasants and beginning peace negotiations...

Then up leaped Volodarsky, shouting harshly that the Executive Committee, on the eve of the Congress, had no right to assume the functions of the Congress. The Executive Committee was practically dead, he said, and the resolution was simply a trick to bolster up its waning power...

'As for us, Bolsheviks, we will not vote on this resolution!' Whereupon all the Bolsheviks left the hall and the resolution was passed...

Towards four in the morning I met Zorin [Gumberg's brother] in the outer hall, a rifle slung from his shoulder.

'We're moving!' said he, calmly, but with satisfaction. 'We pinched the Assistant Minister of Justice and the Minister of Religions. They're down cellar now. One regiment is on the march to capture the Telephone Exchange, another the Telegraph Agency, another the State Bank. The Red Guard is out...'

On the steps of Smolny, in the chill dark, we first saw the Red Guard – a huddled group of boys in workmen's clothes, carrying guns with bayonets, talking nervously together.

Far over the still roofs westward came the sound of scattered rifle fire, where the *yunkers* [cadets] were trying to open the bridges over the Neva, to prevent the factory workers and soldiers of the Vyborg District from joining the Soviet forces in the centre of the city; and the Kronstadt sailors were closing them again...

Behind us great Smolny, bright with lights, hummed like a gigantic hive...[24]

11

The Bolsheviks Take Over

November 7 (9 a.m.) to November 8 (6 a.m.)

At 9 a.m. on the morning of November 7, Bessie Beatty was in her blue and white bedroom at the Astoria Hotel when the servant came in with tea and told her that the building had that minute been occupied by the Bolsheviks. This astounding news sent her hurriedly into the hall and into the arms of a squad of soldiers, but when she explained to the young officer in charge that she was an American correspondent and would like to go downstairs, he bowed low and motioned to his men to let her pass.

> At the head of the winding staircase groups of frightened women were gathered, searching the marble lobby below with troubled eyes. Nobody seemed to know what had happened. The Battalion of Death [which she had watched the previous evening file through the whirling door and encamp on the marble floor] had walked out in the night, without firing so much as a single shot. Each floor was crowded with soldiers and Red Guards, who went from room to room, searching for arms, and arresting officers suspected of anti-Bolshevik sympathies. The landings were guarded by sentries, and the lobby was swarming with men in faded uniforms. Two husky, bearded peasant soldiers were stationed behind the counter, and one in the cashier's office kept watch over the safe. Two machine-guns poked their ominous muzzles through the entry-way. My letter of credit was inside the safe, and the only other money I had was an uncashed cheque for eight hundred roubles.

She hurried off to the National City Bank and reached it just in time, for within the hour the Bolsheviks captured the State Bank, whereupon all the other banks promptly closed their doors. On her way back she walked through Palace Square. Four armoured cars were drawn up under the shadow of the mighty granite shaft (the Alexander Column) in front of the Winter Palace, their guns pointing significantly at the palace windows.[1]

General Knox had been due to leave for the front on November 5, but postponed his departure on learning at the District Staff that 'there would certainly be interesting developments in Petrograd in the next few days'. On the 6th he heard that the Cossack regiments in Petrograd had decided to remain neutral because of Kerensky's refusal to declare the Bolshevik organization illegal. Walking to the Embassy on the morning of the 7th, he was left in no doubt that the Bolsheviks were having it all their own way: 'The Government troops of the night before had disappeared; everywhere were patrols of the local garrison. Trams were running and there was perfect order.' He had sandwiches at the Embassy and walked down to the District Staff.

> Polkovnikov, the Commander of the District... said that he was certain he would be able to turn the whole situation round in favour of the Provisional Government... He was a very brave but rather pathetic optimistic!
>
> Poor Bagratuni made less concealment. He had not slept for three nights, neither had he shaved, and when an Armenian does not shave it is noticeable. He told me that he had never been in such a position, for he could not depend on any single order being carried out. The troops called in from the front had gone over in the night... Troops were on their way from the front, but had been delayed... I got the same impression at the District Staff as I had gathered at the Prefecture on the first day of the big Revolution – forced optimism with nothing to go on.

At the Winter Palace he saw the *yunker* garrison working half-heartedly at the construction of a breastwork of firewood in front of the main entrance. Entering the Palace by the garden gate, he went to look for the Chief of Kerensky's Military Cabinet.

> He had gone. On the stairs many workmen were busy cutting down and removing the tapestries.

As I walked back across the Square to the General Staff building
a fusillade broke out and the crowd ran. No bullets came my way.

Nearly all the officers had left the Staff Building, as the
Pavlovsky Regiment had announced that it was about to occupy
the building...

My officers sealed up the door of our room and took our ciphers
to the Embassy.

At the Embassy I heard that Kerensky had borrowed a car from
the Americans... and had escaped to Pskov. He was forced to
borrow a car; as all the magnetos from the cars collected in the
Palace Square had been stolen by the Bolsheviks in the night...
In my opinion he will not return.[2]

After two late nights, John Reed did not rise early on Wednesday
morning. The noon cannon boomed from the Fortress as he went
down the Nevsky on a raw, chill day. The shops were open, and
there seemed even less uneasiness among the street crowds than on
the day before, though soldiers with fixed bayonets were standing at
the closed gates of the State Bank, and the Astoria Hotel was picketed by armed sailors. In the hotel lobby many of the smart young officers were walking up and down or muttering together; the sailors
wouldn't let them leave. Before the door of the Marinsky Palace
stood a crowd of soldiers and sailors. Reed stopped to listen to a
sailor describing the end of the Council of the Republic.

'We walked in there,' he said, 'and filled all the doors with comrades. I went up to the counter-revolutionary Kornilovist who sat
in the President's chair [the SR, Avksentev, who was also chairman
of the Peasants' Soviets]. 'No more Council,' I says. 'Run along
home now!'[3]

In the early afternoon Reed made his way towards the Winter
Palace with Louise Bryant and Rhys Williams.

All the entrances to the Palace Square were closed by sentries, and
a cordon of troops stretched clear across the western end, besieged
by an uneasy throng of citizens. Except for far-away soldiers who
seemed to be carrying wood out of the Palace courtyard and piling
it in front of the main gateway, everything was quiet.

We couldn't make out whether the sentries were pro-
Government or pro-Soviet. Our papers from Smolny had no effect,

however, so we approached another part of the line with an important air and showed our American passports, saying, 'Official business!' and shouldered through. At the door of the Palace the same old *shveitsari*, in their brass-buttoned blue uniforms with the red-and-gold collars, politely took our coats and hats, and we went upstairs. In the dark, gloomy corridor, stripped of its tapestries, a few old attendants were lounging about, and in front of Kerensky's door a young officer paced up and down, gnawing his moustache. We asked if we could interview the Minister-President. He bowed and clicked his heels.

'No, I am sorry,' he replied in French. 'Alexander Feodorovich is extremely occupied just now...' He looked at us for a moment. 'In fact, he is not here...'

'Where is he?'

'He has gone to the Front. And do you know, there wasn't enough gasoline for his automobile. We had to send to the English Hospital and borrow some.'

'Are the Ministers here?'

'They are meeting in some room – I don't know where.'

'Are the Bolsheviks coming?'

'Of course. Certainly they are coming. I expect a telephone call every minute to say that they are coming. But we are ready. We have *yunkers* in the front of the Palace. Through that door there.'

'Can we go in there?'

'No. Certainly not. It is not permitted.' Abruptly he shook hands all round and walked away. We turned to the forbidden door, set in a temporary partition dividing the hall and locked on the outside. On the other side were voices, and somebody laughing. Except for that the vast spaces of the old Palace were as silent as the grave. An old *shveitsar* ran up. 'No, *barin*, you must not go in there.'

'Why is the door locked?'

'To keep the soldiers in,' he answered. After a few minutes he said something about having a glass of tea and went back up the hall. We unlocked the door. [Bryant's version does not mention a forbidden door: 'When we left Kerensky's office we walked straight to the front of the Palace.'[4]]

Just inside a couple of soldiers stood on guard, but they said nothing. At the end of the corridor was a large, ornate room with gilded cornices and enormous crystal lustres, and beyond it several smaller ones, wainscoted with dark wood. On both sides of the parqueted floor lay rows of dirty mattresses and blankets, upon which occasional soldiers were stretched out; everywhere was a litter of cigarette butts, bits of bread, cloth, and empty bottles with expensive French labels. More and more soldiers, with the red shoulder-straps of the *yunker* schools, moved about in a stale atmosphere of tobacco smoke and unwashed humanity. One had a bottle of white Burgundy, evidently filched from the cellars of the Palace. They looked at us with astonishment as we marched past, through room after room, until at last we came out into a series of great state-salons, fronting their long and dirty windows on the Square. The walls were covered with huge canvases in massive gilt frames – historical battle scenes... '12 October 1812' and '6 November 1812' and '16/28 August 1813.'... One had a gash across the upper right-hand corner.

The place was all a huge barrack, and evidently had been for weeks, from the look of the floor and walls. Machine-guns were mounted on window-sills, rifles stacked between the mattresses.[5]

They spent about three hours there. The boys were all young and friendly, Bryant writes,

and said they had no objection to our being in the battle; in fact, the idea rather amused them... One of them was not over eighteen. He told me that in case they were not able to hold the Palace, he was 'keeping one bullet for himself'. All the others declared that they were doing the same.

Someone suggested that we exchange keepsakes. We brought out our little stores. I recall a Caucasian dagger, a short sword presented by the Tsar and a ring with this inscription: 'God, King and Lady.'...

Once while we were quietly chatting, a shot rang out and in a moment there was the wildest confusion; *yunkers* hurried in every direction. Through the front windows we could see people running and falling flat on their faces. We waited for five minutes, but no troops appeared and no further firing occurred. While the *yunkers* were still standing with their guns in their hands, a solitary figure emerged, a little man, dressed in ordinary citizen's clothes, carrying a huge camera. He proceeded across the Square until he reached the point where he would be a good target for both sides and there, with great deliberation, he began to adjust his tripod and take pictures of the women soldiers who were busy turning the winter supply of wood into a flimsy barricade before the main entrance. There were about two hundred of them and about fifteen hundred *yunkers* in the whole place. There was absolutely no food and a very small supply of ammunition.[6]

While the three Americans were spending the afternoon at the Winter Palace, Philips Price was at Smolny, where an extraordinary session of the Petrograd Soviet had been convened.

Trotsky was in the chair, and on the tribune stood the same short, bald-headed little man that I had seen six months before leading the tiny Bolshevik group in the First Soviet Congress. It was Lenin without his moustache, which he had shaved off, in order to change his appearance during his period of forced concealment, now drawing to a close. The Petrograd Soviet was now one solid phalanx of Bolshevik Deputies, and roar after roar of applause swept the hall, as Lenin spoke of the coming Soviet Congress as the only organ which could carry through the Russian workers', soldiers' and peasants' revolutionary programme.[7]

All our witnesses now converge upon Smolny. Bessie Beatty left the hotel at three, but ran into a company of military cadets, 'strapping, handsome fellows', trying to recapture the Telephone Exchange from the Bolsheviks, and did not reach Smolny until nearly five.[8] After leaving the Winter Palace, Bryant, Reed and Williams went to the Hotel France for dinner. By the time they came out, it was quite dark, except for one flickering street light on the corner of the Nevsky. They walked back up to the Red Arch, where a knot of soldiers was gathered staring at the brightly lit Winter Palace. Here, Reed writes, 'the street-cars had stopped running, few people passed, and there were no lights; but a few blocks away we could see the trams, the crowds, the lighted shop-windows and the electric signs of the moving-picture shows – life going on as usual.' They had tickets to the Ballet at the Marinsky Theatre, but it was too exciting out of doors. Up the Nevsky the whole city seemed to be out promenading. 'Pickets of a dozen soldiers with fixed bayonets lounged at the street crossings, red-faced old men in rich fur coats shook their fists at them, smartly-dressed women screamed epithets; the soldiers argued feebly, with embarrassed grins...'

The massive façade of Smolny was blazing with lights as they drove up. Inside there was an atmosphere of recklessness. The extraordinary session of the Petrograd Soviet had just finished.

A crowd came pouring down the staircase, workers in black blouses and round black fur hats, many of them with guns slung over their shoulders, soldiers in rough dirt-coloured coats and grey fur *shapki* pinched flat, a leader or so – Lunacharsky, Kamenev – hurrying along in the centre of a group all talking at once, with harassed anxious faces, and bulging portfolios under their arms.

Reed stopped Kamenev, who read out in rapid French a copy of the Petrograd Soviet's resolution saluting the victorious Revolution of the Petrograd proletariat and garrison, and outlining the programme of the new Workers' and Peasants' Government.

They pushed their way through the clamorous mob at the door into the great meeting-hall, where the Second Congress of Soviets was waiting to begin.

In the rows of seats, under the white chandeliers, packed immovably in the aisles and on the sides, perched on every window-sill, and even the edge of the platform, the representatives of the workers and soldiers of all Russia waited in anxious silence or wild exultation the ringing of the chairman's bell. There was no heat in the hall but the stifling heat of unwashed human bodies. A foul blue cloud of cigarette smoke rose from the mass and hung in the thick air. Occasionally someone in authority mounted the tribune and asked the comrades not to smoke; then everybody, smokers and all, took up the cry, 'Don't smoke, comrades!' and went on smoking.[9]

They had been waiting there since five. Bessie Beatty describes how a delegate from the Menshevik group came on to announce that his party was still in caucus, unable to come to an agreement.

Another hour passed. Suddenly through the windows opening on the Neva came a steady *boom! boom! boom!*

'What's that? What's that?' asked the sailor of the soldier, and the soldier of the workman.

A man with pale face and blazing eyes fought his way through the crowd on the platform.

'The cruiser *Aurora* is shelling our comrades in the Winter Palace. We demand that this bloodshed shall be stopped instantly!' he shouted.[10]

Others, too, heard the sound of gunfire. At the British Embassy Meriel Buchanan thought she heard it in the distance 'a little before nine'; the English officer who was sitting in her room said it was only the trams on the bridge, but the words were hardly out of his mouth when the sudden boom of a big gun shook the windows. According to Sir George, delegates from the revolutionary committee had demanded the unconditional surrender of the Palace, but since no answer was returned,

> the signal for attack was given by the firing at 9 p.m. of a few blank rounds by the guns of the Fortress and of the cruiser *Aurora*. The bombardment which followed was kept up continually till ten o'clock, when there was a lull for about an hour. At eleven o'clock it began again, while all the time, as we watched it from the Embassy windows, the trams were running as usual over the Troitsky Bridge.[11]

The attention of the waiting crowd at Smolny was diverted, Beatty writes,

> by the arrival of a man of medium height, square-shouldered, lean, dark, and tense-looking. His face was white, and his black hair, brushed back from a wide forehead, his black moustache and small black beard, his black jacket and flowing black tie, still further emphasized the alabaster whiteness of his skin. He stood within a few feet of me, one hand in his pocket, and with sharp, quick glances took the measure of that strange sea of faces.
> 'Here's Trotsky!' whispered the man beside me. 'Come, I want you to meet him.'
> Before I had time to acquiesce or protest, I found a lean hand grasping mine in a strong, characteristic handshake. We stood there for a few moments, talking of inconsequential things, but all of us charged with the tensity of the hour. There was keen intelligence here, nerve, a certain uncompromising streak of iron, a sense of power; yet I little suspected I was talking to the man whose name within a few brief weeks would be a familiar word on every tongue – the most-talked-of human being in an age of spectacular figures.[12]

At 10.40 their conversation was abruptly cut short by the appearance of Dan – described by Reed as 'a mild-faced, baldish figure in a shapeless military surgeon's uniform' – who opened the Congress. A new Presidium of twenty-five members was elected, of whom fourteen were Bolsheviks, and the old Executive Committee stepped down. Kamenev announced the order of the day: organization of power, war and peace, and the Constituent Assembly. But suddenly, Reed writes, 'a new sound made itself heard, deeper than the tumult of the crowd, persistent, disquieting – the dull shock of guns' (the fresh bombardment, presumably, that Buchanan heard at about eleven). Martov demanded the floor and in his hoarse tubercular voice, scarcely audible above the gunfire, protested that the question of power was already being settled without discussion or consultation – 'by means of a military plot organized by one of the revolutionary parties'. The spokesmen for the Mensheviks and the SRs protested along similar lines. Then came Abramovich for the *Bund*, the organ of the Jewish Social Democrats, his eyes snapping behind thick glasses, trembling with rage. 'Our duty to the Russian proletariat doesn't permit us to remain here and be responsible for these crimes.' Better to go unarmed to the Winter Palace and die alongside their colleagues. He invited all delegates to leave the Congress.

> Kamenev jangled the bell, shouting, 'Keep your seats and we'll go on with our business!' And Trotsky, standing up with a pale, cruel face, letting out his rich voice in cool contempt, 'All these so-called Socialist compromisers, these frightened Mensheviks, SRs, *Bund* – let them go! They are just so much refuse which will be swept away into the garbage-heap of history!'[13]

How many delegates left the Congress at this point varies according to each witness: 'fifty' (Reed), 'about eighty' (Rhys Williams), 'a hundred or more of the conservative revolutionists' (Bryant), 'about twenty per cent of the whole Congress', i.e. over a hundred (Philips Price).[14]

Eager not to miss any of the action, the Americans decided to try to reach the Palace themselves. It would be useless, Gumberg warned, to expect to get through Bolshevik lines without a pass from the Military-Revolutionary Committee. He led them down to the far end of a dimly lit corridor, where a young fair-haired boy, Beatty writes,

> met us in an outer office, took our names and request, and disappeared into the next room, shutting the door behind him. We

stared curiously after him. Beyond that door were the men who were directing the siege and capture of Petrograd – directing it so efficiently that in the days that followed, the enemies of the Bolsheviks insisted the committee was composed of Germans, because Russians were incapable of such perfect organization.

When the inside door opened again the fair-haired boy reappeared with the passes in his hand. Mine was typewritten on a bit of paper torn from a scratch-pad, numbered 'Five', and stated simply:

'The Military-Revolutionary Committee of the Council of Workmen's and Soldiers' Deputies allows Miss Bessie Beatty free passage all over the city.'

That scrap of paper was to prove the open sesame to many closed doors before the grey dawn of morning. It bore the blue seal of the committee, the only signature capable of commanding the slightest sign of respect from a Russian bayonet that night.

The Smolny Institute is excellently located to provide seclusion for a young women's seminary, but in the middle of a cold night it seemed a long dark way from anywhere. Walking down the stairs, we speculated upon the improbability of finding an *izvozchik* abroad at such an hour.

Down in the courtyard a huge motor-truck was cranking up for departure. Its only occupants were three sailors, a young Cossack soldier with a cape of shaggy black fur that hung to his heels, and a Red Guard. We hailed them, and Mr Gumberg shouted a request to be taken to town. It was drowned by the sound of the engine. He repeated it in louder tones. The sailor looked dubiously at me and at Louise Bryant, the other woman member of the party.

'It's a dangerous trip,' he said. 'We are going out to distribute proclamations, and we are almost certain to be shot at.'

We looked at one another for a moment, considered that it was probably our only chance to reach the Winter Palace, and asked to be allowed to take the risk. [Louise Bryant was told to remove an eye-catching yellow hatband.[15]] Two strong hands came over the side to pull me up, and two sailors sitting on a board across the body of the truck arose to give us their seats. They held a hurried consultation, then asked us to stand again. They had decided that this exposed position would be too dangerous for women. The Cossack lad in the shaggy cape spread some proclamations on the floor of the car.

'Sit here,' he said, 'and when the shooting begins you can lie flat on your backs and keep your heads low.'

A bundle of rifles lay on the floor under my knees, and as we started off over the cobbles I grabbed a chain and held fast to keep from being bumped out. The streets were like black canyons. Apparently there was not a human being abroad; yet every time the sailor tossed a handful of white leaflets into the air, men came darting mysteriously from doorways and courtyards to catch them.

The Cossack towered above me, rifle in hand, with eyes searching the dark for signs of danger. At the street intersections we slowed up, and groups of soldiers gathered around the bonfires crowded close to the truck for news from Smolny. They peered with curious and startled eyes into our unexpected faces, then hurried back to the circle of light around the blazing birch-wood logs. During one of these pauses Mr Gumberg grabbed a proclamation [drafted by Lenin first thing that morning and also broadcast by wireless] and read it to us:

TO THE CITIZENS OF RUSSIA

The Provisional Government is deposed. State power has passed into the hands of the organ of the Petrograd Soviet of Workers' and Soldiers' Deputies, the Military-Revolutionary Committee, which stands at the head of the Petrograd proletariat and garrison.

The cause for which the people have been struggling – the immediate proposal of a democratic peace, the abolition of the landlords' ownership of land, workers' control over production, the creation of a Soviet Government – that cause is assured.

LONG LIVE THE REVOLUTION OF WORKERS, SOLDIERS AND PEASANTS!
> Military-Revolutionary Committee,
> Petrograd Soviet of Workers' and Soldiers' Deputies

It was one by the clock in the steeple of the Moscow Station when we turned into the Nevsky. The great circle was deserted. Earlier in the day there had been fighting here, but no trace of it was visible now.

'Put your heads down!' the Cossack ordered, catching sight of a group of unidentified men ahead.

We obeyed; but when they proved to be Bolshevik soldiers and Red Guards, we peeped cautiously out again. At the bridge across the Moika Canal we were turned back by the barricade erected early in the afternoon, and by the command of the guard, who said there was fighting just ahead and no one could pass. From the direction of the Winter Palace came the occasional *boom!* of a big gun, followed by the short, sharp crack of the rifles.

Reluctantly we retraced our way. In front of the Kazan Cathedral the guards again ordered us to halt. In the darkness across the wide street, we saw a crowd of black figures lined up in marching order against the curb. We had come suddenly upon that little band of men and women who left Smolny to make a demonstration of passive resistance and die with their comrades at the Winter Palace. They had been joined by the Mayor of Petrograd, members of the City Duma, and the Jewish *Bund*. There were four or five hundred of them in all, and here, within a few blocks of their destination, they had been stopped.

In that crowd were many of the men and women who had been the firebrands of Russia, the Socialist revolutionists, the terrorists, who were quietly walking forth to oppose themselves unarmed to the force of these new revolutionists who, to their way of thinking, were murdering the cause of Russian freedom for which most of them had suffered years of imprisonment and the unspeakable hardships of exile in Siberia. Here and there in the crowd was a young officer or a cluster of students; but more of them were veterans who had grown grey in the service of revolution, and their faces were grim and set.[16]

John Reed depicts the crowd somewhat differently: 'There were about three or four hundred of them, men in frock coats, well-dressed women, officers – all sorts and conditions of people'. They included many of the leading Menshevik and SR delegates from the Congress, white-bearded old Schreider, Mayor of Petrograd, and Prokopovich, Minister of Supplies in the Provisional Government, arrested that morning and released. Reed caught sight of Malkin, reporter for the *Russian Daily News*. 'Going to die in the Winter Palace,' he shouted cheerfully.

All the threats and entreaties of the unarmed demonstrators fell on deaf ears, however, and eventually Prokopovich mounted some sort of box, and waving his umbrella, made a speech:

'Comrades and citizens! Force is being used against us! We cannot have our innocent blood upon the hands of these ignorant men! It is beneath our dignity to be shot down here in the streets by switchmen –' (What he meant by 'switchmen' I never discovered.) 'Let us return to the City Hall and discuss the best means of saving the country and the Revolution!'

Whereupon, in dignified silence, the procession marched around and back up the Nevsky, always in column of fours.[17]

According to Reed, the five of them took advantage of the diversion to slip past the guards, but Beatty recalls that they presented their passes and were allowed through without a word. 'The blue seal of the Military-Revolutionary Committee had done for us what eloquence and argument could not do for the old revolutionists.'[18]

Inside the Winter Palace, meanwhile, the situation had changed since the afternoon. The details are given by Knox, who heard them from Ragosin, a Russian officer sent that evening by the District Staff to report on the Palace defences.

The garrison of the Palace originally consisted of about 2,000 all told, including detachments from *yunker* and ensign schools, three squadrons of Cossacks, a company of volunteers and a company from the Women's Battalion. It had six guns and one armoured car, the crew of which, however, declared that it had only come 'to guard the art treasures of the Palace and was otherwise neutral'!

The garrison had dwindled owing to desertions, for there were no provisions and it had been practically starved for two days. There was no strong man to take command and to enforce discipline. No one had any stomach for fighting; and some of the ensigns even borrowed great coats of soldier pattern from the women to enable them to escape unobserved.

The greater part of the *yunkers* of the Mikhail Artillery School returned to their school, taking with them four out of their six guns. Then the Cossacks left, declaring themselves opposed to bloodshed! At 10 p.m. a large part of the ensigns left, leaving few defenders except the ensigns of the Engineering School and the company of women. . .

The defence was unorganized and only three of the many entrances were guarded. Parties of the attackers penetrated by side entrances in search of loot. At first these parties were small and were disarmed by the garrison, but they were succeeded by larger bands of sailors and of the Pavlovsky Regiment, in addition to armed workmen, and these turned the tables by disarming the garrison. This was, however, carried out, as an officer of the garrison afterwards stated, 'in a domestic manner', with little bloodshed. The garrison fired little and is said to have only lost three *yunkers* wounded...

At 2.30 a.m. on the 8th the Palace was 'taken'...[19]

It was 2.45, according to Beatty, when they halted in the shadow of the great Red Arch and peered cautiously out into the dark square.

There was a moment of silence; then three rifle shots shattered the quiet. We stood speechless, awaiting a return volley; but the only sound was the crunching of broken glass spread like a carpet over the cobblestones. The windows of the Winter Palace had been broken into bits.

Suddenly a sailor emerged from the black.

'It's all over!' he said. 'They have surrendered.'

We picked our way across the glass-strewn square, climbing the barricade erected that afternoon by the defenders of the Winter Palace, and followed the conquering sailors and Red Guards into the mammoth building of dingy red stucco. On the strength of our blue-sealed passes, they permitted us to enter unquestioned. A commissar of sailors motioned us to a bench beside the wall.[20]

Reed tells it differently:

Like a black river, filling all the street, without song or cheer we poured through the Red Arch, where the man just ahead of me said in a low voice: 'Look out, comrades! Don't trust them. They will fire, surely!' In the open we began to run, stooping low and bunching together, and jammed up suddenly behind the pedestal of the Alexander Column.

'How many of you did they kill?' I asked.

'I don't know. About ten...'

After a few minutes huddling there, some hundreds of men, the Army seemed reassured and without any orders suddenly began again to flow forward. By this time, in the light that streamed out of all the Winter Palace windows, I could see that the first two or three hundred men were Red Guards, with only a few scattered soldiers. Over the barricade of fire-wood we clambered, and leaping down inside gave a triumphant shout as we stumbled on a heap of rifles thrown down by the *yunkers* who had stood there. On both sides of the main gateway the doors stood wide open, light streamed out, and from the huge pile came not the slightest sound.[21]

Separated, it seems, from their companions, Reed and Williams were swept into the right-hand entrance, opening into a great vaulted room – the cellar of the East wing. It was full of huge packing cases. 'A terrible lust lays hold of the mob,' Williams writes, 'the lust of loot. Even we, as spectators, are not immune to it... With the butts of their rifles, the soldiers batter open the boxes, spilling out streams of curtains, linen, clocks, vases and plate.'[22] One man, according to Reed,

went strutting around with a bronze clock perched on his shoulder; another found a plume of ostrich feathers, which he stuck in his hat. The looting was just beginning when someone cried, 'Comrades! Don't take anything. This is the property of the People!' Immediately twenty voices were crying, 'Stop! Put everything back! Don't take anything. Property of the People!' Many hands dragged the spoilers down. Damask and tapestry were snatched from the arms of those who had them; two men took away the bronze clock. Roughly and hastily the things were crammed back in their cases, and self-appointed sentinels stood guard. It was all utterly spontaneous. Through corridors and up staircases the cry could be heard growing fainter and fainter in the distance, 'Revolutionary discipline! Property of the People...'

They crossed back to the left entrance in the West wing, where they appear to have rejoined their companions. Here, too, order was being established.

Two Red Guards, a soldier and an officer, stood with revolvers in their hands. Another soldier sat at a table behind them, with pen and paper. Shouts of 'All out! All out!' were heard far and near within, and the Army began to pour through the door, jostling, expostulating, arguing. As each man appeared, he was seized by the self-appointed committee, who went through his pockets and looked under his coat. Everything that was plainly not his property was taken away, the man at the table noted it on his paper, and it was carried into a little room. The most amazing assortment of objects were thus confiscated: statuettes, bottles of ink, bedspreads worked with the Imperial monogram, candles, a small oil-painting, desk blotters, gold-handled swords, cakes of soap, clothes of every description, blankets. One Red Guard carried three rifles, two of which he had taken away from *yunkers;* another had four portfolios bulging with written documents. The culprits either sullenly surrendered or pleaded like children.[23]

The *yunkers* came out in bunches of three or four. No violence was done to them, although they were terrified. They, too, had their pockets full of small plunder. 'When those we had been with in the afternoon recognized us,' Louise Bryant writes, 'they waved friendly greetings. They looked relieved that it was all over, they had forgotten about the "one bullet" they were keeping for themselves.' Clamouring voices demanded: 'Now, will you take up arms against the people any more?' 'No,' answered the *yunkers*, one by one, whereupon they were allowed to go free.[24]

There was a clatter on the stairs, and Bessie Beatty turned to see the members of the Provisional Government file slowly down. Although the Bolsheviks had disconnected telephone lines from the Winter Palace, they missed two of them, and the Ministers had remained in contact with the outside world. At midnight, according to Knox's informant, they were elated by a message from the front that troops were on the march for their relief.

During the bombardment the Ministers moved about from room to room. Ragosin afterwards related that when he had to report on some subject he found 'the Minister of Marine sitting in a window smoking a pipe and spitting. Other Ministers were seated at a table. Tereshchenko walked up and down like a caged tiger. Konovalov sat on a sofa nervously pulling up his trousers till they were finally above his knees.'[25]

They eventually took refuge in the Malachite Room. All of a sudden, the Minister of Justice recalled, they became aware of a noise that was different from all previous noises, a noise that intensified and rolled swiftly towards them, seizing them with intolerable fear like the onslaught of poisoned air. They hastily ordered the *yunker* in charge of the guard not to offer the insurgents any resistance.[26]

Some of the Ministers, Beatty writes,

walked with defiant step and heads held high. Some were pale, worn, and anxious. One or two seemed utterly crushed and broken. The strain of that day of anxious waiting, and that night under the capricious guns of the cruiser *Aurora*, coupled with the weeks when Cabinet crisis had followed Cabinet crisis, had proved too much for them.[27]

Towering above his companions, Tereshchenko stood out. To Louise Bryant 'he looked so ridiculous and out of place; he was so well groomed and so outraged.' Reed describes him glancing sharply round and staring at them with cold fixity, while Beatty writes of 'the tall, dark, slender, handsome figure of the young Foreign Minister, Tereshchenko, who cast an amazed glance in my direction as he passed.' The Ministers were marched off to the Peter & Paul Fortress.[28]

Silently watching them go, Beatty wondered what the night's work would mean in the future of Russia and the world. But then the commissar who had motioned them to the seat indicated that they might now go upstairs (in Reed's version, 'unrebuked we walked into the Palace') and they passed quickly to the council chamber.

We made our way through the shattered rooms, blazing now with a million lights from the twinkling crystal chandeliers. The silk curtains hung in shreds, and here and there on the walls was the ugly scar of a recent bullet. On the whole, the destruction was much less than we had expected to find it. The attacking force had gone about its work, determined to take the Palace, but to take it with as little bloodshed as possible, and in the lulls between storms they had made frequent attempts to break the resistance by fraternization. None of the defenders had been killed, but six of the sailors who had fought in the open square had paid with their lives for their revolutionary ardour, and many others had been wounded.

As we passed the door of Kerensky's office, formerly the study of the last of the Romanovs... I recalled, with a little sigh of regret, that this day in this very spot I was to have lunched with the Minister-President of Russia.

Reed confirms that the paintings, statues, tapestries, and rugs of the great state apartments were unharmed;

in the offices, however, every desk and cabinet had been ransacked, the papers scattered over the floor, and in the living-rooms beds had been stripped of their coverings and wardrobes wrenched open. The most highly prized loot was clothing, which the working people needed. In a room where furniture was stored we came upon two soldiers ripping the elaborate Spanish leather upholstery from chairs. They explained it was to make boots with. . .

The old Palace servants in their blue and red and gold uniforms stood nervously about, from force of habit repeating, 'You can't go in there, *barin*! It is forbidden – ' We penetrated at length to the gold and malachite chamber with crimson brocade hangings where the Ministers had been in session all that day and night, and where the *shveitsari* had betrayed them to the Red Guards. The long table covered with green baize was just as they had left it, under arrest. Before each empty seat was pen, ink and paper; the papers were scribbled over with beginnings of plans of action, rough drafts of proclamations and manifestoes. Most of these were scratched out, as their futility became evident, and the rest of the sheet covered with absent-minded geometrical designs, as the writers sat despondently listening while Minister after Minister proposed chimerical schemes. I took one of these scribbled pages, in the handwriting of Konovalov, which read, 'The Provisional Government appeals to all classes to support the Provisional Government – '[29]

In one of the rooms where they lingered, looking curiously about them, Beatty noticed a crowd of soldiers talking together excitedly.

Once I caught the proletarian word of scorn, 'Bourgeoisie!' But it never occurred to me that we could be the object of their discussion. Suddenly a young commissar came up to us.

'These men can not understand,' he said, 'who you are, and why you are here. They are quite excited and angry about it. They think perhaps you may have come to rob. I told them I would question you, and if you had no right to be here we would arrest you.'

We presented our passes. He examined them, and turned to the men, who were by this time quite obviously casting unfriendly glances in our direction.

'Comrades,' he said, 'these passes are stamped, just as my own is, with the blue seal. See it! You may be sure that if they had not the right they would not be here with this.'

The men examined the paper quizzically, and nodded. They took an informal vote upon the subject, and it was agreed that we should be allowed to go free.

According to Reed, the room was the great picture gallery where they had talked to the *yunkers* in the afternoon, and the whole incident is made to sound considerably more alarming:

About a hundred men surged in upon us. One giant of a soldier stood in our path, his face dark with sullen suspicion...[...] I produced our passes from the Military-Revolutionary Committee...[...] The mass slowly began to close in, like wild cattle around a cow-puncher on foot. Over their heads I caught sight of an officer, looking helpless, and shouted to him...[...]

'Comrades! Comrades!' appealed the officer, sweat standing out on his forehead. 'I am a Commissar of the Military-Revolutionary Committee. Do you trust me? Well, I tell you that these passes are signed with the same names that are signed to my pass!'

He led us down through the Palace and out through a door opening on to the Neva quay, before which stood the usual committee going through pockets... 'You have narrowly escaped,' he kept muttering, wiping his face.[30]

According to his biographer, the sheet on which Konovalov had been scribbling was not the only thing that Reed took out with him.

As the group left the Palace, the guards who had been stationed at the exits to prevent looting started to search them. Reed insisted that he and his friends were above suspicion, and finally grew so convincingly indignant that the guards let them all pass. As soon as he was safely out in the street, he flung back his coat, and showed the others a jewelled sword. And when they turned on him, saying that he had risked their lives as well as his own, he chuckled and refused to believe they were in earnest.[31]

Was this what Rhys Williams had in mind when he wrote that even they, as spectators, were not immune to the lust of loot; or was the sword one of the 'keepsakes' given to Reed and Bryant earlier in the day by the *yunkers*?

Bessie Beatty, who was near her hotel, seems to have decided to call it a day. Not so the other three. At the City Hall they heard Skobelev urging that the Committee of Public Safety be expanded to include all anti-Bolshevik elements. At Smolny Kamenev was reading out the names of arrested Ministers; that of Tereshchenko was greeted with thunderous applause, shouts of satisfaction and laughter. Then a big SR peasant, his bearded face convulsed with rage, mounted the plat- form and pounding on the table, demanded the immediate release of the Socialist Ministers from the Fortress. They didn't use much ceremony with us in July, Trotsky countered. At exactly 5.17 a.m. Krylenko climbed to the tribune with a telegram announcing the formation of a Military-Revolutionary Committee at the Northern Front.[32]

'This historic session ends at six o'clock in the morning,' Rhys Williams concludes. 'Outside it is still dark and chill, but a red dawn is breaking in the East.'[33]

And Reed:

So. Lenin and the Petrograd workers had decided on insurrection, the Petrograd Soviet had overthrown the Provisional Government, and thrust the *coup d'état* upon the Congress of Soviets. Now there was all great Russia to win – and then the world! Would Russia follow and rise? And the world – what of it? Would the peoples answer and rise, a red world-tide?

Although it was six in the morning, night was yet heavy and chill. There was only a faint unearthly pallor stealing over the silent streets, dimming the watch-fires, the shadow of a terrible dawn grey-rising over Russia...[34]

Downfall of Kerensky

Morning of November 8 to November 13 (3 a.m.)

As he walked down the Nevsky not many hours later, it was clear to Philips Price that power in Petrograd was actually in the hands of the Military-Revolutionary Committee, acting in the name of the Second All-Russian Soviet Congress. This all seemed to him at the time very ridiculous.

> I tried to imagine a committee of common soldiers and workmen setting themselves up in London and declaring that they were the Government, and that no order from Whitehall was to be obeyed unless it was countersigned by them. I tried to imagine the British Cabinet entering into negotiations with the Committee for the settlement of the dispute, while Buckingham Palace was surrounded by troops and the Sovereign escaped from a side entrance disguised as a washerwoman. And yet something of this sort in Russian surroundings had actually happened. It was almost impossible to realize that the century-old Russian Empire was actually dissolving before one's eyes with such extraordinary lack of dignity.[1]

'November' had certainly been a very different kind of event from 'March'. For General Knox March was 'the big Revolution'. In November Petrograd was not convulsed, adjectives like 'elemental', 'spontaneous', 'uncontrollable', are inappropriate, and no sense of universal rejoicing was felt afterwards. 'There are not even any of the usual lorries with their loads of *tovariches* in heroic poses,' Louis de Robien notes on November 7.[2] The Bolsheviks had learned the lesson of the July Days: that without an overall plan there was no point in having masses of armed demonstrators milling around the streets. Instead, they carried out their *coup d'état* so discreetly that on the morning of the 7th, as the *Daily Telegraph* correspondent wrote, 'Petrograd awoke and went about its normal business, and only towards midday realized, except in the centre, that the old Government had been painlessly replaced.'[3] That they succeeded with such ease was due not to overwhelming support (only a small part of the garrison troops were willing to fight), but, in Buchanan's opinion, to the simple fact that the Government 'had neglected to organize any force for their own protection'.[4] As for the heroic storming of the Winter Palace later made famous by Eisenstein's film, that turns out on closer examination to have been not at all heroic. What seems most surprising is that it took so long to dislodge the pathetic handful of defenders; had it not been for the two or three hundred Red Guards who finally took the lead, the soldiers might have been waiting under the Red Arch all night. John Reed makes it sound more dramatic by the skilful deployment of some vivid verbs ('In the open we began to run, stooping low and bunching together, and jammed up suddenly behind the pedestal of the Alexander Column... Over the barricade of fire-wood we clambered, and leaping down inside gave a triumphant shout as we stumbled on a heap of rifles...'), but since the Palace had already surrendered, it is clear that they ran very little risk in crossing the Square.

On November 8 General Knox had 'a busy day'. At the General Staff nothing had been touched, but on crossing Palace Square to the District Staff Building he found it occupied by a large guard of mutineers. An N.C.O. assured him that 500 men had been killed and wounded. 'He was of a truculent type, very different from the N.C.O. of the Preobrazhensky who had helped me on March 12.' After lunching at the Embassy, he went to the City Hall in search of a new Embassy guard. The previous guard of eight cadets had distinguished themselves, according to Buchanan,

by appropriating a case of whisky and a case of claret belonging to the secretaries. Most of them were ill the next day, and some were sick in the hall. So far from their protecting us, it is rather we who are protecting them. Luckily an extra guard of Polish soldiers with an officer was given us on Friday [the day after Knox's visit], and we have managed to send the cadets safely home dressed up as civilians.[5]

At the City Hall Knox was told that the Committee of Public Safety had no power behind it, but was hoping for support from the troops coming from the front. Avksentev said he gave the Bolsheviks 'about two days'.

When I returned to the Embassy I found Lady Georgina in great excitement. Two officer instructors of the Women's Battalion had come with a terrible story to the effect that the 137 women taken in the Palace had been beaten and tortured, and were now being outraged in the Grenadersky barracks. ['I did not see the women soldiers,' Beatty writes. 'They were in another wing of the palace.' Philips Price met a batch of them being marched off to the Fortress, 'from which, however, they were to be speedily released and sent home to their mothers'.[6]]

I borrowed the Ambassador's car and drove to the Bolshevik headquarters at the Smolny Institute. This big building, formerly a school for the daughters of the nobility, is now thick with the dirt of revolution. Sentries and others tried to put me off, but I at length penetrated to the third floor, where I saw the Secretary of the Military-Revolutionary Committee [Antonov] and demanded that the women should be set free at once. He tried to procrastinate, but I told him that if they were not liberated at once I would set the opinion of the civilized world against the Bolsheviks and all their works. [Later Knox confessed to William Gerhardie that he had no arguments at hand and came out with the first thing that happened to enter his head.[7]] He tried to soothe me and begged me to talk French instead of Russian, as the waiting-room was crowded and we were attracting attention. He himself talked excellent French and was evidently a man of education and culture. Finally, after two visits to the adjoining room, where he said the Council was sitting, he came back to say that the order for the release would be signed at once.

I drove with the officers to the Grenadersky barracks and went to see the Regimental Committee. The commissar, a repulsive individual of Semitic type, refused to release the women without a written order, on the ground that 'they had resisted to the last at the Palace, fighting desperately with bombs and revolvers'. He said that they were now under a guard apart from the soldiers, unmolested and quite safe. He refused to let me see them, though I asked twice. It was an extraordinary scene, the officers speaking French, which the commissar probably understood, and urging me not to believe a word he said; the half-dozen soldiers of the Regimental Committee, not of a bad type, but stolidly indifferent and taking no part in the discussion; the commissar of a race which has been oppressed for centuries but now holding all the cards, not arrogant but determined. We tried to telephone to the Smolny to ascertain if the order had been dispatched, but could get no reply. I returned to the Embassy and, telephoning through to the Soviet, was told that the order for the release had been sent by special messenger.

The Bolsheviks in this instance were as good as their word. The order arrived at the Regiment soon after my departure, and the women were escorted by a large guard to the Finland Station, where they entrained at 9 p.m. for Levashovo, their battalion headquarters. As far as could be ascertained, though they had been beaten and insulted in every way in the Pavlovsky barracks and on their way to the Grenadersky Regiment, they were not actually hurt in the barracks of the latter. They were, however, only separated from the men's quarters by a barrier extemporized from beds, and blackguards among the soldiery had shouted threats that had made them tremble for the fate that the night might bring...

The heroic effort of these women had had no effect on the men, who were past all shame. They were insulted by the soldiers whenever they came to Petrograd, so kind women friends provided them with civilian clothing and they dispersed to their homes.[8]

On the evening of November 8 Lenin made his first 'public' appearance at Smolny. Once again, the Congress delegates had been kept waiting many hours, and it was just 8.40, according to Reed,

when a thundering wave of cheers announced the entrance of the presidium, with Lenin – great Lenin – among them. A short, stocky figure, with a big head set down on his shoulders, bald and bulging. Little eyes, a snubbish nose, wide generous mouth, and heavy chin; clean-shaven now but already beginning to bristle with the well-known beard of his past and future. Dressed in shabby clothes, his trousers much too long for him. Unimpressive, to be the idol of a mob, loved and revered as perhaps few leaders in history have been. A strange popular leader – a leader purely by virtue of intellect; colourless, humourless, uncompromising and detached, without picturesque idiosyncrasies – but with the power of explaining profound ideas in simple terms, of analysing a concrete situation. And combined with shrewdness, the greatest intellectual audacity.

After various other speakers had been heard, including some protesting against the Bolsheviks' uncompromising attitude, Lenin stepped forward,

> gripping the edge of the reading stand, letting his little winking eyes travel over the crowd as he stood there waiting, apparently oblivious to the long-rolling ovation, which lasted several minutes. When it finished, he said simply, 'We shall now proceed to construct the Socialist order!' Again that overwhelming human roar...[...]
> His great mouth, seeming to smile, opened wide as he spoke; his voice was hoarse – not unpleasantly so, but as if it had hardened that way after years and years of speaking – and went on monotonously, with the effect of being able to go on for ever... For emphasis he bent forward slightly. No gestures. And before him, a thousand simple faces looking up in intent adoration.[9]

On Philips Price, however, Lenin made a different impression. 'His voice was weak, apparently with excitement, and he spoke with slight indecision. It seemed as if he felt that the issue was still doubtful, and that it was difficult to put forward a programme right here and now.'[10]

Lenin read out the proclamation by the Workers' and Peasants' Government, calling upon all the belligerent peoples and their governments to take immediate steps to bring about peace. The Government renounced all previous secret treaties and abolished all secret diplomacy. 'This proposal of peace will meet with resistance on the part of the imperialist governments – we don't fool ourselves on that score. But we hope that revolution will soon break out in all the belligerent countries; that is why we address ourselves to the workers...'

It was exactly 10.35, Reed noted, when Kamenev asked all in favour of the proclamation to hold up their cards.

> One delegate dared to raise his hand against, but the sudden outburst around him brought it swiftly down... Unanimous.
> Suddenly, by common impulse, we found ourselves on our feet,

mumbling together into the smooth lifting unison of the *Internationale.* A grizzled old soldier was sobbing like a child. Alexandra Kollontai rapidly winked the tears back. The immense sound rolled through the hall, burst windows and doors and soared into the quiet sky. 'The war is ended! The war is ended!' said a young workman near me, his face shining. And when it was over, as we stood there in a kind of awkward hush, someone in the back of the room shouted, 'Comrades! Let us remember those who have died for liberty!' So we began to sing the Funeral March, that slow, melancholy and yet triumphant chant, so Russian and so moving.

Lenin went on to the Decree on Land. There were protests from some of the peasants' representatives, and the Left SRs asked for a half-hour intermission. As the delegates streamed out, Lenin urged them not to waste time, but almost two and a half hours passed before they came straggling back. At 2 a.m. the Decree was put to the vote: only one against. So the Bolsheviks plunged ahead, Reed comments, 'irresistible, overriding hesitation and opposition – the only people in Russia who had a definite programme of action while the others talked for eight long months.' At 2.30 Kamenev announced that until the Constituent Assembly was convened, a Provisional Workers' and Peasants' Government, to be known as the Council of People's Commissars, would take charge. He read out the commissars' names. They included Vladimir Ulyanov (Lenin) as President of the Council, L.D. Bronstein (Trotsky) as Commissar for Foreign Affairs, A.V. Lunacharsky for Popular Education, and at the very end of the list, as Chairman for Nationalities, I.V. Dzhugashvili (Stalin).

Far from emptying, the room seemed to become even fuller. 'The air was thick with cigarette smoke, and human breathing, and the smell of coarse clothes and sweat.' The debate continued, and there were more protests against the Bolsheviks' tyrannical conduct. Someone questioned whether it was realistic to expect help from the proletariat in the Allied countries, to which Trotsky replied: 'There are only two alternatives; either the Russian Revolution will create a revolutionary movement in Europe, or the European powers will destroy the Russian Revolution.'

Finally, the Second All-Russian Congress of Soviets was dissolved. It was almost seven when they woke the sleeping conductors and motor-men of the street-cars waiting to take the delegates home. In the crowded car, Reed thought, there was less happy hilarity than on the night before, and many people looked anxious.[11]

Their anxiety was not without cause. The civil servants in Petrograd and a number of big trade unions were refusing to co-operate with the Bolsheviks. Kerensky was reported to be advancing rapidly on Petrograd from the south. The Red Guards were political-ly reliable, but an unknown quantity as a fighting force; the garrison soldiers could be easily swayed in either direction, while the Cossacks and peasants were even more doubtful quantities. Not only the bourgeoisie, but all the left-wing political parties, with a few minor exceptions, had ranged themselves against the Bolsheviks. The news from Moscow was uncertain. To plunge irresistibly ahead, rejecting compromise and overriding hesitation and opposition, was all very well, but if Kerensky were to move on Petrograd, the Bolsheviks would need all the help they could get from the other left-wing parties and their supporters, whom they were so busy alienating.

The Committee of Public Safety, now known as the Committee for the Salvation of the Country and the Revolution, was hard at work attracting to itself all these anti-Bolshevik elements. John Reed plied energetically between the two camps, noting the contrast between the great masses of shabby soldiers, grimy workmen and peasants at Smolny and their well-fed, well-dressed opponents at the City Hall, where there was scarcely a proletarian in sight.[12]

A battle of the printing-presses broke out, as each side issued appeal after appeal, proclamation after proclamation. When Philips Price went upstairs at Smolny to the office of *Izvestiya*, formerly the official organ of the Soviet, he found the Bolsheviks already in pos-session.

The Menshevik editor had packed up and was just leaving as I came in. The Bolshevik leader, Steklov, was engaged in earnest conversation with someone, whom I did not know. Akselrod was trying to put some sort of order into a pile of papers. Someone else was picking with a bradawl at the lock of a drawer, from which the keys had evidently been removed by the Mensheviks before they left. Along one side of the room Lenin was walking up and down, sunk in deep thought. I looked on this scene of untidy bus-tle and wondered; could it last? Was this really the intellectual nucleus of a new ruling power in the world, or was it only an amusing incident – a 'fuss in the mud', so to say?

'They have just issued a proclamation, calling on the people to recognize only them,' I heard the voice of Steklov, indignantly proclaiming. 'Has anyone seen it?' he added. I presumed that he referred to the leaflet issued by the ejected Menshevik Soviet leaders earlier in the day. I happened to have picked it up in the street, and went across the room to Steklov and gave him a copy. He looked at me. I had spoken with him once earlier in the year, but he did not recognize me now. 'That man is certainly a spy from the counter-revolution,' I seemed to hear him think. But he took the pamphlet and roared out to someone in the next room: 'Come over here and write a leader on this leaflet.' A lean individual appeared, took it and began to scribble off an article.[13]

On the morning of Saturday, November 10 all was excitement at City Hall. Hundreds of copies of a proclamation by Kerensky, claiming (prematurely) that he had taken Tsarskoe Selo and would be entering Petrograd on the following day, had been dropped from an aeroplane flying low down the Nevsky.

Smolny, too, was busier than ever, but beneath all the breezy assurances Reed sensed a feeling of uneasiness. As they left the Military-Revolutionary Committee, Antonov entered, 'a paper in his hand, looking like a corpse'. It was an order from Trotsky and Podvoisky calling upon the workers to defend the capital against counter-revolution by stopping work in the factories immediately, and going out to dig trenches and erect barricades. 'All available arms must be taken.' In response to this call, Bessie Beatty writes, Petrograd poured out to fight.

> The factory gates opened wide, and that amazing army of the Red Guard, ununiformed, untrained, and certainly unequipped for battle with the traditional backbone of the Russian military, marched away to defend the 'revolutionary capital' and the victory of the proletariat.
>
> Women walked by the side of men, and small boys tagged along on the fringes of the procession. Some of the factory girls wore red crosses upon the sleeves of their thin jackets, and packed a meagre kitbag of bandages and first-aid accessories. Most of them carried shovels with which to dig trenches.[14]

Sunday, November 11 proved to be the critical day in Petrograd. Acting on the assumption that Kerensky's arrival was imminent, the Committee encouraged the *yunkers* to seize the Telephone Exchange and to take action throughout the city.

Philips Price was awakened early by the sounds of rifle-firing.

I dressed and went out on to the embankment of the Fontanka Canal. Hardly had I gone outside the gateway when the nerve-racking clatter of a machine-gun at close quarters pierced the foggy air. The next minute the dull sound of bullets, embedding themselves in the stucco of the building outside which I was standing, showed me that it was healthier under cover than in the open. From the safety of the door-keeper's lodge I then surveyed the scene of battle. It had begun indeed – the trial of strength between the Smolny Soviets and the 'Committee for the Salvation of the Country and the Revolution'. In the big red building on the other side of the canal, the Military Academy [of Engineering], a force of *yunkers* and students had fortified themselves. Machine-gun fire was spurting out of several of the windows in the direction of the Nevsky Prospect. It was being answered by another machine-gun and sporadic rifle-fire from Sadovaya Street, and some of the bullets were striking the house where I lived. The besiegers were apparently not strong, and presently their firing ceased altogether. In the pause I emerged from my cover and with gingerly steps crept down the side of the Fontanka Canal towards a bridge, which I crossed. When I was opposite the Circus a violent fusillade broke out again from the windows of the Military Academy. Rifle bullets whistled overhead, and suddenly everyone vanished from the streets. I got into a side entrance of a house along with a number of other people and waited. Everyone was silent and depressed and trying to hide his inner feelings beneath an outward calm. I kept on wondering if the next fusillade would cause a bullet to ricochet from the adjoining building into our midst. Here indeed was the front, not the national but the class front, and the remarkable thing about it was that there was no sharp line of division between the opposing forces. Among the people where I was standing were persons of the middle class, and beside them a workman and two soldier deserters from the now fast-melting Tsarist army. 'Why are you hiding?' said a well-dressed man to one of the soldiers. 'You have been at the war, and ought not to be afraid of bullets.'

'Had two years of it against the Germans and wounded twice,' said the soldier; 'think I have had enough.'

'Why don't you go and help these *yunkers* against the Red ruffians? Or are you one of our brave deserters who have sold Russia to these Bolsheviks and to the Germans?' asked the well-dressed man.

'Give me a rifle, and I will go and fight against those *yunkers*,' replied the soldier.

'And I will see to it that you don't get a rifle,' said the well-dressed citizen, as though he was sorry he had raised the subject. Apparently he and his class in Petrograd that day were, on reflection, as anxious to take arms away from the common people as they had been to force arms into their hands three years before, when the war with Germany began.

During an interval of quiet I crept out. Soldiers with red cockades on their hats and Kronstadt sailors had brought up a field-gun. Detachments of Red Guards were arriving. A motor-car from the Smolny came along. Someone in a leather overcoat, apparently from the Military-Revolutionary Committee, called to one of the soldiers:

'What detachment is this?'

'We are from the Putilov Works,' said a young man in civilian clothes with a rifle on his shoulder and a red band on his arm.

'Who is your officer?' asked the Commissar.

'There is none; we are all officers,' said the Red Guard. 'Smolny summoned us by telephone from the works at eight o'clock this morning; we found no one here to give us any orders, so we took up these positions.'

Boom! went the field-gun and a couple of seconds later a three-inch shell crashed into the red walls of the Military Academy. I was standing not far from the Circus, which protected me from the window in the Academy whence the *yunkers* were pouring out their worst machine-gun fire. How could that machine-gun be silenced? It swept three streets and made approach from three sides impossible. Another one was posted at the north entrance. The Red Guards were evidently not anxious to wreck the great building with artillery fire. And yet to storm it would mean heavy loss. Already a dozen wounded Red Guards were lying groaning on the ground at the entrance to the Circus. There was no first aid, although the Smolny had been urgently telephoned. But the Red Cross was working for the 'Committee for the Salvation of the Country and the Revolution', and the staff of the private and municipal hospitals were sabotaging. The soldiers belonging to a regiment supposed to be sympathetic to Smolny were said to be wavering. They had taken up positions on the Field of Mars north of the Academy. Having lost eight men, and seeing no chances of silencing those machine-guns, they were losing heart. About three o'clock I saw a large detachment of sailors march up from the direction of the Neva. Their arrival was the signal for much bustling, cursing, and even kicking. The wavering soldiers on the Field of Mars were told to prepare for attack or clear off home, if they did not want to face a revolutionary tribunal. Two more field-guns were brought up. I was summarily expelled from the point of vantage and of safety I had secured under the wall of a small public garden by the canal. There was nothing for me to do but to bolt back to my rooms on the other side of the Fontanka. I set out, but as I got to the bridge – boom! went the sailors' field-gun, and a terrific clatter of machine-gun fire came from the Academy. Bullets made the air hideous, and looking back I saw a storming party of Red Guards advancing across the garden, where I had just been, in the direction of the Academy. After dodging the bullets by hiding in areas and side entrances, when the fusillades commenced, I reached my rooms at last. Shortly after this all was quiet. The sailors had done their work. The *yunkers* capitulated, and were marched off to the Peter & Paul Fortress, but not before a number of them were selected from the rest and done to death with the butt-ends of rifles.[15]

Louise Bryant found herself in even greater danger. On reaching the corner of Gogol Street and St Isaac's Square, she and her Bolshevik companion from Smolny saw an armoured car coming along at full speed (Reed, who was not present but describes the incident at second-hand, claims that it was one of five or six belonging to the disbanded British Armoured Car Division, being used by the Committee).

We did not have time to seek shelter. We found ourselves crammed against a closed archway that had great iron doors securely locked. We hoped that the car would go on, but directly in front of us it stopped with a jerk as if something had gone wrong with the machinery [Reed: 'the engine stalled']. Its destination was quite evidently the Telephone Exchange. We had no way of knowing which side it was on until it began to spout fire, shooting up the street and occasionally right into our midst. Then we knew that it belonged to the *yunkers*. There were twenty in our crowd and about six were Kronstadt sailors [according to Reed, the sailors, who were ambushed behind woodpiles, began shooting].

The first victim was a working man. His right leg was shattered and he sank down without a sound, gradually turning paler and losing consciousness as a pool of blood widened around him. Not one of us dared to move. A man in an expensive fur coat kept repeating monotonously: 'I'm sick of this revolution!'

All that happened in the next few minutes is not exactly clear – we were all so excited. One thing that I remember, which struck me even then, was that no one in our crowd screamed, although seven were killed. I remember also the two little street boys. One whimpered pitifully when he was shot, the other died instantly, dropping at our feet an inanimate bundle of rags, his pinched little face covered with his own blood. I remember the old peasant woman who kept crossing herself and whispering prayers. . .

The hopelessness of our position was just beginning to sink in on me when the sailors with a great shout ran straight into the fire. They succeeded in reaching the car and thrust their bayonets inside again and again. The sharp cries of the victims rose above the shouting, and then suddenly everything was sickeningly quiet. They dragged three dead men out of the armoured car and they lay face up on the cobbles, unrecognizable and stuck all over with bayonet wounds. ['Among the dead,' Reed claims, 'was a British officer. . . Whatever the official attitude of the Allied Embassies, individual French and British officers were active these days, even to the extent of giving advice at executive sessions of the Committee for Salvation.']

Only the chauffeur escaped. He begged for mercy and my companion from Smolny said to the sailors: 'For God's sake let him go – let's not kill any more of them than we have to.' It was a most characteristic remark. Russians hate violence and they hate to kill. At a time like that Anglo-Saxons or almost any other race would have been insane with rage at the death of their seven comrades. But the Russians let the chauffeur go. . . ['to run to the City Hall,' Reed adds, 'and swell the tale of Bolshevik atrocities'].[16]

Bessie Beatty was sitting in her hotel bedroom shortly before noon and wondering at the quiet, broken only by the ringing of the church bells, when two shots abruptly shattered the silence.

They were followed by the noise of excited voices, and the clatter of many feet in the hall.

I hurried out to the stairs, but an officer turned me back at the first landing.

'They are fighting downstairs – you had better keep to your room,' he said.

I retraced my steps, and on the floor above caught the elevator and dropped swiftly down. The lobby was swarming. Soldiers were running about everywhere, men and officers were shouting, and nobody could tell what was happening. I walked to the door in time to see an armoured car turn the corner and make for the hotel. Several other people saw it at the same moment, and there was a rush for the stairs. The car came to a halt at the entrance.

Suddenly a boy officer, a cigarette hanging nonchalantly from the corner of his mouth and a revolver in his hand, lined the Bolshevik guards up against the wall and disarmed them. He had come with the password of the Military-Revolutionary Committee, and the paper he carried in his pocket was stamped with the blue seal. It did not occur to anyone at that moment that either the password or the seal could have been stolen. The soldiers obeyed every command of the Military-Revolutionary Committee without question. Not until they were prisoners and had heard the lock on the basement door turn behind them did they realize that they had been tricked.

'Who are they?' everybody asked. 'Has Kerensky come? Is Kornilov here?'

I put the question to a Russian admiral standing near me. He shook his head in despair. 'God knows, madame. I don't.'

The boy officer and his squad departed as suddenly as they had come, carrying most of the rifles with them. Quiet settled on the hotel. The old guard was in prison, and there was no new one. Two small boys picked up a couple of rifles left behind, and slung them across their shoulders in imitation of the armed workmen.

'*Krasnaya gvardiya*! (Red Guard),' one said, hunching down into his coat. A woman laughed hysterically.

Leaving the hotel, Beatty followed the officer down the Morskaya to the Telephone Exchange, where she saw Albert Rhys Williams talking to a group of soldiers. They were evidently not Bolsheviks but *yunkers*, and they were expecting a counter-attack at any moment by the Red Guard and the sailors.

A tall, dark-eyed boy, one of the ten who had stood guard over the

Provisional Government in the Winter Palace, related in perfect English the events of the morning.

At daybreak an automobile drove up to the door, and two officers stepped out. They said that Kerensky was on his way to Petrograd and would arrive in a short time with two regiments. They provided the boys with the seal of the Military-Revolutionary Committee and the proper passwords, told them to go to the first cluster of guards gathered around one of the street-corner fires, surprise them, over-power them by numbers, and take their guns away. Their orders then were to take the Telephone Exchange and the Astoria Hotel by means of the password, and hold them until Kerensky arrived.

The boys started blithely forth, convinced that they were prepar-ing the way for the restoration of the Provisional Government and it was merely a matter of an hour or two before the victorious troops of Kerensky would come to relieve them.

'I don't see why he does not come,' he ended plaintively. 'We can't hold out long alone.'

At this time there was only an occasional volley, but at two o'clock the firing began in earnest from both ends of the street. The *yunkers*, mere children in this business of war, built barricades of boxes and boards across the sidewalks, and when the supply of these was exhausted they carried logs from a wood-pile. They took up positions behind these frail protections and fired at the attacking forces, which came at them from two directions. Some hid behind the motor-trucks, resting their guns upon the engines. Some lay flat in the mud upon the wooden cobbles, and fired underneath the cars.

I watched the fight, first from behind the barricade in the court-yard, then went upstairs to a front window where I could look down upon the street.

In a room on the second floor, Antonov, the Bolshevik War Commissar, was a prisoner [taken by surprise and seized earlier while making a routine round of inspection].

The crowd outside the building, led by a factory worker and reinforced by sailors, learned that Antonov was in the building, and were mad to be at the throats of the men who were holding their leader. They had still another grievance against the *yunkers*. Many of these same boys had been captured once in the Winter Palace, and allowed to go free. They had broken their parole, and the sailors especially were bitter to think they had to sacrifice more of their comrades to re-arrest them.

In the middle of the afternoon the *yunkers* suggested a peace parley, offering to surrender Antonov if they were allowed to go free.

'We'll take Antonov ourselves, and kill every last one of you,' came back the answer.

The boys grew desperate.

'Why doesn't Kerensky come? Why doesn't Kerensky come?' they asked again and again.

There was no one to answer. The older officers, who had been directing them, completely disappeared. The stock of ammunition diminished. A Red Cross automobile dashed up to the building at half-past two, left a box of hand-grenades, and departed again. [This was an automobile disguised as a Red Cross car, in which officers from the Telephone Exchange had bluffed their way through the Red Guard lines; Rhys Williams had accepted an invitation to accompany them on their mission.[17]]

A machine-gun had been set up on a wooden box in the street, and in the courtyard a woman with a shawl over her head loaded and reloaded the tape. The attacking forces were pressing closer and closer upon the building. The street barricades were abandoned. A few of the *yunkers* poured up the stairs and into the front rooms. At four o'clock I was moved from my place at the window.

'We want to shoot from here,' one of the *yunkers* explained.

With that they smashed the glass with the butts of their rifles, and took their places behind the yellow silk curtains. I walked across to a window overlooking the court. Two *yunkers* passed into the building bearing a wounded comrade, who lay limp in the arms of his bearers.

'Come away from here. They're down in the courtyard at the foot of the stairs!' somebody shouted.

With that the hall was deserted. Men and girls [the telephonists] fled to the back of the building. In a pantry I found a boy officer with a huge breadknife, trying to cut the buttons from his coat with hands that trembled so they made a long job of it. Still another was tearing frantically at his epaulettes. In an ante-room behind the switchboard three more discovered the street clothes of some mechanics, and were quickly stripping themselves.

Suddenly the thing for which these boys had striven – the coveted gold braid and brass buttons of an officer's uniform, symbol of their superiority – had become their curse. Any one of them would have given the last thing he possessed on earth for the suit of a common working-man. Stripped bare of every scrap of the pride and tradition of their class, they were caught in the grip of a fear that drained every drop of blood from their faces and every bit of courage from their hearts.

Wandering about from room to room, stopping here and there to say '*Kharasho!*' or '*Nichevo!*' to some poor girl dissolved in tears upon a bench, I came out finally in a corridor where Mr Williams was standing with his interpreter. A *yunker* officer had hold of the lapels of his overcoat, and was pleading with him to take it off and let him escape. The boy's bronze face was grey with fear, and his words tumbled over each other in jumbled incoherence. I glanced from him to the American, and saw a pair of eyes full of pain and indecision. A tense, silent moment followed – a moment in which I held my breath and waited.

The shooting outside had stopped. Dark was closing in around us. Everything for me was obliterated but the one man asking for something that might save his life, and the other to whom it was second nature to give, torn between conviction and desire. I knew the tumult in his soul.

The coat of rough brown cloth and American cut was strikingly different from any other in Russia, and it had become a familiar garment in revolutionary Petrograd. Its owner was an excellent speaker, and he had talked to the men at the front, on the fleet, and in the factories, and wrapped in the brown coat he had slept in peasant huts from Moscow to Kiev.

The Russian workmen loved him and trusted him, and he had come to know them and to believe in the integrity of their idealism. He had pity for these frightened fellows, but he was almost as bitter as a Red Guard at the breaking of parole, the stealing of passes, and the illegitimate use of the Red Cross car.

'If I give him my coat they will recognize it and think me a traitor,' he said.

I did not answer. I felt I had no right to plead with him against his principles. His Russian had completely deserted him. He turned to his interpreter:

'Tell him I can't give him my coat, but perhaps I can help in some other way,' he said.

The interpreter obeyed, and the officer walked away with a hopeless, despairing shake of the head.

We stood for a moment looking after him, both of us possessed of a frantic consciousness that something must be done to save these boys doing the bidding of the men who had left them in a trap.

'Oh, if I could only speak this language!' I said, in a futile explosion of protest against my helplessness.

'What would you do?' my companion asked.

'I don't know what I'd do, but I'd do something!' I answered, and started down the hall, deserted a few minutes earlier. Mr Williams followed me.

'Find him,' he said. 'I can't give him my coat, but I will leave it here, and he can come and take it.'

I hurried past the stairway, with one swift glance toward the dark courtyard, where men from the street were crowding thicker and thicker. I went from corridor to corridor, jostling groups of frightened men and women, and stumbled at last into a back room, where most of the *yunkers* had gathered. They had thrown down their guns and were waiting for the end. I searched the faces. The officer was not among them.

Mr Williams, by this time possessed of a passion to find him, had been hunting in another part of the building. At the moment, for both of us, the whole tragic situation was done up in the plight of this one feeble human being trying to save his life. Every second we expected to hear the rush of men on the stairway.

'Perhaps I can do something with Antonov,' Mr Williams suggested. 'Where are the boys?'

I led him back to the room where I had found them, and he offered to go to the imprisoned Minister of War and try to make terms of surrender that would guarantee their safety.

'*Pazhal'sta, barin!* Please help us! Please save us!' they cried in chorus.

With two *yunkers* to guide him and unlock the door, he disappeared. We waited a breathless two minutes. When he returned, a queer, emaciated little fellow, stoop-shouldered and pale, walked beside him. A very long nose and a fringe of long pale hair were almost all of him visible below the wide brim of his soft felt hat. Surely the War Minister had none of the traditional appearance of a Russian military man.

'Comrade Antonov, save our lives!' cried the *yunkers* in unison. 'On the word of the good revolutionist that we know you are, save our lives!'

'Where are your officers?' Antonov asked.

'They have all left us,' they answered.

The terms of surrender were quickly made, and Antonov and Williams started downstairs to face the crowd. The men of the Red Guard recognized their leader.

'Antonov! Antonov!' they shouted. '*Nash, nash!* (Ours, ours!)' 'Where are the *yunkers*?'

With this the men in the lead made for the stairs. Antonov stopped them.

'I have given my word of honour as a revolutionist that these men in there shall not be killed, and as revolutionists you must keep that word.'

Some of the Baltic Fleet sailors, who had come down from the *Respublica*, recognized the American.

'The American comrade!' one of them shouted.

Mr Williams began speaking to them [in English, through his interpreter].

'I know the temptation you have,' he said, 'but the ideals of your Revolution will be sullied if you yield to it. If you insist on fighting till you kill the last *yunker*, it will be a useless massacre, and I will make it known around the world.'

He explained the case of the boys and their desertion by their officers, and when he finished a vote was taken. All the sailors lifted their hands. A few of the Red Guard murmured dissent.

Antonov turned to them.

'I have made my terms of surrender,' he said, 'and I will myself shoot the first man who harms one of the *yunkers*.'

There was a ring of finality in his tone. The men looked at him in astonishment.

'Shoot us?' they cried incredulously.

'Yes,' he answered. 'I would rather that we should all die than that this American should say that revolutionists of Russia were base and revengeful!'

This time all the hands went up.

A committee from the City Hall arrived at that moment, and as the *yunkers* filed down the stairs, the leader took the hand of the first one and placed it in the hand of a sailor.

'This is prisoner number one, and I trust his life into your hands. Guard it for the honour of the Revolution,' he said.

When the last man was delivered, the sailor who brought him downstairs tossed a contemptuous glance in his direction and said: 'The last of the trash!' He was quickly hushed by one of his companions.[18]

It was midnight when Beatty returned to the hotel, to find that in her absence it had been recaptured by the Bolsheviks. This time they were taking no chances.

> The lobby and the upper floor swarmed with sailors. There were hundreds of guards where the day before there had been twenty. They had commandeered the entire second floor, and with machine-guns had taken positions in the front windows. The servants had fled. The beds were unmade. There had been no food in the hotel all day. Most of the residents had departed...
>
> I found my desk covered with messages from kindly members of the American colony, bent on rescuing me from the storm-centre of Revolution. I read them over with a sense of pleasure... but I had not the slightest intention in the world of obeying any of the well-meant advice or accepting any of the gracious hospitality.[19]

So ended the *yunker* rising of November 11. Philips Price comments that it had been planned to break out at the moment when Kerensky was nearing Petrograd, but broke out too soon. Knox agrees that the rising was badly organized, and adds that only a handful of the thousands of officers in the city took any part.

> A few of them joined in the defence of the Telephone Exchange, but very few. While the firing was in progress there I met an officer I knew walking in the next street arm-in-arm with a lady friend. I expressed my astonishment that he took no interest in the fighting, and he said that it had nothing to do with him![20]

The Committee, however, continued to pin all its hopes on Kerensky. John Reed describes November 12 as 'a day of suspense'. That evening an SR friend drew him aside and asked if he would like to be taken to the Committee's secret headquarters.

> At Number 86 Nevsky we went through a passage into a courtyard, surrounded by tall apartment buildings. At the door of apartment 229 my friend knocked in a peculiar way. There was a sound of scuffling; an inside door slammed; then the front door opened a crack and a woman's face appeared. After a minute's observation she led us in – a placid-looking, middle-aged lady who at once cried, 'Kyril, it's all right!' In the dining-room, where a samovar steamed on the table and there were plates full of bread

and raw fish, a man in uniform emerged from behind the window curtains, and another, dressed like a workman, from a closet. They were delighted to meet an American reporter.

They would not give their names, but both were SRs. As Reed discussed the current crisis with them, he and his companion were aware of people constantly entering and leaving – most of them officers, their shoulder-straps torn off.

We could see them in the hall, and hear their low, vehement voices. Occasionally, through the half-drawn portières, we caught a glimpse of a door opening into a bathroom, where a heavily-built officer in a colonel's uniform sat on the toilet, writing something on a pad held in his lap. I recognized Colonel Polkovnikov, former commandant of Petrograd [the 'very brave but rather pathetic optimist', as Knox had called him on November 7], for whose arrest the Military-Revolutionary Committee would have paid a fortune.

Out again on the Nevsky they swung on the step of a street-car bulging with people, 'its platform bent down from the weight and scraping along the ground, which crawled with agonizing slowness the long miles to Smolny'. Here the Petrograd Soviet was in full swing. Trotsky reported that heavy fighting was going on against Kerensky's forces at Pulkovo.

'Why aren't you out there with the Red Guards?' shouted a rough voice.
'I'm going now!' answered Trotsky, and left the platform. His face a little paler than usual, he passed down the side of the room, surrounded by eager friends, and hurried out to the waiting automobile.

Kamenev spoke, then Lenin appeared for a moment to answer the accusations of the SRs: 'They charge us with stealing their land programme... If that was so we bow to them. It is good enough for us...'

So the meeting roared on, leader after leader explaining, exhorting, arguing, soldier after soldier, workman after workman, standing up to speak his mind and his heart... The audience flowed, changing and renewed continually. From time to time men came in, yelling for the members of such and such a detachment, to go to the front; others, relieved, wounded, or coming to Smolny for arms and equipment, poured in...

It was almost three o'clock in the morning when, as we left the hall, Holtzman, of the Military-Revolutionary Committee, came running down the hall with a transfigured face.

'It's all right!' he shouted, grabbing my hands. 'Telegram from the front. Kerensky is smashed. Look at this!'

The telegram was from Trotsky. Kerensky's move against the capital, it announced, had been decisively repulsed. 'Glory to the warriors of the Revolution, the soldiers and the officers who were faithful to the People!'[21]

Next day Buchanan wrote in his diary:

Kerensky has again failed us, as he did at the time of the July rising and of the Kornilov affair. His only chance of success was to make a dash for Petrograd with such troops as he could get hold of; but he wasted time in parleying, issued orders and counter-orders which indisposed the troops [as did an aerial attack by the Bolsheviks with revolutionary pamphlets] and only moved when it was too late. The Bolsheviks have reoccupied Tsarskoe and are now confident of victory...

Nobody at the Embassy or in the colony has so far suffered, but we are still having a very anxious time. Yesterday a report reached us from two sources that an attack was to be made on the Embassy in the course of the night. In addition to our Polish guard we have six British officers sleeping in the house, and Knox, who acts as commander-in-chief, is a tower of strength in these troublous times. Though the Bolsheviks, who want to stand well with the Allies, are hardly likely to encourage such an attack, there is always the danger that German agents may incite the Red Guard to raid the Embassy in order to cause friction between Great Britain and Russia. In spite of the measures taken for the maintenance of order, life is not very secure at present, and this morning a Russian petty officer was shot dead in front of our windows for refusing to give up his sword to some armed workmen.[22]

*

Looking back later, Buchanan drew a parallel between Kerensky's fate and that of Nicholas.

Kerensky's Government had fallen, as the Empire had fallen, without a struggle. Both the Emperor and he had been wilfully blind to the dangers which threatened them, and both had allowed the situation to get beyond their control before taking any measures for their own protection... If I had to write the epitaphs of the Empire and the Provisional Government, I would do so in two words – lost opportunities.

From the very first Kerensky had been the central figure of the revolutionary drama and had, alone among his colleagues, acquired a sensible hold on the masses. An ardent patriot, he desired to see Russia carry on the war till a democratic peace had been won; while he wanted to combat the forces of disorder so that his country should not fall a prey to anarchy. In the early days of the revolution he displayed an energy and courage which marked him out as the one man capable of securing the attainment of these ends. But he did not act up to his professions, and every time that a crisis came he failed to rise to the occasion. He was, as subsequent events proved, a man of words and not of action; he had his chances and he never seized them; he was always going to strike and he never struck; he thought more of saving the revolution than of saving his country, and he ended by losing both.

Some blame, Buchanan felt, also attached to the moderate Socialists, so obsessed by the fear of a counter-revolution that they shrank from the adoption of measures that alone could make the army an effective fighting force, and to the Kadets, who went out of their way to create the impression that they were secretly working for a counter-revolution, in which the army was to be the dominant factor. 'The inability of Russians to work cordially together, even when the fate of their country is at stake, amounts almost to a national defect.'[23]

Other witnesses, however, like Bessie Beatty, took the view that it was precisely men like Buchanan himself and his advisers who must shoulder much of the blame for Kerensky's downfall:

His uncomprehending military partners, the Allies, were urging the impossible, and refusing to grant the demand of the Russian masses for a statement of war aims and a publication of the secret treaties, without which Kerensky could no longer hold the faith of his followers... Those who should have been behind him, with every energy and influence they possessed, were secretly willing his downfall, and some of them were plotting to bring it about. Individual members of the Allied military missions, still clinging to the old belief that Russia could be saved by a man on horseback, in spite of the Kornilov fiasco, were meeting behind closed doors, where they discussed, not the way to save Kerensky, but the way to put a dictator in his place.[24]

John Reed, concentrating on the forward movement of his story, treats Kerensky with studied indifference, but Louise Bryant writes that she had 'a tremendous respect' for him when he was head of the Provisional Government: 'He tried so passionately to hold Russia together, and what man at this hour could have accomplished that?' Beatty, too, is sympathetic: 'Kerensky, trying like the true democrat he was to please everyone, succeeded in pleasing no one.' Philips Price's verdict is in a similar vein: 'He remained true to himself to the end, spending his time honestly trying to reconcile two irreconcilables, and being finally abandoned by both.'[25]

'The true democrat he was', 'true to himself to the end', 'honestly trying to reconcile. . .': such phrases suggest that Kerensky was not only a man of integrity, but also an integrated individual. But there were many who felt that the trouble with Kerensky, as Buchanan wrote on September 20, was that he had *two* souls —

one as head of the Government and a patriot and the other as a Socialist and Idealist. So long as the former is in the ascendant he issues orders for strong measures and talks of establishing an iron discipline; but, as soon as he listens to the promptings of the latter, he relapses into inaction and allows his orders to remain a dead letter. I fear, moreover, that, like the Soviet, he has never wished to create a really strong army, and that, as he once remarked to me, he will never lend a hand to forge a weapon one day to be used against the revolution.

According to Verkhovsky, Kerensky's Minister of War until his resignation on November 3, 'Kerensky had not wanted the Cossacks to suppress the rising by themselves, as that would have meant the end of the revolution' (Buchanan's diary entry for November 14).[26]

An intriguing analysis of Kerensky, which suggests how these two conflicting views of him might be reconciled, is provided by E.H. Wilcox. Of Kerensky during those heady weeks in the spring of 1917 he writes:

He became the personification of every thing that was good and noble in Russia. He was no longer the leader of a political party, but the prophet of a new faith, the high priest of a new doctrine, which were to embrace all Russia, all mankind. Whatever he may have been before or after, during this dazzling and intoxicating interlude he had in him true elements of greatness. He ceased to be what he had been, and became different, not only in degree, but also in kind. What a man is and does depends on the medium in which he works and the motive that actuates him, as well as upon his inherent powers. Kerensky may have been by nature little more than a mediocrity, but he had been fired by the revolutionary enthusiasm which surrounded him and inspired by a fervent and profound belief in the religion of freedom. Russia had a new and great message of hope for the world, and he was to be its bearer. Under the sense of his high mission, his physical and mental powers were purified and enhanced. He knew exactly what he believed in, and what he wanted to be at. The path lay straight ahead, and there was no need for vacillation or temporizing. His decisions were instant, peremptory, irrevocable, and nearly always right. His very oratory participated in his rebirth. It lost its artificiality and diffusiveness, and became the spontaneous expression of intense feeling passing through a well-trained mind. In brief and pungent phrases, it spoke the hearts of his deliriously enthusiastic audiences.

At the front he achieved miracles in encouraging the troops. 'How his feeble frame supported the Herculean work of those days none could imagine who had seen him step down from the Duma tribune [before the Revolution] limp and shaking after a single speech.' But when his great effort failed, there disappeared also the forces which had made it possible.

It was like the pricking of an iridescent bubble, and nothing was left behind. All the bright hopes of himself and others vanished, and their place was taken by disillusionment, depression, and despair. The medium of popular enthusiasm which had reacted on him, and on which he, in his turn, had reacted, was no more. The burning faith in the cause which he had personified was extinct. All that remained was the old Kerensky, gifted and sincere no doubt, but without the inward inspiration and the outward stimulus that had made him for a few weeks the great champion of a great idea. The road in front of him was no longer a broad and straight one, along which he could march boldly, looking neither to right nor left, in the consciousness that everything good in Russia was following in his footsteps. Public opinion now divided sharply into two parties, and it was his impossible task to find a fresh course which would be acceptable to both of them. The advocates of discipline pulled him in one direction, the advocates of 'democratization' in the other. In the search for a reconciliation of their demands, heroic gestures, fine sentiments and resonant appeals were of little avail. It was now a question of delicate negotiation and what the other side always calls 'intrigue'. Kerensky ceased to be a prophet and priest, and once more became a mere politician.

Everyone at the Moscow Conference – the last serious effort to restore national unity – noticed the change that had come over Kerensky. He was now playing a part for which he was not suited, and he did not play it well. Instead of the storm of passionate words which had shaken vast audiences like a hurricane, there was a forced and stilted speech, with no ring of sincerity or fervour, and jarring by its continued insistence on the speaker's own power, authority and determination. Meanwhile, in his attempts to pick his way between two conflicting extremes, he had become involved in the meshes of the Kornilov Affair, which was soon to bring him down. It would, however, be a mistake to attribute his eclipse entirely, or even mainly, to that incident. The radiant Kerensky, who had dazzled the world with his brilliance, came to an end with the disaster and disgrace of Tarnopol, and in all probability could never have been again.

At the same time, one is tempted to speculate what Kerensky would have now been had he succeeded. He was not so far from success as to make the hypothesis ridiculous. If he had been able to work upon the Army with his intoxicating eloquence a few weeks earlier, if the demoralization of the troops had not gone quite so far... it is possible that the brilliance of the opening of the Galician advance might have been maintained. In that case, the momentum of victory would probably have carried forward the armies on all the other Russian fronts, the triumph of the Allies would have come much sooner, and Kerensky would have stood out as the most potent statesman of the War, for his individual contribution to victory would then have appeared greater than that of any other civilian.[27]

Moscow

The Battle of Moscow (November 10–15) and the Red Burial (November 23)

In contrast to the March Revolution, in November there was considerably more fighting and bloodshed in Moscow than in Petrograd. One reason for this was that the Bolshevik leaders in Moscow, who inclined towards the long-term strategy of Kamenev and Zinoviev, did not expect to have to seize power so soon and had not made such careful plans for a swift and painless takeover. Another was that they encountered stiffer opposition. It came once more from the *yunkers*, helped by a few volunteers and a few ('a very few', Knox again stresses) officers.

One of those who found himself uncomfortably close to the centre of the Battle of Moscow was an Englishman, Reginald Bennett, who worked for William Miller & Co.[1] His family had already returned to England and he was being looked after by a Russian servant, Annushka. He had a large flat overlooking Lubyanskaya Square, a strategic point to the north-east of Red Square and the Kremlin.

Guarding the Kremlin, he writes, were some Cossacks and the 56th Infantry Regiment, which was supposedly loyal to the Government, but then mutinied and went over to the Bolsheviks. The Cossacks, however, though absolutely outnumbered, held the gates, enabling the *yunkers* to run a gun into the Kremlin and fire two or three rounds, whereupon the 56th surrendered. This happened in the early hours of Saturday, November 10. Continuous firing also went on all night in the streets.

Under our bedroom windows there was a fierce fight, and when I looked out in the morning, there were heaps of dead and wounded on both sides on the pavement who lay there till the Red Cross ambulance removed them at about 9 o'clock. All Saturday the fire of machine-guns and rifles was incessant, but the streets were fairly full of people taking no part but intensely interested. It did not seem to strike them that there was any danger in watching the combat. Heaps of curious onlookers have been killed. I have seen four killed today... Annushka tells me that she has heard that hundreds of children have been killed, their parents (mostly their mothers) having taken them out to see the fun. I went out myself on Saturday afternoon for a bit, but came back when I found bullets whizzing uncomfortably all round.

On Sunday we first began to hear big guns, 4" and 6", and since then the roar and boom of artillery has been continuous. Now the Bolsheviks have got a gun on to the Sparrow Hills and are firing from there into the Kremlin. A very fierce engagement has been going on all day on the Nikitsky Boulevard, both sides employing guns, machine-guns and rifles, but I don't think there has been any bayonet work. Of course all works, offices, etc. are closed, as well as all the railways, and there are no provisions at all in the town. The Town Council hopes to be able to ration out ¼ lb. bread per day for the next few weeks, but how it is going to get it I don't know. Of course we don't know how things are going to end, but in spite of the immense disparity of force, I am convinced that the Government will win, for the Bolsheviks are merely an armed mob, and cowards at that.

It is reported that two Divisions of Terek Cossacks are arriving this evening; that means about 16,000 men; and also 1,500 men of one of the shock battalions.

Sunday 10.30 p.m. For the last two hours, since writing the above, there has been a most uncanny silence; not a shot; not a gun. I wonder what it means. It is pitch dark outside, not a lamp lit, not a house that shows a light, and it is raining heavily. But last night it was the same, yet the firing went on all the time. There is apparently not a soul in the streets. All day long pickets of five or six Bolsheviks have been strolling about and loosing off their rifles at the corners of the streets at nothing in general. What for I can't make out as there is no return fire and no opposition of any sort. I can only imagine that it is with a view of terrorizing the people. They know that public sympathy is entirely against them, and I think they must be afraid of a hostile crowd and are therefore determined to prevent people coming out. That can be the only explanation of this wanton and random firing about the streets at anyone who happens to be there.

The town is declared to be in a state of siege, and no one is allowed to be in the streets without a pass; but unfortunately the Government authorities have no means for the present of enforcing this edict, for the few troops they have are all engaged in fighting the Bolsheviks and there is no police or militia at all. It is the Bolsheviks who are enforcing the edict that their opponents have promulgated. The first thing the Bolsheviks did was to shoot down the Town Militia, the new Police, very few and an absolutely rotten lot at any time. Those who were not shot disappeared at once. The Bolsheviks' system of promiscuous shooting in the streets has effectually cleared them.

Sarnia came here yesterday in great glee and fearfully excited. She is an out-and-out Bolshevik, and told Annushka that their day was come at last and that they were going to alter and improve the whole order of the universe. She said with great pride that though the men seemed to be afraid of going about, she and her friend (another girl) went everywhere and were afraid of nothing. Annushka told her she was a fool, and I should not be in the least surprised myself to hear that she had been killed.

There goes a machine-gun again! – another! What a rabble! There go the rifles and guns. The whole symphony is starting again after a two hours' lull.

We have a house guard of Special Constables from amongst the lodgers. My time on guard is from 2 to 4 at night – 2 hours for those on night duty, 3 hours on day duty; three of us at a time in the yard, though what effective use we could be in case of an attack I am sure I don't know. However, it gives a certain sense of security. All the front doors of the house are locked, no one is allowed to enter or leave except by the gates in the yard, and everyone has to get in and out of their flats by the back stairs. There is only one gate for the whole house, so that the guard can be sure that no one can get in without their knowledge, but of course there would be no difficulty in forcing any of the front entries if half a dozen men tried to do so, nor the back gates for the matter of that, in spite of our guard, if the attackers were armed with rifles. All the houses have been organizing these house guards throughout the town, and it is really a very sound thing in principle.

In his flat near Arbat Square, another strategic point to the west of the Kremlin, Mr Urch the schoolmaster was woken on Saturday morning by the voice of his wife saying: 'I think it has begun.'

'That's good,' I replied, 'tell me if it goes out again.'

How could I guess that my wife was not referring to the kitchen fire, but to the Bolshevik street fighting? She informed me of my mistake with a little more vigour, and I got up in the dim dawn to see about it.

True enough. There were creeping men on the other side of the street, creeping in single file towards Arbat. No doubt there were some on our pavement, too, but they kept so close under the wall that we could not see them.

As it became lighter, they saw that the figures consisted of a mixture of soldiers, railwaymen, tramwaymen and men without uniform.

'They are Bolsheviks,' I said decisively at last, though that should have been clear to all from the beginning. For, apart from the uniforms, why should Government troops creep towards the centre of the town they themselves held?

With his friend and lodger, Professor Clark, Mr Urch was summoned to a meeting where the residents of the ten houselets in their house-group were working out a common approach to the coming period of strife.

Without any debate, the meeting decided unanimously that we should be 'strictly neutral', whatever happened. But as the ordinary laws were necessarily suspended, our premises might be troubled by bandits, thieves, burglars, and must organize a system of self-defence.

'How are we to know who is a bandit and who a Bolshevik?' asked one old lady, but the meeting could give her no satisfactory answer.

It was a very mixed company – over one hundred adults of both sexes. We did not know them all by sight. There was General Voronov, a man of about seventy years. He and his wife were living very modestly on his pension. Three or four younger men were in military uniform, but none of us asked why they did not join in the fight. People were naturally reticent, as it was not discreet to speak in favour of the Government with our street in the hands of 'the enemy', and those who leant the Bolshevik way were not sure that it was yet safe to show their colours. There were certainly adherents of both sides at our meeting. The atmosphere was therefore one of doubt and mistrust.

As a measure of self-defence against bandits, the House Committee decided to keep a day and night guard on the gate. The instructions to the guard were inconveniently vague, except in one point: no resistance was to be offered to the belligerents of either side.

Armed with a sabre and revolver apiece, Messrs Urch & Clark made a fearsome pair.

The premises were large and the yard-wall low, so our watch might have been anything but a sinecure. Every time our turn came round, we were together, for the Committee allowed us that privilege.

Professor Clark is a versatile man, and it was interesting to be on guard with him. For all the notice he took of the battle, we might have been on one of our walks in search of rare lepidoptera, as we paced up and down our spacious yard or sat to rest under shelter at the gate. Through the long dark watches I learnt much from him on many subjects, from the building of ice-breakers and violins to the catching of tiger-moths at night with a bait of apple-pulp and beer.

During the day watches they could take glimpses up the street to the point 100–150 yards away where the Bolsheviks had dug a trench across the road and erected a barricade behind it. Convinced that this small minority of extremists would be beaten, Mr Urch felt uncomfortably aware that the 'front' was bound to move their way, but as time went on and the barricade remained intact, he had to revise his opinion.

Each day they had another chance of looking round without much danger.

This came as a more or less regular lull every morning, when the firing would cease for about two hours. There must have been a 'gentlemen's agreement' about this between the belligerent sides. Whether or not it was arranged for the purpose of giving non-combatants a chance to do their shopping, the daily lull was interpreted in this sense.

The street became a curious sight at this time. As if a signal had been given, housewives and cooks, with here and there a man, would come out of the houses and scurry along furtively to shops in the vicinity. Admitted through side-doors or back-doors, they would buy what they could and scurry home again.[2]

On Monday, November 12 Mr Bennett reports that a fight has been going on round the Works where he is employed between the Bolsheviks and the *yunkers,*

who have their school just on the other side of the street, over the bridge. As each side has a couple of guns, one 4" and one 6" each, the shooting is quite lively. There are only 40 *yunkers* against about 1,000 Bolsheviks, but the latter are such cowards that they don't try to storm the school. The Bolsheviks fired a 6" shell at the warehouse in the yard of the Works, where there are 150 Cossacks quartered, but it struck the cashier's house 50 yards away and burst in the wall on the ground, doing little damage except that it happened to strike the main electric light cable and put out all the lights everywhere. Close to the *yunkers'* school is the cadets' academy, boys under 16 years old. These also, about 150, put up quite a good fight, but I hear this evening that after having suffered heavy casualties, they have surrendered.

It is a horrible thing that though others can ring me up by telephone, I can't ring up myself. The explanation is that the telephone staff is so depleted that they can't serve all the numbers and so have cut off about three-quarters of the subscribers from calls. I am thus dependent upon others ringing me up, but all the same I get a fair amount of news of what is going on. There are of course no papers, and we don't know what is happening abroad or outside Moscow... It is true that the Bolsheviks have been publishing a paper, but it is of course absolutely unreliable.

Tuesday evening. I did not get to bed till 5 o'clock this morning; heavy firing all night. During my watch almost incessant rifle fire just outside the yard gates in the Malaya Lubyanka. I did not get up till 11 o'clock; the firing was then more intense. The Bolsheviks had brought up a 4" gun to try to capture the Telephone Station. The telephone has ceased to work at all today. I attended the House Committee which sat from 3 to 8 discussing measures of self-protection and provisioning. Fifty-five occupiers of flats attended. All agreed that there is no possibility of obtaining protection from any authority, as there is none, and that we must organize our own protection. Also that we must consider ourselves in a state of siege, pool provisions and ration them out as it may be a fortnight or more before we can get any more. Few have any revolvers or know how to use them. All day long big guns have been firing, but we are cut off and no one knows in the least what is happening. Six people were killed in the Square this morning, walking along the pavement, one of them a Red Cross man. I saw two shot. As there is practically no one in the streets and I don't suppose a hundred people have been through the Square during the day, this is a high percentage of casualties. I am more than ever amazed at the extraordinary foolishness or dense stupidity of the few people who now go about the streets. They seem to stroll about in an aimless way, totally unconscious that the shooting is in the least dangerous. The two I saw killed were loafing along casually, apparently totally unconscious of danger.

This evening is again pitch dark; not a light to be seen, and I have been watching a big fire, evidently the result of shell fire. It looks to be somewhere in the neighbourhood of the Arbat Square. One can see the violet flashes of the guns reflected in the smoke above the red glare beneath. No one knows anything of what is happening, or who is getting the best of it. The curious thing is that no soldiers are to be seen anywhere. Firing all round, and nothing to be seen. This absolute ignorance of what is going on around one is terribly trying for the nerves. It seems evident that no Government troops have come in, or if they have come, they are unable to do anything. Our windows here don't rattle from the gunfire, but they vibrate in an extraordinary way. There are big guns booming continuously now, but they must be a considerable distance off. What on earth they can see to fire at in a night like this I am sure I can't think. There is a continuous firing of volleys from a squad of Bolsheviks in the Malaya Lubyanka. They fire every 15 seconds, but I am absolutely positive they have nothing to fire at, and I can only suppose that it is to keep up their spirits. The shots draw no reply and there is never any return fire from across the Square. During the day I think their object is to terrorize, and at night to keep up their own spirits.

As the days passed, it became clear to Mr Urch that the Bolshevik grip on their locality was tightening.

Their men came from time to time to inspect our house, and some of our menfolk were taken away... Later it became known to some of us that one or two of the young men in our house-group had taken part in the fighting on the side of the *yunkers*, though we were unaware of it at the time. They would get round to the other side of the barricades to use a rifle now and then, and come back to sleep at home in the Bolshevik camp. Movements of this sort were possible during the earlier stages of the fighting, provided one made a detour and had a good pretext for being out if challenged; but it must have been decidedly risky as a practice towards the end of the fighting week.

All day and all night, except for occasional lulls, sometimes for a few minutes, sometimes for an hour or more, the din of artillery fire and exploding shells continued.

We did not manage to sleep well any night, on account of the noise. More disturbing to our rest than the artillery was the machine-gun fire, such a spiteful sound which would keep on for hours at a time with scarcely a pause, and it was so near. This became intensest towards the end of the battle, and it was all the more disturbing to our feelings, as we knew the spot where this particular part of the fighting was going on – at the *yunker* school some 300 yards from our house.

The promised Government reinforcements never arrived. The few who did come in joined the Bolsheviks, who were able to tighten the net around the *yunker* strongholds by bringing in more Red Guards from the suburbs. At 2 a.m. on Friday, November 16, according to Mr Bennett, the *yunkers* surrendered, peace terms being effected by the Metropolitan of Moscow, Tikhon. 'Surely,' Mr Urch comments, 'Russia must some day produce a poet or historian to give this gallant band – largely mere youths in their teens – their meed of glory for the plucky stand they made.'

It was now possible to walk about freely again both indoors and out. 'The bodies of the fallen', Mr Urch writes, 'had all been removed from the streets, but blood was still in the tramway grooves, and small pools here and there in the streets, as well as gruesome smears on some of the walls.' Few houses nearby were free of bullet marks, but theirs had scarcely been touched.[3]

At the Bennetts' flat, however, it was a different story:

We have one bullet-hole through the dining-room window, and in the drawing-room the plate glass window looking over the Square has three shots through it and the glass is entirely smashed. Every window in each room along the Bolshaya Lubyanka has been smashed by shrapnel fragments, or possibly H.E. shell, so I am now living in the study at the back, sleeping on the sofa which makes a most comfortable bed. The Bolsheviks put a machine-gun on the roof of our house, and fired it for some time, which no doubt explains why we got such a dose in reply, otherwise we should not have been in the line of fire as far as I can make out.

Now that the Bolsheviks have a complete victory, he wonders what they are going to do with it. There is talk of them confiscating all the banks and factories.

Of course this state of things can't last, and I expect to see a violent swing round very shortly. Meanwhile, however, they may do a lot of damage. If the people find themselves duped, as they undoubtedly will, if they find they are no nearer to peace, that not only is there less food but absolute starvation, that they are no nearer a practical division of the land and that none of the promises made them are being fulfilled, then I fear we shall see the people turn and rend their false leaders, and there will be no leaders at all and complete anarchy followed by pillage, rapine and murder. This is a very real fear. That will be the ultimate and final swing of the pendulum, after which it must swing back in the other direction.

Mr Urch likewise expected the Bolshevik rule to be short.

'The worse the better,' was a saying one often heard. It was intended to mean that the Bolshevik victory would prove a good thing in the long run, that a period with Bolshevism at the helm would unite the moderate elements against them, and their attempt to rule could not last long.[4]

On Sunday, November 18 Moscow's wide pavements were thronged with sightseers who had come to inspect the damage to the buildings. Among them was the Moscow Art Theatre's famous young actress, Maria Gérmanova, accompanied by her husband, their six-year-old son, his recently recruited English governess Emma Dashwood ('Miss Emmie'), and an Indian friend of the family,

Suhravardi. For six days they had been cooped up in the vestibule of their flat in the Arbat district, living on a diet of sugar, black rusks made from rye, and as many cups as they liked of China tea. Now, as the five of them walked along in a line, Miss Emmie became aware of fingers pointed in their direction. Then she caught the words:

'*Vot Germanova*! Look, there's Germanova!' They were friendly, excited voices – well, you know the Russians, they don't say things softly – and I thought to myself: good gracious, she *is* well known, and I hadn't realized! I think people were reassured at seeing her. Look, they seemed to be saying, there's Germanova, *she's* all right.[5]

Meanwhile, in Petrograd, the news that the Bolsheviks were bombarding the Kremlin had passed from mouth to mouth, as John Reed puts it, 'almost with a sense of terror'. Lunacharsky, aware that many of the country's most important art treasures had been removed from Petrograd to the Kremlin for safe-keeping from the Germans, was so upset by this development that he resigned as Commissar of Education. Reed and Bryant decided to go to Moscow to see for themselves.

They arrived late on November 22. The Governor-General's palace was now the headquarters of the Moscow Soviet, and Reed describes how its splendid state salon was filled with 'a low-voiced hum of talk, underlaid with the whirring bass of a score of sewing machines. Huge bolts of red and black cotton cloth were unrolled, serpentining across the parqueted floor and over tables, at which sat half a hundred women, cutting and sewing streamers and banners for the Funeral of the Revolutionary Dead.' They were invited to march with the Executive Committee in the funeral procession next morning. Later that night they walked through the empty streets to Red Square. Along one side stood the Kremlin, still intact despite all the fearful reports circulating in Petrograd that it had been razed to the ground. In front of the Kremlin wall, by the light of huge fires, two massive burial trenches were being carved out of the frozen ground. 'The tall figures of soldiers,' Bryant writes, 'the smaller and more gaunt figures of factory workers cast distorted silhouettes across the snow as they bent over their gruesome task... It was terrifyingly still and lonesome. There was no sound but the clatter of spades and the sputter of torches.' Exhausted workers, running with sweat in spite of the cold, climbed wearily out, to be replaced by a fresh band of silent volunteers. The mounds beside the trenches grew into little hills. About 5 a.m. Bryant and Reed climbed stiffly over them and straggled wearily home. The task was completed; the trenches were ready to receive five hundred coffins.

Two hours later they were up again, drinking tea and eating black bread at the Hotel National before hurrying through the dark streets to the Soviet. At eight the procession set out down the Tverskaya, the banners flapping overhead. Forcing their way through the dense mass packed near the Kremlin wall, they stood on one of the mounds of newly turned earth. 'It was bitter cold,' Bryant writes. 'Our feet froze to the ground and our hands ached under our gloves. But the spectacle before us was so magnificent that we forgot everything else.' Gigantic banners, red, with great letters in gold and in white, had been suspended from the top of the Kremlin wall to the ground. Reed noted some of the inscriptions: 'Martyrs of the Beginning of World Social Revolution' and 'Long Live the Brotherhood of Workers of the World'. The coffins, made of unplaned wood and stained red as if in blood, were borne on the shoulders of fine-looking young giants of soldiers in towering grey caps. Some of the coffins, according to Reed,

> were open, the lid carried behind them; others were covered with gilded or silvered cloth, or had a soldier's hat nailed on the top. There were many wreaths of hideous artificial flowers...[...]
>
> Slowly the marchers came with their coffins to the entrance of the grave, and the bearers clambered up with their burdens and went down into the pit. Many of them were women – squat, strong proletarian women. Behind the dead came other women – women young and broken, or old, wrinkled women making noises like hurt animals...

A woman near Bryant tried to hurl herself after a coffin as it was being lowered.

> She forgot the revolution, forgot the future of mankind, remembered only her lost one.
>
> With all her frenzied strength she fought against the friends who tried to restrain her. Crying out the name of the man in the coffin, she screamed, bit, scratched like a wounded wild thing until she was finally carried away moaning and half unconscious. Tears rolled down the faces of the big soldiers.

One by one, Reed writes, the five hundred coffins were laid in the pits.

Dusk fell, and still the banners came drooping and fluttering, the band played the Funeral March, and the huge assemblage chanted. In the leafless branches of the trees above the grave the wreaths were hung, like strange, multicoloured blossoms. Two hundred men began to shovel in the dirt. It rained dully down upon the coffins with a thudding sound, audible beneath the singing...[...]

I suddenly realized that the devout Russian people no longer needed priests to pray them into heaven. On earth they were building a kingdom more bright than any heaven had to offer, and for which it was a glory to die...[6]

Neither Bryant nor Reed describes how the *yunkers* were buried. Bessie Beatty spares them a thought after describing the Red Burial (though her account does not sound first hand):

There was another day, another funeral, another crowd of broken-hearted men and women. Their crumbs of comfort were more meagre, for theirs was the bitterness of defeat; but they also hugged the faith that the stalwart boys who lay stretched in their coffins had died defending an ideal.

Worlds of space lay between those two groups of mourners – they had no single thing in common but their grief. Their dead lay in the darkened recesses of great churches, and priests in funeral robes of black and silver said many masses for the repose of their souls. There were no red coffins, no crimson banners, no singing multitudes – only prayers and silent tears.[7]

*

'Worlds of space lay between the two groups': this aptly describes how our witnesses reacted to the November Revolution as a whole. The British and American official representatives were bound to be uncompromisingly hostile, for whatever else might happen, Bolshevik Russia would never make an effective ally against the Germans. 'Everyone has forgotten the war!' Knox complains in his diary on November 8.[8] Even more virulently hostile were the members of the resident British and American communities. For them, as for the Russian bourgeoisie, a whole world was at stake: the comfortable world of capital, class and property, of servants to be given orders, of status and of privilege. In the privacy of her diary Mrs

Marie Smith, the widow of a British businessman, does not mince words about the Bolsheviks:

> The latter are all the scum & hooligans from everywhere & all they care for is to create a panic & then to start looting and robbing... Everyone is disgusted to think of being ruled by such scum. The life here promises to be as hard as hatred can make it; they loathe the higher classes & are going to make us feel it... Yesterday [November 23] was the funeral of all the victims or rather of the 'beasts', they made a great fuss & had a military funeral with pomp & red coffins. They were all put into 2 huge graves under the Kremlin walls but no church service was read over them, they were buried like dogs![9]

In the other group were idealists like John Reed and Louise Bryant. When General Knox visited Smolny, he saw only a building that was 'thick with the dirt of revolution', whereas for Reed the dirt – the air 'thick with cigarette smoke, and human breathing, and the smell of coarse clothes and sweat' – was more real than all the frock-coats at the City Hall. 'How impressive it was!' Bryant comments on the Red Burial. 'No ceremony, no priests; everything so simple and so real!' And of the November Revolution itself Reed writes that it had not come as the political martyrs of the past expected it would come, 'nor as the intelligentsia desired it; but it had come – rough, strong, impatient of formulas, contemptuous of sentimentalism; real...'[10] They saw the Revolution as the first genuine expression of the will of the people (and not only of the Russian people): the underdogs, the exploited, the proletariat, had spoken at last and taken their destiny into their own hands. It did not matter that the Bolsheviks were isolated, even from their fellow Socialists, that when two thousand Red Guards marched through Petrograd on November 16, the crowds were silent, and that the Red Burial (unlike the burial of the victims of the March Revolution on the Field of Mars in Petrograd) had been an occasion on which no one unknown to the proletariat dared to venture out of doors: it could not have been otherwise.[11]

At the time of the March Revolution, our witnesses differed only in the degree of their enthusiasm and in their assessment of what the future might hold, though as the months went by, these divisions became wider and more obvious. The effect of the November Revolution, however, was suddenly to accelerate this process of division, so that attitudes became polarized. 'Bolshevism admits no com-promise', Harold Williams wrote. 'Either you are for it or you are against it.'[12] The Bolshevik Revolution was – and still is – a profoundly divisive event.

14

The Constituent Assembly

Attempts to convene the Constituent Assembly
(December 11–13 and January 18, 1918)

Harold Williams and his wife were still in Kislovodsk when rumours came through on November 8 of a successful rising in Petrograd. 'Faith in Kerensky had grown very slender,' Harold comments, 'but it was assumed that as he had been so clamorously forewarned, even he must be forearmed.'[1] They returned at once to Petrograd, and on November 19 Harold writes:

> Days drag on to winter, and still no decision, no issue. There is a conflict that is furious, but diffuse, violent, up to within an ace of the decisive point, perpetually and desperately inconclusive. If only one could point to a man or a group and say: 'Here is the hope of salvation; here is the promise of a new day!' But there is no concentration as yet, no visible organizing centre.
>
> I hear the Socialists talking, gloomily depressed beyond all measure, contemplating the wreck of all their hopes, bewailing their own errors, loathing their own verbiage, and taking refuge in a lingering instinct of patriotism that for months they have passionately denied. I listen to them, but they proffer no solution. They are afraid of the Bolsheviks and are afraid of a dictatorship, and are yet half inclined to make common cause with some of the Bolsheviks even now against the coming dictator, wherever and whoever he may be.
>
> Every moment is instinct with catastrophe. Problems of food and fuel grow daily more menacing. Further anarchy and starvation loom ahead. Yet the moments are linked by some stubborn

substratum of habit. Life goes on in an unintelligible way, defying bold plots and amazing negations, cheating all the prophets, baffling all calculation. Trains still run, electric light still burns, tradesmen still hand over goods in return for the scraps of paper that are called money, and even the postman goes his daily round. There is no Government in Russia, and yet Russia still exists by force of habit, by virtue of some common, irrefutable, irrational belief. The Russians are certainly at bottom a most extraordinarily law-abiding people, considering the continual opportunity for and provocation to excess.

The problem of Russia's future is now not a matter for speculation, but for the liveliest imagination, and the probabilities are fantastic.

Two days later, he has come to the conclusion that Blondin was not a remarkable man.

Here we are all Blondins now, balancing on a tightrope over an abyss. The sensation is peculiar at first, but human beings are adaptable creatures, and we are growing habituated. In the abyss below we see glimmering forms and dim outlines, and are learning that even the abyss is not a void.

Children are at school today, crossing sweepers are cleaning the streets and business offices are open. The Government departments are empty; the officials remain grimly on strike. The much-maligned Russian official is displaying heroic qualities.

The Council of the People's Commissars is distinctly embarrassed. Lenin tries to ignore the boycott, and issues tonight a proclamation to the peasants and workers, saying the government is in their own hands. He orders the local peasant soviets immediately to take over the estates and to guard them from all injury till details of the partition have been arranged. The revolution, he says, has conquered in Petrograd and Moscow, and 'the great majority of the Russian people is on the side of the peasants' and workers' Government'...

Lenin is an interesting figure.

It is absurd to regard him as a mere German agent. I imagine that in pursuit of his ends Lenin is willing to use all available means, and if the Germans like to supply money or officers for the purpose of effecting a social revolution in Russia he gladly accepts even their services.

Mere money for his personal use could not tempt such a man. He is utterly headstrong, oblivious of realities, oblivious of what he regards as bourgeois morality, oblivious of immediate consequences. He sees only his goal, the complete and forcible establishment of Socialism in Russia. And the Germans who are helping him now may repent of their bargain; they may not find it so easy to lay the destructive spirit they have called forth from the valleys of Switzerland. They have promised anarchy in Russia, but are they quite sure that the infection may not spread among their own exhausted population?

In the meantime Lenin persists in his fantastic enterprise. He does not see that he is isolated, does not see that his army is fading away, that the forces that availed for destruction are incapable of any constructive work.

And even Lenin's right-hand man, Trotsky, who is much more astute and worldly-wise than his chief, is showing signs of wavering. There are rumours that he is resigning his thankless post as Commissar for Foreign Affairs.[2]

This is Harold Williams' first assessment of Lenin. Its strangely impersonal quality becomes more comprehensible in the light of his wife's remarks apropos of the period before the July Days:

Harold never went to the Bolsheviks. They disgusted him.
  Sometimes he would say with a guilty air:
  'What do you think? Perhaps I ought to go and listen to Lenin?'
  And he gave a sigh of relief when I firmly answered:
  'Of course you need not.'

Eventually he did go to see Trotsky, describing him afterwards to Bruce Lockhart as 'one of the most evil men I have ever met'; the enigmatic Lenin was 'a problem in nightmare psychology'; and both were the 'fantastic products of the underworld of our civilization'.[3]

Lockhart was to have considerably more contact with the two Bolshevik leaders. In character, they were 'as far apart as the two poles'. Lenin was a convinced Marxist who had adapted Marxism to Russian conditions, had no interest in Western concepts of liberty and nationalism, and regarded the proletarian revolution as the necessary prelude to Socialism. 'Having made up his mind, he was inflexible.' E.H. Wilcox likewise comments that both friends and foes speak of Lenin's 'iron will' and 'iron nerve', and adds that 'it is these qualities, coupled with the rather mechanical smoothness and precision of his mental processes, which have made him unchallenged chief over the associates of his work'.

In conversation with foreigners, Lockhart goes on, Lenin 'never lost his temper, nor was he personally vindictive like Stalin', while Wilcox quotes the case of an English merchant who, in order to extricate his family from a critical situation, had to seek Lenin's personal aid, and 'was astonished to find the "bloodthirsty tyrant" a mild-mannered man, courteous and sympathetic in his bearing, and almost eager to afford all the assistance in his power.' If he promised anything, according to Lockhart, he fulfilled it – 'but, regarding capitalists as criminals, he considered it legitimate to deceive them.'[4]

On meeting Lenin for the first time, Lockhart was reminded more of a provincial grocer than of a leader of men. 'Yet in those steely eyes there was something that arrested my attention, something in that quizzing, half-contemptuous, half-smiling look which spoke of boundless self-confidence and conscious superiority.' Dressed, according to the American, Raymond Robins, in 'a woollen shirt and a suit of clothes bought, one would think, many years ago and last pressed shortly afterward', Lenin was quite indifferent to his personal appearance. Not so, Trotsky. Bessie Beatty had noted how the alabaster whiteness of his skin was enhanced by his black jacket and flowing black tie. To Lockhart he seemed unmistakably Jewish: 'dark with vast forehead, flashing eyes, sensuous mouth with well-trimmed beard and moustache, and beautiful well-manicured hands... Like Lenin he was short in stature with broad shoulders. Temperamentally he was an individualist with all the enthusiasms and depressions of an artist. When the sun smiled on him, he could be affable and even charming. When things went wrong, the clouds darkened his forehead, and his eyes flashed.' Trotsky 'does not flatter an audience,' Robins writes. 'He will even go to the other extreme. He will openly sneer at it. He will freeze it with contempt... His face then is the face of a Mephistopheles, diabolically intelligent, diabolically scornful...'[5]

At Smolny Lenin kept himself aloof, never visiting the huge canteen on the ground floor or even the little upstairs tea-room, whereas journalists could always be sure of an interview with Trotsky.[6] Like Lenin (but unlike Kerensky), Trotsky had acquired an international outlook from his many years abroad. In political philosophy, Lockhart thought, he was no match for Lenin, though he had often taken a line of his own between 1905 and 1917, and did not become a Bolshevik until the July Days. What brought the two men together was their passion for revolution. The qualities that made Trotsky indispensable to Lenin were his great administrative ability (this Lenin had also), and – something that Lenin did not have – his superb physical courage, well illustrated during the July Days by his rescue of Chernov from the Kronstadt sailors.[7]

Buchanan acknowledges that he underestimated the strength of the Bolsheviks; perhaps he might not have done, had Harold Williams overcome his feeling of disgust (or fear of offending his wife) and kept him better informed about Lenin. 'Much as I deplore the ruin and misery which they have brought on their country,' he writes,

> I readily admit that Lenin and Trotsky are both extraordinary men. The Ministers, in whose hands Russia had placed her destinies, had all proved to be weak and incapable, and now by some cruel turn of fate the only two really strong men whom she had produced during the war were destined to consummate her ruin. On their advent to power, however, they were still an unknown quantity, and nobody expected that they would have a long tenure of office.[8]

One major problem facing the Bolsheviks was the attitude towards them of the peasants, most of whose leaders had supported the Committee of Public Safety. On November 26 the Second All-Russian Peasants' Congress opened in Petrograd with what Philips Price describes as 'one of the stormiest three hours' debates which I have ever witnessed in Russia'. Finally a new Executive Committee was elected under the chairmanship of the leader of the Left SRs, Marie Spiridonova, whose pale bespectacled face and hair drawn flatly down reminded John Reed of a New England schoolteacher. Chernov, whose programme of land nationalization had once seemed so dangerously radical to Harold Williams, now attempted to check the drift of the Congress towards the left, but was unable to prevent the Left SRs, after a series of secret conferences at Smolny, from agreeing to enter into a coalition with the Bolsheviks. This provided John Reed with the happy ending that he needed for *Ten Days That Shook the World*, which climaxes (though not on the tenth day) with the 'wedding' between the Peasants' Soviets and the Workers' and Soldiers' Soviets.

On the steps of Smolny about a hundred Workers' and Soldiers' Deputies were massed, with their banner, dark against the blaze of light streaming out between the arches. Like a wave they rushed down, clasping the peasants in their arms and kissing them; and the procession poured in through the great door and up the stairs, with a noise like thunder...[9]

Even more urgent of solution, though, if the Bolsheviks were to remain in power, was the problem of the war. When the news broke that Lenin was proposing peace terms to the Germans, Harold Williams was at first filled with indignation.

Of constructive power the Bolsheviks have none, but they have enormous power for destruction. They can make a wilderness and call it peace. They can finally demoralize the army and reduce it to a rabble of hungry, looting bands, who will stream across the country, block the railways, reduce the civil population to starvation and the extreme of terror, and will fight like wolves over their prey. That they can do in the name of peace...

A few days later indignation gives way to despondency and a vicarious feeling of shame.

There is still no news of truce negotiations... In this fantastic topsy-turvy world where logic has gone bankrupt, where boundaries are effaced between life and death, one involuntarily looks for signs and symbols; men and women, helpless, hopeless and bewildered, go to wizards and conjurers trying to read the books of fate. Even the posters seem to have mystic meaning now. About the time of the Kornilov affair the town was placarded with bills bearing in red letters the words: *The Ruin of a Nation...* Who knows whether there is any hope for Russia, whose fate seems almost sealed? If you in England knew the suffering of Russia now, you would be merciful in spite of the great wrong.

You may say it is the Russians' own fault. Perhaps it is and they say so themselves. They repeat again and again in bitter humiliation, 'We have brought this on our own heads through our credulity and weakness.' They believed with all their hearts in a free Russia, and now they see Russia and freedom crumbling together into ruin.

Strong men are heartbroken and suffocated by the consciousness that they are Russians. It is not physical suffering, or physical danger, or material ruin that counts. Other nations have been trampled on and almost annihilated in this war, but no great nation, with hundreds of thousands of sensitive high-spirited citizens has suffered such a violation of its honour.[10]

Potentially the most dangerous of the problems facing the Bolsheviks, however, was that of the Constituent Assembly. In opposition, they had consistently presented themselves as the Assembly's only genuine champions. Ransome had often stressed that it was the right that had most to fear from free elections. As recently as October 20, in his speech to the Pre-Parliament before the Bolsheviks walked out, Trotsky had violently attacked the new Government in which the tax-paying classes were 'grossly over-represented', and had accused it of planning to stifle the Constituent Assembly. On the other hand, the Bolsheviks knew that they had little chance of winning a general election because of the massive peasant support for the SRs.

Voting began on November 25, as the Coalition Government had arranged. When Philips Price spoke to a Bolshevik leader on the evening of the 29th, he was told that they did not expect to win more than 300 of the 700 odd seats.[11] In the event, they won only 175, whereas the SRs had 370. Even with the support of those among the 370 who identified themselves as Left SRs, the Bolsheviks were very much in a minority. As expected, they did well in urban areas, although the Kadets, with only 17 seats overall, came a strong second in Petrograd and Moscow. The Bolsheviks also did well among the soldiers and sailors, especially the garrison troops in both cities, whose support was crucial.

The Government's timetable had also specified that the opening session of the Assembly should be held on December 11. The Bolsheviks announced a postponement, on the grounds that there would not be enough time for a quorum to gather. Some of the elected deputies, however, decided to ignore this order. 'There is a restless feeling in Petrograd this evening,' Williams writes on the 10th. 'It is still highly debatable whether the Assembly will actually meet... The Electoral Board, which was to have completed the arrangements, is now imprisoned in Smolny.' However, they were released in time, and on Tuesday December 11 Williams made his way to the Taurida Palace along with many others.

Today is a festival. That is to say, shops and factories are closed, bunting is waving, and processions are marching all over the town; and, for a wonder, in this grey and gloomy month sunshine is glittering on the snow. Round the Taurida Palace the scene was like that of the first days of the Revolution – the crowds, the workmen, the soldiers, the banners, the speeches, the cheering. But I listened to the crowds singing a revolutionary funeral hymn, and watched in the procession old men who had spent years of exile in Siberia, and could not rid myself of the impression of complete somersault. The shadow of tyranny was very near, and it was quite possible that the guns might go off at any moment, and the crowds would go scattering down the street. There was nervousness in the air, a plaintive insistence on liberties that are slipping away; and it was from old comrades of the exiles that the menace came, and the crowd that was shouting for liberty and acclaiming the Constituent Assembly were contemptuously branded as counter-revolutionary by those very powers that be, who, a month ago, were crying that the Constituent Assembly must be convened at the appointed date. Is the wheel coming full circle, and so soon?

My head is dizzy with the arguments I have heard today, the everlasting arguments of the soldiers about peace, the bandying of words between bourgeoisie and proletariat, the strange mixture of cynicism, sentimentalism, naiveté, and hard sense that one hears in all the whirling eddies of street talk. When I came up to the Taurida Palace a procession had just arrived from the Obukhov works with banners, and the crowd was cheering a speaker who bitterly attacked the Bolsheviks...

In the meantime a meeting was going on inside the rails, and I jumped over the fence into the snow and listened to a poem by a young Siberian, and to a speech of an SR peasant who raised a howl of indignation by suggesting re-elections if the Constituent Assembly proved unsatisfactory. The crowd was very jealous, pathetically jealous, of the honour and dignity of the Constituent Assembly, and would hear of no Bolshevik heresies. All the time, on the swirling outskirts, the unceasing argument went on. I tried to make my way into the building, and inside the door I found myself held up with some Russian and two or three foreign journalists before obdurate sentinels.

No papers, no persuasion availed. Finally a Russian journalist from inside managed to lead us on to the next sentry, but here a soldier rudely pushed the foremost of the party, and shouted

'Back, back,' and put his hand to his revolver, whereupon the Russian journalist shouted back, and told the soldier he had never had such treatment in the time of autocracy, and there was a hubbub and violent altercation, which ended in the youthful commandant stammering lame explanations, and the crestfallen soldier handing in his resignation. After long waiting and much argument, as always in Russia, we got inside, to find the Palace clean and spick and span, with new paint and plaster, and in the hall of the sitting a new and not very pleasant scheme of decoration in red and brown, with depressing faces in medallions, and festoons in yellow on a ceiling once seemly, and effectively white.

But the Assembly! Where was it? We saw a little group of men gathered at the foot of the speakers' tribune, and after a time they drifted to the seats and appeared as about fifty out of all the 800 for whom preparation had been made. Four Kadets sat on the right, and in the centre sat forty or so SRs, of whom the only prominent figures were Schreider, Mayor of Petrograd, and Rudnev, Mayor of Moscow. I saw one Menshevik, the former Minister Skobelev, while the left, where the Bolsheviks should sit, was empty. Then there was a quiet little meeting, the voices sounding like whispers in the empty hall, and it was decided, as there was no quorum, to meet every day at one till there was one.

Schreider announced that during the night three members of the Constituent Assembly, the Kadets Shingarev, Kokoshkin, and Prince Dolgorukov, had been arrested, and someone made a speech and a protest or a demand. Then the little assembly melted quietly away. 'We're all waiting for our turn,' said one member, with a bitter smile, as we walked out... So passed the day to which generations of revolutionaries have looked forward with longing.[12]

Next morning the Bolsheviks published an order for the arrest of all the Kadet leaders. The Assembly met again and decided, as before, to adjourn until the following day. On the afternoon of Thursday, December 13, Williams writes, the curtain fell on the first act of the drama of the Constituent Assembly.

About twenty SR delegates arrived, and attempted to hold a meeting. Entrance to the hall was prohibited by numerous armed sailors guarding all the doors. The members therefore entered the library, with the intention of holding a formal session. Ensign Blagonravov, the officer charged with the defence of the Taurida

Palace, appeared, and read a long instruction sent by Lenin, declaring that all meetings inside the palace were illegal until the Constituent Assembly was permitted to meet. Lenin authorized the ensign to use force if necessary.

Rudnev, Mayor of Moscow, speaking for the delegates, refused the demand that they should not meet. Blagonravov, a handsome young fellow with an undecided manner, went out, threatening to return 'with bayonets'.

The members unperturbably proceeded with their business. They decided to issue a protest to the whole world, and defer their next meeting until a substantial number of delegates is present at Petrograd. They had already adjourned when the ensign returned, with a small number of sailors with fixed bayonets and cutlasses, and ordered the delegates to leave; but they refused, behaving with dignity. The sailors were ordered to remove the members, and gave in answer an exhibition of the present state of discipline, looking sheepish under the crossfire of harangues from their own officers and the indignant delegates. But the bayonets won, and the library emptied slowly.

This incident is perhaps trivial, but it is intensely characteristic of the prevalent conditions. The bayonet rules Russia. The accepted conventions of a democratic Government do not exist. Lenin is said to have described the inviolability of the elected representatives of the people as a 'bourgeois prejudice'.[13]

Bessie Beatty, however, defends the attitude of the Bolshevik leaders at this time:

They said, quite truthfully, that the Assembly was chosen according to election laws made by the Coalition Government, and conducted by officials representative of that group, and of the political rather than of the economic ideal.

The Revolution that overthrew Tsarism was basically a political revolution. That which established the dictatorship of the proletariat was fundamentally economic. Between the political and the economic revolutions, the demands of the masses had undergone a sweeping change. The Constituent Assembly, in spite of its socialistic membership, and its claim of being the only elective group in Russia, was a bequest of the political Revolution.[14]

*

For the British and American people still left in Russia, life in the closing weeks of 1917 was difficult and uncertain. Not even the British Ambassador felt safe. Buchanan had been instructed by the Foreign Office to abstain from any step that might imply recognition of the Bolsheviks, so that when Trotsky sent him a note demanding the release of two Bolsheviks interned in Brixton Prison for anti-war propaganda, he ignored it. Trotsky retaliated by refusing British subjects permission to leave Russia. Then General Niessel, the French military representative, came to warn Buchanan that Trotsky might arrest him.

> General Niessel did not think that Trotsky would dare arrest me in the Embassy, but as he knows that I am in the habit of taking a daily walk he might do so when I was out of doors. By way of cheering me, the General added that, from inquiries which he had made, he believed that the most comfortable cells in the Fortress were between the Numbers 30 and 36 and that should the worst happen I had better bear this in mind.
>
> I did not take Trotsky's threats too seriously and continued my walks as usual without any unpleasant consequences.

The affair blew over when the British Government agreed to repatriate the interned Russians, provided that freedom of movement was restored to British subjects in Russia.

On December 8 Buchanan gave what amounted to a press conference (the term was not yet in use), with Harold Williams as his interpreter. Answering questions afterwards proved 'rather a trying ordeal'. Three days later his health broke down badly, and he received permission from London to return whenever he liked.[15]

On Christmas night there was a farewell party at the Embassy. Fortunately the electricity was not cut off that evening, so the great glass chandeliers, Meriel writes,

> blazed with light, the big rooms were crowded and filled with laughter, and though every officer present had a loaded revolver in his pocket, though there were rifles and cartridge cases hidden in the Chancery, for the moment we tried to forget the ever-present lurking danger...
>
> We began the evening with a variety entertainment got up by Colonel Thornhill and ended with a supper... We danced old Russian folk-dances, we sang English songs, we drank each other's

health and wished each other a Merry Christmas and a happy meeting in England during the coming year. . . but it was impossible not to feel a chill of foreboding, a presage of tragedy, underlying the wishes for 'Good Luck' one heard on every side.[16]

For William Gerhardie the star of the evening was Sir G. himself, who 'stood at the top of the staircase receiving the guests as they came up, and with his monocle which dangled down from his neck and broad ribbon, looked as much an Ambassador as any Ambassador can look'. At supper, when everyone stood up and sang 'For he's a jolly good fellow', the Ambassador responded by saying that he could not accept all the nice things that were said of him,

> and like some person who was told that it was hoped he was 'pretty well', will reply that he is 'neither pretty, nor well', to which all laughed; and as for being 'a jolly good fellow', he was 'neither jolly nor good', and that all he could say of himself was that he was 'a fellow'. I did not know that our old Ambassador could speak like that, and that evening 'H.E.' was really brilliant.[17]

Buchanan had intended to stay on until the next meeting of the Constituent Assembly, but shortly after Christmas he had a relapse, and it was decided that he and his family, accompanied by seven British military and naval personnel, including General Knox, should leave on January 7. Gerhardie, however, was to remain in Petrograd.

> In parting, General Knox thanked me for my work for him and supposed that when he saw me again I'd be a general. He gave me a mock punch in the ribs and said that if I did not come to see him in England he would kill me. I was so attached, so devoted, to the man that when I was alone in the street I hurried against the biting blizzard, which blinded me as I tore on, and sobbed.[18]

'Our last day in Petrograd!' Buchanan writes in his diary on the 6th,

> and yet, in spite of all that we have gone through, we are sad at the thought. Why is it that Russia casts over all who know her such an indefinable mystic spell that, even when her wayward children

have turned their capital into a pandemonium, we are sorry to leave it? I cannot explain the reason, but we *are* sorry.

Meriel, too, felt profoundly miserable all through the last week.

People used to ask me, 'But surely you must be glad to get away from this desolation and chaos, to go back to civilization and order, to clean streets, and shops and comfort?' And I could only say that 'Yes, of course I was glad to be going back to England, but – '

It was the very difficulty of explaining that 'but' that was part of Russia's spell.[19]

*

Arthur Ransome arrived back in Petrograd on Christmas Day, and in a telegram to the *Daily News* three weeks later he describes living conditions in the city:

The central power station is not working owing to the complete absence of coal. Electric light, which is supplied by various separate companies, is increasingly irregular. In some parts of town it only begins at seven in the evening, while other parts yesterday had none at all. No candles are to be found and it is difficult to secure oil. The bread allowance is at a minimum and that minimum is sometimes unobtainable. It is feared that the water supply will also cease. Sledges are growing rarer, because there is no forage. Food is sometimes impossible and always difficult to secure, though today I got a good chicken for little more than a sovereign. This, however, was unusual luck. Petrograd has long forgotten the taste of milk, though now and again it is possible to secure inferior butter at twenty one shillings a pound. Naturally the absence of lighting helps thieves who pay most attention to those shops with any kind of food for sale and ready-made clothes shops. Also for the sake of warm clothes they have the unpleasing habit of holding up people and stripping them naked in the street. Extremely unfair attempts are made to put down these conditions to the rule of the Bolsheviks and to use them as political propaganda. Kerensky would have had to face the same conditions.[20]

Ransome, at least, could afford to buy a chicken. Philips Price was living on a bank balance from abroad, and during the latter part of

December and the first two weeks of January all private banks were closed. The bread ration from the Food Commissariat fell to one-eighth of a pound a day, sugar to half a pound a month, and butter to a little pat no bigger than a half-crown piece. In three weeks he lost a stone and a half and started with fright when he looked at himself in the glass. The only way to escape starvation was by making purchases on the free market.

> I had to ration the money that I already had, and cut myself down to ten roubles a day for expenditure on food and other necessaries. I had to go round and search in the bazaars for smoked fish and listen for news of someone who had brought a sack of flour from the country and was selling it privately. I began to find that a considerable part of my day was being spent in providing myself with the barest necessities of life. I scrutinized the menu-card of the vegetarian restaurant, where I used to go, to find the cheapest possible fare. I ate the skins of smoked herrings, bought in the streets. As a great luxury, I occasionally allowed myself a piece of chocolate. I began to think of food, to dream of food, to think of all politics in terms of food.

'I sometimes doubt', he writes to his aunt on December 22, 'if I shall live through the winter and see the spring.' He thought of going to Sweden, where he could pass on the latest Russian news and get money from the *Manchester Guardian*, but decided to stick it out. 'It would be something for me to say in after life that I was one of the very few who saw the great Russian Revolution as an eye-witness.' By the middle of January his weight had dropped from twelve stone to about eight.

> When I walked up to the Smolny to attend a meeting of the Soviets from my flat I had to sit down every hundred yards on a doorstep because I was so weak. I remember about this time having a bath and being so shocked at my physical state of skin and bones that in my weakness I burst into tears... With the few copecks that I still had, I went to one of the wharfs on the Neva every morning and generally found a woman who sold smoked herring from the Murman coast. How on earth she got them and how they were not all swallowed up at once I never found out. But there she was nearly every morning and I have often thought since that she and her smoked herring really saved my life.

Relief came with the return to Petrograd of Chicherin, one of the two Bolsheviks interned in Brixton Prison whose repatriation Trotsky had obtained. On hearing of Price's plight, he immediately made arrangements for him to draw money from the State Bank.[21]

In his first telegram to the *Daily News* (December 29), Ransome gives a very favourable account of the Bolsheviks.

> I arrived in Petrograd to find that the reports of disorder appearing in the English press are based mainly on wilful misrepresentation by the opposition newspapers here. The city is more orderly than it had been for some months before the Bolsheviks took control. For the first time since the Revolution the Government in Russia is based on real force. People may not like the Bolsheviks, but they obey them with startling alacrity. The present Labour Government is extremely efficient, energetic and decisive, though faced by the noisy opposition of the privileged classes, who, though quite unable to replace this Government by one of their own, are doing all that they can to shake it by means of sabotage and libel.

As regards the Constituent Assembly, the Bolsheviks, he states, have nothing against it meeting once a quorum of 400 delegates is present; so far, there are only 391. In any case, they have nothing to fear from the Assembly, since the SRs 'divide, I believe, approximately half and half, the left half definitely supporting the present Labour Government'. The important thing for English people to realize is that by weakening the Government at home, the Assembly may also weaken it in its dealings with the Germans. 'Any attempt to turn out the present Government by force, supposing such force were available, which it is not, or any acts of violence against it, can have no result except a state of anarchy favourable to nobody but the Germans.'[22]

Next day he writes to his mother that 'there is a lot that must be done unless we are to throw up our hands and leave Russia to the Germans'. He has been so busy seeing people – 'yesterday for example... something like eighteen or nineteen various folk, ranging from the present dictator of Russia [Trotsky] to our ambassador through pretty well every shade of contradictory Russian opinion' – that he is afraid his telegraphing may suffer. He had, in fact, only managed to get off his eagerly-awaited telegram the day before through a stroke of luck. Finishing it very late, he went round to the

Commissariat of Foreign Affairs on the off chance of finding a censor, and wandering unchallenged through its corridors, came at last to a room with a few people in it. He recognized one of them from his visit earlier in the day to Smolny to interview Trotsky. She recognized him and when Ransome explained that he wanted to find a censor to stamp his dispatch, 'instead of remarking that it was long after office hours, she said she thought he was in the building. This was Evgenia, the tall jolly girl whom later on I was to marry...'. Though not a member of the Bolshevik Party, she was working as Trotsky's personal secretary. Through her, and even more through his friendship with Karl Radek, 'a little light-haired spectacled revolutionary goblin of incredible intelligence and vivacity', Ransome came into contact with many leading Party members.[23]

There had been a hitch in the Bolsheviks' negotiations with the Germans. At first, all seemed to be going well. An armistice was signed on December 15, the Germans apparently accepting the five points put forward as a basis for peace by the Russians. December 30 was proclaimed a day of public celebration. From the early morning hours of the wintry Petrograd day, which began at ten o'clock, to dusk, which came on about half-past three, Philips Price stood in the snow and watched an endless procession of factory workers, Red Guards and garrison soldiers making their way to the Field of Mars.[24] Unknown to the demonstrators, however, the German generals had already overridden the diplomats and told the Russian delegates at Brest-Litovsk that Germany could not give up the occupied territories of Poland, Lithuania and Courland, previously part of the Russian Empire. This clear violation of the sacred principle of 'no annexations' put the whole Bolshevik Revolution in jeopardy. To accept the terms would be a humiliating climb-down; to reject them meant that the people's hopes of peace would be disappointed and the Germans would advance further into Russia.

Trotsky could do little but play for time and try to involve the Allies. But the Allied Governments did not recognize the Bolsheviks. To get his message through to them, he had to make use of friendly journalists. Ransome was at Smolny three times within four days. ('You ought to be shot!' Knox exclaimed, breaking into a conversation between Ransome and Buchanan, but 'the Ambassador quietly waved him away and went on with what he was saying'.[25]) Trotsky's room was just as John Reed had seen it two months earlier: unfurnished except for a writing-table, two chairs and a telephone. Like other witnesses, Ransome was struck by Trotsky's 'very broad high forehead above lively eyes, fine-cut nose and mouth, and small cavalier beard'. He also got the impression of 'extreme efficiency and definite purpose. In spite of all that is said against him by his enemies, I do not think that he is the man to do anything except from the conviction that it is the best thing to be done for the revolutionary cause which he has at heart.'

At the interview on December 29 Trotsky kept quiet about the occupied territories and gave Ransome the impression that the Bolsheviks were still negotiating from a position of strength. The Germans had been forced 'by democratic pressure to throw aside their grandiose plans of conquest and to accept a peace in which there is neither conqueror nor conquered,' though 'this can hardly be achieved unless the Allies join the conference'. On December 31, however, the tone of Ransome's telegram is far more urgent:

> I wonder whether English people realize how great is the matter now at stake and how near we are to witnessing a separate peace between Russia and Germany, which would be a defeat for German democracy in its own country, besides ensuring the practical enslavement of Russia. A separate peace will be a victory not for Germany but for the military caste in Germany. It may mean much more than the neutrality of Russia. If we make no move, it seems possible that the Germans will ask the Russians to help them in enforcing Russian peace terms on the Allies.

Ransome stresses that Trotsky is adopting a truculent attitude and leaving no stone unturned in his efforts to thwart Germany's plans, but he needs help: 'I am convinced that our only chance of defeating these designs is to publish terms as near the Russian terms as possible and by taking a powerful hand in the proposed conference.'

Not until the third interview on January 1 did Trotsky make public for the first time that negotiations had broken down over the occupied territories, thereby giving Ransome a marvellous scoop and the *Daily News* a chance for dramatic headlines. The version that Trotsky gave Ransome of the Russian reaction to the German claim that Poland, Lithuania and Courland had already 'defined themselves' was clearly designed to appeal to Western sympathies.

> The Russian delegation, acting on the most unequivocal instructions from Smolny, took up an uncompromising attitude. They

said self-definition was impossible until the last German soldier had left the country... They asked what they [the Germans] proposed to say to their own democracy which protested a couple of months ago against the proposed annexation of Poland and Lithuania. They remarked that they were surprised that 'even Prussian Junkers had such audacity'. The Germans asked for time to consider and begged that this stage of negotiations be unpublished. The Russians refused to allow this and left Brest-Litovsk.[26]

Ransome had acted as a perfect vehicle for Trotsky's message to the Allies. At its meeting on January 2 the British War Cabinet did indeed discuss his *Daily News* articles. They sensed that 'possibly Mr Arthur Ransome's despatch [of December 31] was a signal that M. Trotsky would like to get into touch with the Allies with a view to extricating himself from his difficulties', but they thought that he was anxious about the implications of a general peace, not a separate one.[27] How such an interpretation could be put on Ransome's articles it is hard to imagine. Had Trotsky known about this crass reaction, it would have provoked him, in the words of Ransome's biographer, Hugh Brogan, 'to rage, astonishment and scornful laughter'.[28] Trotsky himself took charge of the Russian delegation, and on January 6 left for Brest-Litovsk with the aim of keeping the negotiations going as long as possible.

While Ransome was very much part of the Bolsheviks' world – 'seeing these people every day, drinking their tea, hearing their quarrels, sharing with them such sweets as I had, going now with one and now with another to meetings from which most foreigners stayed away' – Harold Williams belonged just as clearly to the world of their opponents. 'We went on living in our old flat,' Ariadna writes, 'more or less in the same conditions. But things were growing more and more sinister.' After the outlawing of the Kadet Party on December 24, several more of its leaders were arrested or had their homes raided. Well-meaning friends refused to let Ariadna go home to sleep. 'As a means of self-defence this was very naïve, but my staying in other people's flats got on Harold's nerves. I had never seen him in such a state. He changed colour if a motor-car drew up by our door, especially at night.' Life in Petrograd, he reports on December 23, 'is a succession of curious anecdotes and fantastic rumours and menaces, which fall as thickly as the snowflakes which now descend steadily day after day on the beleaguered city that was once the capital of a great country called Russia, and perhaps some day will be again. For Russia is not dead, but is in marvellous travail to a new birth.'[29]

Ransome and Williams had come to a parting of the ways. Williams had always been well to the right of centre and Ransome well to the left, pouring scorn on the Kadets for imagining that a revolution could be conveniently stopped at the point where they wanted to get off; but so long as there existed a middle ground in Russian politics, the divide between the two men did not seem unbridgeable. Now it had become absolute.

Hugh Brogan writes of Williams that 'his temperament was, compared with Arthur's manic bounce, depressive, which made it easy for him to see the dark side of events'.[30] He had welcomed the March Revolution with more enthusiasm than anyone, as the realization of a dream that it seemed would never come true. Disillusionment quickly followed, especially with the Petrograd politicians, whose constant bickering fell so far short of the generous ideals of the Revolution, and by the end of September his feeling of depression was already intense. He saw only too clearly the dark side of the events of December 11: that 'the shadow of tyranny was very near' and that 'the bayonet now rules Russia'; yet always there was the lingering hope that out of this travail a new and better Russia would be born.

The buoyant Ransome, by contrast, had shown a remarkable capacity for looking on the bright side of events throughout 1917, and this did not stop with the November Revolution. Previously, he had had few good things to say about the Bolsheviks. The outcome of the July Days had been 'a triumph for the moderate party' and might have a result 'exactly opposite to German wishes, in unifying Russia, in destroying the Bolshevik organization'; while of the Bolsheviks in September he had written that they brought to the Democratic Assembly 'the irresponsible nonchalance of the debating society, sitting there smiling, indifferent to words that to their speakers represented blood and tears', and had pointed out that fear of the ballot was 'an unfortunate characteristic' of theirs. All these objections are now engulfed by his new-found enthusiasm. For Ransome, as for the American witnesses, the Bolsheviks are the only genuine revolutionaries: guided by the principle of 'All Power to the Soviets', they alone are walking hand in hand with the Russian people. ('When opinion in the country really changes,' he writes on January 20, 'we shall find the character of the Soviets changes.') Theirs is an audacious, unprecedented undertaking. After November he still sees them as the underdogs. Inexperienced, few in number, and conscious that failure will expose them to the same fate as the Communards in 1871, they are working frantically round the clock in an effort to keep their regime functioning in the face of 'the noisy opposition of the privileged classes'. He approves of the strongarm tactics being used – 'People may not like the Bolsheviks, but they obey them with startling alacrity' – and of the uncompromising measures being introduced to quell opposition by a Government that has the great advantage of knowing its own mind. 'Nationalization of the banks', he writes on December 31, 'puts a weapon almost more powerful than the guillotine in the hands of the Government and will probably put an end to much of the present sabotage'. He takes the idea of class warfare in his stride, writing on January 10: 'The civil wars now proceeding in Russia are not wars of one part of Russia against another, but attempts to spread class warfare into those parts of the country where the proletariat or its equivalent has not yet got the upper hand.' Nor does he balk at the idea of world revolution, Trotsky having left him in no doubt that his ultimate aim was 'to stimulate the revolutionary movement throughout the world'.[31]

At the same time Ransome's desire to preserve the Anglo-Russian friendship and thereby contribute to the crushing of 'Prussianism' is as strong as ever. His first thought on returning to Petrograd is not of the Revolution, but of all that must be done 'unless we are to throw up our hands and leave Russia to the Germans'. Here, he feels, he has a unique contribution to make: enjoying the confidence of both Buchanan and Trotsky, he can act as the Anglo-Russian go-between. Given that Russia is unable to continue the war, Trotsky's manner of making peace is 'likely to do more damage to Germany than would be done by any more respectful and polite person in his place'.[32] Ransome in his own way is no less ardent a patriot than General Knox. The astute Trotsky knew that he was dealing with that kind of Englishman.

Philips Price's position is different again. He was not so preoccupied as Ransome with 'Prussianism'; millions of lives were being sacrificed because of the stupidity and wickedness of the ruling classes in all the belligerent countries. Holding such views, it is surprising that he 'always found Trotsky the most difficult of the Commissars to make contact with', but it was through Trotsky that he obtained *his* big scoop: the text of the secret treaties between the Allies, published in the *Manchester Guardian* on November 28. Towards the Bolsheviks his attitude fluctuates. Describing the reign of terror inaugurated by them to his aunt on November 30, his tone is exultant:

> We have got the dictatorship of the proletariat with a vengeance this time!! But I rub my hands and chuckle with glee. May the day soon come when the proletariat of Western Europe does the same. I am rapidly coming to the view that the armed forces of a country ought to be used only for the purposes of fighting the landlords and capitalists!!!

Earlier, though, he had predicted that a Bolshevik Revolution 'would lead to the most indescribable anarchy', and these feelings surface again in his letter of December 22. Though the Bolsheviks have done very well in destroying the war, 'they are destructive Jacobins who believe that by flaming decrees, passionate speeches, terrorism and the guillotine they can create a worldly paradise. They will have to go and make way for more constructive people.' This was the time, though, when his own private circumstances were so desperate that he could only think of politics in terms of food. Once that problem had been solved, his mood seems to have changed again, and he came down firmly on the side of the Bolsheviks.[33]

*

> 'This year, next year, sometime, never.' Will the Constituent Assembly open tomorrow or not? The SRs say it will, the Bolsheviks now say it will, now it will not. (Harold Williams, January 17)

The Bolsheviks finally decided that it would be more dangerous not to let the Assembly meet at all than to let it meet in circumstances over which they exercised strict control. The SRs, Ransome reports, were planning great demonstrations, but these had been forbidden by the Soviet Government, 'who well knew that conflict between the parties might easily end in uncontrollable anarchy'. Feeling in the town was therefore 'fairly tense'. January 18 he describes as a particularly fine day, with a clearer sky than usual because of the enforced stoppage of the factories from lack of coal. As he walked across town to the Taurida Palace, Ransome met Red Guard and sailor patrols, but comparatively few people. The so-called barricades 'were not barricades at all, but such impediments as in England we place across the head of a street under repair to divert the traffic'. In spite of the Government ban, however, processions did in fact form and one or two of them refused to disperse and tried to force their way to the Duma, where the Constituent was meeting. On several occasions there was shooting, mostly on the Liteiny Prospect, which must be crossed by anybody going towards the Duma. In all about fifteen were killed and about 100 wounded.[34]

Bessie Beatty and her companions came upon the aftermath of one of the shootings.

We drove along the Liteiny in the direction of the firing. At the Kirochnaya, we came suddenly upon a group of Red Guards and soldiers, brandishing ominous guns. They rushed about, tossing orders at one another, their faces flushed with excitement.

'Murderers! Murderers!' shouted a woman, shaking a fist in their direction.

'Murderers! Murderers!' echoed a dozen other women, who turned blazing eyes upon them.

Scattered all over the snow were broken and splintered poles – all that remained of the proud banners that a few minutes before had proclaimed 'All Power to the Constituent Assembly'.[35]

Harold Williams was reminded by the shootings of an earlier episode in Russian history:

Meantime, all the day long in the snow-heaped streets beyond the Palace, the apostles of pacifism revived the memories of that Sunday, almost exactly thirteen years ago, when the Tsar's troops shot down processions of workers.

From various quarters of the town processions, carrying red flags with insciptions for the Constituent, marched towards the centre and one by one were fired on and dispersed by Red Guards and sailors. Barricades were erected near the Taurida Palace, sailors and Red Guards were stationed in convenient courtyards: all the methods so familiar under the old regime were brought into play.

Most of the shooting took place on the Liteiny Prospect...   The number of killed and wounded apparently was not large, considering the amount of ammunition expended. Among those killed and wounded were several workmen and students and one member of the Constituent, the peasant Loginov. Indignation is intense.

The approaches to the Palace itself, he reports, were also lined by sailors and Red Guards. 'Two guns were mounted in the snow before the Palace, and shivering Red Guards stood sentinel over them in the bitter wind.'[36] (Even the weather that day seems to vary according to the witness!) Behind the upper windows, Beatty writes,

> hidden from public gaze, were six machine-guns, with tapes loaded for use. Within a moment's call, the gunners waited for action. Behind the ornate iron fences, Red Guards and sailors paced ceaselessly back and forth.
>
> We made our way through a procession of sentries into the Palace... There were guards and more guards, stairs and more stairs, until at last a sailor politely forced us into a box overlooking the Assembly.
>
> The auditorium was a great square room surrounded by balconies and roofed with glass. The seats were arranged like a fan in widening circles. They were cushioned with red leather, and strips of red carpet ran like ribs towards the tribunal, where slender bay trees stretched their green arms against the white columns.[37]

Towards midday the deputies slowly assembled and wandered about the building. Williams describes them as mostly of the type made familiar by the Soviets:

> a large proportion of young men in the late twenties and thirties, returned political refugees, workers in the Revolutionary parties, two or three obvious peasants, possibly a working man or two, several soldiers, a sailor, a priest, three or four women, and a sprinkling of middle-aged professional men and veteran Revolutionaries. A few Tartar deputies in skull caps gave a faint touch of the picturesque.
>
> The SRs numbered about 240, the Bolsheviks over 90 [a low figure compared with other sources], and their allies, the Left SRs, over 30. The Kadets, of whom only 15 have been elected, were absent, several of their number having been arrested at the last attempt [December 11]. Neither the imprisoned Kadets nor the SRs who were arrested a few days ago were released for the opening day.

Beatty comments merely that the Kadets 'had all remained away', while Ransome found it 'ironic' that having been anxious to postpone the Assembly as long as possible till opinion should have swung to their side, the Kadets had only eleven deputies, 'and it was impossible even for one to take his seat'; he does not explain why.[38]

At 2 the Assembly was still unopened, and since Taurida could offer nothing but glasses of tea, Ransome went off to Smolny, where he got some soup. The building was garrisoned by Red Guards and Lettish riflemen, and 'fully prepared in case of attack which at one time was expected. There were field guns under the portico of the building and plenty of machine-guns upstairs.'[39]

Everything was quiet on his way back to Taurida, where the Assembly opened at 4. The Bolsheviks sat on the left, Williams writes,

the SRs and their associates in the centre, while the seats on the right were vacant. The galleries were crowded, mostly with Bolshevik supporters. Sailors and Red Guards, with their bayonets hanging at various angles, stood on the floor of the House. [Ransome was 'amused to observe a Red Guard on more than one occasion lean his rifle against the wall in order to be able more enthusiastically to applaud.']

To right and left of the Speaker's tribune sat the People's Commissars and their assistants. Lenin was there, bald, red-bearded, short, and rather stout. He was apparently in good spirits, and chatted merrily with Krylenko [Commander-in-Chief of the Army]. There were Lunacharsky and Mme Kollontai [the Commissar of Public Welfare, who arrived first, according to Beatty, carrying a large briefcase under her arm, and pausing for a moment to search the crowd for comrade faces], and a number of dark young men who now stand at the head of the various Government departments and devise schemes for the imposition of unalloyed Socialism on Russia.

After a long wait an SR proposed that the senior deputy, Shvetsov, should open the proceedings. The Bolsheviks in the House and galleries raised a howl of indignation, banged the desks, and with whistles and catcalls accompanied the slow, heavy tread of an elderly gentleman with long hair towards the tribune. Shvetsov rang the bell, but the din continued. The Bolsheviks shook their fists, several rushed towards the tribune, two or three young men in uniform put their hands on Shvetsov, and the brawl only ceased when, after the appearance on the scene of Sverdlov, president of the Executive Committee of the Bolshevik Soviet, the old gentleman retired.

According to Ransome, Shvetsov lost his bell, while Beatty describes the white-haired, white-whiskered old man looking from left to right in a bewildered way before finally yielding the gavel.[40]

Sverdlov then opened the proceedings in the name of the Soviets, reading out a declaration of the rights of working people, followed by a statement of the Bolshevik programme, which demanded that the Assembly recognize the Soviets as the supreme power. The Bolsheviks, Beatty writes,

> punctuated his speech with vigorous applause. The Right SRs expressed themselves equally emphatically by stolid silence. When he finished, a delegate proposed that the Assembly sing the *Internationale*. It was a challenge that no Socialist could refuse. They arose to a man.

Ransome, however, notes that the SRs 'were a little unwilling to stand and only in twos and threes joined in the singing', while Williams has them all rise and sing, but discordantly and heavily, as if the Internationale were a funeral dirge.[41]

Then came the election of a chairman, which Ransome says took an hour and a half. To count the vote, the tellers had to drop tiny marbles from one bowl into another. While this was going on, the hall began to fill up again with Commissars, among whom Ransome noticed Lenin, talking and laughing. At last the click-click of the marbles ended and there was silence for a moment before the announcement: 244 votes for Chernov (Right SRs) and 153 for Spiridonova, the left nominee.[42]

None of our witnesses is enthusiastic about the long opening address by Chernov that followed. The Constituent, he announced, must take the initiative in summoning an international socialist conference to secure a general democratic peace. Otherwise, 'he hardly said a word', Williams writes, 'that could offend the susceptibilities of the Bolsheviks.' Philips Price agrees, adding only that Chernov was careful not to say anything to imply recognition of the Soviets' authority.[43]

While the speech was going on, another American witness, Edgar Sisson, noticed that the Bolsheviks 'lolled in their seats, taking their cue from Lenin, who stretched himself full length on a settee on the presidium, and pretended to sleep'. Simultaneously the empty space in the back of the Americans' box filled up with men, one of whom sat just behind Beatty, 'a dark, swarthy-skinned factory worker, with sullen eyes, that flamed red and went black by turns', while poised on the railing was a Bolshevik sailor, who interrupted frequently with shouts of 'Kornilov! Kaledin! Kerensky! Counter-revolutionist!'[44]

Far more impressive than Chernov, however, was Tsereteli, leader of the handful of Mensheviks, even though his speech, according to Sisson, lasted less than ten minutes. For Beatty he was 'the heroic figure of the day', although his position was impossible. Philips Price dismisses him finally as a middle-class revolutionary, but not before doing justice to the man and his speech:

> In this swan-song apology for the history of the previous eight months, Tsereteli was the same as ever – thoughtful, unemotional, philosophic, calm, like some Zeus from Olympus, contemplating the conflicts of the lesser gods. 'The Constituent Assembly,' he said, 'elected democratically by the whole country, should be the highest authority in the land. If this is so, then why should an ultimatum be sent to it by the Central Soviet Executive? Such an ultimatum can only mean the intensification of civil war. Will this help to realize Socialism? On the contrary, it will only assist the German militarists to divide the revolutionary front. The break-up of the Constituent Assembly will only serve the interests of the bourgeoisie, whom you (the Bolsheviks) profess to be fighting. The Assembly alone can save the Revolution.'

Tsereteli put his criticisms of the Bolsheviks into language that any Russian could understand. The proof of this, Sisson writes, 'was the action of the sailor in our box. He cursed in monotone and several times raised his rifle threateningly. I doubt if he really meant to fire, and enough were near to prevent him, but he was tempted.'[45]

After further discussion the Bolsheviks demanded the right of intermission for party caucus. Harold Williams decided to leave. It was nearly midnight. According to his wife, 'he came home as depressed and worn out as though he had been to the funeral of someone he loved'. Ransome, too, left around this time. He found the streets perfectly calm and was pleased to see plenty of sledges, 'since they disappear like magic at the first sign of serious trouble'.[46]

Bessie Beatty stayed on. Two hours passed. Nothing happened. Chernov reopened the meeting, and Skobelev demanded the appointment of a commission to investigate the bloodshed of the day. Representatives of the left then filed back to their seats. A

Bolshevik member read out a statement declaring that since the Constituent Assembly had refused to accept the demands of the People's Commissars, it had become a counter-revolutionary body. With that the Bolsheviks left the hall. The Left SRs then offered a resolution that the Assembly recognize the peace steps taken by the People's Commissars. The delegates refused, whereupon the Left SRs also got up quietly from their seats and departed. For half an hour the meeting continued. The question of land nationalization was introduced, but before the discussion had progressed very far, the Palace guard ordered the meeting to close, saying it had become no more than a party caucus.

> The guard yawned. President Chernov demurred. The guns once more began to assume ominous positions.
>
> 'Why should we wait? We should arrest all! We should kill the counter-revolutionist Chernov!' came in angry murmurs from factory workers and soldiers.
>
> The delegates looked from one to another. Some one moved a resolution to adjourn until five that afternoon. It was promptly adopted.
>
> The murmurs of 'Counter-revolutionist!' grew louder and louder. The soldiers and sailors flocked down the stairs, and crowded round the delegates. Some of the Bolshevik members who had remained in the ballroom surrounded Chernov, and took him in safety through the hostile throng to the gate.[47]

The Assembly did not meet at five that afternoon. The curtain had already fallen on its final act. Next morning Smolny ordered it to be dissolved. No attempts were ever made to reconvene it.

In his telegram of January 19 Harold Williams writes that 'the day of the opening of the Constituent Assembly, that was to have solved all the problems of the Revolution, inaugurated a fresh phase of terror. The pall is settling still more heavily on Petrograd.' For Ransome, though, calling the Assembly had been 'little more than a move in political chess', and had the Bolsheviks not ordered its dissolution, what remained of it could only have provided a cover for the efforts of bourgeois counter-revolution. 'People in England have not realized that whereas the March Revolution was an elemental rising without a definite aim, the November Revolution was a real revolution with a definite aim and definite ideas. The Constituent Assembly in its present form must be considered as a belated last act of the March rising accidentally persisting into the new era begun by the November Revolution.' For Philips Price, too, the Assembly 'passed like a meteor across the horizon of the Russian Revolution. No one seemed prepared for its coming, and no one seemed to miss it when it was gone. With it vanished the last relics of middle-class democracy in the territories of the Soviets.'[48]

Bessie Beatty, never so wholeheartedly committed as her fellow-Americans, comes down on the side of the Bolsheviks, albeit a little hesitantly: 'I have never met in any country any group of men possessed of such power as theirs who would have acted otherwise.' She concludes by quoting an exchange that took place at midnight between Rhys Williams and Mme Kollontai:

> 'How long do you think the Constituent Assembly will last?' he asked.
> 'Comrade, don't you think it has lasted too long already?'[49]

No answer could be given then to her rhetorical question. Only the subsequent history of the November Revolution would do that.

On one point all our witnesses seem to agree: that the March Revolution, having come in like a thief, slipped out just as unobtrusively.

Afterword

Our witnesses leave us in no doubt about the very different nature of the two revolutions in Russia in 1917. The March Revolution can be described as popular in four senses. It was popular in that very large numbers of people, as if by some common impulse, were willing to defy authority and risk their lives by coming out on to the streets in order to overthrow their oppressors. It was popular in that it contained the vital element of fraternization (absent in 1905), when instead of obeying orders, the servants of authority – not the Tsarist police, but the garrison soldiers of Petrograd, and even more critically, the Cossacks, traditional quellers of all kinds of disturbance – started fraternizing with the insurgents and went over to their side. It was popular in not being planned or master-minded. Various political groups were busy during the war years stirring up revolutionary feelings and were quick to exploit the movement once it gathered strength, but this falls far short of saying that they planned it; Lenin, in exile in Switzerland, was as much taken by surprise as anyone. Finally, it was popular in the colloquial sense that it was greeted with obvious rejoicing by all but a small section of Russian society. British eye-witnesses vividly convey the euphoria, the sense of regeneration, of a new era dawning, that followed the March Revolution. Their descriptions seem especially poignant in the light of what was to happen later.

The March Revolution is not to be seen, however, as a nice clean bloodless middle-class affair. Not until two or three days after the main action did the middle classes venture on to the streets, by which time most of the dirty work had been done. Dirty work was needed because the Tsarist police put up fierce resistance, believing that loyal troops would soon be drafted into Petrograd. One should not lose sight of this strong element of violence, brutality and bloodshed without which the March Revolution might not have succeeded.

The man whose name has become synonymous with the Provisional Government period is Alexander Kerensky, one of history's most famous or infamous losers, the man who let the Russian Revolution slip through his grasp, and then had the misfortune to live on for more than half a century. The accepted wisdom about Kerensky is that his downfall was inevitable and due largely to his own weakness.

By the Bolsheviks Kerensky was predictably despised and ridiculed, but in Bolshevik Russia he was quickly forgotten. It was in the West and among émigré Russians that a more subtle character assassination of Kerensky was carried out. He was portrayed as highly emotional, as a vain theatrical man always striking poses, seeing himself as a second Napoleon or a new Tsar, and who when things went wrong, became hysterical and unbalanced, only managing to keep going at all by resort to drugs: in short, as a weak unstable character who had ruined Russia.

It suited everyone to vilify Kerensky, to seize upon and magnify his defects, because he was such a convenient scapegoat. This appalling disaster that had overtaken Russia was all his fault. Rightwing Russian émigrés conveniently forgot that they had been bitterly opposed to the socialist Kerensky from the start. The Allied governments conveniently forgot that their support for him had always been lukewarm. Though they held back from open support of General Kornilov, they would have much preferred to see him in Kerensky's place. It was the fiasco of the Kornilov Affair that revived the Bolsheviks' waning political fortunes in the autumn of 1917. How different it might have been if the West had been able to look into the future and foreseen Stalin, mass terror, the Cold War and everything else that was to follow.

Our witnesses on the spot at the time give little support to this commonly held view of Kerensky. He was theatrical, true, but in his eloquence and ability to move large audiences lay his strength as a politician; he was emotional, too, but no one doubted the sincerity of his concern for the future of Russia (in contrast to Lenin and Trotsky, who were far more internationally-minded). Had Kerensky succeeded, we should have heard no more about his defects of character. Trotsky was flamboyant and theatrical, but because he was on the winning side, no one holds these qualities against him.

The Provisional Government failed because they tried to play by the book, to follow correct democratic procedures and abide by the rule of law. But the people could not wait. Kerensky fatally undermined his own position by committing himself to an impossibly difficult task, that of keeping the Russian army in the war. He tried to do this by moral persuasion, arguing that it would be dishonourable to let down the Allies, that the good name of the Revolution would be sullied for all time. The failure of the summer offensive turned Kerensky from a charismatic leader into a politician fighting for survival.

The November Revolution was not popular in any of the four senses mentioned above. It did not involve large numbers, indeed many people remained ignorant of what had happened. In place of fraternization there was widespread popular apathy and indifference, a feeling of 'let the politicians get on with it'. It *was* planned by the Bolsheviks, and it was *not* followed by universal rejoicing, as witnesses again make clear. This was a seizure of power by the Bolsheviks from the Provisional Government, not a popular Revolution. If we talk of the Bolshevik Revolution, we do so by virtue of its impact and revolutionary consequences, not only for Russia but the whole world; but as a description of what took place in November 1917 the word 'Revolution' is inappropriate.

Whatever we may think of Lenin and his ideology, in the West we have come to feel a grudging admiration for the man and his political genius, for the ruthless efficiency with which the Bolsheviks seized power under his direction and for the heroism of the Red Guards who stormed the Winter Palace.

The heroic storming of the Palace was a myth to which John Reed contributed in *Ten Days that Shook the World* and which was handed down to posterity by that brilliant film-maker, Sergei Eisenstein. As for the Bolsheviks' ruthless efficiency, that proves on closer examination to have been something of a myth, too. Successful *coups* depend on secrecy, but there was no secrecy about this one, which had been openly discussed in the press for days beforehand. They also depend on making sure that your opponents are cut off from the outside world and unable to summon loyal troops. The Bolsheviks disconnected telephone lines to the Winter Palace but missed two of them, so that members of the Provisional Government were able to remain in contact with Kerensky, who had fled the night before and was trying to rally support; just as in August 1991 the conspirators isolated Gorbachev, but failed to move against Yeltsin, who immediately alerted the outside world to what was going on.

As for Lenin's political genius, one is more impressed at this point in his career by his exceptional political good fortune. So much had already been done for him, by the war, by the March Revolution, and by the failure of the Provisional Government to deliver what the people wanted. The hand that he had to play was far easier than Kerensky's. He was holding three trump cards, the promises of peace, bread and land: peace to satisfy the soldiers, bread the workers, and land the peasants. He was unencumbered by what he would have seen as the hypocritical bourgeois morality that made Kerensky reluctant to let down the Allies, or the hypocritical democratic scruples that would have made it impossible for Kerensky to dissolve the Constituent Assembly.

Since the 1960s there has been a movement among Western historians of the Russian Revolution away from 'political' history – dealing with the decisions and actions taken by individuals at the top – towards 'social' history, which concentrates more on mass movements and looks at events from the viewpoint of the factory floor or the peasant hut, the front-line trench or the army barracks. Richard Pipes has remained faithful to the older tradition. 'In the eyes of the revisionists,' he writes, 'events are driven by unstoppable and anonymous forces; in my eyes, the decisive factor is human will.'[1] To a Russianist like myself who does not have a foot in either camp, it seems obvious that neither the 'top-down' nor the 'bottom-up' approach to history can be adequate in itself, and that the historian is bound to consider how the 'political' and the 'social' interact and try to strike the right balance between them.

Here the two revolutions provide another striking contrast. The story, however bizarre, of the drama that was played out at the top – involving Rasputin, the Tsarevich, the Empress Alexandra and the Emperor Nicholas – is not in itself going to provide an adequate explanation of the March Revolution. The Emperor's individual will and personality are significant only in a negative sense. Tsarism might have survived if the autocracy had been demolished and a new constitutional monarchy put up in its place; but Nicholas and those round him were constitutionally incapable of such a radical change. Orlando Figes puts this more bluntly: 'The Tsarist regime's downfall was not inevitable; but its own stupidity made it so.'[2] No event or sequence of events, however, can be shown to have led inevitably to the March Revolution; it just happened. At a particular moment the ancient structure collapsed without warning. 'Bottom-up' explanations that take into account the many and various underlying factors – social, economic, historical, cultural and so on – are likely to be far more useful and persuasive in analysing this historical event.

In the case of the November Revolution the balance seems to have shifted. The underlying factors, though still relevant, no longer seem to carry the same explanatory weight. In contrast to Nicholas, the personalities of those most closely involved are very positively charged. These individuals are strong and wilful: they know exactly where they want to go and they are determined to make things happen. But the outcome of this clash of wills and ideologies could not have been predicted. Far from obeying the forces of historical necessity, as Soviet historians once wanted us to believe, the November Revolution now strikes me as an unpredictable, improvised, haphazard sequence of events in which elements of luck and timing and personality predominate.

*

'It was almost impossible to believe,' Philips Price wrote in November 1917, 'that the century-old Russian Empire was actually dissolving before one's eyes with such extraordinary lack of dignity.' Similar words might have been used in 1991. Soviet Russia, like its Tsarist predecessor, was looking more and more ill-adapted to face the modern world, but no one in the early 1980s thought that it was in danger of imminent collapse. Motivated by the desire to put the Communist Party house in order, Gorbachev did not seem to appreciate the risks that he was running in tampering with the foundation stones. Events spun out of his control until finally the unthinkable happened and the Soviet Empire collapsed just as the Russian Empire had done seventy-four years earlier.

During the Cold War years it seemed to me important to make a distinction between 'Soviet' and 'Russian' and to think of oneself as 'anti-Soviet' but 'pro-Russian'. To be nothing more than 'anti-Soviet' meant to adopt a complacently superior attitude that lumped all Russians together under that inept term, 'the Soviets'. To be 'pro-Russian' meant admiring the distinctive contribution to world culture made by a talented and creative people, and to recognize that the Russians seemed to have retained a greater warmth, emotional spontaneity and communality in their everyday life than was to be found in the West.

When the Cold War ended, the peculiarly Soviet atmosphere of fear and suspicion, of censorship and surveillance, that had become only too familiar to Western visitors, was finally dispelled. Russian citizens acquired the kind of basic freedoms that had long been taken for granted in the West: freedom to take part in genuine elections and engage in independent political activity, freedom to speak one's mind openly on any subject, and freedom to travel at home and abroad.

Yet at the same time, as G.D.G. Murrell writes, 'there has been no real coming to terms with the communist past'.[3] *Glasnost* or openness on Soviet history 'was intense but too short-lived perhaps for the message to sink fully home'. Whereas German consciences are still troubled by the events of sixty years ago and Holocaust literature shows no signs of abating, Russian labour camp literature is no longer read. There was no Russian equivalent of the Court of Reconciliation in South Africa; on the contrary, 'those whose crimes were exposed in the media remained aggressively unrepentant'. In 1997 members of the reconstituted Russian Communist Party celebrated the 80th anniversary of the 'Great October Socialist Revolution' as if nothing had happened in the previous ten years and there was no historical case for them to answer. Perhaps it was too much to expect the bemedalled old Soviet veterans, who not surprisingly survive in greater numbers than the prisoners released from the camps, to have a change of heart, but the Party has hundreds of thousands of members and millions of voters. 'The historical lesson,' Murrell concludes, 'was not fully learned, there was no repentance and nostalgia for the USSR soon re-emerged.' What John Lloyd calls the life of 'secure indolence' in Soviet times[4] was felt by many to be preferable to the insecure, stressful life generated by a market economy.

Russia's new-found democratic freedoms would be defended more vigorously now, but only by the urban middle classes. Such freedoms are too abstract to mean much to the underprivileged; being free to travel abroad is important only if you have the money to do so. What is felt more keenly by ordinary Russians is a sense of national humiliation: Russia has ceased to be a world power, its influence in the world generally is much reduced, and from time to time it has to be bailed out by the richer nations. 'Russia's identity crisis is the dominant political factor in its post-Communist history' (Murrell).[5] This crisis fuels both the nationalist and neo-communist movements and increases the danger of a new authoritarian regime.

When *Witnesses of the Russian Revolution* was first published in 1994, I felt sure that only by coming fully to terms with their Soviet past, in which 1917 occupied such a central position, would the Russians be able to shape a better present or plan a better future for themselves. That still seems true. But it is now nine years since the collapse of Communism in the Soviet Union, and the distinction between 'Soviet' and 'Russian' no longer looks so convincing: features of life that we took to be 'Soviet' now appear to be much more deeply seated in Russian life than we had imagined. No new 'Russian' morality has emerged to replace the threadbare morality and double standards of Soviet life; no new culture of honesty and intrinsic moral values seems capable of counteracting the widespread philosophy of corruption. Youthful idealism quickly evaporates. It is generally assumed, and with justification, that anyone who has made a lot of money is bound to be corrupt, or at best entirely self-seeking.

This sense of a vacuum in Russian life has to be seen within the context of the peculiar historical relationship of Russians to authority. 'In Tsarist times,' Richard Pipes writes, 'all power was concentrated in the Crown. The lines of authority ran from the top down; there were hardly any lateral lines.'[6] Of the Soviet period John Lloyd writes: 'All of work and social life fell into formal and informal groupings which were commanded to relate vertically, up towards the apex. Horizontal relations were both proscribed and shunned. The "us" and "them" were absolute categories in the Soviet system,' Lloyd goes on, 'and remained so afterwards.'[7] Poor people in Russia will often ask: 'Why do they make our lives so miserable?' Who 'they' are is unspecified. The same unfocused complaint that was heard in Tsarist times and in Soviet times is still being heard today.

Traditionally it has been assumed that 'they', the masters, the bosses, the people in power, will behave arbitrarily and unfairly towards 'us' and make our lives a misery. If that is so, why should 'we' be expected to behave responsibly, to be made accountable for our actions, towards 'them'? People who are resistant to authority in this way are unlikely to develop any sense of authority within themselves. To make a democracy work requires a degree of self-discipline, a kind of inner sense of law and order, that seem to be lacking from the ordinary Russian mentality.

Is change going to come from the top down, from those in power? Traditionally, the people have never been looked upon as 'partners'; that was a fiction of Soviet society; the people needed always to be tightly controlled. Here, too, we see that those in power have never been checked by any inner restraints. There was only one possible message to be derived from Soviet society, John Lloyd writes: that life was a game of winners and losers, and the winner 'took all and held the losers at bay . . . The Soviet lesson was to grab and hold; the post-Soviet experience was that flaunting wealth could be done with impunity as long as you bought or created protection from behind which to do so.'[8] Where do exercising power with responsibility, or being held accountable for decisions affecting other people's lives, come into the picture? They don't. As I write, news of the Russian submarine disaster is still coming in. The whole issue of accountability in Russian life is being highlighted in a powerfully emotional way. Public outrage is being expressed with a vigour that would have been unthinkable in Soviet times, and the Russian leadership is having to respond to public opinion as never before. If the idea of responsibility and accountability begins to take root in Russian life, that would be one positive outcome of the tragedy of the 'Kursk'.

Russians have always been adept at circumventing authority, evading officialdom and finding ways of beating the system. Life in Soviet times could not have functioned as smoothly as it did without *blat*. To obtain something *po blatu* meant obtaining it 'under the counter' or 'on the quiet' by making use of influence or connections. It differed from the ubiquitous bribery of Tsarist Russia in that no money changed hands. In today's market economy, Jonathan Steele writes, 'while *blat* is no longer needed to obtain goods, it is used to get jobs and services . . . In many cases, *blat* has been given a price tag. People pay high prices in cash for favours which used to be done free or for small presents.'[9] But life is still made more tolerable for ordinary Russians by what Steele describes as a 'culture of private solidarity' that also survives from Soviet times. Local networking is strongly developed: towards family, friends and friends of friends. Here co-operation continues as it did before, governed not by the exchange of money but by a recognition of mutual need: today I am in a position to lend you money, help you obtain a privilege or enable you to jump that queue, knowing that tomorrow you may be able to do the same for me. This is a fine tribute to friendship. Friends in Russia are greatly cherished, they 'add the salt' to day-to-day living, and for a Westerner this 'culture of friendship' remains perhaps the most attractive feature of Russian life. But there is another aspect to this. If the system worked better and more fairly, a culture of private solidarity would not be necessary; and in the final analysis, jumping a queue is unfair to all the others left behind. Here is a deep-seated feature of Russian life: friendship and emotional warmth flourish (more than in the West), but at the expense of believing in or identifying yourself in any way with the system or with authority.

Returning to Russia early this year after a five-year interval, I was struck more than ever by the inequalities in Russian society. The contrast between rich and poor, between those who seem to have more money than they know what to do with, and those who are worse off than in Soviet times, is much more blatant than in the past.

How these New Russians acquired their wealth – enabling them to build luxurious country houses in large grounds and to send their children to be educated at expensive schools abroad – does not bear much scrutiny. As in Tsarist times this wealthy new upper class looks to the West for models and fashions to follow. Even the Russian language is becoming saturated by this Western influence; new flats in Moscow are advertised as *elitnyi dom v prestizhnom raionye* ('an elite block in a prestigious area'). Professional people on whom a civilized society depends, like teachers, doctors and architects (but not lawyers who are doing very nicely) are falling further and further behind, both financially and in terms of social prestige. 'The largest change which affected Russian society through the 1990s,' John Lloyd writes, 'was an adaptation to new ways of getting by. Bit by bit, it was made plain to people that state or enterprise could not provide for a decent living standard – but that their own efforts could supplement the miserable wages they received. This was patchy and, like so much in the new Russia, desperately unequal.'[10] Fine to turn your car into a taxi – so long as you had a car in the first place. While these inequalities last, it is impossible to see how Russia is going to become a more integrated society. 'Us' and 'them' is bound to persist.

Whatever may have happened to the Soviet Union, the Russian Revolution of 1917 has lost none of its power to challenge and disturb. It threw down a challenge to the unfair distribution of wealth and privilege within a society. Confronted by the gross inequalities of their new capitalist system, where the rich seem to get richer and the poor poorer, the majority of Russians are bound to conclude that this situation has got worse, not better. The same situation, as the ideologists in 1917 pointed out, is reproduced at a global level, in the gross inequalities between nations. These are all problems, it has to be said, that the Western world has scarcely begun to address, let alone resolve, and that are going to become increasingly urgent. At an even more fundamental level, the Revolution challenged the whole idea of property and ownership. The abolition of private property was a central part of the huge experiment in social engineering that was initiated in 1917. The experiment failed and the cost was enormous; but did this happen because the experiment was fatally flawed from the outset or because the notion of private property is one that we cannot do without? This is a question of how we view ourselves.

How do Russians view themselves? Many years ago I argued that there were two strains in popular Russian behaviour: one was 'collective' and 'submissive', the other 'independent' and 'self-asser-tive'.[11] Contemporary Russian society exhibits this same tension between collectivism and individualism, as two of the best recent commentators on Russia point out. 'The attempt to impose a Protestant ethic of competitive individualism,' Jonathan Steele writes, 'and a new psychology of market attitudes is diluted by the old practices of informal networking, solidarity among friends, and distrust of accumulation.'[12] And John Lloyd foresees a 'long and continuing struggle' between on the one hand, 'an egalitarianism which was as much a result of pre-communist communal village life as it was the socialist ideology which had sanctioned and enforced it, and which is still clung to or appealed to by millions,' and on the other, 'a Darwinian hierarchy in which the new rich and powerful are contemptuous, overtly and covertly, of those who fail to see that the world is changing, and cannot even adapt, let alone master it.'[13] In 1917 Soviet Russia began a collectivist experiment in which the forces of individualism fought a rearguard action; today the situation is reversed and it is collectivist forces that are fighting back. Like so much else in her history, the outcome of Russia's 'experiment with individualism' is quite unpredictable.

Sources and Bibliography

The Arthur Ransome Archive in the Brotherton Collection (University of Leeds) contains a full series of Ransome's own typewritten dated copies of his telegrams to the *Daily News* from Russia during 1917, with a break between October 7 (No.262) and December 29 (No.263), due to his absence from the country.

Unless otherwise indicated, all material from newspapers and journals was consulted at the British Library Newspaper Library.

Published eye-witness accounts

Listed below are all the published eye-witness accounts of the Russian Revolution which have been used in the text, but not all those consulted. Details of further titles may be found in Philip Grierson's *Books on Soviet Russia 1917–1942* (Methuen, 1943; reprinted, Anthony C. Hall, Twickenham, Middx., 1969). Unless stated otherwise, the place of publication is London. An asterisk after a title indicates that the book was reprinted in *Russia Observed*: An Arno Press/New York Times Collection, 1970–71.

Beatty, Bessie, *The Red Heart of Russia*, Century, New York, 1918
Bryant, Louise, *Six Red Months in Russia*, George H. Doran, New York, 1918; Heinemann, 1919*
Buchanan, Meriel, *Petrograd the City of Trouble 1914–1918*, Collins, 1918
— *The Dissolution of an Empire*, John Murray, 1932*
Buchanan, Sir George, *My Mission to Russia and Other Diplomatic Memories*, 2 vols., Cassell, London and New York, 1923*
Dawe, Rosamond (née Dowse). *Looking Back: A Memoir of an English Governess, 1914–1917*, Bishop Otter College, Chichester, 1973; revised edition, Unwin Brothers, Old Woking, 1976
Farson, Negley, *The Way of a Transgressor*, Gollancz, 1936
Francis, David R, *Russia from the American Embassy, April 1916–November 1918*, Scribner, New York, 1921*
Gerhardie, William, *Memoirs of a Polyglot*, Duckworth, 1931; reprinted, Robin Clark, 1990. A Revised Definitive Edition of all Gerhardie's works was published by Macdonald between 1970 and 1974

Hanbury-Williams, Major-Gen. Sir John, *The Emperor Nicholas II as I knew him*, Humphreys, 1922; Dutton, New York, 1923

Hard, William, *Raymond Robins' Own Story*, Harper, New York and London, 1920*

Jones, Stinton, *Russia in Revolution: being the experiences of an Englishman in Petrograd during the upheaval*, Herbert Jenkins, 1917

Knox, Major-Gen. Sir Alfred, *With the Russian Army, 1914–1917*. 2 vols., Hutchinson, 1921*

Lockhart, R.H. Bruce, *Memoirs of a British Agent*, Putnam, London and New York, 1932; new edition, Macmillan, 1974

— *The Two Revolutions: An Eye-Witness Study of Russia 1917*, The Bodley Head, 1967

Marcosson, I.F., *The Rebirth of Russia*, John Lane, The Bodley Head, 1917

Paléologue, M., *An Ambassador's Memoirs*, translated from the French by F.A.Holt. 3 vols., Hutchinson, 1923–25

Pares, Sir B., *My Russian Memoirs*, Jonathan Cape, 1931

Pitcher, Harvey, *When Miss Emmie was in Russia*, John Murray, 1977 (includes recollections of the Revolution by Louisette Andrews, Marguerite Bennet, Emma Dashwood, Rosamond Dowse and Edith Kerby)

— *The Smiths of Moscow*, Swallow House Books, Cromer, 1984 (includes recollections of the Revolution by Harry Smith and other members of the Smith family)

Pollock, J., *The Bolshevik Adventure*, Constable, 1919

Poole, Ernest, *The Village: Russian Impressions*, Macmillan, New York, 1918

— *'The Dark People': Russia's Crisis*, Macmillan, New York, 1919

Price, M. Philips, *My Reminiscences of the Russian Revolution*, George Allen & Unwin, 1921

— *My Three Revolutions*, George Allen & Unwin, 1969

— *Dispatches from the Revolution: Russia 1916–18,* edited by Tania Rose, Pluto Press, 1997

Ransome, Arthur, *Autobiography*, edited and with an introduction by Rupert Hart-Davis, Jonathan Cape, 1976

Reed, John, *Ten Days That Shook the World*, Boni and Liveright, New York, 1919; Modern Books, London, 1926; many subsequent editions

Robien, Louis de, *The Diary of a Diplomat in Russia*, translated from the French by Camilla Sykes, Michael Joseph, 1969, originally published by Editions Albin Michel, Paris, 1967

Sisson, Edgar, *One Hundred Red Days*, Yale University Press, New Haven, Connecticut, 1931

Stebbing, E.P., *From Czar to Bolshevik*, John Lane, The Bodley Head, 1918

Stopford, Albert. *The Russian Diary of an Englishman: Petrograd, 1915–1917*, Heinemann, 1919. (Published anonymously, but the author is identified by Obolensky in *One Man In His Time*, p.141: see below)

Tyrkova-Williams, Ariadna, *Cheerful Giver: The Life of Harold Williams*, Peter Davies, 1935

Urch, R.O.G. *'We Generally Shoot Englishmen': An English Schoolmaster's Five*

Years of Mild Adventure in Moscow (1915–20), George Allen & Unwin, 1936
Wilcox, E.H., *Russia's Ruin*, Chapman & Hall, 1919
Williams, Albert Rhys, *Through the Russian Revolution*, Labour Publishing Co., 1923; reprinted, Monthly Review Press, New York, 1967
Wilton, Robert, *Russia's Agony*, Arnold, 1918

Unpublished eye-witness material

The letters of Marguerite Bennet (Mrs Thomson), Reginald Bennett, Kenneth Metcalf and Mrs Nellie Thornton are deposited with the Leeds Russian Archive (MS Nos. 790/20, 1090/7, 1224/1 and 1072/24), and Sir George Bury's account of the March Revolution with the Department of Manuscripts and Records of the National Library of Wales at Aberystwyth (Lord Davies of Llandinam Papers, C2/23). William Gerhardie's letter is in the Gerhardie Archive at Cambridge University Library (Add. MS 8292, Box 1).

Additional select bibliography

Brogan, Hugh, *The Life of Arthur Ransome*, Jonathan Cape, 1984
Davies, Dido, *William Gerhardie: A Biography*, Oxford University Press, 1990
Figes, Orlando, *A People's Tragedy: The Russian Revolution 1891–1924*, Jonathan Cape, 1996, Pimlico, 1997
Figes, O. and Kolonitskii, B., *Interpreting the Russian Revolution: The Language and Symbols of 1917*, Yale University Press, New Haven, 1999
Hicks, Granville, with the assistance of John Stuart, *John Reed: The Making of a Revolutionary*, Macmillan, Toronto, 1936; reissued, Benjamin Blom, New York, 1968
Hoare, Sir Samuel, *The Fourth Seal*, Heinemann, 1930
Lloyd, John, *Rebirth of a Nation: An Anatomy of Russia*, Michael Joseph, 1998
Murrell, G.D.G., *Russia's Transition to Democracy: An Internal Political History, 1989–1996*, Sussex Academic Press, Brighton, 1997
Obolensky, Serge, *One Man In His Time*, Hutchinson, 1960
Oktyabr 1917 goda i bolshevistskii eksperiment v Rossii ('October 1917 and the Bolshevik experiment in Russia'). Proceedings of a conference held on 5 November 1994. Moscow, 1995
Pethybridge, Roger (ed.), *Witnesses to the Russian Revolution*, George Allen & Unwin, 1964, Citadel Press, New York, 1967
Pipes, Richard, *The Russian Revolution 1899–1919*, Knopf, New York, and Collins Harvill, London, 1990
— *Three Whys of the Russian Revolution*, Vintage Canada, 1995, Pimlico, 1998
Pitcher, Harvey, *Understanding the Russians*, George Allen & Unwin, 1964
Steele, Jonathan, 'Blatting order', *The Guardian*, 8 August 1998
Sukhanov, N.N., *The Russian Revolution 1917: A Personal Record*, edited, abridged and translated by Joel Carmichael, Oxford University Press, 1955, reprinted 1984.
Williams, Harold, *Russia of the Russians*, Pitman, 1914

Notes and References

The dates used throughout are those of the New Style (Western) calendar, which in 1917 was thirteen days ahead of the Old Style (Russian) calendar.

In the original texts the rendering of Russian proper names into English is very variable. For instance, the name of the building where the Duma met – in Russian the *Tavricheskii dvorets* – may appear in at least six different ways. All proper names have therefore been standardized in accordance with appropriate modern usage.

Omissions from the original text are indicated by three-dot ellipses, but since John Reed himself frequently uses three dots as a stylistic device, in his case this was increased to six. Where several sources have been used within a paragraph, the references are collected together at the end of the paragraph; in the case of extracts consisting of several paragraphs, the reference will be found at the end of the extract.

Newspaper articles are referred to by the date of publication, followed by the date-line in brackets. Arthur Ransome's telegrams are referred to by their number in the Brotherton Collection series, followed in brackets by the date which he wrote on his copies, i.e. the date of dispatch.

The following abbreviations have been used: AR Arthur Ransome; HW Harold Williams; JR John Reed; PP Philips Price.

FOREWORD TO THE PIMLICO EDITION

1 *Oktyabr 1917 goda,* p.39
2 Figes, xix
3 Hoare, p.239
4 See the articles by Christopher Andrew, 'Swallows and Bolsheviks', *The Times,* 31 December 1994; Paul Foot, 'Cold War gold undermines our independence', *The Guardian,* 2 January 1995; and Andrew Rosthorn, 'Ransome was not a spy, say Swallow fans', *Independent on Sunday,* 8 January 1995
5 Pares, p.482

INTRODUCING THE WITNESSES

1 Biographical details from Tyrkova-Williams. Pares (p.479) also wondered why Williams' dispatches had never been reprinted.
2 AR, *Autobiography,* p.167
3 Sisson, p.182
4 PP, *My Three Revolutions,* pp.23–4
5 Buchanan, vol. 1, p.1
6 Hoare, pp.241–3; Pares, p.366

7 Pares, p.426
8 Evelyn Miller, 'The British Embassy in Petrograd', *Lady's Pictorial*, 24 October 1914, Buchanan Papers, Hallward Library, University of Nottingham
9 Meriel Buchanan, *Petrograd*, p.228
10 Davies, p.71, quoting Rodzianko, Paul. *Tattered Banners: An Autobiography* (1938), p.169; Knox, p.367
11 This is how Gerhardie describes the fictional character of Admiral Butt, who is based on Knox, in *Futility* (Macdonald edition, p.72).
12 Gerhardie, *Memoirs of a Polyglot*, p.115
13 Biographical details from Hicks
14 The memorable title was suggested to Reed by Arthur Garfield Hays (see Hicks, p.325). *Which* ten days it refers to is unclear!

CHAPTER 1: RED MONDAY

1 PP, *Reminiscences*, p.11
2 Knox, pp.334, 388
3 Buchanan, vol. 2, pp.43–9
4 Obolensky, p.87
5 Stopford, p.94; Meriel Buchanan, *Dissolution*, pp.153–4
6 Stopford, p.101
7 Leeds Russian Archive, MS 790/20
8 Stopford, pp.101–2
9 HW, March 13 (10)
10 AR, 50 (March 10), 52 (March 15)
11 Stopford, pp.102–4
12 Stinton Jones, p.98; AR, 52 (March 15)
13 *The Times*, March 16 (12)
14 Wilton, pp.109–11
15 Stopford, pp.107–8
16 Meriel Buchanan, *Petrograd*, pp.92–6
17 Knox, pp.553–9
18 Stinton Jones, p.viii
19 Stinton Jones, pp.105–16, 121
20 Stinton Jones, pp.119–20
21 Meriel Buchanan, *Petrograd*, pp.97–8
22 Stinton Jones, pp.123–4, 131
23 AR, 52 (March 15)
24 Stinton Jones, p.127; AR, 52 (March 15)
25 Stinton Jones, pp.132–5
26 HW, March 17 (15)
27 See Tyrkova-Williams, pp.178–9 (quoting from Harold Williams' unfinished history of the Revolution?)
28 Tyrkova-Williams, p.179

29 See Tyrkova-Williams, p.179
30 Tyrkova-Williams, p.180
31 Stinton Jones, p.158

CHAPTER 2: THE BIRTH OF FREEDOM

 1 Meriel Buchanan, *Petrograd*, pp.101–2
 2 Knox, p.560
 3 AR, 52 (March 15)
 4 *Daily Telegraph*, March 16
 5 Stinton Jones, p.166
 6 Bury, pp.xv–xvi
 7 Stinton Jones, pp.165–6
 8 Bury, p.xvi
 9 Knox, pp.561–3
10 HW, March 17 (15); Knox, p.563; Bury, pp.xix–xx
11 *The Times*, March 16 (14)
12 Knox, p.563
13 AR, 53 (March 15)
14 *Daily Chronicle*, March 16
15 Bury, pp.xxii–xxiii
16 Francis, p.83; HW, *Russia of the Russians*, p.85
17 AR, 53 (March 15)
18 Stopford, pp.111–2
19 *The Times*, March 17 (15)
20 Leeds Russian Archive, MS 1224/1
21 Stinton Jones, p.193
22 *The Times*, March 17 (15)
23 AR, 55 (March 15)
24 HW, March 17 (16)
25 Knox, pp.565–70
26 AR, 55 (March 15)
27 Stopford, pp.115–6
28 Stinton Jones, pp.222–3; Marcosson, p.115
29 HW, March 17 (16)
30 Knox, pp.572–3
31 Bury, pp.xxi–xxii
32 *The Times*, March 19 (17)
33 AR, 59, 62, 63, 64 (March 17)
34 HW, March 19 (16)
35 HW, March 21 (17)

CHAPTER 3: ASSUMING OFFICE

1 Hanbury-Williams, pp.167–70
2 AR, 81 (March 23)
3 HW, March 27 (23)
4 AR, 63 (March 17); Lockhart, *Memoirs*, p.175; Marcosson pp.151–2
5 Hoare, p.256; Lockhart, *Memoirs*, p.175
6 Francis, p.87; HW, *Russia of the Russians*, p.89
7 HW, March 20 (17); Pares, pp.434–5
8 Marcosson, pp.165–6
9 HW, March 19 (15)
10 Wilcox, p.191
11 HW, March 22 (19); Knox, pp.576–8
12 Knox, pp.578–9
13 AR, *Autobiography*, p.216; AR 72 (March 19)
14 Buchanan, vol. 2, p.91
15 Francis, p.94
16 Buchanan, vol. 2, pp.91–2, 108
17 Knox, pp.584–6
18 Pollock, pp.178–9
19 *The Times*, March 20 (18)
20 AR, 62 (March 17)
21 AR, 66 (March 17); *The Times*, March 20 (18)
22 AR, 52 (March 15), 81 (March 23)
23 AR, 72 (March 19)
24 *The Times*, March 19 (15)
25 HW, March 21 (18)

CHAPTER 4: 'WALK AND TALK'

1 HW, March 28 (25)
2 See Pares, p.444
3 Buchanan, vol. 2, p.113
4 Stopford, pp.147, 148
5 Marcosson, p.110
6 HW, *Russia of the Russians*, p.401
7 Stopford, p.147
8 HW, April 9 (5)
9 Robien, p.27
10 Hanbury-Williams, p.211
11 Meriel Buchanan, *Petrograd*, 114
12 Buchanan, vol. 2, p.113
13 See Robien, p.38
14 Knox, p.575
15 Pares, p.423

16 Knox, p.610
17 AR, 83 (March 27), 90 (April 2), 91 (April 3)
18 Buchanan, vol. 2, pp.99, 111, 114
19 Dawe, p.19; Pitcher, *Miss Emmie*, p.142
20 Farson, pp.276–7
21 Pollock, p.184
22 AR, 91 (April 3)
23 See Marcosson, p.114
24 Knox, pp.579–82
25 Sukhanov, pp.202–3
26 Knox, pp.591–2
27 Buchanan, vol. 2, p.111
28 Knox, pp.589–90
29 AR, 88 (March 30), 92 (April 8)
30 HW, April 12 (10)
31 AR, 94 (April 10)
32 AR, 96 (April 12), 205 (August 7)
33 AR, 96 (April 12)
34 AR, 97 (April 13)
35 AR, 98 (April 14)
36 HW, April 18 (16)
37 AR, 99 (April 18); PP, *Reminiscences*, pp.19–20
38 See Knox, pp.582–3
39 PP, *Reminiscences*, pp.12–13, 14
40 AR, *Autobiography*, pp.220–1
41 PP, 'The Background of the Revolution', *The U.D.C.* [Union of Democratic Control], vol. 2, No.9, July 1917, pp.97–9, Hull University Archives: U.D.C. Collection
42 Buchanan, vol. 2, p.115

CHAPTER 5: KERENSKY IN THE ASCENDANT

1 AR, 109 (May 4)
2 Buchanan, vol. 2, pp.137–9 (slightly adapted)
3 Buchanan, vol. 2, p.136
4 Wilcox, p.241
5 Based on Russian sources, especially Sukhanov
6 Meriel Buchanan, *Dissolution*, p.202
7 Wilcox, p.240; Francis, p.136
8 AR, 101 (April 22); HW, April 20 (18)
9 AR, 105 (May 1); Robien, p.48
10 PP, *Reminiscences*, p.21; Pares, p.433
11 PP, *My Three Revolutions*, pp.52–3
12 AR, 106 (May 3)
13 PP, *Reminiscences*, p.30

14 AR, 108 (May 3), 109 (May 4)
15 Pares, p.435; AR, 111 (May 5); Buchanan, p.124
16 Buchanan, vol. 2, pp.126–7; AR, 121 (May 16)
17 AR, 124 (May 20), 125 (May 23)
18 *Manchester Guardian*, August 7 (written about the end of May)
19 Buchanan, vol. 2, p.118
20 Pares, p.444; Meriel Buchanan, *Petrograd*, pp.116–7
21 Pares, pp.433–4
22 *Daily Telegraph*, May 15; AR, 119 (May 13)

CHAPTER 6: ONE ISLAND, TWO ORATORS

1 Knox, pp.610, 613, 616–7
2 Pitcher, *Miss Emmie*, pp.146–7
3 Knox, p.618; AR, 130 (June 1); *Daily Telegraph*, June 2
4 HW, June 8 (6), June 11 (8)
5 HW, June 12 (10)
6 *Manchester Guardian*, July 17 (date-lined 'June'); PP, *Reminiscences*, pp.34–41, *My Three Revolutions*, pp.55–6. The *MG* article, being written nearer the time, is factually more reliable, but *Reminiscences* has more detail. This account is a conflation of the two.
7 AR, 134 (June 7)
8 *Daily Telegraph*, May 21 (19)
9 *Manchester Guardian*, August 7 (written about the end of May)
10 PP, *My Three Revolutions*, p.55
11 Wilcox, p.241
12 PP, *Reminiscences*, p.42
13 AR, 139 (June 14)
14 AR, 141 (June 19)
15 *Common Sense*, August 4 (date-lined June 26); PP, *Reminiscences*, pp.44–6

CHAPTER 7: JULY DAYS

1 Buchanan, vol. 2, p.135
2 AR, Letters to his mother, May 27–July 23
3 *Daily Telegraph*, July 6
4 *Daily Telegraph*, June 26
5 HW, June 28 (23); AR, 146, 148 (June 23)
6 AR, 149 (June 24), 151 (June 26)
7 HW, July 4 (1); AR, 154 (June 28), 157 (July 2)
8 AR, Letter to his mother, July 1
9 Leeds Russian Archive, MS 1072/24 (slightly adapted)
10 Buchanan, vol. 2, pp.151–2
11 Meriel Buchanan, *Petrograd*, pp.130–5

12 AR, 175 (July 17)
13 AR, 174 (July 17)
14 Knox, p.657
15 HW, July 19 (17)
16 AR, 177 (July 17); Knox, p.657; AR, 178 (July 17)
17 AR, 179 (July 17); Knox, p.657; Meriel Buchanan, *Petrograd*, pp.136–7
18 Buchanan, vol. 2, p.153
19 Knox, pp.657–8
20 Meriel Buchanan, *Petrograd*, pp.139–42; Knox, pp.658–9
21 Knox, p.659
22 Buchanan, vol. 2, p.154; AR, 185 (July 18)
23 Knox, p.661
24 HW, July 23 (19)
25 Meriel Buchanan, *Petrograd*, pp.148–53, with some details from *Dissolution*, pp.226–7
26 Stopford, p.177
27 Knox, pp.662–3
28 Knox, p.661
29 AR, 188 (July 20)
30 Knox, p.663
31 HW, July 24 (22)
32 AR, 186 (July 19), 189 (July 21)
33 HW, July 24 (22)
34 AR, 173 (July 16), 186 (July 19), 189 (July 21)

CHAPTER 8: THE PLAIN PEOPLE

1 All the material used here is from *The Village*, mainly Chapters II and III
2 *Manchester Guardian*, December 6; PP, *Reminiscences*, pp.108–14

CHAPTER 9: KORNILOV

1 Pares, p.472
2 AR, 203 (August 6)
3 AR, Letter to his mother, August 12
4 Urch, p.42
5 Pares, p.451
6 PP, *Reminiscences*, pp.70–1
7 Urch, pp.56–7, 62
8 Stebbing, p.158
9 Urch, p.60
10 HW, August 29 (26)
11 Wilton, pp.287–8
12 PP, *Reminiscences*, pp.73–7

13 HW, September 1 (August 29), September 5 (2)
14 Stopford, p.192
15 Buchanan, vol. 2, pp.171–3
16 Beatty, pp.316–8
17 Buchanan, vol. 2, pp.175–6, 181–2
18 Meriel Buchanan, *Dissolution*, pp.238–9
19 Buchanan, vol. 2, p.184
20 Buchanan, vol. 2, p.185
21 PP, *Reminiscences*, pp.69, 79
22 AR, 233 (September 10); HW, September 17 (13); Buchanan, vol. 2, pp.178, 185; Knox, p.692; Stopford, p.202
23 AR, 233 (September 10)
24 AR, 238 (September 13)
25 HW, September 20 (18)
26 HW, September 29 (26)
27 HW, October 2 (September 27)
28 AR, 248 (September 27)
29 HW, October 2 (September 27)
30 AR, 248 (September 27), 249 (September 28); HW, October 2 (September 27)
31 PP, *Reminiscences*, p.130
32 AR, 254, 255 (October 2), 258 (October 4), 261 (October 6)
33 HW, October 5 (September 30)

CHAPTER 10: 'SOME MAD SCHEME'

 1 JR, p.9
 2 PP, *Reminiscences*, p.133
 3 Bryant, pp.37–8, 42
 4 JR, p.12; Hicks, p.261; Francis, pp.166–9
 5 PP, *Reminiscences*, p.130; Stebbing, p.91; HW, September 18 (15); AR, 254 (October 2)
 6 Buchanan, vol. 2, pp.188–9
 7 PP, 'Memorandum on the State of Russia between August and November 1917', date-lined November 2 (Price Papers)
 8 JR, pp.15, 19, 26
 9 AR, 215 (August 4)
10 JR, pp.26–9
11 JR, pp.40–1
12 JR, pp.41–3
13 Bryant, p.117
14 Hicks, p.268
15 JR, pp.32, 279
16 JR, p.46
17 Knox, p.702; JR, p.34; Buchanan, vol. 2, p.201

18 Buchanan, vol. 2, p.203; Meriel Buchanan, *Petrograd*, p.188
19 Buchanan, vol. 2, pp.203–4
20 JR, pp.47–8, 49–51
21 Knox, p.705
22 JR, pp.52–5
23 Meriel Buchanan, *Petrograd*, pp.191–2
24 JR, pp.57–61

CHAPTER 11: THE BOLSHEVIKS TAKE OVER

 1 Beatty, p.186
 2 Knox, pp.704–8
 3 JR, pp.62–4
 4 Bryant, p.80
 5 JR, pp.65–7
 6 Bryant, pp.80–1
 7 PP, *Reminiscences*, p.143
 8 Beatty, pp.190–2
 9 JR, pp.69–73
10 Beatty, pp.193–4
11 Meriel Buchanan, *Petrograd*, p.193; Buchanan, vol. 2, p.207
12 Beatty, pp.194–5
13 JR, pp.74–9
14 JR, p.79; A.R.Williams, p.103; Bryant, p.200; PP, *Reminiscences*, p.144
15 Bryant, p.83
16 Beatty, pp.201–7
17 JR, pp.81–2
18 JR, p.82; Beatty, p.209
19 Knox, pp.709–10
20 Beatty, pp.209–10
21 JR, p.83
22 A.R.Williams, p.109
23 JR, pp.84–5
24 JR, p.85; Bryant, pp.86–7
25 Knox, p.709
26 See Pipes, p.496, quoting Maliantovich in *Byloe*, No.12, 1918, pp.129–30
27 Beatty, p.212
28 Bryant, p.87; JR, p.85; Beatty, p.212
29 Beatty, pp.212–4; JR, pp.85–6
30 Beatty, pp.214–5; JR, pp.87–8
31 Hicks, pp.274–5
32 JR, pp.88–92
33 A.R.Williams, p.104
34 JR, p.92

CHAPTER 12: DOWNFALL OF KERENSKY

1 PP, *Reminiscences*, p.147
2 Robien, p.131
3 *Daily Telegraph*, November 11 (8)
4 Buchanan, vol. 2, p.206
5 Buchanan, vol. 2, p.212
6 Beatty, p.216; PP, *Reminiscences*, p.146
7 Gerhardie, p.129
8 Knox, pp.711–4
9 JR, pp.103–5
10 PP, *Reminiscences*, p.144
11 JR, pp.105–19
12 JR, pp.88, 99
13 PP, *Reminiscences*, pp.149–50. Price's dates are very confused here.
14 JR, pp.144–8; Beatty, p.221
15 PP, *Reminiscences*, pp.151–4
16 Bryant, pp.231–2; JR, 161
17 A.R.Williams, pp.129–33
18 Beatty, pp.225–239
19 Beatty, pp.240–2
20 PP, *Reminiscences*, p.154; Knox, p.717
21 JR, pp.171–80
22 Buchanan, vol. 2, pp.212–3
23 Buchanan, vol. 2, pp.215–7
24 Beatty, pp.183–4. See Kettle, pp.81–2
25 Bryant, p.115; Beatty, p.183; PP, *Reminiscences*, p.142
26 Buchanan, vol. 2, pp.186, 214
27 Wilcox, pp.196–205

CHAPTER 13: MOSCOW

1 The letters used here are in the Leeds Russian Archive, MS 1090/7
2 Urch, pp.68–77
3 Urch, pp.78–83
4 Urch, p.84
5 Pitcher, *Miss Emmie*, p.170
6 JR, pp.205–18; Bryant, pp.187–91
7 Beatty, pp.269–70
8 Knox, p.707
9 Pitcher, *The Smiths*, pp.124–7
10 Bryant, p.190; JR, p.109
11 JR, p.204; Bryant, p.188
12 Tyrkova-Williams, p.229

CHAPTER 14: THE CONSTITUENT ASSEMBLY

1 HW, December 4 (November 14)
2 HW, November 21 (19), November 22 (21)
3 Tyrkova-Williams, pp.190, 204; HW, November 26 (24), December 28 (26)
4 Lockhart, *Two Revolutions*, p.108; Wilcox, p.242
5 Lockhart, *Memoirs*, pp.237–8, *Two Revolutions*, p.108; Hard, pp.65, 156
6 Bryant, pp.47–8, 145
7 Lockhart, *Two Revolutions*, pp.108–9
8 Buchanan, vol. 2, p.217
9 PP, *Reminiscences*, p.168; JR, pp.257–61
10 HW, November 26 (24), December 6 (4)
11 *Common Sense*, December 1, *Manchester Guardian*, December 3 (November 29)
12 HW, December 12 (10), December 14 (11)
13 HW, December 15 (12)
14 Beatty, pp.410–1
15 Buchanan, vol. 2, pp.226–8, 231, 239
16 Meriel Buchanan, *Dissolution*, pp.273–4
17 Letter of December 31 to his parents, Gerhardie Archive (Add. MS 8292, Box 1)
18 Gerhardie, pp.131–2
19 Buchanan, vol. 2, p.247; Meriel Buchanan, *Petrograd*, p.244
20 AR, 291 (January 15)
21 PP, *Reminiscences*, pp.208, 211, *My Three Revolutions*, pp.109–10; letter of December 22 to his aunt, Anna Maria Philips (Price Papers)
22 AR, 263 (December 29)
23 AR, Letter to his mother, December 30; *Autobiography*, pp.228–9; AR, 275 (December 29)
24 PP, *Reminiscences*, p.192
25 Brogan, p.162
26 AR, 265 (December 31), 266 (January 1), 276 (written December 29, but not sent until January 6)
27 Kettle, p.179
28 Brogan, p.160
29 AR, *Autobiography*, p.230; Tyrkova-Williams, p.199; HW, December 26 (23)
30 Brogan, p.164
31 AR, 265 (December 31), 279 (January 10), 301 (January 20), *Autobiography*, p.230
32 AR, 265 (December 31)
33 PP, *My Three Revolutions*, p.96; letters of November 30 and December 22 to Anna Maria Philips (Price Papers)
34 HW, January 19 (17); AR, 299 (January 19)
35 Beatty, p.415

36 HW, January 21 (19)
37 Beatty, pp.417–8
38 HW, January 21 (19); Beatty, p.421; AR, 296 (January 19)
39 AR, 299 (January 19)
40 HW, January 21 (19); AR, 297, 298 (January 19); Beatty, p.420
41 Beatty, p.421; AR, 296 (January 19); HW, January 21 (19)
42 AR, 297, 298 (January 19)
43 HW, January 21 (19); PP, *Reminiscences*, p.219
44 Sisson, p.244; Beatty, p.423
45 Sisson, p.245; Beatty, p.424; PP, *Reminiscences*, p.220
46 Tyrkova-Williams, p.201; AR, 299 (January 19)
47 Beatty, pp.425–7
48 HW, January 21 (19); AR, 297 (January 19), 301 (January 20); PP, *Reminiscences*, p.221
49 Beatty, pp.428–9

AFTERWORD

 1 Pipes, *Three Whys*, p.2
 2 Figes, p.810
 3 Murrell, pp.22–3
 4 Lloyd, xix
 5 Murrell, p.15
 6 Pipes, *Three Whys*, pp.17–18
 7 Lloyd, xxiii
 8 Lloyd, xxiii–iv
 9 Steele, 'Blatting order'
10 Lloyd, xviii
11 Pitcher, *Understanding the Russians*, p.184
12 Steele, 'Blatting order'
13 Lloyd, xxv

INDEX

Index

Abramovich, 201
Admiralty, 17, 18, 35, 37, 40
Akselrod, P.B., 219
Aladin, A.F., 171
Alexander Column, 194, 206, 214
Alexandra, Empress, 11, 12, 54, 61
Alexandrinsky Theatre, 173, 174
Allen (Thornton driver), 124
Anarchists, 86, 102, 107, 120–2, 126, 128, 129
Anderson, Mr, 13
Anglo-Russian (English) Hospital, 36, 196
Anichkov Palace, 17
Antonov (Antonov-Ovseyenko), V.A., 189, 215, 220, 226–7, 229–30
Arbat Square, 241, 244
aristocracy, fate of, 150–1, 158–9
Armoured Car Division, British, 168, 223
Arsenal, 24–5
artel, ploughing, 156
Artillery Department, 20–2
Associated Press, 185–6
Astoria Hotel, 35–7, 136, 168, 193, 195, 224–6, 231
Aurora (cruiser), 199–200, 209
Avksentev, N.D., 195, 215

Babcock & Wilcox, 44
Bagratuni, 194
Balaban, 136
Balmont, K.D., 162
Baltic Fleet, 92
Barter, General, 167–8
Battalion of Death, 193
Battle of Moscow, 238–47

Beatty, Bessie, 7, 168, 179, 193–4, 198, 199, 200, 201–4, 205, 206, 208–9, 210–11, 215, 220, 224–31, 234–5, 249, 255, 261, 273, 274, 275–9
Belyaev, General M.A., 23
Bennet, Marguerite, 13
Bennett, Reginald, 238–40, 243–4, 245
Birkenheim, 178
Blagonravov, Ensign, 260, 261
Blondin, 253
Bologoye, 43, 47
Bolshevik Central Committee, 182, 184, 186
Bolsheviks (also referred to as 'Leninites'), 86–8, 92, 93, 95, 111–15, 121–2, 123, 127–9, 130, 131, 137–9, 149–50, 154, 160, 161, 166–7, 169, 171, 173–7, 180–2, 185, 187, 188, 190, 191, 192, 193–4, 198, 201, 213–14, 215, 218–19, 233, 252, 256–61, 262
Bolsheviks (Moscow), 238–46
Bolshoi Theatre, 161–2
bourgeoisie, 78, 79, 81, 120
Breshko-Breshkovskaya, Ye.K., 80–1, 83
Brest-Litovsk, 267, 269
British Embassy, 17, 20, 22, 28, 37, 43, 71, 89, 116, 127, 130–5, 187, 188, 200, 214, 215, 216, 233, 262–3
British Labour delegation, 82–3
Brixton Prison, 262, 266
Brogan, Hugh, 269, 270
Bryant, Louise, 7, 179, 180, 185–6, 195, 196, 197–8, 201, 202, 208, 209, 211, 223–4, 235, 247–50

Bublikov, 165
Buchanan, Lady Georgina, 19, 169–70, 215
Buchanan, Meriel, 4–5, 19–20, 28, 34, 71, 89, 96–7, 126–7, 130, 131, 133–5, 169–70, 187, 189, 200, 262–3, 264
Buchanan, Sir George, 3–4, 17, 19, 22, 23, 37, 43, 47, 63–4, 69, 71–2, 73–4, 77, 85, 86–8, 93–4, 95, 96, 100, 119, 126–7, 132, 133–4, 160, 167–9, 170, 171, 181, 187–8, 200, 201, 214, 233–4, 235, 256, 262–3, 266, 267, 271
Bury, Sir George, 35–7, 40, 41–2, 49–50

Cachin, 82–3
Cadet Corps (building), 111
cadets, see *yunkers*
Carlotti, 64
Catherine Hall (Taurida Palace), 38, 44
Chernov, V.M., 87–8, 94, 130, 137, 256, 276–8
Chernov Group, 154
Chicherin, G.V., 266
chinovniks, 102
Chkheidze, N.S., 32, 57, 88–9, 90, 165
Circus, 221, 222
City Hall, 93, 102, 129, 205, 211, 214–15, 219, 220, 224, 230, 250
Clapham Junction, 128
Clark, Professor, 241–2
Co-operative movement, 142–4
Co-operators, 162, 178
Coalition Government, First, 94–5, 115, 126, 139; Second, 160, 172; Third, 177, 258, 261
Commissariat of Foreign Affairs, 266–7
Committee of Public Safety / Committee for the Salvation of the Country and the Revolution, 212, 215, 219–24, 231–2, 256
Common Sense, 111
Communards, 271

Constantinople, 57, 78, 83, 91–2, 94
Constituent Assembly, 47, 50, 55, 62, 63, 65, 88, 114, 119, 122, 157, 166, 177, 179, 181, 190, 201, 218, 258–61, 272–9
Cossacks, 13–14, 15, 23, 71, 111, 131–2, 135, 138, 165, 194, 205, 219, 235, 238, 243
Council of Five, 172
Council of People's Commissars, 218, 253
Council of the Republic, 182, 185, 186, 189, 191, 195

Daily Chronicle, 2, 13–14, 31–2, 39, 43, 66, 117
Daily News, 2, 15, 43, 50, 62, 117, 179, 264, 268, 269
Daily Telegraph, 3, 214
Dan, F.I., 112, 190, 191, 200–1
Dashwood, Emma, 246–7
Decree on Land, 218
Democratic Assembly, 172–8, 181, 186, 270
Den, 102
District Court, 23, 25
District Staff, 194, 205, 214
Dolgorukov, Prince P.D., 260
Donon's, 13, 15
Dostoievsky, 175
Dowse, Rosamond, 74
dual authority, 61, 80, 81, 84–5, 94
Duma, 9, 16, 29, 31–3, 37–40, 41–4, 46–7, 51, 55, 56, 61, 72, 73, 75
Duma Committee, 31, 32, 38, 47, 48
Duma, First, 114
Duma, Fourth, 58
Durnovo, General P.N., 120
Durnovo palace, 120–1, 123, 126
dvorniks (yard-keepers), 30, 75, 128

Ehrlich, 191
Eisenstein, S.M., 214
Emancipation, 145–6
Engelhardt, Colonel, 22–3, 39
Engineering School, ensigns of, 205
Europe Hotel, 15
'extravagant humanitarianism', 99

fabrichny komitet (factory committee), 108–9
Field of Mars, 17, 70–1, 131, 222–3, 267
Finland Station, 88–9, 216
Fontanka Canal, 26, 221, 223
Foreign Office (London), 4, 94, 96, 181
Foreign Office (Petrograd), 22, 57
Francis, David R., 42, 56, 63, 89, 180
French Embassy, 13, 22
Funeral March, 218, 249
Funeral of victims of March Revolution, 69–71

Gardiner (*Daily News*), 117
Garvin, J.L. (*Observer*), 117
General Staff, 127, 195, 214
Gerhardie, William, 5, 215, 263
German General Staff, 131
Germanova, Maria, 246–7
Golitzin, Boris, 18
Gots, A.R., 190, 191
Grand Duke Boris, 18
Grand Duke Cyril, 23, 44
Grand Duke Mikhail Alexandrovich (Michael), 47
Grand Duke Nicholas, 60
Grenadersky Regiment, 215–16
Grenfell, Captain, 63
Guchkov, A.I., 38, 57, 60, 62, 64, 94
Gumberg, Alexander, 179, 201, 202, 203

Hanbury-Williams, Sir John, 53–4, 64, 71
Hicks, Granville, 6
Hoare, Samuel, 56
Holtzman, 233
Hotel France, 198
Hotel National (Moscow), 248
house committees, 241–2, 243–4
Hypatiev, General, 20, 21

Iberian Chapel, 163
Internationale, 218, 276
Izvestiya, 38, 191, 219

Jewish *Bund*, 204

Jones, Stinton, 16, 24–31, 33, 36–7, 45
July Days, 5, 123–39, 171, 214

Kadet (Constitutional Democrat) Party, 2, 56, 62, 66, 79, 80, 87, 126, 139, 159, 172, 176–7, 188, 191, 234, 258, 260, 269, 270, 274–5
Kaledin, General A.M., 165–6, 277
Kamenev, L.B., 177, 182, 199, 201, 212, 217, 218, 232, 238
Karakhan, L.M., 184
Karelin, V.A., 188
Kazan Cathedral, 15, 93, 204
Keksgolmsky Regiment, 23
Kerby, Edith, 100
Kerensky, A.F., 1, 32, 38, 40, 50, 57–62, 64, 66, 68, 69, 77–8, 79, 80, 84, 87, 88, 90, 94–8, 99–101, 110, 123, 128–9, 135–6, 137, 154, 160, 161, 162–6, 167, 169–70, 171, 173–6, 180, 182, 185–6, 187, 188, 189, 191, 194, 195, 196, 209, 219, 220, 225, 226, 227, 232, 233–7, 252, 255, 264, 277
Khabalov, General S.S., 18, 23
Kislovodsk, 179, 252
Knights of St George, 96, 165–6, 170
Knox, Major-General Sir Alfred, 5–6, 20–4, 29, 34–5, 37–40, 46–7, 48–9, 58–62, 63–4, 65, 72, 73, 75–8, 83, 84, 99–101, 127, 129, 130, 132, 133–4, 135–6, 138, 171, 187, 188–9, 194–5, 205, 213, 214–16, 231, 232, 233, 238, 249, 250, 263, 267, 271
Kokoshkin, F.F., 260
Kollontai, A.M., 218, 275, 279
Konovalov, A.I., 187, 208, 210, 211
Kornilov, General L.G., 62, 94, 101, 160, 163–76, 225, 235, 237, 257
Kremlin, 163, 238, 239, 241, 247, 248
Krestovsky Prison, 22, 25, 33
Kronstadt, 103–10, 180
Kronstadt sailors, 35, 92, 107–8, 130, 132, 192, 222
Kropotkin, Prince P.A., 52
Krylenko, N.V., 212, 275
Kshesinskaya's house, 89, 102, 121, 127, 129–30, 132, 135

Lakhta, 160
land nationalization, 88, 137, 256, 278
Lavergne, Colonel, 22
Left SRs, 218, 256, 266, 274, 278
Lekhovich, General, 21
Lenin (Ulyanov), V.I., 85, 86, 87, 88–90, 99, 102, 110–11, 112–15, 126, 130, 132, 137, 138, 171, 182, 186–7, 198, 203, 212, 216–18, 219, 232, 253–6, 257, 261, 275, 276
Lessney, 125
Levashovo, 216
Liberty Loan, 142
Lieber, M.I., 112
Liteiny Prospect, 20, 22, 23, 129, 273
Litovsky Regiment, 16, 23, 92
Lloyd George, 64
Lockhart, R.H. Bruce, 6, 55, 56, 96, 254–6
Loginov, 273
Lubyanskaya Square (Moscow), 238
Lunacharsky, A.V., 177, 199, 218, 247, 275
Lvov, Prince G.E., 43, 55–6, 58, 77, 84, 94, 136, 137
Lvov, Vladimir, 170

Macdonald, Ramsay, 119
Machine-Gun Regiment, 1st, 138, 139
Makarov, Admiral, 105
Malachite Room (Winter Palace), 208, 210
Malkin (*Russian Daily News*), 204
Manchester Guardian, 2, 3, 92, 265, 271
Manikovsky, General, 20, 21, 64
Marble Palace, 131
March Revolution, 9–52, 213; in Moscow, 161; reaction of witnesses, 64–7
March SR, 87
Marcosson, Isaac, 55–6, 57, 70
Marinsky Palace, 37, 84, 93, 182, 188, 189, 195
Marinsky Square, 92, 93
Marinsky Theatre, 41, 69, 198

Markozov, 24
Marseillaise, 13, 14, 43, 69, 70
Martov (Tsederbaum), Yu.O., 191, 201
Marxism, 87, 88, 107, 111, 114, 183, 254
May Day celebration, 90–1
meetings, 101
Menshevik Internationalists, 191
Mensheviks, 57, 86–8, 112, 166, 170, 185, 189, 191, 199, 201, 204, 219–20, 277
Metcalf, Kenneth, 44
Metcalf, Leslie, 44
Mikhail Artillery School, 205
Military Academy of Engineering, 221
Military-Revolutionary Committee, 188, 189, 191, 201, 202, 203, 205, 211, 213, 220, 222, 225, 226, 232
Miller, William, & Co., 238
Milyukov, Pavel N., 56–7, 63–4, 78–9, 84, 91–4, 112, 172
Mitava Hussars, 135
mitingovat, 72
Mogilev, 12, 53
Moika Canal, 35, 130, 203
Monks' Soviet, 159
Morning Post, 2
Morskaya, 20, 225
Moscow Art Theatre, 246
Moscow Soviet, 171, 247
Moscow State Conference, 161–6, 167, 170, 237
Moscow Station (Petrograd), 15, 17, 18, 25, 31, 203
Moskovsky Regiment, 24
Moutet, 82–3
Murino, British golf course at, 169

Nagaev, Esaul (Cossack), 165–6
Nat Pinkerton, 173
National City Bank, 194
nationalization of banks, 264, 271
Neilson, Captain J., 64
Nekrasov, N.V., 137
Nevsky Prospect, 13, 15, 16–17, 18, 24, 43, 44, 46, 61, 63, 68, 93, 102,

128, 130, 195, 198, 203, 205, 213, 220, 231–2

Nicholas II, Emperor, 9–12, 31, 40, 43, 47, 53–5, 60, 61, 65, 102, 113, 185, 233–4

Niessel, General, 262

Nikitsky Boulevard (Moscow), 239

Nizhny Novgorod, 170

'no annexations or indemnities', 81, 95, 113, 267

Northcliffe Press, 85

Noulens, Joseph, 169

November Revolution, 182–212; compared with March, 213–14; reaction of witnesses, 249–51

Novoe Vremya, 102, 129

Obolensky, Serge, 12

Observer, 117

Obukhov Works, 259

Ochta, 126

Octobrists, 43, 57

O'Grady, Sir James, 82–3

Oldenburg, 160

Opera House, 41

Order No. 1, 45–6, 49, 60, 65, 66

Ostrovsky, A.N., 144

Palace Square, 43, 138, 188, 194, 195, 214

Paléologue, M., 64, 69

Pares, Sir Bernard, 6, 57, 72, 83, 91, 93, 97, 160, 161

Pavlovsky Guards Regiment (Pavlovtsy), 17–18, 23, 132, 195, 205, 216

Peasants' Congress, First, 96, 110; Second, 256–7

Peter & Paul Fortress, 20, 28, 34, 71, 116, 130, 131, 132, 133, 134, 135, 195, 200, 209, 212, 215, 223

Peters, Will, 43

Petrograd Soviet, 171, 185, 188, 189, 198–9, 203, 212, 232–3

Pitirim, Metropolitan, 39

Plekhanov, G.V., 52, 82–3, 87

Plekhanov Group, 48, 87, 184

Podvoisky, N.I., 189, 220

Pokrovsky, 22

police, Tsarist, 16, 18, 26–7, 71

police-stations, 25–6

Polkovnikov, Colonel G.P., 194, 232

Pollock, Sir John, 64–5

Polovtsev, General P.A., 136

Poole, Ernest, 140–54, 159

Pravda, 62, 66, 78, 92

Pre-Parliament, 177, 182, 258

Preobrazhensky Regiment, 20, 23, 38, 44, 214

Price, Morgan Philips, 3, 66, 83, 84, 85, 91–2, 103–15, 154–9, 161–2, 164–6, 177, 179, 180, 181–2, 198, 201, 213, 215, 217, 219–20, 221–3, 231, 235, 256, 258, 264–6, 271–2, 276, 277, 279

prisoners of war, 99

Progressive Bloc, 56

Prokopovich, S.N., 204–5

Protopopov, A.D., 11, 26, 35, 39–40, 56, 66

Provisional Government, 33, 48–50, 55–67, 91–4, 172, 182, 185, 194, 203, 208–9, 212, 234, 235

Prussianism, 51, 66, 83, 271

Pulkovo, 232

Pushkin, A.S., 159

Putilov Works, 222

queues, 168

Radek, Karl, 267

Radziwill, Léon, 18

Ragosin, 205, 208

Ramsden, 24

Ransome, Arthur, 2, 15, 16, 29–30, 35, 40–1, 43, 45, 47, 50–1, 55, 56, 62–3, 65–6, 72–3, 74, 78–82, 83, 84–5, 86, 89, 90, 93, 94, 95, 97–8, 101, 110, 114, 116–20, 122, 123, 128, 129–30, 132, 136, 138–9, 160–1, 170, 171, 174, 175–7, 179, 180–1, 183, 258, 264, 266–71, 272–3, 275, 276, 277, 278–9

Ransome, Evgenia (née Shelepina), 267

Red Arch, 198, 206, 214

Red Burial (Moscow), 247–50
Red Cross, Russian, 222, 227, 228
Red Cross Store, British, 169
Red Guard, 93, 138, 187, 192, 193,
    203, 206, 207, 210, 214, 219, 220,
    222, 223, 225, 230, 232, 233, 245,
    250, 267, 272, 273–4, 275
Red Monday, 19–33
Red Square, 163, 238, 247
Reed, John, 6–7, 179, 180, 182, 183–7,
    188–92, 195–9, 200–1, 204–5,
    206–8, 209–12, 214, 216–20, 223–4,
    231–3, 235, 247–50, 256–7, 267
Reuter's, 2, 41
Revolution of 1905, 66, 88, 105, 173
Riga, 168
Right SRs, 276
Robien, Louis de, 71, 91, 213
Robins, Raymond, 255
Rodzianko, M.V., 9, 31, 33, 38, 42,
    44, 46, 55, 167
Roshal, S.G., 136
Rudnev, V.V. (Mayor of Moscow),
    260, 261
Russia of the Russians, 2, 43, 56
Russkaya Volya, 121, 122
Ryazanov, 165

Sadovaya, 17, 221
St Isaac's Cathedral/Square, 20, 223
Salvation Army, 102
Samara Soviet, 154–5, 157
San Francisco Bulletin, 7
Sanders, W.W., 82
Schlüsselburg, 180
Schreider (Mayor of Petrograd), 204,
    260
Scott, C.P., 3
Secret Police, Tsarist, 24, 26
secret treaties, 271
selsky skhod (village meeting), 156–8
servants, 75
Sestroretsk Works, 21
Shcheglovitov, I.G., 32, 59
Shepherd, W.G. (United Press),
    120–1
Shingarev, A.I., 260
Shvetsov, 275–6

Simbirsk, 88
Singer sewing machine, 145
Sisson, Edgar, 276, 277
Skobelev, M.I., 94, 110, 181, 211–12,
    260, 277
Smith, Mrs Marie, 249–50
Smolny Institute, 183–5, 190–2,
    198–202, 215, 216–18, 232–3, 250,
    255, 256–7, 258, 267, 275
Social Democrats, 38, 47, 62–3, 66,
    86–7
Social Revolutionaries (SRs), 38,
    86–8, 112, 114, 166, 170, 171, 185,
    189, 191, 201, 204, 232, 258, 266,
    272, 274, 275
Sokolov, N.D., 48
Soskice, David, 3
Soviet (Council of Workers' and
    Soldiers' Deputies), All-Russian,
    33, 38, 45–6, 48–9, 52, 57–8, 60, 61,
    67, 74, 77–8, 79, 84–5, 86, 92, 93–4,
    112, 130, 137–8, 139, 168, 171, 172,
    181, 183, 187, 188, 190–2, 235;
    Executive Committee, 57–8, 77,
    93, 112, 119, 190–2, 201
Soviets, Conference (April), 80–3;
    First All-Russian Congress,
    111–15, 122; Second All-Russian
    Congress, 182, 184, 186–7, 188,
    198, 199–201, 212, 213, 216–18
Sparrow Hills, 239
Spiridonova, Marie, 256, 276
Stalin (Dzhugashvili), I.V., 218, 255
State Bank, 194, 195
Stebbing, E.P., 180
Steklov, Yu.M., 219–20
Stopford, Albert, 12, 15–16, 18, 43,
    47, 69–70, 71, 135, 167, 171
Struve, Peter, 2
Stürmer, B.V., 39, 40, 56, 83
Suhravardi, 247
Sukhanov, N.N., 77
Summer Garden, 17
Sverdlov, Ya.M., 275

Tarasov, 141–54
Taurida Palace, 31–3, 40, 44, 55, 84,
    129, 130, 183, 258–61, 272, 273, 275

Telephone Exchange, 198, 220, 223, 225–30, 231
Tereshchenko, M.I., 13, 21, 22, 39, 57, 94, 100, 126, 130, 135, 169, 182, 187–8, 208, 209, 212
The Ruin of a Nation, 257
Thorne, Will, 82–3
Thornhill, Colonel C.M., 62, 75–6, 133–4, 135, 136, 262
Thornton, Mrs Nellie, 123–6
Thornton's Mill, 74, 123
Tikhon, Metropolitan, 245
Times, The, 3, 43, 45, 50, 85, 163, 171, 188
Tolstoy, L.N., 1, 76, 159
Trans-Siberian Express, 100
Tretiakov, 187
Troitsky Bridge, 34, 127, 130, 189, 200
Trotsky (Bronstein), L.D., 2, 103, 130, 137, 171, 182, 184–5, 187, 188, 191, 198, 200, 201, 212, 218, 220, 232, 233, 254, 255–6, 258, 262, 266–9, 271
Trudoviks, 58
Tsarevich, 47, 53, 54
Tsaritsyn, 180
Tsarskoe Selo, 10, 54, 55, 220, 233
Tsereteli, I.G., 88, 94, 110, 112, 113, 137, 165, 177, 181, 277
Tumanov, General Prince, 36
Turcomans (Kornilov's bodyguard), 163, 167
Turgenev, I.S., 159
Tverskaya, 248
Tyrkova-Williams, Ariadna, 2, 31–3, 56, 179, 252, 256, 269, 277

Urch, R.O.G., 161, 162–3, 241–3, 244–6

Veren, Admiral, 107
Verkhovsky, General A.I., 235
Vickers, 13
Volodarsky, V., 186, 192

Volynsky Regiment, 20, 23, 31, 62, 69
von Meck family, 13
Vyborg District, 35, 43, 58, 121, 122, 132, 182, 192

War Cabinet, British, 171
Watson, Mrs, 13
Westinghouse, 24
Wilcox, E.H., 3, 58, 88, 89, 110–11, 235–7, 254–5
Williams, Albert Rhys, 7, 179, 180, 195, 198, 201, 207, 211, 212, 225, 228–30, 279
Williams, Harold, 1–2, 4, 6, 31–3, 39, 43, 45, 48, 50, 51–2, 55, 56–7, 57–62, 66–7, 68, 70–1, 79, 83, 84, 85, 86, 89–90, 101–3, 117, 120, 121–3, 127–9, 137–8, 139, 163, 166–7, 170–1, 171–6, 177–8, 179, 180, 251, 252–4, 256, 257–8, 258–61, 262, 269–70, 272, 273–4, 275–7
Wilson, Edmund, 88
Wilton, Robert, 3, 16–18, 40, 43–4, 45, 50, 65, 85, 163–4, 171
Winter Palace, 6, 23, 57, 135, 185, 194, 195–8, 201, 202, 204, 205–11, 214
Women's Battalion, 188–9, 197–8, 205, 215–16
Workmen's Group of Central Military Industrial Committee, 33, 62

yunkers (cadets), 192, 194, 196–8, 205–6, 207, 208, 220, 221–3, 225–30
yunkers (Moscow), 238, 243, 245, 249

Zankevich, General, 23
Zavoiko, V.S., 170
Zinoviev, G.E., 137, 182, 238
Znamenskaya Square, 18
Zorin, 192